Expert Systems

Knowledge, Uncertainty and Decision

Ian Graham, M.Sc., MBCS

and

Peter Llewelyn Jones, B.Sc., ARCS

LONDON   NEW YORK

Chapman and Hall

First published in 1988 by
Chapman and Hall Ltd
11 New Fetter Lane, London EC4P 4EE
Published in the USA by
Chapman and Hall
29 West 35th Street, New York, NY 10001

© 1988 Ian Graham and Peter Llewelyn Jones

Printed in Great Britain by
St Edmundsbury Press Ltd
Bury St Edmunds, Suffolk

ISBN 0 412 28510 X

British Library Cataloguing in Publication Data

Graham, Ian
  Expert systems: knowledge, uncertainty
  and decision.
  1. Expert systems (Computer Science)
  I. Title   II. Jones, Peter Llewelyn
  006.3′3   QA76.76.E95
  ISBN 0-412-28510-X

Library of Congress Cataloging in Publication Data

Graham, Ian, 1948–
  Expert systems.

  Bibliography: p.
  Includes indexes.
  1. Expert systems (Computer science)   I. Jones,
Peter Llewelyn, 1945–   II. Title
QA76.76.E95G73 1988   006.3′3   87-29910
ISBN 0-412-28510-X

This book is dedicated to
Peggy, Natalie and Simon

Contents

Acknowledgements

It is almost impossible to acknowledge adequately all the people who have made contributions, great or small, to this book. They fall into four main categories. There are those workers in artificial intelligence, decision support systems, fuzzy sets and other areas whose ideas have provided the ground on which we have been able to build. These are the authors of the many books and papers from which we have borrowed or synthesized ideas. I hope that the bibliography will be viewed as sufficient acknowledgement. We are in debt to the many, many people who have discussed, argued and debated our ideas with us. Thirdly, there are all those who have contributed to the physical production and publication of this work. Last, but not least, there are our colleagues and co-workers whose ideas and encouragement have been invaluable.

Above all, we want to make some acknowledgement to those people whose lectures at meetings of the British Computer Society Specialist Group in Expert Systems and the Information Technology Research Centre at Bristol University formed the basis of substantial sections of this book. Among these we would single out Dr. Janet Efstathiou's analysis of the various kinds of uncertainty which we used extensively in Chapter 4, and her earlier contribution to the volume edited by Mike Small of ICL [190] which influenced the structure and content of the early part of Chapter 7. The section in Chapter 7 on AI Planning is largely based on the presentation of Dr Nigel Shadbolt of Nottingham University, and the one on Nonmonotonic Logic in Chapter 6 owes much to a lecture by Dr V Homolka of Bristol University. Parts of Chapter 8 are influenced by the presentations in [190] of Drs C. Martin and G. Winch of Durham University Business School.

Mostly, we have acknowledged written sources in the text as they are mentioned, but on occasion, where we felt that too many numbers in the text would impair its readability, the reader is expected to use the reference numbers to trace the reference. This should not be too difficult because of the structure of the reference section.

Peggy Thomas helped in retyping part of the manuscript, finding many spelling errors in the process. Phyllida Culpin, Susan Dixon and Gail Swaffield proofread parts of the manuscript and Vi Jones did a sterling job on all of it. Richard Forsyth of Warm Boot Ltd first put us in touch with Chapman and Hall. Our sincere thanks are due to all these people.

Also among those who deserve special thanks are our colleagues and friends at Tymshare Inc. and later Logica and Creative Logic. In particular, Graham Young,

Ron Chestnut and Amy Okuma for many good ideas, Richard Lelliott, and the rest of the ARIES team for their practical insights, David Millar for his patience and Gail Swaffield, whose short sabattical at Logica gave at least one of us some ideas, for sharing some of her thoughts during the preparation of a Ph.D. thesis at Thames Polytechnic.

Introduction

THE SCOPE AND PURPOSE OF THIS BOOK

Why the title *Knowledge, Uncertainty and Decision?* This is a book with two distinguishable but interwoven themes: the centrality of uncertainty management in practical knowledge based or expert systems, and the need to locate knowledge engineering within the corpus of decision support theory and practice.

The first theme reaches a climax in Chapter 5 where we deal with the neglected field of Fuzzy Sets theory, which we believe is central among a range of better understood methods for handling uncertainty. This emphasis on Fuzzy Sets immediately gives the book a controversial flavour, as there are strongly opposing views in the artificial intelligence community on the soundness of these methods. Thus, in places, we adopt a consciously polemical style in anticipation of a hostile reaction from some entrenched positions. However, we do go beyond the rather elementary coverage of the subject to be found in most books on knowledge engineering. In particular, we go beyond the simple use of Fuzzy Sets to model *and, or* and *not* and introduce fuzzy inference rules and quantifiers. We also cover most other methods of managing uncertainty: probabilities, certainty factors, nonmonotonic logic, etc.

The second subject permeates most of the book, from the first chapter onwards, reaching a climax in Chapter 8. Uncertainty management in artificial intelligence systems is generally considered an advanced topic; therefore we were faced with a choice as to whether to defer its discussion to the end of the book or introduce it as appropriate when discussing other topics. We have chosen to do the latter in order to preserve the force of the polemic. The price we pay is that some readers who do not begin with a sound background may have to reread certain sections after completing the text. However, we have included guidance on this in the text, and it should pose no real difficulty if the book is not regarded as a course textbook.

In embarking on this work, the authors noticed some rather irritating gaps in the literature of Artificial Intelligence (AI), Management Science and Fuzzy Sets. Whilst it is possible to learn from books about any of these subjects from their own classical and accepted points of view, the necessary background for a critical appreciation of each area or a combination of them requires a great deal of effort in the library, selecting fragments from scattered references.

In many cases, having found the appropriate volumes, themselves written from the viewpoint of some specific tradition, it becomes necessary to regress further to home in on exactly the techniques required. For example, many authors on Fuzzy Sets introduce some connections with other logical systems but do not have the space or the inclination to expose the theories at a level suitable for the beginner. When the beginner turns to the literature of formal logic for solace, he or she is confronted with books written either for neophyte logicians where the introduction is as slow as an apprenticeship and the essence of the subject is lost under a welter of detail, or for those already having served their time who are not particularly interested in the application of logic to remote fields such as AI or Fuzzy Sets.

The result is that the exposition is usually selective of precisely those points which are of least interest. In a similar way, books on AI represent the prejudices of the AI community; too often, scant attention is paid to connections with other disciplines such as Management Science. In the one worthy exception we have found, *Foundations of Decision Support* by Bonczek, Holsapple and Whinston [28], the treatment of logic represents all the most entrenched prejudices of AI; that logic is always two-valued and first order and that its main value is as a language for database or proof theoretic searches.

In Turner [201] there is a good survey of the basic material but the exposition suffers from brevity in that merely stating the formal description of, say, first-order logic does not give any real feel for the subject, and the treatment of fuzzy logic in particular is too scant to be of practical value. We aim to remedy this situation in our Chapters 5 and 6.

Having spent some time talking about logic let us now return to a more general perspective. We are aiming in this book to be very practical. Readers should have their ability to build real systems of practical significance enhanced after digesting the material of some chapters. At the same time, we want to clarify the status of both knowledge engineering in general and fuzzy reasoning in particular in the formal world of the mathematician, computer scientist, logician and philosopher.

THE SUBJECT MATTER COVERED

After Chapter 1, which is of a purely introductory character and sets the scene for what is to follow, we begin with KNOWLEDGE. This is, for us, the central problem in building intelligent computer systems. Most of the artificial intelligence literature has concentrated hitherto on problems of inference and search. For this reason, problems such as knowledge representation, knowledge base management and knowledge acquisition have only recently received the attention they deserve. Books on the subject are therefore fairly scarce. In this section we cover basic epistemological questions and the pros and cons of the various representations that have been used. We introduce a totally new concept; that of a Fuzzy

Frame. The next chapter gives a thorough coverage of relational database theory, leading on to extensions into fuzzy database enquiry, (library) information retrieval with fuzziness, and returns to the exposition of the fuzzy frame concept. Lastly, we survey developments in natural language computing from this point of view.

Part III covers theories of uncertainty, first in general and then fuzzy sets theory in detail. The latter coverage is split into an informal, non-mathematical development, followed by a section giving a much more mathematical treatment.

Part IV is about decision making, in which we include search and inference methods; methods of applying knowledge to a particular problem. The theme of uncertainty runs strongly through the chapters in this part. In fact the chapter on Logics includes a deal of material on knowledge representation and the mathematics of Fuzzy Sets. Chapter 7 comes down from the abstract heights reached at the end of the preceding chapter to reach a more elementary level again. We repeat the basic material on artificial intelligence search strategies, introduce rule induction as a method of building expert systems – again concentrating on how the induced rules can include uncertainty – and move on to deal with AI planning before ending on a more practical note. This chapter includes a totally new method of fuzzy backward chaining. Chapter 8 concerns itself with the classification and evaluation of decision support systems, drawing on much of the preceding material on fuzziness and logic.

The last part of the book attempts to synthesize all the preceding material by looking at practical issues. First, knowledge acquisition, on which there still is no decent textbook, and secondly, practical application systems.

Each chapter, with the exception of the first one, which is quite short, ends with a summary and pointers for further study.

THE INTENDED READERSHIP

The essential character of this work might be described as pedagogical, but equally, it is not simply a training manual, including as it does a unique coverage of its domains of discourse.

The book is aimed at several readerships. Fuzzy sets and the theory of approximate reasoning are treated with the formalism necessary to support an undergraduate or graduate course in these topics as background reading. They are compared and contrasted with other methods of representing uncertainty. Furthermore, the place of fuzzy relations and approximate reasoning in mathematics is explored, both from the viewpoint of the logician and the category theorist.

At the same time, the utility of fuzzy sets theory in knowledge engineering and the relationship between the latter and Decision Support Systems (DSS) theory is covered from the standpoints of both the practitioner and the user, and the book is supportive of courses in knowledge engineering and decision support.

Having mentioned all these detailed interest groups, we can summarize by saying that this volume will be of interest to three broad categories of reader:

(1) managers seeking to gain a deeper insight into the commercial possibilities for expert decision support systems;
(2) systems designers and knowledge engineers faced with building such systems, and
(3) advanced undergraduate or postgraduate students of computer science or artificial intelligence.

The organization of the work separates the formal, mathematical treatments of the topics from the introductory and motivational material, and makes the key arguments and examples accessible to the non-mathematical reader. This structure has been selected to ensure that the work is of value to the general reader interested in obtaining an overview of the application of fuzzy and expert systems techniques to the problems of the business world.

The Reveal system is introduced in some places merely as a vehicle for presenting fully worked examples of knowledge-based decision support systems in practice. This system, which is already extensively referenced in the literature, provides an environment for the development of knowledge-based systems utilizing fuzzy reasoning within the context of DSS. Thus the pedagogic character referred to above is largely based on the wide compendium of background knowledge provided, organized in a way suitable for a student of the *application* of logic, fuzzy sets and AI to management and OR problems, and supported by much sound practical material and many exercises.

ALTERNATIVE READING PATHS

Having given this emphasis to the application orientation of the work, we would like further to justify this claim by pointing out the other aspects of the book which will be of value to the non-student readership. The table of contents will show that some sections are highly practical in character. These can be read independently of (or as an introduction to) the other chapters, which fall into three classes.

The practical chapters are those on knowledge engineering (9), decision support systems (8) and applications (10), and on database systems and methods (3).

The balance of the material addresses various segments of the requisite theoretical backgrounds. These are principally chapters which explain at a beginner's level (but not thereby avoiding advanced topics in some sections) all the background techniques of AI and Fuzzy Sets in a unified manner (these are Chapters 1, 2, 3, 4, 5 (the first part), 7, 8 and 9). Chapter 6 deals with the connections between logic and the remainder of the book and addresses the problem of collecting all the material required at a level suitable for the non-logician, whilst remaining readable and concise.

Logicians, however, may find some of the polemical remarks of interest. It is not a rigorous development and the emphasis is on intuitive understanding rather than proof. Every reader should read Chapters 1, 10 and 11 which are simply written and will further cover the *philosophy* of the book and give a taste for research directions and the future of applications.

COMPARISON WITH OTHER WORKS

It may be useful to compare the approach adopted in this book with that of other recent works. In comparison for example with Hayes-Roth, Waterman and Lenat [91] which essentially reports at the outline level on previous work, we are both providing more detailed and complete information on the internals and construction of complete applications, and adding the all-important theoretical and formal background.

Our purpose is to present a unified account of a body of knowledge which is sufficient to provide both the techniques and the underlying mathematics to those engaged in practical work and the context and perspective to those managing or reviewing projects. We will not attempt to cover ground that is covered by the other works mentioned here except in the briefest outline or where our point of view differs appreciably. Our book may be seen as complementary in this respect. The Hayes-Roth book is principally concerned with building systems with expert system shells. We take a more critical and impartial look at the problems of shells and offer different types of solution with our opinions. As indicated above, our objective is to equip the reader with the tools to construct serious expert system solutions at a low (albeit not very low) level of difficulty.

We regard Winston's *Artificial Intelligence* [210] as wholly complementary to our book. It is, after all, still the basic reference on classical LISP-based AI for the beginner, even if it does overstate the case somewhat; an error we are at pains to avoid. Very little of its content will be duplicated by us, and where this is not possible, as in dealing with frames, scripts, etc., our approach is stylistically totally different. However, because of the author's background and viewpoint *Artificial Intelligence* does not emphasize the role of AI techniques in DSS, nor indeed is any intention paid to fuzzy modelling or fuzzy inference or to links with conventional modelling and database design cultures. This book sets out to fill precisely that gap in the literature.

REFERENCE SECTION

The references are very extensive, although it was not our intention to produce an exhaustive bibliography (mainly due to our breadth of coverage). There are also directions for further reading and some bibliographical notes at the end of each chapter.

We have introduced a further innovation, which seemed particularly appropriate in a book concerned in some way with artificial intelligence. That is a

Computer Systems Index, separate from the more usual Subject and Name Indexes.

The authors' aim has been to produce an informative, stimulating, controversial but above all enjoyable text. We hope you enjoy reading it as much as we have enjoyed working on its production.

Ian Graham
Peter Llewelyn Jones

Part one
Overview

1

Knowledge engineering and decision support

'Who shall decide, when doctors disagree?'
Alexander Pope

1.1 COMPUTING AND ARTIFICIAL INTELLIGENCE

What has nearly thirty years of research into Artificial Intelligence brought us?
And what is Knowledge Engineering? And is that the same as Expert Systems?
And is any of it really practical? And why haven't the data processing
departments done anything with it in the past? And is the whole area really so
shrouded in the mystery and the arcane technology as we are led to believe?

In this book, we try to answer these and allied questions. We try to place the
entire discipline of Artificial Intelligence into the context of mainstream data
processing development, and to look at its future in the commercial environment,
short and long term. First, a brief history – very condensed, for this has always
been a broad field.

1.1.1 Whence it came

They called them 'electronic brains' when the first vacuum tube machines were
brought into existence. The sheer computational power of those devices of the late
1940s exceeded the existing electro-mechanical comptometers by two orders of
magnitude. But much more importantly, these were 'stored program computers';
devices which could modify their own succeeding actions on the basis of their
current state – surely the epitome of intelligent behaviour.

Babbage [133] had explained how to do it a century before. Turing [200] had
speculated on the nature of artificial intelligence as instantiated in such
machines, seven years after he worked with Wilkes in Bletchley Park where the
latter was involved in the creation of COLOSSUS.

It was therefore not at all unnatural that researchers, when in the immediate
aftermath of the second world war computers became available for non-military
tasks, should have undertaken projects which implied replicating intelligence in
these new and powerful artifacts.

Haemertia followed hubris; and not for the last time in the story of artificial intelligence. It rapidly became clear that the computational power of the new tools was not even partially sufficient to handle the complexities arising in solving real-world problems on a generalized basis. The jargon phrase 'combinatorial explosion' described the fact that the number of possibilities to be examined, even in problems which human intelligence could solve readily, expanded far faster than the ability of the increasingly powerful processors could handle. And so, in what we may term the second cycle of AI research, the focus lay on the development of general methods of navigating efficiently through this sea of possibilities. Newell, Shaw and Simon described their 'Logic Theorist' [160] program in 1956, which was developed into the 'General Problem Solver' [161] in 1959. These seminal programs introduced vital approaches to structuring solution strategies which permeate AI to this day. Yet beyond a very limited range of problems, these programs failed to perform effectively. Computational power alone was not enough. Computational power allied to general search strategies was not enough. It transpired that to solve real-world problems effectively, knowledge about the domain of the problem at hand was needed. And this recognition ushered in the third cycle of research into AI, along with the birth of the concept of knowledge engineering as a discipline.

During the period from 1967 to 1977, the first effective knowledge-based systems began to emerge from the laboratories. Although highly domain-specific, these systems were for the first time able to out-perform human beings in their selected areas of expertise.

These early examples of knowledge-based programs, mimicking human experts, were not unreasonably termed *Expert Systems*. DENDRAL [36] and MYCIN [186] are two of the best known and most successful, dealing with the domains of organic chemistry and medical diagnosis respectively. We can note parenthetically that to separate itself from ordinary mortals the artificial intelligence community, like other such groupings, has its own argot; here we find them referring to *domains* where everyone else talks about *applications*.

These systems, along with many others, were written in LISP. This language has been the workhorse of AI research in the United States since its definition by McCarthy [144] in 1960. Weissman [207] described it in his then standard text on the language in 1966 as 'not an easy language to learn, because of the functional syntax and the insidious parenthetical format'.

During a quarter century, the language and its support environments, both in terms of software and special-purpose computer hardware, has undoubtedly become more tractable in usage. This allied with the succeeding generations of graduates from the schools specializing in AI has led to its almost universal acceptance as the sole language of choice for AI in the United States.

But following the successful demonstration of the early Expert Systems, written from the ground up in LISP, it became clear that higher-level tools would be needed if there was to be commercialization of the new technology. This led to research in two directions – the design of higher-level 'knowledge representation languages' such as KRL [25], ROSIE [66], and OPS5 [68]; and the design of 'Expert System Shells'.

The knowledge representation languages are typically developed themselves on top of a LISP environment, and exist to provide a more natural formalism for expressing knowledge than as LISP functions. The shells are typically derived from completed expert systems, whereby the domain-specific knowledge which provides the power of the system in its chosen domain is removed, allowing knowledge from a new domain to be entered. This admittedly cuts down considerably on the building time of the new system, but experience has shown that, if the new problem is not a good paradigm of the problem for which the original shell was developed, the predefined shell structure will prove restrictive.

This brings us essentially up to date. There are at present available on the market around two dozen commercially available shell systems, and a smaller number of knowledge representation languages.

1.1.2   Attitudes to artificial intelligence

For much of the period outlined above, AI has lived the existence of a pariah amongst disciplines. Funding has tended to be scant and irregular (though DARPA has an outstanding record in long-term support) and the attitude of the world at large has varied from indifference to hostility.

There is a not unnatural antipathy towards the concept of a 'thinking machine' that has coloured responses. Tesler's Lemma says that 'AI is anything that has not been done yet'. In other words, to the justifiable chagrin of AI researchers, there has been a long-term tendency to devalue anything that has been demonstrated (once it has been explained) with the dismissive observation that 'that's not really intelligence, anyway'.

This negative attitude, coupled with the lack of visible progress at various stages in its history, has tended to leave AI out in the cold. In 1974, the Lighthill Report commissioned by Her Majesty's Government in the UK concluded that there was no future in AI research, and recommended that all funding should be terminated forthwith!

In the last few years, there has been a dramatic reversal of attitude. To a large degree, this has been stimulated by the Japanese Fifth Generation Computer initiative. In Japan, MITI are funding pre-commercial co-operative research into the development of a Knowledge Information Processor – a fifth generation computer which will be qualitatively different to the previous four generations by being concerned with the manipulation of knowledge. The goals of the project are ambitious, to say the least. One measure is to say that by the 1990s, the aim is to have a processor of 100 000 times the power of say a DEC PDP-10 (the vehicle of much of AI research in the US to date).

Worldwide responses to the challenge of the Japanese initiative have been equally dramatic. The European Economic Community have funded the ESPRIT project, allocating 800 000 ECUs over the next five years to stimulate the research in the countries of the EEC. In the UK, the Alvey Directorate has been established with the same mission, and a budget of £3 50 000. West Germany has recently announced a similar level of support for West German industry. And in the USA, we see the unprecedented collaboration under the aegis of MCC of the majority of the computer industry outside of IBM.

What are the key challenges and obstacles to be faced if the commercialization of knowledge engineering is to succeed?

1.1.3 Data processing and artificial intelligence

If we compare the history of commercial data processing with that of artificial intelligence and knowledge engineering, as outlined above, a number of striking differences become apparent.

Innovation in mainstream DP has been derived in large measure from the efforts of the vendors and the practitioners. AI, on the other hand, has almost exclusively been practised in the academic environment, with major vendors taking very little interest until recent times.

Secondly, and more technically, the thrust in AI research has been, quite properly, into methods of symbolic computation, whereas mainstream DP has been concerned with numeric computation.

As a result, there is both a culture gap and a technology gap to be bridged if AI techniques are to be used with advantage in the business arena. Typically, AI products rely on the use of special languages, generally derived from LISP, and frequently on special-purpose hardware to operate these languages efficiently. The use of these special-purpose tools not only raises the threshold at which a project becomes viable, but introduces endless problems if there is a need to interface the application to existing databases and programs running on the corporate mainframe.

There is a need to take a balanced look at the discipline of knowledge engineering, and to place it into the context of all the other tools of the practising management scientist – operations research, decision analysis, decision support, simulation modelling and so on.

Knowledge engineering makes tractable many problems which previously could not be tackled on the computer. But equally, it leaves many problems still intractable; and it in no way invalidates the successful solution strategies which have been adopted for many other problems over the last thirty years.

There is also an urgent need to engineer tools for the practice of knowledge engineering which do not require the specialized hardware, software, and training associated with the current generation of tools. Only when this has been achieved will knowledge engineering enjoy the full support of the data processing management of the corporate community.

1.2   THE EMERGENCE OF KNOWLEDGE ENGINEERING

The critical recognition in the development of expert systems technology was the identification of large amounts of domain-specific knowledge as being the key to the development of programs which could perform adequately in complex fields.

Thus the archetypal expert system is generally described as comprising two fundamental, indeed defining, components: the 'knowledge base', analogous in some ways to a database in commercial data processing; and an 'inference engine', analogous in some ways to the algorithmic program in commercial data processing. (Nearly every expert system will contain further identified components: modules to handle the user dialogue, to provide rational explanations of its actions, to maintain and extend its knowledge base and so on – but the paradigm of knowledge base and inference engine is universal.)

The use of the word 'engineering' clearly implies the existence of some raw material which can indeed be engineered. In this sense of the word, what do we mean by 'knowledge'? Clearly, we mean the representation of human knowledge, gathered from an acknowledged expert in the field under study (the 'domain expert') by the 'knowledge engineer' – the developer of the expert system.

There seems to be little agreement on how knowledge is represented in the human mind. Without an agreed objective model, it is inevitable that many competing and complementary formalisms will be proposed and used with varying degrees of success in the endeavour to create adequate computerized replications. Indeed, it is recognized [189] that many formalisms are necessary, and will tend to be used in parallel, each having its own strengths and weaknesses under various circumstances.

One of the more frequently employed formalisms is that of the 'production rule'. A production rule represents some separable chunk of knowledge, in the form:

'IF ⟨some set of antecedent conditions is true⟩ THEN ⟨some set of consequent conclusions can be drawn⟩'.

A typical expert system will consist of from some ten to many hundreds of such rules.

One of the complicating factors in representing knowledge in this way is the issue of confidence in the knowledge itself, and thus in the deductions which can be made. In any worthwhile field of expertise, there will be the need to capture judgement under uncertainty, for not all data will be available to the expert, and some of the data may be ambiguous or vague. Various approaches have been used to mechanize this management of uncertainty. One method is to assign a 'certainty factor' to any rule, and then to combine these certainty factors as information is aggregated. Bayesian probabilities have also been employed in a number of notable expert systems.

The usage of 'fuzzy sets theory' or 'approximate reasoning' provides a further method of capturing uncertainty. Fuzzy sets are a new mathematical concept, originated in 1965 by Professor Lotfi Zadeh at Berkeley [238]. It is interesting that in parallel with the development of the theory during the 1970s, some of the prototypical expert systems such as MYCIN [245] which were being developed at the same time in fact used the arithmetic of fuzzy sets theory to aggregate the uncertainty in the knowledge base.

The methods used for encoding knowledge are closely bound up with methods used to manipulate knowledge in the presence of facts pertaining to some problem under examination – the 'inference engine' or control strategy mentioned above. A number of control strategies exist, and in many applications a mixed approach utilizing features from more than one will be adopted. There is, for example, the 'backwards chaining' or goal-directed approach, where a hypothesis is formulated, and evidence is sought to sustain or refute the hypothesis. In direct contradiction, there is the 'forwards chaining' or data-directed aproach, where inferences are drawn from the evidence currently available, leading forward to the establishment of some final conclusion.

'Bi-directional' and the closely related 'blackboard' approaches work more opportunistically. The 'blackboard' is a representation of everything that is known to the program at any instant, and modules trigger and add further data to the blackboard once there is enough information present to allow them to function.

1.3   THE DEVELOPMENT OF DECISION SUPPORT THEORY AND PRACTICE

If we try to build up a taxonomy of computer applications, we might finish up with something along the lines illustrated in Fig. 1.1. Here, on the left-hand side,

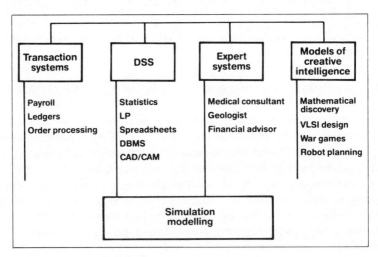

Fig. 1.1   A taxonomy of business computing

we see what is still perhaps the most widespread use of the digital computer: the replacement of 'armies of clerks by book-keeping systems. These are the straightforward commercial applications of computing, typically implemented in COBOL, processed in batch mode, and only visible to the end user in the form of printed reports.

During the 1960s and 70s we witnessed the development of the decision support systems referred to in the second block of our chart. Boulden [32] documents a number of systems from this era. These followed the introduction of timesharing and interactive computing, and were characterized by two things. The accessibility of the computer via terminal interaction meant that the user could be in direct contact with the program, rather than its output. Also, to support the user, the facilities began to include richer data structures which eased the programming task. The introduction of callable models in SPSS made statistics accessible to far more programmers, as did various linear programming and engineering 'packages'. The key here is the introduction of extra primitive data types. These might vary from simple vectors of numbers, as in many financial modelling packages, through relations in database products, program templates in 4GLs, callable modules in scientific packages, right up to the paradigm implicit in the 'VISI-clones'; packages such as Symphony; where the spreadsheet data structure effectively means that the program *per se* disappears altogether.

The third block in the diagram refers to the models of intelligent behaviour which have come to prominence even more recently; the knowledge-based, expert systems such as MYCIN (medicine), PROSPECTOR (geology), DENDRAL (chemistry) and PlanPower (personal financial planning).

The final category, here labelled Creative Intelligence, essentially refers to the leading edge research in artificial intelligence. The first three examples cited refer to the work of Lenat whose doctoral dissertation was concerned with the development of AM, an 'artificial mathematician', which, given a few pre-numerical set theoretic concepts, set out to propose interesting ideas in mathematics, and in doing so 'rediscovered' large parts of number theory, including the prime number concept itself and Goldbach's conjecture that every even number is the sum of two primes. A development of the AM structure, involving self-modifying heuristics, is the EURISKO system, which has been used in a number of areas to carry out the exploration of concepts, including the design – invention? – of new three-dimensional tesselated VLSI components and participation – winning – in the annual US navy war game.

These latter programs take ages to run and it is not even suggested that they are commercially viable. The specialization that permitted commercial applications of artificial intelligence techniques was the incorporation of domain-specific knowledge; and richer primitive knowledge structures. This is analogous to the liberation of scientific computing referred to above and summarized in Fig. 1.2.

The two central columns of Fig. 1.1 are unified by the observation that both are

---

Program = algorithm + data structure

- **Richer data structures permit higher levels of user interface**

    - DBMS   - relations

    - Financial modelling   - vectors and arrays

    - 4GLs   - templates

    - Engineering packages - modules

Expertise = inference + knowledge

- **Richer knowledge structures permit more intelligent systems**

    - Object knowledge   - frames

    - Causal knowledge   - rules

    - Process knowledge   - procedures

    - Knowledge of relationships   - logic

Fig. 1.2   Conventional *versus* knowledge based programming

special cases of simulation modelling; decision support systems assist with model building whereas knowledge-based systems are themselves often simulations of human experts. In fact the correct analogy is with expert systems shells which are tools to assist in model building.

Sprague [246] suggested that any decision support system should be analysed in terms of its abilities in three dimensions: those of logic management, data management and dialogue management. Knowledge-based decision support systems introduce the need to look at a fourth dimension: that of uncertainty management.

As with decision support systems, knowledge engineering applications – if they are to be successful – will need to perform tasks in all four areas at least as well as existing 4GLs.

Chapter 8 goes into the classification and evaluation of decision support systems in great detail. In a sense, the whole of this book will be concerned with methods for managing uncertainty in knowledge-based and decision support

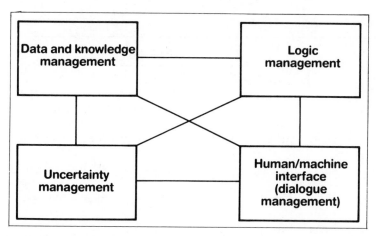

Fig. 1.3   The dimensions of decision support systems

systems. For now we turn to a comparison of knowledge engineering and decision support methods.

1.4   THE RELATIONSHIP BETWEEN DECISION SUPPORT SYSTEMS AND KNOWLEDGE ENGINEERING

If we begin with Anthony's famous pyramid of information structures (Fig. 1.4 and Table 1.1) we recall that traditional computing is concerned with the processing of large volumes of data, and that each datum is of relatively low value. These are the transaction-based book-keeping systems again. Management Information Systems (MIS) filter and classify these data into lower volumes of higher value information. However, this is a one-way process. Only with the introduction of decision support systems (DSS) were managers able to interact with the data and carry out 'what-if' tests, sensitivity analyses, etc., and thus begin to manage the uncertainty inherent in the information. Either way the manager can be regarded as an 'expert' who is able to take the data and information provided by such systems and turn them into decisions – thus the terminology 'decision support' systems rather than 'decision making' systems. In the domain of financial planning, for example, the expert is an accountant who can be said to apply various types of knowledge and experience in order to arrive at management or strategic decisions.

Knowledge-based expert systems remove this decision making stage to a higher level still, by applying stored knowledge to the information to produce 'advice'. Note that the onus is still with the human to take the decision, and that therefore the expert system will have to be able to explain its reasoning if required.

Table 1.1   The decision matrix

	Nature of decision		
	Operational	*Tactical*	*Strategic*
Life of decision	Short (1–60 days)	Medium (3–24 months)	Long (1–5 years)
Span of decision	Narrow (department)	Broad (multi-dept)	Corporate
Nature of data			
Source of data	Internal	Mostly internal	Internal and external
Level of data	Detailed	Some aggregation	Mostly aggregation
Precision of data	High	Mostly high	Low
Varieties of data	Few	More	Many
Nature of analysis			
Style of analysis	Quantitative	Largely quantitative	Largely qualitative
Problem definition	Tightly defined	Defined	Loosely defined

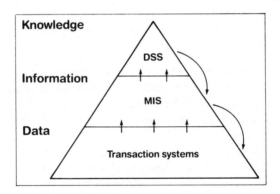

Fig. 1.4   The great pyramid of computing

The first famous medical expert system, MYCIN, had this property. A typical consultation where this facility has been invoked is shown below.

15) Is the patient's illness with ORGANISM-1 a hospital acquired infection?
**WHY?
[i.e. Why is it important to determine whether or not the infection with ORGANISM-1 was acquired while the patient was hospitalized?]
[1.0] This will aid in determining the category of ORGANISM-1.
  It has already been established that
    [1.1]the gram stain of ORGANISM-1 is gramneg, and

[1.2]the morphology of ORGANISM-1 is rod, and
[1.3]the aerobicity of ORGANISM-1 is facultative
Therefore, if
[1.4]the infection with ORGANISM-1 was not acquired while the patient was hospitalized
then
There is strongly suggestive evidence (.8) that the category of ORGANISM-1 is enterobacteriaceae
ALSO:
There is weakly suggestive evidence (.1) that the identity of ORGANISM-1 is pseudomonas-aeruginosa
[RULE037]

In this case MYCIN is rule based and is able to say (in pseudo-Anglicized form) which rule it is currently using. It could also answer a HOW type of question by regurgitating the rule it had used during the search that had led to the current rule. The other point to note in the above consultation is the way MYCIN is able to give an indication of how much confidence it attaches to each diagnosis. The techniques which make this possible and the search methods used will be the subject of later chapters. For now, the important point is that here is a decision support system which can:

(1) incorporate practical, judgemental human knowledge as rules;
(2) select relevant rules and combine the results in appropriate ways;
(3) use these independent components to solve problems;
(4) adaptively determine the best sequence of rules to apply;
(5) explain its conclusions by retracing the line of reasoning;
(6) talk to the user in a reasonably friendly manner.

It has often been claimed that such systems display intelligence. We categorically refuse to debate this issue in this book. The reason should be made clear. We are not cognizant of any adequate essential, operational or functional definition of the concept of intelligence. We will however have a few words to say about the academic discipline of artificial intelligence. For now, artificial intelligence will be regarded as research into human psychology via the analogy with computers, while knowledge engineering (our chief concern) is the practical application of the techniques from *all* parts of computer science to solving a range of problems in the construction of better decision support systems. See Fig. 1.5.

MYCIN contained specialist knowledge on one area of medicine. It was soon realized that similar reasoning processes could be applied to other medical diagnosis problems, and this led to the development of EMYCIN, standing for Empty-MYCIN, which was one of the first expert system 'shells'; the inference engine with the knowledge base carefully excised. New rules concerning some other branch of medicine could then be substituted with less development effort.

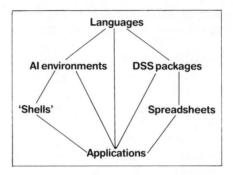

Fig. 1.5   The analogy between knowledge engineering and decision support software packages

Perhaps unsurprisingly the most successful use of such shells was in applications similar to the original problem faced by their progenitor expert systems.

Similar requirements for more generalized high-level development tools have led to the production and marketing of specialized software products, usually running on hardware optimized to run LISP. It seems not unreasonable to draw the analogy between these 'AI development environments' and the 4GLs of mainstream computing: the aims are the same, only the applications differ. In the same way we can view the shells, with their restricted applicability but higher productivity, as analogous to spreadsheet products.

Thus, in both knowledge engineering and decision support systems, the choices facing the developer now range from basic and totally general languages, through higher level development environments, up to application specific kernels, and finally to bespoke applications.

This question of the level of a language is often confused with its 'generation', perhaps due to the non-procedural character of the fifth generation language PROLOG. To put this in perspective it is only necessary to note that the third generation language LISP (yes, it predates COBOL by about a year!) also has a non-procedural flavour. See Fig. 1.6.

In other words newer isn't always better. Some would still make a case for the 0GL of the abacus for certain applications.

The concept of the fifth generation is essentially concerned with the development of new fast, parallel architecture computer hardware. This book is about software and applications. We will thus not discuss these matters further.

The reasons for the need to extend decision support with knowledge-based techniques are manifold. We have already mentioned the need to process the available information into the form of advice (at least in the routine cases) and thus free the decision maker for planned, rational work – as opposed to fire-fighting. This decision maker may or may not be an 'expert'; a physician or a postgraduate in chemistry for example. Or she or he may be merely a valued operative; a skilled machine operator, currency trader or salesman perhaps.

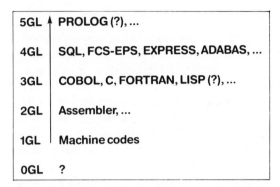

5GL	PROLOG (?), ...
4GL	SQL, FCS-EPS, EXPRESS, ADABAS, ...
3GL	COBOL, C, FORTRAN, LISP (?), ...
2GL	Assembler, ...
1GL	Machine codes
0GL	?

Fig. 1.6   The genealogy of programming languages

Many highly skilled decision makers use specialist knowledge, where they would not normally be described as 'experts' in normal speech. Thus we duck the distinction between expert systems and knowledge-based systems. Despite the claims made in the literature, we have seen nothing that convinces us that there is a significant technological difference.

One final remark on the definition of knowledge-based systems will be necessary to distinguish our view from that of other authors. We believe that there is a profound sense in which a payroll system, for example, is a knowledge-based – or even expert – system. However, its knowledge is represented in the form of procedures – because that is how payroll clerks express their knowledge. We believe that procedures are an important, necessary form of knowledge representation, as will emerge in later chapters. Having said this, we should point out that the average payroll system usually fails to be genuinely knowledge based since its control structure is hopelessly mixed up with the knowledge. That this is not necessarily a good thing can be seen from the recent introduction of statutory sick pay in the UK, where most systems had to undergo major rewrites.

Returning to the reasons for introducing knowledge engineering techniques we end this chapter with a list of some of the more obvious benefits.

(1) Experts retire, taking their knowledge with them.
(2) Experts may be in short supply.
(3) Humans need sleep and can fall ill.
(4) Humans are sometimes forgetful or inconsistent.
(5) Experts can be impatient if required to repeat themselves in training situations.
(6) Expert systems can often be more cheaply delivered to where their advice is required.
(7) Experts may be better employed on the more difficult cases.

1.5   FURTHER READING

Introductory books on expert systems are as numerous as good ones are rare. We will recommend only two introductory texts, Harmon and King [87] and Forsyth [69], and three more substantial references. These latter are: Barr and Feigenbaum [16] which is a huge, comprehensive but by now dating reference also containing much material of an introductory nature, Winston [210], the best basic text on artificial intelligence and Hayes-Roth, Waterman and Lenat [91]. Each chapter of this book will end with additional recommendations as new material is introduced. Alexander [5] gives a more engineering oriented introduction.

The historical background to artificial intelligence is covered in a delightful book by McCorduck [147]. The dimension of social responsibility is introduced in the classic work by Weizenbaum [236]. Other important and entertaining background material may be found in Hodges [98] and Hofstadter [99]. All these last four books have influenced us greatly in the production of this one.

Dreyfuss [58] writes entertainingly from the sceptic's point of view and provides, *inter alia*, an excellent summary of the major trends of the last thirty years in AI research. Hofstadter [100] and [99] covers many other topics in his *tour d'horizon*, but the core of his concern is the machine representation of [105] cognition and Koestler [118]. Johnson-Laird, Watson and Boden [27] provide radically different and thought-provoking perspectives on the nature of cognitive process.

Some of the classic early papers (from the 1960s) on the development of techniques are summarized in Minsky [150].

Part two
Knowledge

2

Knowledge representation

'Say first, of God above or man below,
What can we reason but from what we know?'
Essay on Man, Alexander Pope

2.1 INTRODUCTION

2.1.1 Knowledge-based systems

There are essentially three components of a knowledge-based computer system. Firstly, the underlying environment of symbol and value manipulation which all computer systems share and which can be thought of as the programming languages and support environment: editors, floating point processors, data structures, compilers, etc. Secondly, we have the structure of the knowledge itself including methods of representation and access, and lastly there must be some techniques for applying the knowledge in a rational manner to the problem at hand. This third element has been called the 'control strategy', the 'inference engine' and, as we prefer, the 'knowledge application system'. Note that some authors restrict the usage 'control strategy' to a component of the inference engine devoted to search.

The architecture which has emerged in recent years as favourite in knowledge-based and expert systems is precisely what we have described in Fig. 2.1. The point is that the knowledge base and the inference strategy are best separated from one another to facilitate maintenance. After all, in most cases knowledge will change over time and one does not want to rewrite the application system whenever a new rule is added. In real systems this separation is achieved to a greater or lesser extent and may be regarded as an ideal to be strived for.

In this chapter we will deal with the notion of a knowledge base. To do this we will need to ask 'What is knowledge?' and 'How may it be represented on a computer?'. The question of how human beings store and manipulate knowledge is a question we only touch upon and we more or less ignore the philosophical problems of epistemology. The question of how knowledge comes about, what philosophers call the problem of cognition, is decidedly beyond the scope of this book, but we shall take up a related question in Chapter 9 – that of knowledge

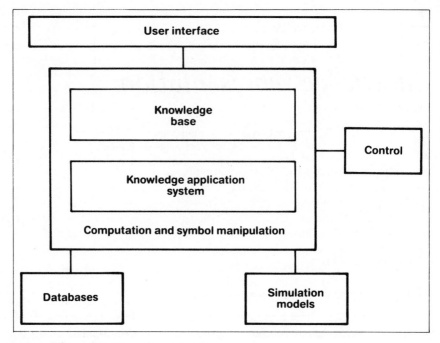

Fig. 2.1   The architecture of expert systems

acquisition; the techniques by which knowledge is obtained from humans and other sources and incorporated in a knowledge-based system.

2.1.2   What is knowledge?

Most of us are familiar with the notion of data, that is unstructured sets of numbers, facts and symbols. These data can convey information only by virtue of some structure or decoding mechanism. In the limiting case this distinction can be illustrated by two people who may communicate via a channel which may only carry one message consisting of a single symbol. The datum, the symbol itself carries no information except by virtue of the presence of the channel whose structure determines that the receiver may learn from the absence of a symbol as well as from its transmission. Two points emerge from this example. Information always has a context while data may be context free; thus if I say 'she shot up' that is a datum for which I would need to explain whether the person in question was an astronaut or a heroin addict to convey information. Knowledge is usually seen as a concept at a higher level of abstraction, and there is a sense in which this is true. For example, '1000' is a datum, '1000 isobars at noon' could be information about the weather in some situations but 'Most people feel better when the pressure rises above 1000' is knowledge about barometric information and people. The realization that much knowledge is expressed in the form of heuristic descriptions or rules of thumb is what gives rise to the conception of knowledge as more abstract than information. However, this evades the need for a really precise definition. We offer a philosophically contentious one here.

Quite apart from its ability to be abstract at various levels *knowledge is concerned with action*. It is concerned with practice in the world. Knowing how people feel under different atmospheric conditions helps us to respond better to their moods, work with them or even improve their air-conditioning (if we have some knowledge about ventilation engineering as well). Knowledge is a guide to informed practice and relates to information as a processor; that is, we understand knowledge but we process information. It is no use knowing that people respond well to high pressure if you cannot measure that pressure. Effective use of knowledge leads to the formation of plans of action and ultimately to deeper understanding. This leads to a subsidiary definition that knowledge is concerned with using information effectively. The next level of abstraction might be called 'theory', but now we are getting on to really contentious ground and well outside of the concerns of this book; so back to knowledge.

Apart from asking what it is, epistemologists have been concerned with several other issues concerning knowledge:

(1) How may it be classified?
(2) How is it obtained?
(3) Does it have objective reality?
(4) Is it limited in principle?

As a preliminary attempt at classification we might note that there are several evidently different types of knowledge at hand: knowledge about objects, events, task performance, and even about knowledge itself. If we know something about tomatoes we will probably know that tomatoes are red; however, we are still prepared to recognize a green tomato; so that contradictions often coexist within our knowledge. Object knowledge is often expressed in the form of assertions, although we shall see later, when we come to discuss frames, that this is by no means the only available formalism. Some assertions:

Tomatoes are red.
This bottle is made of glass.
Zoe is very lively.

Knowledge of causality, however, is expressed typically as a chain of statements relating cause to effect:

If you boil tomatoes with the right accompaniments chutney results.

To perform a task as commonplace as walking in fact requires a very complex interacting system of knowledge about balance, muscle tone, etc., much of which is held subconsciously and is deeply integrated in with our biological hardware. Knowledge about cognition, often called meta-knowledge, is in some sense the subject of Chapter 7 on inference methods, but also needs to be represented when such questions as 'What do I know?' and 'How useful or complete is a particular knowledge system or inference strategy?' are raised. This, we hope, leads to a clear perception that there is no clear boundary between knowledge and inference as practices. Each interpenetrates the other; we have inference with knowledge and knowledge about inference.

In Fig. 2.2 which we have borrowed from Chinese philosophy, we have a representation of the interpenetration of these opposites: knowledge and inference. Borrowing now from German Idealism we must identify the mediations by which each is posited, or 'sublated', in the other. In one direction we have reasoning and in the other intuition or logic according to how the knowledge arises.

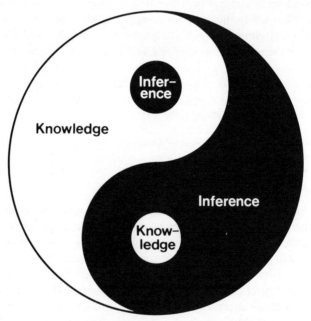

Fig. 2.2   The interpenetration of opposites

There are various dimensions along which knowledge can be evaluated:

Scope   – What does it cover?
Granularity   – How detailed is it?
Uncertainty   – How certain or plausible is it?
Completeness   – Might we have to retract conclusions if new knowledge
                 comes to light?
Consistency   – How easily can we live with its contradictions?
Modality   – Can we avoid it?

All these dimensions give rise to some sort of uncertainty and this too will be important in our study of inference. The dimension of uncertainty will be covered extensively in Part III, but we remark here that in some senses all the above dimensions are to do with some form of uncertainty. This arises from the contradictory nature of knowledge. Knowledge presents itself in two basic forms as absolute and relative. To understand this consider the whole of the history of science, which is an attempt to arrive at a knowledge of the environment we inhabit. The scientist develops this or that theory or paradigm which explains experimental evidence and is further verified in practice. He or she never suspects that any theory is comprehensively correct, at least not nowadays; Newton's models overthrew the theories of earlier times and were in their turn overthrown by Einstein's. If nature exists beyond, before and apart from us then it represents, in all its complexity, an absolute truth which is (in principle) beyond knowledge because nature is not in itself human and knowledge is. To assume otherwise is to assert that nature is either a totally human construct or that the whole may be totally assimilated by a fragment of itself. This is not to say that the finite may not know the infinite, only that the knowledge may only be relative, otherwise the finite would contain the infinite and thus become infinite itself. Thus all truth-seeking aims at the absolute but achieves the relative and here it is that we see why all knowledge must perforce be uncertain. This is why it is the primary thesis of this book that the correct handling of uncertainty is one of the primary concerns for builders of knowledge-based systems of any sort.

2.1.3 Representing knowledge

The dimensions mentioned above will all have some bearing on the techniques used to represent knowledge. If we choose logic as the representation then, if our knowledge is incomplete, nonmonotonic logic will be required in preference to first-order predicate logic, and in the presence of uncertainty a logic capable of handling it will be requisite. Similar remarks apply to inconsistent knowledge where contradiction must be handled either by the logic or the control structure or meta-logic. Modality will require the use of a logic which can deal with necessity and possibility.

If, on the other hand, we choose frames or network representations the scope and granularity will affect the amount of storage we can expect to use. For this it is useful to have some metrics. Granularity is often measured in 'chunks'. Anderson [9] defines a chunk to be a learned configuration of symbols which comes to act as a single symbol. How this learning might take place is covered in Chapter 7, Section 3. The passage between levels of representation is an important theme in AI research and is covered well by Hofstadter [99]. It has great bearing on the practical question of efficiency of storage and execution. Generally speaking, you should choose a granularity close to that adopted by human experts, if this can be discerned, and use chunking whenever gains are not made at the expense of understandability.

There are two important questions about the representation of knowledge.

First there was the question of how knowledge is represented in the human or animal brain, and now there is that of what structures may be used for computer representation. The first question is the concern of cognitive psychology and psychoanalysis and will not exercise us in this book greatly. However, the theories of the cognitive psychologists have much to offer in the way of ideas and cognitive simulation has been an important issue in research on expert systems. The inter-disciplinary subject of artificial intelligence has indeed been defined as 'the study of mental faculties through the use of computational models' (Charniak and McDermott, [41]); exactly the reverse of what interests us as builders of knowledge-based systems. Perhaps this is why there is such a considerable overlap and confusion between the fields of artificial intelligence and knowledge engineering today. One important point to make categorically is that no one knows how the human brain works and no one can give a prescription for the best computer knowledge representation formalism. Until some pretty fundamental advances are made, our best bet as system builders is to use pragmatically whatever formalism best suits the task at hand.

2.2   REPRESENTATION METHODS

2.2.1   Procedural and logic representations

The representation scheme most prevalent in existing computer applications is the procedure. Knowledge of how and in exactly what order to perform a certain task or calculation is stored and then applied to data and/or information to produce results which are put out in a form predetermined and readable by the user. For example, if the machine is required to perform as if it had knowledge of management accounting one might store the 'program':

```
1 INPUT PRICE, VOLUME, COST

2 REVENUE = PRICE * VOLUME

3 COSTS = COST * VOLUME

4 MARGIN = REVENUE - COSTS

5 PRINT MARGIN
```

which prompts us for three numbers and correctly computes and prints the product margin. The knowledge stored is principally about the order in which to perform the calculations, and if line 4 were to appear anywhere other than as line 4 the output would be incorrect. Of course, this is a very simple problem and the program is correspondingly easy. Procedural programs of vast complexity exist ranging from integrated business systems carrying out payroll, accounting and reporting functions to esoteric scientific and engineering systems to predict the weather, calculate stresses and strains or guide spacecraft to their destinations among the stars. To come a little closer to reality consider the REVEAL program shown in Fig. 2.3 which 'knows' how to construct magic squares of odd order using the technique devised, or at least imported to the West, by De la Loubere.

This program illustrates some of the tools of the trade of procedural representation: repeat loops, if . . . then . . . else constructions, assignment, etc. The point is that the knowledge is obscured by the representation; such programs can be intensely difficult to understand and maintain. True knowledge-based systems aim at a more transparent representation and we shall now examine alternatives to the procedural one.

We shall, throughout this book, have occasion to mention formal logic. In particular, in Chapter 6 we introduce the first-order predicate calculus. A subset of this logic can be used to represent knowledge, and this is the purport of the

```
MODE >INSPECT
  1:   print('')
  2:   print('...magic square generator')
  3:   type('...enter the size of the square')
  4:   imax=tty
  5:     if imax lt   1 then goto notpos:
  6:     if max gt 19 then goto toobig:
  7:     if int(imax/2)*2 eq imax then goto notodd:
  8:
  9:   print('...the magic number is',(1+imax*imax)/2*imax like'xxxxx')
 10:   print('')
 11:
 12:   repeat i=(1,imax)
 13:     repeat j=(1,imax)
 14:        k=j-i+int(imax-1)/2
 15:        1=2*j-i
 16:        if k ge imax then k=k-imax
 17:                  else do
 18:                        if k lt 0 then k=k+imax
 19:                        enddo
 20:        if l gt imax then 1=1-imax
 21:                  else do
 22:                        if 1 le 0 then 1=1+imax
 23:                        enddo
 24:        type(k*imax+1 like'xxxx')
 25:     endrep
 26:     print ('')27:  endrep
 27:     endrep
 28:   print('')
 29:
 30:   exit
 31:
 32:   notpos: print('---square side must be positive');exit
 33:   toobig: print('---maximum square side is 19');exit
 34:   notodd: print('---square must have an odd number of rows');exit

MODE >
```

Fig. 2.3 Magic squares algorithm

programming language PROLOG. If one wishes to store knowledge about a data structure PROLOG is particularly appropriate. An example might be the structure of kinship relationships among the Trobriand Islanders of Melanesia (Levi-Strauss [129]):

```
brother(X,Y) :- male(X),mother(Z,X),mother(Z,Y)
maternal_uncle(X,Y) :- mother(Z,Y),brother(X,Z)
dislikes(X,Y) :- maternal_uncle(Y,X)
dislikes(X,Y) :- (brother(X,Y); sister(X,Y))
likes(X,Y) :- father(Y,X)
likes[X,Y) :- (husband(X,Y); wife(X,Y))
etc.
```

This particular fragment describes one of the possible structures observed by Levi-Strauss and (if completed) would allow the user to inquire whether two individuals traditionally liked each other by generating questions such as 'Are they married?' and so on. This is possible by virtue of the built-in goal-seeking of the PROLOG language which works through the logical connections attempting to find instances of a variable for which a goal is satisfied. More will be said of this method of inference in Chapter 7. For those not already familiar with the PROLOG syntax the above code could be translated as saying:

Someone is someone else's brother is they share a mother.
A maternal uncle is a brother of a mother.
X dislikes Y if Y is their maternal uncle, brother or sister.
If two people are married then they like each other.

Any reader mystified by these seemingly odd statements is highly recommended to read *Structural Anthropology*, not merely for the explanation which is irrelevant to the present work, but because it is a delightful book.

In fact, there are several different syntaxes for different implementations of PROLOG. The one in which the above rules were expressed is known as the 'Edinburgh' or DEC 10 syntax and is emerging as a standard. Clocksin and Mellish [47] describe the syntax in detail. A strikingly different syntax for micro-computer versions of PROLOG originates from Imperial College, London. In Fig. 2.4 we illustrate the Levi-Strauss kinship structures for five nations using this syntax, together with some interactive queries about whether certain roles are hostile or tender towards one another. Details of this syntax can be found in Clarke and McCabe [45]. Note here the distinction between facts (Sonny is a male role) and rules (a parent is either a father or a mother). All these statements are Horn clauses, since they possess only one consequent. Horn clauses are defined in Chapter 4 to which the reader should refer for further details.

Having said that PROLOG is an easier way to represent this kind of knowledge, it would not be entirely fair to conceal some very real difficulties. The order in which the statements occur can (sometimes) have a striking effect on efficiency; to the extent that a reordering of the program shown can easily exhaust the

```
------------------------------------------
X parent-of Y if
    (either X father-of Y or X mother-of Y
X sibling-of Y if
    Z mother-of X and
    Z mother-of Y and
    not (X EQ Y)
X sibling-of Y if
    Z father-of X and
    Z father-of Y and
    not (X EQ Y)
X brother-of Y if
    male (X) and
    X sibling-of Y
X sister-of Y if
    X female and
    X sibling-of Y
Gran female
Mum female
Dad married-to Mum
Gran mother-of Mum
Gran mother-of Nunc
Mum mother-of Sonny
X maternal-uncle-of Y if
    Z mother-of Y and
    Z sister-of X
X father-of Y if
    X married-to Z and
    Z mother-of Y
X tender-to Y if
    Trobriand people and
    (either X married-to Y or X parent-of Y)
X tender-to Y if
    Siuai people and
    (either X sibling-of Y or X parent-of Y)
X tender-to Y if
    Cherkess people and
    X sibling-of Y
X tender-to Y if
    Kubutu people and
    (either X parent-of Y or X sibling-of Y)
X tender-to Y if
    Tonga people and
    X married-to Y
X hostile-to Y if
    X maternal-uncle-of Y and
    Z father-of Y and
    Z tender-to Y
X hostile-to Y if
    Trobriand people and
    X sibling-of Y
X hostile-to Y if
    Siuai people and
    X married-to Y
X hostile-to Y if
    Cherkess people and
    (either X married-to Y or X father-of Y)
------------------------------------------
```

Fig. 2.4 Anthropology in PROLOG

Fig. 2.4 *contd*

```
------------------------------------------

X hostile-to Y if
      Tonga people and
      (either X sibling-of Y or X father-of Y)
X hostile-to Y if
      Kubutu people and
      X married-to Y
male (Dad)
male (Sonny)
Cherkess people
&is(Dad tender-to Sonny)
NO
&is(Nunc hostile-to Sonny)
NO
&is(Dad hostile-to Nunc)
NO
&is(Mum tender-to Dad)
NO
&add(Trobriand people)
&is(Dad tender-to Sonny)
YES
&is(Dad hostile-to Sonny)
YES
&is(Nunc hostile-to Sonny)
YES
&is(Dad hostile-to Nanc)
NO
&is(Mum tender-to Dad)
NO
&which(x:x hostile-to Dad)
No (more) answers
&which(x:x tender-to Dad)
No (more) answers
&which(x:x hostile-to Sonny)
Nunc
Dad
No (more) answers
&.

------------------------------------------
```

memory of the 256K machine on which it was written. Furthermore, the programmer who is tempted to insert a rule which says that marriage is a commutative relation will soon come to grief if the rule is expressed in the obvious manner: X married-to Y if Y married-to X. Like most conventional languages, PROLOG demands great skill of its users for anything but very simple problems.

The positive points to note about the knowledge representation are that it is extremely concise and readable compared with procedural code and that no statements as to procedure are explicit. Also, the order of the lines of the program does not affect the outcome except in terms of execution efficiency in some implementations. It is often quite natural to express knowledge in this way, say when a complex decision tree has to be represented. Unfortunately, real PROLOG programs usually depart from the simplicity of examples and are highly procedural which leads to a loss of separation of knowledge from inference. It should become obvious to the reader after studying Chapter 4, that higher-order statements will be dealt with only tortuously and that the language is not well suited to handling uncertainty, especially if we add that computation is not a strength of the extant implementations of the language.

The only natural way to deal with uncertainty is to predefine a fixed set of linguistic terms such as 'tall' or 'sunny' and explicitly pattern match for them as is done, for example in the Xi shell product [65]. In general this is unsatisfactory although some small applications suit this approach. Furthermore, as has been pointed out elsewhere, this approach merely avoids the whole question of uncertainty by increasing the granularity of the description so that 'sunny' is really a certain but coarse predicate. Of course, in real implementations of PROLOG higher order structures are permitted but this is not consonant with the theory any more than the 'cut' construction is, resulting in maintenance and comprehension problems.

Baldwin's team at Bristol University has introduced 'fuzzy PROLOG' which holds great promise but is not yet commercially available [15, 141]. This system has the additional advantage of interfacing with FRIL (Fuzzy Relational Inference Language) which is a fuzzy set based query language using relational algebra to answer queries. We will have more to say about FRIL in Chapter 3. Predicates in fuzzy PROLOG have an extra argument to represent the uncertainty measure associated with the predicate. The user may choose their own multivalent or fuzzy logic depending on the problem in hand and the interpreter includes a fuzzy backtracking algorithm. Many of the weaknesses of PROLOG are overcome in this way; the logic is inherently higher order; uncertainty is coped with well, naturally and flexibly.

2.2.2   Networks, frames, scripts and cognitive emulation

Another natural way to represent knowledge about objects and their class relationships is as a semantic network. This concept arose first in studies of human cognition. A semantic network is a collection of objects and relationships between objects together with some interpretation. We illustrate a semantic network which shows that Chaucer wrote a tale about someone who told a cock and hen story (Fig. 2.5).

Here we have represented the statements 'every chicken is a bird' and 'every hen is a chicken' directly and thus have made it easy to infer that every hen is a bird. The reader will, we hope, forgive our restriction of the usage of 'hen' to female chickens.

Semantic networks (or nets) are very good at expressing knowledge about class inheritance properties, demons, defaults and perspectives; for details see Winston [210]. A particularly important point is that learning can be simulated by creating explicit links for commonly used compound links. Thus if we are using the above network to solve crosswords or engage in general knowledge contests we might well find our pattern matcher constantly having to associate Chaucer

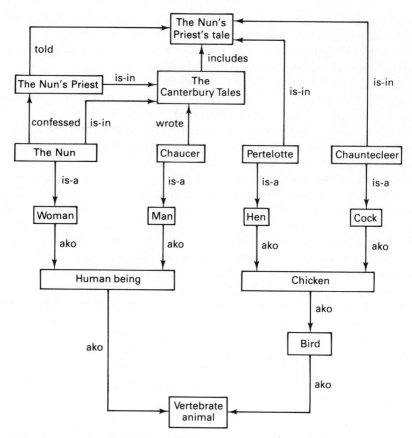

Fig. 2.5 A semantic network

with Chanticleer, so the learning algorithm must introduce a 'wrote about' link between them. The advocates of this model of associative memory in humans might well assert that this sort of thing goes on when people link Shakespeare with Hamlet whilst having forgotten everything else about the play; this example seems to indicate that primitive links may be allowed to wither away in humans but we don't know of any computer systems where this happens. A recent critique of such models is discussed below.

Two strong weaknesses of this formalism can be immediately identified. First there is no formal semantics available as there is for logic representation which means that the choice of inference methods is highly arbitrary. There is no guarantee that inferences drawn are *valid* as with logic and no built-in distinction between class and individual. This leads to the need for exceedingly complex inference strategies such as property inheritance, or the spreading activation of Quillian [142]. Secondly it is awkward to represent uncertain or partial linkages such as 'Chaucer is very famous' by links or operations on links in the absence of a semantic model. For this, a second-order structure of fuzzy values or probabilities attached to links needs to be introduced together with the appropriate modifier rules to cope with hedges like 'very' or 'slightly'. As far as the authors know no-one has done this, but the approach is more in keeping with the spirit of 'frames' discussed below. The idea of a 'fuzzy semantic net' would assign a degree of membership to each link or allow fuzzy sets as objects. All this drives us towards the concepts of category theory introduced in Chapter 6 where the latter approach will be explored and where we shall see that the links themselves become complex mathematical objects in their own right.

Minsky [151] introduced and popularized the notion of an aggregated network structure called a 'frame' where the links associated with a particular object are called 'slots'. These frames are not to be confused with the frames of Section 6.6 or indeed with the 'frame problem' mentioned in Chapter 7. The word frame is a little overworked and some authors prefer to use 'schema' for the present notion [210, 41], but since this too has other overtones when we come to database theory we will stick with 'frame' for the remainder of this book. Slots can be of various types. Just as with links we have IS-A, IS-IN, OWNS, etc. The idea is that to describe our knowledge of an *object* we introduce a data structure associated to the object which includes declarative, procedural and property-inheritance information. In this sense frames represent a partial unification of the procedural and semantic net approaches. Let us look at a typical frame.

Name: Golf club
Is_a: Club, Place, Licensed Premises
Type: String variable
Value:
Derived_from:
Default: Boondoggle
Membership_fee:
Member: Person
  (If_needed find a Person with Belongs_to = Value:)

The slots can be filled in in various ways; by giving a value, by prescribing another frame to supply the value or by assigning a procedure to compute a value if so required. In the above example a golf club inherits the more general properties of being a place, for example it has a location, from the place frame. The member slot can be filled by firing up a search procedure and the value slot can be filled by a specific instance either as a result of the execution of some program, by inheritance from a higher frame, or by taking the default value. The derivation slot is there to record how a particular value came about. Slots can be filled by other frames; thus a member is something which the person frame 'understands' about. Understanding is said to take place when all the the slots are filled. The frame can contain explicit knowledge about what to do when a slot cannot be filled or how to reassign the frame when a minor difference of detail is detected. For example, if we are trying to understand a perceived object using our 'golf club' frame but find that it has no greens we could assume that it was a country club and try that frame. Minsky calls this using an 'excuse'. In this sense frames are capable of dealing with certain kinds of uncertainty, but traditional frames do not permit fuzzy objects to fill their slots. We take up this point in Section 2.2.4.

Computer scientists will be more at home with the concept of a relational database with variable length records with the additional freedom to mention procedures as data. We return to the connection between these concepts in Chapter 3 and Section 2.2.4.

Hayes [90] has pointed out that the constructions which are possible with frames can be represented in first order logic, but it is by no means clear that this is a natural way to deal with such constructions. The idea of defaults leads to attempts to deal with nonmonotonic logic, so that clearly there will be alternative higher order logics which could be used. The outstanding advantage of frames however remains their abilities in respect of chunking at a higher level of abstraction, leading to considerable computational advantages.

Whereas frames are primarily useful for capturing knowledge about objects there is a related structure called a 'script' which is designed to be more appropriate to the description of event knowledge. Scripts, according to Schank and Abelson [180], are structures that describe sequences of events pertinent to a context. They are particularly useful in forming the internal representation of meaning in a universal form suitable for understanding stories written in natural language and summarizing them. Consider, for example, the following story.

> 'Gill went to her golf club. She stayed there for three hours. Next day she needed an aspirin.'

It is difficult to understand the meaning of this story unless we refer to our knowledge of golf clubs as places where hangovers can be acquired and indeed of drinking alcohol. Scripts (assuming that they are part of our cognitive repertoire) enable us to leave out the boring details when relating a story in the safe knowledge that our auditors can fill in the gaps from their own knowledge of what is normal or expected. Like a frame a script is made up of slots and requirements as to what can fill those slots. The structure is an interdependent whole, in which the contents of one slot can influence what can be in another. As with frames, 'understanding' occurs when all the slots are filled. Scripts are predetermined, stylized, stereotyped sequences of actions that define well known situations and are not subject to much change once stored. This fixed nature means that intelligent behaviour requires some methods for handling exceptions and, indeed, for learning new scripts as the need arises. Thus planning and goal seeking are important adjuncts to any script based system.

Every script has associated with it a number of roles which the actors can assume. The script is written from the point of view of a particular role and this role is the stereotype for the default actor, if unnamed. Schank and Abelson break down all actions to a set of primitive actions and evaluate them according to predefined 'scales' such as HEALTH (dead, ill, average, well, superfit). Their theory of conceptual dependency is not our chief concern here, but we will introduce a fragment of it to speed our discussion of scripts as a form of knowledge representation. The primitive actions of conceptual dependency theory are:

ATRANS – Transfer abstract relation between actors
PTRANS – Transfer object
MTRANS – Transfer mental state
PROPEL
MOVE
GRASP
INGEST
EXPEL
MBUILD – Construct new mental state
SPEAK – Display information
ATTEND
DO – Perform unknown act

The meanings of the unlabelled primitives should be obvious. The assumption is that this is a complete list, which is probably not the case but seems to have worked well in the limited domain in which Schank and Abelson worked. The theory enables sentences to be understood as sequences of causal primitives consisting of:

r – an ACT results in a STATE
E – a STATE enables an ACT
dE – a STATE disables an ACT
I – a STATE initiates a M(ental)STATE
R – a MSTATE is a reason for an ACT

It allows two abbreviated combinations of these primitives:

IR – an ACT or STATE initiates a thought which is a reason for an ACT.
rE – an ACT results in a STATE which enables an ACT.

For example the sentence 'Jan gave Gill an aspirin for her hangover' is represented by the causal chain:

Jan ATRANS aspirin to Gill
      rE
Gill INGEST aspirin
    r
Gill HEALTH(positive change)

Fairly complex stories can be handled this way.

To aid understanding let us have a look at a fragment of the script system for golf clubs.

Script: Golf club
Track: Boondoggle
Props: Irons,Fairway,Chairs,Drinks,Glasses,Plates,Food,Money,...
Roles: M – member
      G – guest
      O – official
      S – staff
      C – caddy
Entry conditions: M has money,...
Results: M has less money, O happier, M happier, ...
Scenes:
  Scene 1: Entering(member)
      M MBUILD M thirsty(high)
      M DO (SIGN-IN-GUEST script)
      M ATTEND eyes to bar
      M MBUILD S(barmaid) present
      M PTRANS M to bar
      M MTRANS signal to S
      ...
  Scene 2: Drinking
      ...

In practice scripts are very complicated indeed and have to allow for many exceptions: what happens when the bill arrives and you find you have lost your wallet? However, the point is that the script describes a well known situation; one that has been encountered many times before. They do not assist in dealing with the unexpected or unusual. For that the ability to form plans is required and this is a major theme in current AI research to which we will return in Chapter 7. Of course the same remark applies to frames: they cannot take account of objects whose properties are not known and cannot be inherited from those of more general objects or computed from default procedures. The key use of scripts up to now has been understanding stories. The SAM program [180] for example understands stories about restaurants and is provided with appropriate scripts to make this possible. It can paraphrase and answer questions about these stories. PAM is a similar system for understanding based on plans rather than scripts. TALESPIN uses similar methods and assigns the actors goals with the result that it can invent children's stories in a limited domain. The most practical use to which scripts have been put is for skimming news stories for new content so that humans don't have to read press releases which say much the same thing as those which came over the wire yesterday. The early work on this was written up in Schank and Abelson [180] but much has been done since that was published in 1977 and currently research is proceeding into how such systems could handle uncertainty.

Recently Morton, Hammersley and Bekerian [154] have criticized semantic nets and frames from the standpoint of cognitive emulation and introduced the notion of headed records. So far this has found no application in the form of computer programs but the ideas are important enough to warrant inclusion here. It is interesting to note that scripts can much more easily resist the criticism from this direction as they may be stored in the form of headed records where the header need not be explicitly accessible to a decoding mechanism and thereby remain totally inaccessible. However the chief difficulty with headed records is that class inheritance becomes difficult to represent and so our headed scripts would need access to undecoded headers.

The theory of headed records was introduced by Morton and his colleagues to explain the familiar phenomenon that occurs when we can remember almost everything about an acquaintance except that we can only recall their name with great difficulty or after the subject has been changed. They propose that memory is stored as indelible decodable records which are accessed via a header which cannot be decoded by our cognitive processes. If facts about a person are accessed via a header which includes the name but that name is not stored explicitly in that record (although it must be in some other record) this will explain the phenomenon. Some experimental studies have been carried out to confirm the plausibility of the theory, but its key interest, for us, is that semantic nets and frames do not explain this kind of phenomenon unless we admit the highly implausible likelihood of all the links to the name being blocked simultaneously and by some obscure mechanism. This is not to say that the headed records theory is not subject to criticism. In a 'frames' approach we could conceive of a part of a frame being copied elsewhere so that someone's academic record might be stored under 'psychology' rather than by name; we then associate ideas with 'someone' who wrote this or that famous paper. The present author has speculated that if there is anything in the headed records approach, it may be that the headers are coded at the RNA level in the brain which would further account for the speed of human recall in some situations and the undecodability of the headers. See Hofstadter [99] for some interesting remarks on how RNA and proteins carry code structures. System builders would do well to attempt to simulate this kind of structure in knowledge representation where access speeds are critical. The same considerations are involved when we decide to store numbers in packed form, i.e. how often do we have to decode or rather unpack them? What they must avoid, however, are computer systems which forget names.

In defence of frames it may be said that the two theories may coexist if we allow that the memory needs sometimes to build mechanisms to short circuit the search through all these billions of remembered images when oft encountered concepts must be dealt with quickly.

The other question raised is the desirability of cognitive simulation in knowledge-based systems. It is worth pausing to summarize the pros and cons.

Because of the emergence of knowledge engineering as a discipline from the AI laboratories, most expert system builders have attempted some form of cognitive emulation in their systems. Whether this is a good thing is still the subject of debate. Slatter [188] provides a useful summary of the cases for and against cognitive emulation, but, like most writers on the subject, neglects one important argument for its use. One of the reasons it may be preferable not to emulate humans is that there may be means to increase the efficiency of computer systems which contradict all known psychological models. However, human experts, reasoning in the presence of uncertainty, take many short cuts because of the representations available to them. They certainly don't think in terms of precise numerical probabilities, but often represent uncertainty by linguistic means and are able to manipulate it at that level in a 'logical' manner. One of the objectives of fuzzy logic is precisely the representation of this kind of knowledge, as we shall see later in this chapter.

Apart from efficiency, the other factors which will influence a system designer in deciding whether or not to attempt direct emulation of human thought processes are as follows. A system which reasons like a person is more likely to gain acceptance among users. To see that acceptance can be a problem with otherwise successful expert systems it is only necessary to ask why MYCIN is so strongly resisted by physicians. Equally important is the relative ease with which a system can be built if its inbuilt representation corresponds well with that of the expert in the form which has been elicited by a knowledge engineer by techniques which we deal with below.

On the other hand human experts are bad at numerical tasks, forgetful, often irrational and contradictory and prone to error. If computers are better at some things than we are we should certainly exploit that fact. Knowledge engineers aim to construct efficient, modifiable, simple, understandable and correct code and it is only to the extent that emulation does not conflict with these goals that it should be employed. Slatter gives a decision rule which we paraphrase below with our own additions.

IF   CONVENTIONAL TECHNIQUES CANNOT MEET ENGINEERING REQUIREMENTS AND
       THERE ARE PERTINENT COGNITIVE PROCESSES IN USE AND
       THESE PROCESSES ARE EMULABLE IN PRINCIPLE AND
       HUMAN PERFORMANCE IS FASTER AS A RESULT OF THEIR USE AND
       THE PROCESSES ARE WELL UNDERSTOOD AND THERE IS A COMPUTATIONAL MODEL OF
         THEM AND
       (SOFTWARE TOOLS EXIST WHICH EMBODY THEM OR RESOURCES EXIST TO DEVELOP
         SUCH TOOLS) AND
       (THE TOOLS MAP ONTO ELICITED KNOWLEDGE OR CAN BE TAILORED TO DO SO) AND
       (EMULATION DOES NOT COMPRISE ENGINEERING OBJECTIVES OR
       (EMULATION DOES COMPROMISE OBJECTIVES BUT THE PROBLEM IS OTHERWISE
         INSOLUBLE))
THEN COGNITIVE EMULATION SHOULD BE USED

The rule just given is an example of knowledge represented in the way which has been most widespread up to now in expert systems; that is, it is a production rule and it is this formalism that we consider next.

2.2.3   Production systems

The concept of reducing systems to a few primitives and production rules for generating the rest of the system goes back to Post, who with Church and Turing all worked on the idea of formal models of computers independently. Post's original work was concerned with the theory of semigroups which is of interest in algebraic models of language [98]. Newell and Simon [162, 161] introduced them in the form in which we find them in knowledge-based systems as part of their work on GPS, the general problem solver, which was an attempt to build an intelligent system which did *not* rely for its problem solving abilities on a store of domain-specific knowledge but would *inter alia* generate production rules as required. For example, Marvin the robot wants to go to MIT. He is faced with an immediate problem before this goal can be satisfied: how to get there. He can fly, walk/swim, ride a bus or train, and so on. To make the decision he might weigh up the cost and the journey time and decide to fly, but this strategy will not work because he is not at an airport. Thus he must solve a sub-problem of how to get to an airfield which runs a service which takes him close to Boston. In production rules his reasoning so far (he hasn't solved the whole problem yet) might look like this:

IF I WANT TO GO TO BOSTON THEN I MUST CHOOSE A TRANSPORT MODE
FLYING IS A MODE OF TRANSPORT WHICH I WILL CHOOSE
IF YOU ARE AT AN AIRPORT THEN YOU CAN FLY
I AM NOT AT AN AIRPORT
IF I WANT TO BE AT AN AIRPORT THEN I MUST CHOOSE A TRANSPORT MODE

The statements above consist of assertions and productions and together these represent some of the knowledge Marvin needs to begin reasoning about his problems. There are many reasoning strategies he can employ, and, however depressing a thought this may be for Marvin, we will deal with them in the chapter on inference methods. For the time being we are interested in the representation of knowledge by production rules as these IF . . . THEN constructions are known.

The left-hand side of a production rule of the form

IF A THEN B

is called its antecedent and the right-hand side its consequent. It may be interpreted in many ways: If a certain condition is satisfied then a certain action is appropriate; if a certain statement is true then another can be inferred; if a certain syntactic structure is present then some other can be generated grammatically. In general the A and B can be complex statements constructed from simpler ones using the connectives AND and OR and the NOT operator. In practice only A is permitted this rich structure so that a typical production would look like this:

IF (animal is hairy AND animal gives milk) OR location is mammal-house
THEN animal is mammal

The parentheses disambiguate the precedence of the connectives and avoid the need to repeat clauses unnecessarily. Production systems combine rules as if there were an OR between the rules; that is between the antecedents of rules with the same consequent. A production rule system may be regarded as a machine which takes as input values of the variables mentioned in antecedent clauses and puts out values for the consequent variables. Clearly it is equivalent to a system with one machine for each consequent variable unless we allow feedback among the variables. When feedback is present we enter the realms of inference and the territory of Chapter 7.

Production rules are easy for humans to understand and, since each rule represents a small independent granule of knowledge, can be easily added or subtracted from a knowledge base. For this reason they have formed the basis of several well known large scale applications such as DENDRAL [16], MYCIN [186] and PROSPECTOR [223] and form the basis of nearly all expert system 'shells'. Because the rules are, in principle, independent from each other, they support a declarative style of programming which considerably reduces maintenance problems. However, care must be taken that contradictory rules are not introduced since this can lead to inefficiency at best and thrashing at worst. Another advantage that has been exploited in expert systems is the ease with which a production system can stack up a record of a program's use of each rule and thus provide rudimentary explanations of the systems reasoning. Lastly, productions make fairly light demands on a processor, although large amounts of memory or secondary storage will typically be required.

Precisely because they are memory intensive, production systems can be very inefficient. Also it is difficult to model association in processes where the use of the network methods described in Section 2.2.2 are more appropriate. This makes the taking of short cuts in reasoning difficult to implement. The declarative style makes algorithms extremely difficult to represent and flow of control is hard to supervise for a system designer. Lastly, the formalism as described so far makes no allowances for uncertain knowledge.

For these reasons it is now becoming more common to find that knowledge-based systems use several different kinds of knowledge representation. The next section shows how the formalism can be directly extended to cope with some kinds of uncertainty, and in this and a following chapter it will be seen that productions can be used to encode knowledge for manipulation through different underlying logical systems. Although most existing shells rely solely on production rules there is a trend for the more recently written packages to include frame representations and procedures as well. REVEAL and LEONARDO, for example, include procedures and fuzzy productions in an integrated manner, the latter offering frames as well.

Generally, representation by productions is appropriate when the task at hand consists of a sequence of independent transformations of state in a problem space in which the knowledge is fragmentary and independent of the inference strategy.

2.2.4 Fuzzy productions and fuzzy frames

One of the key concerns of this book is the effective management of uncertainty in expert and knowledge-based systems. Chapter 5 is an introduction to Zadeh's theory of fuzzy sets which is particularly useful in some implementations. In this section we anticipate some knowledge on the part of the reader in order to locate fuzzy sets within the topic of knowledge representation.

Traditional production rules admit as their antecedent and consequent clauses assignments to or testing of values of variables which take numbers, strings or lists as values. If the antecedent clause is satisfied then so is the consequent, with no shade of uncertainty apart from that expressed in the terms themselves.

The only difference with fuzzy productions is that the variables involved in the antecedent and consequent clauses may be function valued rather than 'value' valued, or point valued if you prefer. In other words a new primitive data type, the fuzzy subset, is permitted. In general, we would also allow probability distributions as primitive types. Normally however, it would be dangerous to allow both simultaneously without some complex supervisory structure to avoid the mixing of different kinds of uncertainty. The most striking advantages of fuzzy productions over the conventional rule formalisms are that hedges may be used and that truth values are automatically propagated through the rules obviating some of the need for a complex control strategy. This is to say that the logic plays a fundamental role as with the predicate calculus systems discussed later. The upshot from the point of view of knowledge representation is that rules may be expressed in a formal language which comes much closer to modelling the process of natural reasoning. Fig. 2.6 is an example of some knowledge represented by fuzzy production rules. The examples are based on the way a career counsellor might express knowledge based on experience and on knowledge about marketing strategy for consumer goods.

Note that there are actually two kinds of knowledge represented. First, knowledge about causality or transformation is represented as with all production systems but in a strikingly clear fashion. The second kind is actually hidden in words such as 'high' and 'very' which are pre-defined by the knowledge engineer in the form of functions which assign truth values to various input values for variables and transformations (hedges) which modify such functions in the presence of words such as 'very'. We shall discuss the representation and manipulation of fuzzy sets and hedges in Chapter 5 in some detail. For the time being we merely note that 'very' is usually represented by an operator such as 'raise every truth value to the power of 2'. Fig. 2.7 illustrates the function describing the value 'high'.

The same kind of extension of functionality can be applied to frames by permitting slots to be filled with fuzzy valued variables. To comprehend this

```
 1:  !Career selection policy
 2:  ! = = = = = = = = = = = = =
 3:
 4:      If maths is excellent and physics is excellent then research is indicated
 5:
 6:      If maths is less than average or physics is less than average then research is
         discouraged
 7:
 8:
 9:      If art is more than good and maths is more than average then architecture is
         indicated
10:
11:      If maths is more than average and economics is more than good then
         accountancy is indicated
12:
13:      If biology is more than good and the worst.science is more than average then
         medicine is indicated
14:
15:      If avge.art is less than good and avge.science is less than good then teaching is
         indicated
16:
17:
18:      If english is more than good and maths is more than average and worst.science is
         more than poor then law is indicated
19:
20:      If english is excellent and worst.art is more than poor then writing is indicated
21:
22:
23:      If english is good and economics is good but maths is less than average then
         politics is indicated
24:
25:
26:      If (worst.art is good or worst.science is good) and maths is average then
         administration is indicated
*>
```

```
MODE >INSPECT

 1:  ! EXAMPLE OF APPLYING
      JUDGEMENT IN A FINANCIAL
      MODEL
 2:  !
 3:  ! Compute the forecast direct cost per
      unit
 4:  !
 5:    direct.cost = compound(base.cost,cost.
      infl,12)
 6:  !
 7:  ! Now apply the rules given in the
      policy Pricing.
 8:  ! = = = = = = = = =
 9:    APPLY(' PRICING' )
10:  ! = = = = = = = = =
11:    margin = price − direct.cost
12:    revenue = price *volume
13:    profit = margin *volume
14:    net.profit = profit − fixed.exp
15:  !
16:    profit%sales = 100 *net.profit/revenue
17:  !

MODE >
```

```
MODE >VOC PRICING
...VOCABULARY INSTALLED

MODE >POLICY PRICING

*>TYPE*

 1:  ! Product pricing rules
 2:  ! = = = = = = = = = =
 3:  !
 4:  ! We want a cheap product to generate
      high sales : =
 5:
 6:    Our price should be low
 7:
 8:  ! We need to adequately cover our
      expenses : =
 9:
10:    Our price should be about
      2 *direct.cost
11:
12:  ! As long as the opposition don't
      overcharge we will try
13:  ! to maximise profits by following their
      price : =
14:
15:    If the opposition is not very high
      then our price should be near the
      opposition

*>QUIT
```

Fig. 2.6 REVEAL programs

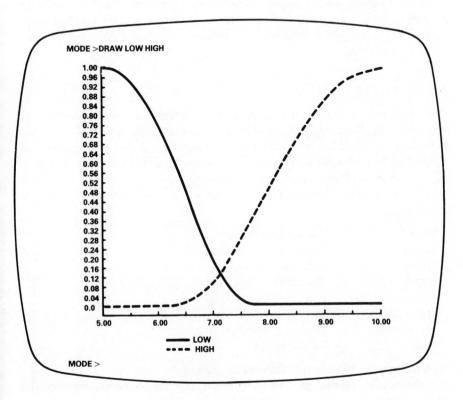

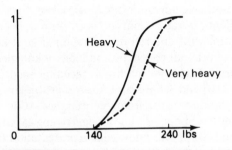

Fig. 2.7 Fuzzy sets and hedges

extension of the usual notion of a frame we will need to introduce some concepts from the theory of relational databases. Thus detailed consideration of this idea is deferred to the next chapter. The general idea is obtained by considering a frame for the notion of a man which might include slots for height, weight and beauty which might contain the 'values': 5'10", 10 stone and 'ugly'. The last value is an array representing a fuzzy subset chosen from a term set of values describing possible levels of beauty which it would be inappropriate to give exact numerical values to. The linguistic variable is, of course, represented on some arbitrary numerical interval.

2.3 SUMMARY

This chapter introduced the fundamental conceptions and apparatus of knowledge engineering. It was shown that knowledge and inference are intimately connected. The importance of choosing efficient and appropriate techniques for representing the various particular kinds of knowledge present in the context of a problem was emphasized. The reader was introduced to a range of knowledge representation formalisms appropriate for representing different kinds of knowledge.

Procedures	Process knowledge
Productions	Causal knowledge
Frames	Object knowledge
Semantic nets	Associative knowledge
Headed records	Associative knowledge
Fuzzy productions	Uncertain inference
Fuzzy frames	Imprecisely defined objects
Logic	Relationships

Each technique has been the subject of a critique.

In the next chapter we go, as it were, behind the scenes and look at databases and how they can contribute to knowledge representation.

2.4 FURTHER READING

Volume 1 of Barr and Feigenbaum's *The Handbook of Artificial Intelligence* [16] provides an excellent, if rather out of date, introduction to most of the representational formalisms covered here. Brachman and Levesque [34] have edited a collection of original papers on the topic of knowledge representation which would be hard to better and it is highly recommended. Other basic reading includes Winston [210] and Schank and Abelson [180]. For an alternative, and highly readable, definition of the frame concept see Atkin [12]. Bartlett [17] provides an excellent summary of knowledge typing. Many of the papers in Webber and Nilsson [206] cover knowledge representation from an implementation perspective, while Woods [213] addresses the nature of semantic networks in some detail.

3

Databases and knowledge-based systems

'It is a capital mistake to theorize before one has data.'
Sherlock Holmes

3.1 AN OVERVIEW OF DATABASE THEORY

This chapter sets out to tackle quite a challenging problem; that of how to integrate knowledge-based systems with that part of decision support theory which is concerned with data. The reader will recall from Chapter 1 the classification of the dimensions of decision support systems into modelling, data, knowledge and interface. Although we are primarily concerned here with the data dimension, it will be seen that it is just as impossible to separate completely these dimensions as it was to separate knowledge from inference in the previous chapter (nor indeed will it prove possible to achieve this separation in Chapter 7).

In this section we give a very cursory explanation of the basic concepts of file handling, network, hierarchical and relational techniques and move on to consider the relational model in more detail in the next. Building on this base we will investigate two directions in which the latter can be extended: in membership and in dimensionality. We then attempt to synthesize the extensions in the theory of fuzzy frames, which has not been done in any other work that we know of, and if it were to be completed might be considered an original contribution at the edge of current human knowledge. Next we consider the use of AI-based inferencing techniques in database navigation, with emphasis on the navigation of the data dictionary, and some related issues. Lastly, we consider the concept of a knowledge base, building on the formalisms developed in this chapter.

Any computer system processes data of some sort, whether those data are composed of numbers or symbols. Data flow into a system, are stored, are combined, are given structure (thus becoming information – they are *informed*) and finally flow out in some modified form. Database theory is concerned with how data are stored both physically and logically; with how those data may be accessed efficiently, meaningfully and simply (i.e. with a view to non-procedurality); with the logic of information structures and its related algebra. It is also concerned, peripherally, with the extent to which programs can be regarded as data and vice versa. A database then is the computer representation of data storage and logical structure in such a way as to define permissible procedures for addition, enquiry, amendment and deletion of groups or individual items of data; i.e. symbols of some sort. We will only be concerned in this book with the logical structure of data. For any given logical structure there are many possible ways of physically implementing it on a computer. The interested reader is referred to the literature of computer science for implementation details. The section on further reading will supply the basic references. Chomsky [44] offers some interesting insights into rules as a form of knowledge representation in the context of linguistics. Searle's influential work [179] is relevant to our study of scripts and several other topics in knowledge representation.

From a certain point of view, that of data processing, the history of commercial computing has proceeded through higher and higher stages of abstraction in data management. Starting with file management and passing on to database management systems of increasing power and abstraction, we have moved from transaction processing, through management information systems up to the top of the organizational pyramid where it is the decision support system that represents the most refined application of data management. The chapter on decision support systems explores this point more fully; but here we need only note that these more complex requirements, even when only small volumes of data are involved, have led to the need for greater flexibility in information processing systems. Thus, the progression, if such it is, from files through hierarchies and networks to relational databases represents a continuing process of bringing computer systems closer to the needs of human information processors (or computers as we used to be known prior to 1948) and decision makers. That the process continues is evidenced by the current interest in knowledge-based techniques applied to database technology. The INGRES and RAPPORT database products now sport interfaces to PROLOG and will be followed, of necessity, by their close competitors such as ORACLE and DB2 in having some such inferencing capability. Some query optimizers use AI techniques to decide on how to perform table joins, and pattern matching techniques have been employed in text processing systems. Also, some of the work which has been done on natural language processing has found expression in products such as INTELLECT, which converts English queries into the formal query languages of a range of commercial database products. The degree to which INTELLECT shows intelligence is a matter of dispute, since like the Eliza system [147] its successful operation depends on recognizing keywords, matching others with the data dictionary and stacking expressions to provide contextual guessing of meaning. This is not to denigrate such systems which achieve a high degree of acceptance among management who are not prepared to learn the formal languages for occasional use only.

Having said this much however, there is a sense in which the relational model is the last word. Network and hierarchical databases were not, in the first place, based on any formal model, the accompanying models being defined by induction, as it were, from existing systems *after* the relational model had been proposed by Codd [48]. Even today the other models have not been fully formally defined. This is because the relational model is based on first-order logic (or set theory if you like to think of it that way) and its limitations are therefore only those of the underlying logic. Developments in the future cannot abandon the relational model for some alternative 'fashion' but extensions can and will emerge. We propose one such later in this chapter.

The only other suggestion to be found in the literature as a competitor to the relational model is the functional data model described in Gray [82] and due originally to Shipman [184]. Gray is obviously a little confused over the exact meaning of the term 'data model' since he states: 'This (Multibase) uses the ability of the functional model to map the same abstract data definition onto both CODASYL and relational databases'. This statement makes the common error of confusing a logical model (the relational one in this case) with the physical implementation mechanism. There is no network data model, and the recommendations of the CODASYL committee are a *post hoc* response to existing physical implementations, no more and no less. The ideas of the functional model are closely related to the ideas of semantic networks discussed in the previous chapter and functional programming (cf Chapter 6). The underlying logic, thus, is closer to the Church–Curry λ-calculus than to first-order predicate calculus. It so happens that IS-A links and functions correspond closely to the owner-member links and 'sets' of a CODASYL database. Languages do exist which exploit this model and these are described in Gray's book: Daplex and Adaplex. In Daplex two entities with the same component values can still be distinguished by having distinct references. This cannot be accomplished in the standard relational model and extensions to the latter have been suggested (Codd [49]) which introduce unique identifiers for tuples so that an expression can denote a unique object which exists separately from its components. This is related to the idea of 'call by reference' in programming languages. As with LISP the functional approach removes the distinction between data and function (or program) and permits abstract data typing; that is, types are defined implicitly by the operations used. For example, the type List could be defined by the operations CAR, CDR and CONS. New types can be generated by generalization [IS-A] and aggregation, so that entities can be defined and arranged in hierarchies or networks. The functional model may, thus, hold out the promise of new developments, especially with the advent of parallel and dataflow hardware architectures when the overhead of non-destructive assignment can be regarded as less important. We will not consider this approach any further in this chapter.

The simplest data structure we can consider is a list, followed closely by lists of lists and the kind of tree structured lists found in languages like LISP. Anyone who has written a computer program will have opened a file of data and read through it record by record until some condition was satisfied. This is just like looking down a list, or list of lists if the file stores more than one kind of symbol. For example, consider a computerized telephone directory which stores name, address and phone number for some defined population. If you have the name and address it is then easy to look up the number. Not so if you have the number and address and want the name. This is because lists or files have logical structure; the structure of being sorted in a particular order. To facilitate our task we would have to read the file in a different order. The telephone book is a list of lists which can be viewed as a table. The situation can be more complicated in that lists of lists of lists, and so on, can arise. For example, our reverse phone book might have the structure shown in Table 3.1.

Table 3.1

Phone No.	Company	Dept.	No. of exits	Extension	Contact
999–8888	Aardvark Plc	Sales	1	102	Ann T. Eater
777–1234	ABC Ltd	PR	3	110	J. Doe
				111	A. N. Other
				133	T. Codd
123–4567	Blue Inc.	Marketing	1	2001	P. C. Dixon

There are three extensions in the PR department of ABC Ltd, so we have to include a 'repeating group' consisting of a list of extensions and contact names. A little thought will show that this arrangement has the logical structure of a tree or hierarchy. The use of repeating groups derives from the restriction to sequential storage devices such as tape in early computers.

The next level of complexity occurs when we have more than one file. Given random access technology, in the above example we don't need to keep the repeating groups in the same file. We can, instead, arrange for the company file records to merely contain pointers to the extensions file. The structure is now something like that shown in Table 3.2.

Table 3.2

	File–1				File–2	
Phone No.	Company	Dept.	Dept. code	Dept. code	Extn	Contact
999–8888	Aardvark	Sales	17	17	102	A. T. Eater
777–1234	ABC	PR	23	23	110	J. Doe
123–4567	Blue	Mrkting	24	23	111	A. N. Other
				23	133	T. Codd
				24	2001	P. C. Dixon

There are two files with a common field to link them. Logically, this link could be represented differently. It is logically a one-to-many relationship between departments and extensions. An extension cannot be in two departments in this scheme of things, which shows up one major limitation of the hierarchical approach to data structure, that is the difficulty of dealing with general, many-to-many relationships. More complex hierarchies may easily be envisaged.

The astute reader will detect that we have oversimplified in this example, in that two companies may possess the same department code. The key in the second file should be interpreted as company-department code strictly speaking. However, the idea is not compromised by this *abus de langage*.

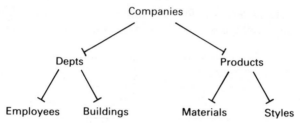

Fig. 3.1   One-to-many relationships

Another approach is to allow these links to go in any direction (see Fig. 3.1). This is achieved in the network model by allowing the links to be named and permitting a descendent node to have more than one antecedent or parent node. The fact that a particular company makes a product can be represented by the storage of a *link* representing, say, the volume of production in that product. Clearly, a product, say widgets, may be manufactured by many companies, just as the consumers of products may obtain them from many suppliers. We can represent this at a purely logical level in Fig. 3.2.

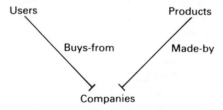

Fig. 3.2   Many-to-many relationships

This Bachman diagram (see [14]) expresses the many-to-many relationship amongst users and products. The nodes, such as Companies, Users, Products, etc., are normally called *entities* and the links, through what is perhaps the most idiotic piece of terminology in computing, are called *sets*. In fact they represent mappings logically, even though, physically, they refer to sets of links, as we will see next.

Consider the simple example shown in Fig. 3.3 where there is only one link.

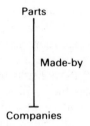

Fig. 3.3   A one-to-many relationship

In particular, and to get a feel for the complexity of the network model, let us suppose that our database is to contain the information shown in Fig. 3.4.

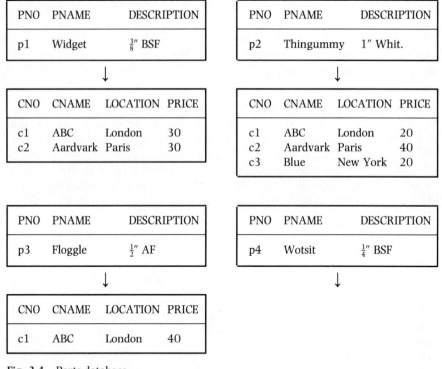

Fig. 3.4   Parts database

The detailed network is shown in Fig. 3.5.

Notice the ring structure of the links and that there are two ways to retrieve the answer to the query 'Find the description of part P2 made by C2': either start with the company and look along the pointers for a connector linked to the part, or

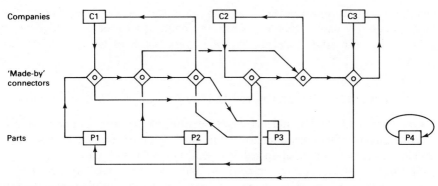

Fig. 3.5   (After Date)

start with the part and look for the company. It is completely non-trivial to decide which is the most efficient strategy.

Most people seeing a diagram such as that in Fig. 3.5 for the first time, would we are sure, agree that it looks a frightful mess. The maintenance costs associated with practical hierarchical databases seem to bear this view out. Fortunately there is a soundly formulated approach which overcomes all the pitfalls we have mentioned and more besides. This is the relational database.

The relational model of data was motivated by several aims. Among them were the desire to use formal methods in database design, enquiry and update; the desire to be able to prove the correctness of programs based on non-procedural descriptions and the urge to meet Occam's razor that the theory be as simple as possible while retaining its expressive power. The basic idea is that data are represented as a series of tables or 'flat files'. No repeating groups or implicit hierarchies are to be allowed, and no fixed structural links are to be a part of the database. Logical relationships between the data are constructed at run time or are held in tables themselves. Thus the same type of object is used to represent both entities and relationships. Also these 'cross reference' tables can be rebuilt without the need to reorganize the basic data. This is a great advantage in databases which model enterprises subject to much organizational change. It is amazing that, even today, many systems' development methodologies still place emphasis on labelling datasets or entities as to whether they are subject to change over time (LBMS for example). In a relational database the assumption is that *everything* can, in principle, change over time unless some exogenous fiat dictates otherwise. This, we assert, is typical of the extent to which the relational model has been misunderstood by its proponents as well as its enemies. The chief source of misunderstanding is the confusion between logical and physical data models. The relational model is a logical one. On the other hand there is no real hierarchical or network model in the logical sense. These are physical designs. In fact many relational database products are implemented in a hierarchical style. The logical relational model allows users to view one data structure in many different ways through so-called user views and thus an important benefit is a higher degree of user acceptance. From the point of view of knowledge-based systems the relational model makes even more sense, as we will see in this chapter.

3.2   THE RELATIONAL DATA MODEL

We have introduced relational databases fairly informally. This common practice has often led to misconceptions so we now turn to a more precise development. The formality of this exposition will be useful later in the chapter.

The relational model consists of three parts: a structural part which uses notions of domains, *n*-ary relations, attributes, tuples and primary and foreign keys; a manipulative part whose main tools are relational algebra and/or calculus and relational assignment; an integrity part in respect of both entities and reference. There is a fourth component normally considered as within the relational model, although this is not strictly the case, and that is the design part consisting of the theory of normal forms and top-down techniques such as Chen's entity-relationship model. We will explain some of this terminology as we go.

A relation, mathematically defined, is any subset of a Cartesian product of sets. This notion is developed more fully in Chapter 6 where it will be found that, given a list of sets $A_1, \ldots, A_n$, their Cartesian product is the set of all lists of *n* elements of the A_i where there can be only one element in the list from each A_i. Such a list is called an ordered *n*-tuple, or just a tuple. The relation is sometimes said to be *n*-ary. Each A_i is called a domain when viewed as a set of elements and an attribute when viewed as a label for that set. There are several notions which are equivalent to that of relation. For example, a *span* is a pair of mappings:

The universal property of products (cf. MacLane [136]) shows that spans are in one-to-one correspondence with relations. Note also that relations can be made into a category using functions as arrows or in other ways (using relations!).

Another equivalent notion is that of a table, and it is this one which is most often used in the context of computers because of the strong physical analogies. The trouble with classical mathematics is that its objects tend to be static, but the tables in our real world databases change with time. Thus we define an *extensional relation* to be the set of members of a relation at any particular time and an *intensional* relation to be set of permissible extensional relations with a given relational frame. A relational frame is (informally since we have not specified a category) a presheaf of relations; in other words a *relational frame* is a relation which varies through time or stages of knowledge. The above uses of the words extension and intension are based on the approach of Date [53]. Addis [3] gives a slightly different nuance to the words, where he points out that the tables with attributes (Name, Age) and (Name, Height) are mathematically isomorphic, the domain of the second attribute being the real numbers in both cases. This, we feel, is a slightly baroque consideration, and may be overcome by considering domains to be pairs consisting of a set and an attribute label. This, anyway, is much closer to the computational notion of a data type (which is what an attribute really is).

The next order of structure in a database concerns the relationships between relations. These, of course, are relations themselves. Chen [42] uses the terminology 'entity-relations' and 'relationship-relations' to distinguish them. We will talk about *links* as a shorthand implying no connection with the links of a CODASYL database. Both kinds of relation must conform to certain integrity constraints. Every entity must have specified at least one primary key set of attributes which uniquely identifies each tuple at any given time. Furthermore, it must be in first normal form; i.e. the attribute values cannot be complex structures but must be atomic relations (numbers, strings, etc.). This is no restriction for data processing applications but in list processing, text and image storage and knowledge processing we will see that extensions are going to be needed. The links have two kinds of property, valency and functionality. The valency of a link may be one-to-one, many-to-one and the functionality may be into (monomorphic) or onto (epimorphic). These four primitives and the notation which we introduce below give rise to the following cases:

one–one	$A \;\text{———}\; B$
many–one	$A \vdash\text{——}\; B$
into	$A \succ\text{——}\; B$
onto	$A \text{———}\!\!\twoheadrightarrow B$
0-implies	$A \rightarrowtail\!\!\text{—}\; B$ many–one and into
1-implies	$A \vdash\!\!\text{——}\!\!\twoheadrightarrow B$ many–one and onto
equivalence	$A \;\equiv\equiv\equiv\; B$ one–one and onto
many–many	$A \vdash\text{——}\dashv B$ no restrictions

These provide a graphical notation for expressing referential integrity checks which is useful during the data analysis stage of building a database. Our notation is based on that of Addis [3] but slightly more in concord with classical notations. We will also need the definition of a foreign key; that is an attribute which is the primary key of some other relation. The integrity rules specify what happens to related relations when a table is subjected to update or deletion operations. The only cases which deserve further elucidation are 0-implies and 1-implies. Recalling our earlier many–many Made-by link we can represent it as follows:

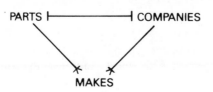

These 0-implies links mean that if a new MAKES tuple is added then both PARTS and COMPANIES must be scanned for the corresponding keys' existence. If either a PARTS or a COMPANIES tuple is deleted then all corresponding MAKES tuples ought to be removed; 1-implies is a stronger condition and were the link between MAKES and COMPANIES of this nature then this would mean that there could never be a company without it makes something.

We now turn to the manipulative part of the model; that is, to the means by which queries and update requests can be expressed. There are essentially two methods and various hybrids of them. The two methods are known as the relational calculus and the relation algebra. A manipulation language is said to be 'relationally complete' if any possible operation over the database may be prescribed within a single (and *a fortiori* non-procedural) statement of the language. This provides us with an operational definition of a relation calculus.

A language permitting all feasible operations over a database to be prescribed, but in more than one statement of the language (and therefore a procedural language), is operationally defined as a relational algebra.

The first method to emerge with Codd's original paper was the relational calculus which is a retrieval and update language based on a subset of the first-order predicate calculus. Later the Berkeley QUEL language was based on it.

Retrieval is done via a tuple-variable which may take values in some given relation. An expression of the tuple calculus is defined recursively as a formula of predicate calculus formed from tuple variables, relational operators, logical operators and quantifiers. In this sense relational calculus is nonprocedural. Consider the following statement of predicate calculus:

$$(\exists x, y) \ (t \in \text{PARTS}] \wedge x = \text{PNAME} \wedge y = \text{DESCRIPTION} \wedge \text{PNAME} = \text{'Widget'}$$

This can be regarded as a query which should return the name and description of all parts whose part name is widget. Note that the tuple variable is free and the bound variables correspond to the attributes. In PROLOG, which can be regarded as a database retrieval language, we would express this as

```
query(X,Y)  :-

parts(T),T=record(Pno,Pname,Description),

X=Pname,Y=Description,Pname='Widget'.
```

In QUEL the syntax would be

```
RANGE OF T IS PARTS

RETRIEVE(PNAME.DESCRIPTION)

WHERE PNAME='Widgets'
```

A similar syntax permits update operations in this nonprocedural style.

The alternative approach is to regard enquiries and updates as expressed by a sequence of algebraic operations. This is more procedural and comes closer, if not very close, to the physical implementation, since the results will depend on the order of evaluation. In actual implementations a query optimizer will usually attempt to select the optimal order of evaluation making use of the referential transparency of algebra. Relational algebra is based on four primitive operations: Selection, Projection, Union and Join. Selection on a predicate yields those tuples which satisfy the predicate; it corresponds to the comprehension scheme of set theory, ($\{x: p(x)\}$), and may be thought of as an horizontal subset operation. The corresponding vertical subset operation is just the projection out of the Cartesian product. If two tables have the same attributes, their union may be formed by appending them together and removing any duplicates in the primary key. The join of two relations A and B over a relational operator (or dyadic predicate p) is obtained by building all tuples which are the concatenation of a tuple from A followed by one from B such that p holds for the attribute specified. In practice duplicates are eliminated here too. The derivative operations such as difference and intersection will not be covered here. Relational algebra can be regarded as defining the scope for operations such as retrieval, update, view formation, authorization and so on. Purely algebraic languages are extremely rare in practice. Gray [82] gives a syntax for such a language, ASTRID.

Several hybrid languages based partly on calculus and algebra exist, the most notable being those based on the IBM System-R language SQL. SQL was partly derived from the motivation to produce a 'structured' language. Later it was found necessary or convenient to add in most of the power of algebra and calculus, so much so that SQL is a highly redundant and thus inelegant language. However, it looks set to become an industry standard so we will introduce its syntax and use it in examples.

The query given above, in SQL, would be

```
SELECT PNAME,DESCRIPTION

FROM PARTS

WHERE PNAME='Widget'
```

The reader is warned not to confuse this SELECT with the selection of algebra defined above. This query might be regarded as saying: Project PARTS over PNAME and DESCRIPTION, and select under the predicate PNAME = 'Widget'. Confused? Don't worry, it's very simple in practice.

We have said that relations must be in first normal form. In fact this condition sits at the bottom of a hierarchy of normal forms as shown in the figure, and of which the most important are the third or Boyce–Codd normal forms. The theory of normal forms is merely a way of formalizing the commonsense notion of a 'good design'. See Fig. 3.6.

To facilitate the definition of the various normal forms we have to define what it means to say that one attribute of a relation is *functionally dependent* on another.

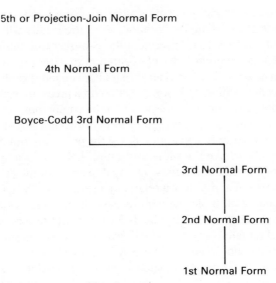

Fig. 3.6   Normalization

An attribute is functionally dependent on another iff (if and only if)* each value of the second one uniquely determines the value of the first. In other words the projection of the relation onto these two attributes is a function (i.e. a single-valued, everywhere-defined relation).

Functional dependency is not symmetrical. For example, if the relation is the set of all points on a parabola, then the y-axis is functionally dependent on the x-axis but not vice versa. For a more concrete example, in most company relations the telephone number will be functionally dependent on the company number (this assumes no party lines). Date [53] points out, interestingly from our point of view as we will see in the next section, that a functional dependence is a special form of integrity constraint, in other words it is a legality condition relating to the semantics of the situation.

Intuitively, a relation is in (third) normal form iff the primary key uniquely identifies a tuple and the other attributes are independent from one another and all functionally dependent on the key. These attributes are properties or descriptions of the entity. In fact, it has been said that the value of an attribute depends upon 'the key, the whole key and nothing but the key'.

Formally then, a relation is in first normal form iff all attributes can only take atomic values; usually numbers or strings, but this actually depends on the underlying logical language. It is in second normal form iff, in addition, every non-key attribute is functionally dependent on the primary key and on no proper

*The strong (two-way, or necessary and sufficient) condition 'if and only if' is used so frequently that it is convenient to abbreviate it: iff. This is a good idea also because the meaning here differs slightly from colloquial usage. Chapter 6 will make use of the abbreviation extensively.

subset of that key. Second normal form designs overcome certain anomalies in respect of the operations of insertion, deletion or modification of tuples. For example consider Tables 3.3–3.7.

Table 3.3

CNO	Location	Currency	PNO	Price
1	London	£	1	30
1	London	£	2	20
1	London	£	3	40
1	London	£	4	20
1	London	£	5	10
1	London	£	6	10
2	Paris	FF	1	30
2	Paris	FF	2	40
3	Paris	FF	2	20
4	London	£	2	20
4	London	£	4	30
4	London	£	5	40

Table 3.4

CNO	Location	Currency
1	London	£
2	Paris	FF
3	Paris	FF
4	London	£
5	New York	$

Table 3.5

CNO	PNO	Price
1	1	30
1	2	20
1	3	40
1	4	20
1	5	10
1	6	10
2	1	30
2	2	40
3	2	20
4	2	20
4	4	30
4	5	40

Table 3.6

CNO	Location
1	London
2	Paris
3	Paris
4	London
5	New York

Table 3.7

Location	Currency
London	£
Paris	FF
New York	$

In Table 3.3 it is not possible to record the existence of a company by its company number (CNO) until it supplies a part unless we allow the key field PNO to take null values. Even worse, if the ninth tuple is deleted we lose all the information about company 3. This phenomenon is often referred to as 'the connectivity trap'. If we try to amend the location of company 1 then all the tuples referring to that company must also be amended or the database will become inconsistent, an error that could easily be made in practice. Table 3.3 shows our database in first normal form but not in second. Decomposing it into Tables 3.4 and 3.5 achieves second normal form and overcomes all these problems. Note, incidentally, that if the layout is conceived of as representing physical storage we may have saved some space on secondary storage too. The reader should also note the functional dependencies implicit in this database: CURRENCY depends on LOCATION, which depends on CNO, and PRICE depends on both the company and the part numbers, which together form the primary key of Table 3.3 and separately the primary keys of Tables 3.4 and 3.5. We have not, with our new design, overcome all problems. It is not possible to record the currency of a location until a company with that location is entered in the database. Similarly if we delete the last tuple of Table 3.4 we lose this information. Since this table still contains some redundancy there are update problems that remain also. To recover from these symptoms we note that the functional dependency of CURRENCY on CNO arises by composing the other dependencies; it is a *transitive dependency*. If we rearrange the database into Tables 3.5, 3.6 and 3.7 we remove all transitive dependencies and thus overcome all the anomalies mentioned.

A relation is in third normal form iff it is in second normal form and every non-key attribute is nontransitively dependent on the primary key. There is a slightly stronger version of this definition due to Boyce and Codd as follows. A relation is in (Boyce–Codd) third normal form iff every attribute on which others depend is a candidate key (i.e. could be the primary key). This definition is not couched in terms of first and second normal forms and is thus slightly more elegant. It can be shown that it implies all the normal forms defined so far, with the possible exception of the first (Ullman [202]).

Note that the join of Tables 3.6 and 3.7 recovers Table 3.4 and the join of Tables 3.4 and 3.5 recovers Table 3.3 without any loss of information in the sense that no spurious tuples are introduced. This need not be the case, although it can be shown that any relation admits such a lossless decomposition. Care must be exercised in database design and manipulation to avoid operations of projection followed by join which lose information in this way. For example, projecting Table 3.4 over (CNO, CURRENCY) and (LOCATION, CURRENCY) would give a 'lossy' join over CURRENCY.

EXERCISE: Verify the last statement.

To overcome this lossy join and other minor problems fourth and fifth normal forms have been introduced. Their precise definition is a fairly complex matter and would be out of place in this text. The reader is referred to the works specified in the section on further reading for these definitions.

The theory of normal forms is an aspect of 'bottom-up' design and is complementary to top-down design methods such as the entity-relationship approach. It is not, strictly, a part of the relational model. We are tempted because of this to disagree with the experts here and say that the whole theory of integrity is also not a part of the model. In order to carry out the remainder of our programme to extend the theory into the area of knowledge engineering this will prove a most fruitful point of view.

One striking weakness of the relational point of view, when it comes to business applications, is the unnatural way in which it handles relations which are directly perceived in multidimensional form. The very best example of this is in the domain of financial modelling. The refusal to recognize as atomic any object of higher type (lists, vectors, etc.) makes the relatively trivial tasks of spreadsheet modelling tortuous within a relational model. The ease of use of such packages as Symphony, Visicalc, Framework, EPS/FCS, Wizard and Express derives from the richness of the data structure and its good match with the way in which the problem is generally perceived by humans. In practice, most organizations will store raw data in relational tables and aggregate it in various ways before passing it to such packages for modelling and decision support applications. This makes it seem as though the relational model is about handling bulk, unrefined data, but this is patently not the case. Some very high level decision support applications suit the relational organization of data perfectly; e.g. checking for likely criminal suspects. Much the same remarks apply in other highly structured fields such as word processing and information retrieval. We will return to this point after we have extended the range of tools at our disposal.

The EXPRESS and REVEAL systems literature both refer to the products supporting a relational data model. This is justified in the sense that the data model is a logical one and that the algebraic operations, such as move, project and so on, are supported. However, the version of the relational model present in these systems differs in important ways from the 'pure' model described above, thus meeting certain practical needs and pointing to deficiencies in the latter. For example, in REVEAL the projection operator is dyadic rather than monadic; one relation is projected over another rather than over a set of attributes. The primary motivation in these products is to support arrays as atomic constructs and, in the latter case, to allow the formation of fuzzy relational enquiries.

EXPRESS, along with several of the decision support systems such as ACUMEN, provides a logical data model to the user which in fact differs from all of the network, hierarchical and relational viewpoints. It is a multi-dimensional data model; i.e. it is concerned with variables scoped over several dimensions. These dimensions need not map into the real line, as in Cartesian geometry, but may themselves be sets. In fact, this data view is simply a transform of the relational model, where instances in a dimension are equivalent to attribute values drawn from a domain.

Figure 3.7 illustrates the equivalence of a relation called SALES, with a primary key SALESMAN/CUSTOMER/PRODUCT and an additional attribute QUANTITY, to the multidimensional model of the EXPRESS kind which deals with the variable SALES (salesman, customer, product).

The benefit of the EXPRESS representation lies, of course, in the syntactic ease with which operations over projections of the relations may be expressed.

We now turn to these and other extensions to the relational model.

3.3   FUZZY RELATIONS AND THEIR APPLICATIONS

3.3.1   Fuzzy information retrieval

A fuzzy relation is thus a fuzzy subset of some Cartesian product, so that a truth value is associated with every point of an ordinary relation. Relating this to the

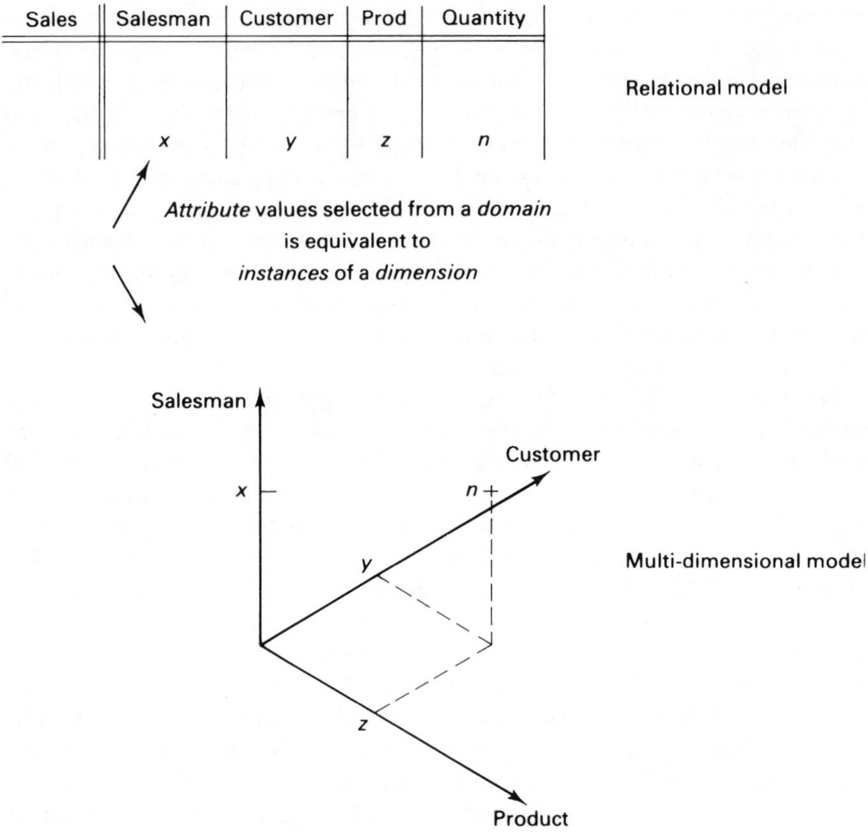
Sales
Salesman
Customer
Prod
Quantity
x
y
z
n
Relational model
Attribute values selected from a domain
is equivalent to
instances of a dimension
Salesman
x
Customer
n
y
z
Product
Multi-dimensional model

Fig. 3.7 Relational and multi-dimensional modelling

notion of tables given in the foregoing section, we must allow every attribute to become associated with a truth value attribute for that attribute. For example, we might have the fuzzy relation BOOKS:

Book	*Subject*	*About that subject*
Dubois and Prade	Fuzzy Sets	0.95
Graham and Jones	Fuzzy Sets	0.35
Date	Databases	0.80
Gray	Databases	0.35

All the remarks we have made about extensionality and intensionality still apply. Clearly also, the operations of algebra and calculus carry over by the extension principle (see Chapter 6). For instance the projection of a fuzzy relation is a fuzzy set although the elimination involved means we must choose some combinators for the truth values. In the example above, projecting onto SUBJECT we could choose the maximum if we were asking 'Print all the subjects in the database' since we might take the view that the answer expresses the information contained somewhere in the database on each subject. If this is a problem we can always treat the *n*-ary fuzzy relation as an at most 2*n*-ary crisp relation. This is all very well for binary fuzzy relations such as the one above, but if we have more than one pair of relationships with an uncertain relationship then the resultant structure is no longer a fuzzy relation in the strict sense. For example, if the attributes were

(BOOK,SUBJECT,AVAILABILITY,APPEARANCE_OF_BINDING)

then we would have to decompose into three fuzzy relations to retain the formalism or treat the relation as a conventional 7-ary relation. The latter course is probably simpler. The point here is that in the Boolean case an *n*-ary relation denotes just one relationship between *n* attributes, whereas in the fuzzy case alluded to above we are denoting three fuzzy relations; specifically those between (BOOK,SUBJECT), (BOOK,AVAILABILITY) and (BOOK,APPEARANCE]. In the terminology of Zimmermann [222] we are dealing with a fuzzy graph. This extra complexity arises because in the classical case the attributes either are related or they are not. In the fuzzy case we have to specify the relation. In practice it is probably wiser to allow only binary fuzzy relations to be used.

Another way to view the fuzzification of relations is to consider fuzzy-valued relations, wherein the elements are themselves fuzzy sets. For example, another version of the BOOKS database might be:

Book	Subject	About that subject
Dubois and Prade	Fuzzy Sets	Very
Graham and Jones	Fuzzy Sets	Quite
Date	Databases	Almost all
Gray	Databases	About a third

This 'relation' can no longer be considered a part of the classical relational model, since it is not in first normal form; it contains a non-atomic attribute. However, in practice, we could overcome this problem by viewing the string 'Very' as a pointer to an object which happens to be a fuzzy set (in its turn a relation). In the case of binary relations, again things are fairly simple; such a relation is a mapping $X \times Y \rightarrow I^A$ and this is equivalent (by the exponential adjointness relationship of Chapter 6) to a mapping from $A \times X \times Y$ to I, which is to say to a fuzzy relation on one extra attribute (the linguistic variable A). For higher dimensional relations the position is not so clear, and again a decomposition into binary relations makes life much easier. Such a higher dimensional 'relation' can, again using

Zimmermann's terminology, be regarded as a family of fuzzy functions. For example, the schema

(BOOK,SUBJECT,DEPTH_OF_TREATMENT_OF_SUBJECT,APPEARANCE)

might have the following elements.

Book	Subject	Depth of treatment of subject	Appearance
1	1 high	shallow	good
1	2 low	deep	good
2	1 avge	deep	poor
2	2 avge	moderate	poor

Notice that the appearance must have the same value for the same book, thus there is an immediate and strong sense in which this table is not in normal form; it's a bad design. This schema is represented by three fuzzy functions whose domains are BOOKS and whose co-domains are the sets of fuzzy subsets of the universe represented by the attributes. Treating these functions independently restores normal form (in our loose, intuitive sense) and each fuzzy function is isomorphic (by adjointness) to a ternary fuzzy relation. In the case above the first such relation has the form

$$\text{BOOKS} \times \text{SUBJECTS} \times \text{RELEVANCE} \to I = [0, 1].$$

There are certain practical consequences of this analysis if a computer application is being considered. In the first case given above, where the truth values are stored in the relation, a fuzzy enquiry gives a fuzzy set as response. In the second case, a fuzzy enquiry can give a crisp answer, which is usually what is required in simulation exercises. The representation by fuzzy functions has a much more convenient syntax which corresponds closely to the way human knowledge is often expressed.

We believe that the correct solution to these problems is to be found in the theory of fuzzy frames to be discussed in the next section.

Baldwin's Fuzzy Relational Inference Language, FRIL, provides a kind of non-procedural logic programming language based on fuzzy relations. Various extensions have since been developed. Support Logic Programming (which is not meant – we are told – to be a slogan) comes closer to the logic programming ideal [15], and CRIL adds conceptual networks to the representational tools available [172].

In relaxing the requirement that relations have only atomic attributes or are in 1st NF, we must ask if we are throwing out the baby with the bath water. The question reduces to asking whether the theory of normal forms is indispensable in the practical activity of building knowledge-based systems, and, if it is, whether that theory can be resurrected by either extending the type properties of the underlying logic or by arriving at a notion of third normal form which need not imply first normal form. At the time of writing it is not clear how these questions will be resolved, but we hope that this discussion will be a modest contribution to arousing interest in their solution.

Among the useful applications of fuzzy relations of the first type discussed, we can identify their use in medical expert systems [172], the extension of the methods of multi-attribute decision making under uncertainty [221] and the use of operations on fuzzy relations in information retrieval.

Kohout, Keravnou and Bandler [119] point out that the key concerns of information processing, and in particular the automatic classification and retrieval of documents, have also been at the forefront of discussions in the field of fuzzy systems. These concerns (inexact matching of terms, relevance of terms to inquiries and to documents, polythetic classification of items, and nondeterministic inductive inference) have led to the separation of information retrieval from database theory because of the inability of the latter to deal with these questions. A typical information retrieval system is concerned with the following structure: a set of documents, a set of terms or keywords used in or about those documents and a thesaurus or structured dictionary showing the relationships between terms, usually based on a statistical formula based on frequency counts. The user of such a system will generally wish to enter queries in the form of a weighted logical combination of descriptors. The 'documents' can be almost anything but would typically be learned papers; they could be textual descriptions of the properties of drugs or references to the case law of torts. The trouble with combinations based on Boolean logical operators is that there is no way to express gradations in the degree of relevance of the terms to the documents or to the individual requirements of users. For example in a legal context one might wish to enquire for 'all papers about road traffic law and injuries and alcohol', but the weightings given to each term will not only be non-Boolean but will be different according to whether the questioner is a solicitor acting on behalf of an insurance company or a researcher looking into the history of the law on drinking and driving. Kohout and his co-workers introduce a fuzzy relation D of relevance between documents and terms wherein each cell represents the relevance of term t_j to document d_i. The triangle sub-product of the transpose of this matrix with itself is the relation giving the mean degree to which term t_j is more *specific* than t_i. The super-product gives the relation of being *broader* in meaning and the square product the degrees of being *synonymous*. From these relations a fuzzy thesaurus can be automatically constructed. The categories broader, more specific and synonymous allow the user of the systems to interact with and control inquiries by specifying a relevance threshold and asking for terms broader or narrower than the ones used in the original query. This introduction of a feedback mechanism into queries can be extremely powerful.

For completeness we repeat the definition of the relational products mentioned above. The triangle subproduct of R with S is given by

$$(R \triangleleft S)_{ik} = (1/n_j) \Sigma_j (R_{ij} \Rightarrow S_{jk})$$

and the super- and square-products are given by replacing the operation of fuzzy implication $\Rightarrow$ by $\Leftarrow$ and $\Leftrightarrow$ respectively. Thus

$$(R \triangleright S)_{ik} = (1/n_j)\Sigma_j(R_{ij} \Leftarrow S_{jk})$$

$$(R \square S)_{ik} = (1/n_j)\Sigma_j(R_{ij} \Leftrightarrow S_{jk})$$

The implication can be chosen according to the application. If it is taken to be $\max(1-x, y)$ then we can illustrate with a numerical example of the subproduct. Suppose we have the following relevance matrix about books.

	DSS	Fuzzy
Graham and Jones	.40	.30
Dubois and Prade	.10	.90

Then

	DSS	Fuzzy	
$D^T \triangleleft D =$	.75	.75	DSS
	.40	.80	Fuzzy

Kohout *et al.* claim that this matrix represents the (unnormalized) degrees to which the two terms are more specific than one another. However, it is difficult to see exactly what this means in the context of the implication we have used here, and in a later version of their paper [120] the same authors are more cautious. They claim only that the subproduct is a relation between terms in which the numbers represent the degree to which if a term is treated in every document then the other term is treated, and correspondingly for the other products. Despite this confusion, which is only to be expected in a subject so new, there is no doubt that fuzzy information retrieval systems will be developed and will make a major contribution to information retrieval systems in general.

Having dealt with fuzzy relations in general and their application to information systems, we now turn to a much simpler application, to database enquiry.

3.3.2 Fuzzy relations and database enquiries

Graham [78] and Negoita [156] quote an example of enquiry on a fuzzy relational database, due originally to Jones. Consider a manager who is posed the problem of a cash surplus and who thus considers the acquisition of another company. He or she can turn to several sources of published information on company performance and may have decided to concentrate initially on two performance measures. Suppose the manager has access to a database which stores, in relational form, the following information on sales and profitability.

Company	Turnover	Profitability (%)
A Ltd	750	7
B Plc	600	14
C Plc	800	17
D Ltd	850	12
E Ltd	999	18
F Inc	1,000	15
G Inc	1,100	14
H Inc	1,200	13

A typical way to express the manager enquiry in a 4th generation language such as SQL might be

SELECT COMPANY, TURNOVER, MARGIN
FROM COMPANIES
WHERE TURNOVER >= 1000 AND MARGIN >= 14

which would return the relation

Company	Turnover	Profitability (%)
F Inc	1,000	15
G Inc	1,100	14

Notice immediately that E Ltd is missing although it is evidently a very interesting candidate for further investigation. The problem is that statements such as 'TURNOVER >= 1000' do not fully capture the intentions of the manager concerned. He or she is more likely to express it in the form *'turnover must be high'*. If we consider turnover as a linguistic variable and define a fuzzy term *high* on this variable by assigning a truth value to each number in the domain and similarly for margins and *acceptable*, then we can express a more realistic enquiry as follows:

IF TURNOVER IS HIGH AND MARGIN IS ACCEPTABLE

This returns not a relation but a fuzzy relation:

Company	Turnover	Profitability (%)	Truth
C Plc	800	17	0.52
E Ltd	999	18	0.80
F Inc	1,000	15	0.36
G Inc	1,100	14	0.19
H Inc	1,200	13	0.10

'Truth' could be interpreted as the degree to which the company is an interesting candidate for acquisition. Here E Ltd receives the highest score as a result of its performance with respect to *both* variables. This example is based on a system written in the REVEAL language. To give a feel for the actual syntactic nicety we reproduce a printout of a session in Fig. 3.8.

MODE >relation	A	B	C	D	E	F	G	H	I
CLASSIFICATN	6	6	12	6	12	6	12	12	6
SALES	200	1,100	1,000	800	500	1,200	1,300	100	400
THOUS.EMPS	3	10	11	9	8	14	12	2	6
PROFITS	40	110	160	120	55	115	200	20	10
TRUTH	13	49	27	4	1	72	87	13	

MODE > relation :: sales are high	B	C	D	F	G
CLASSIFICATN	6	12	6	6	12
SALES	1,100	1,000	800	1,200	1,300
THOUS.EMPS	10	11	9	14	12
PROFITS	110	160	120	115	200
TRUTH	49	27	3	72	87

MODE >relation :: sales are high and profits/sales is acceptable	C	D	G
CLASSIFICATN	12	6	12
SALES	1,000	800	1,300
THOUS.EMPS	11	9	12
PROFITS	160	120	200
TRUTH	5	3	4

MODE >

Fig. 3.8   Fuzzy relations in REVEAL

A similar example is illustrated below which refers to enquiries on a database of suspects. In this example the linguistic description is elicited by prompting the user for values for each attribute of the relevant relation and then a production rule is constructed dynamically and applied to the database. The output is then ranked in order of degree of truth. The generated rule in this particular case is: 'IF AGE IS MIDDLE.AGED AND WEIGHT IS HEAVY AND HEIGHT IS VERY TALL AND HAIR.COLOUR IS 'GREY' THEN AN INTERVIEW SHOULD BE CONDUCTED'. The fuzzy sets MIDDLE.AGED, TALL, HEAVY and CONDUCTED are predefined by the designer, and INTERVIEW is a variable designed to receive the output rankings. HAIR.COLOUR is a crisp string variable corresponding to a stored list of possible conditions of the head. VERY is a hedge, as usual defined by

```
MODE >SHOW. SUSPECTS

                  CRIPIN   MORIARTY   EVANS    TURPIN    JONES    FAGIN

HEIGHT            61.00    76.00      69.00    68.00     70.00    55.00
WEIGHT           150.00   160.00     170.00   155.00    190.00   130.00
AGE               45.00    45.00      35.00    30.00     50.00    65.00

MODE >POLICE
...VOCABULARY INSTALLED
...CONTEXT LOADED
HELLO,
      HELLO,
            HELLO...

How old was the felon        ? >MIDDLE.AGED
How was his build            ? >HEAVY
How tall was he              ? >VERY TALL
What colour was his hair     ? >GREY

The following suspects match your description.
You should interview them in the order given as far as possible

                  MORIARTY      JONES

INTERVIEW         55.00         51.00

MODE >
```

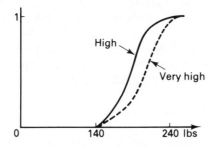

In the diagram we have illustrated how such a qualifier can be 'qualified' to give
VERY HEAVY. From these qualifiers we can now form a new one to represent
HEAVY AND MIDDLE AGED. The rules of inference then permit the formation of
expressions such as:

IF WEIGHT IS VERY HEAVY AND AGE IS MIDDLE-AGED AND HAIR
COLOUR IS 'GREY', THEN AN INTERVIEW SHOULD BE CONDUCTED

based on a witness's statement.

Fig. 3.9   A system to interpret a witness's statement

raising to the power of 2. The figure also illustrates a typical stored fuzzy set hedged in this way.

These very simple examples show, we hope, how much the use of fuzzy sets add to the ease with which database queries can be expressed and the significantly increased sense contained in the answers.

3.4   RELATIONS AND FRAMES

As we saw in Chapter 2 a frame is a structure consisting of slots to be filled in. In some ways this is very like the idea of a relation, but there are some important differences. For one thing the fillers are no longer atomic; they can be any simple or complex data structure or even a procedure. Secondly, we do not know in advance how many slots there will be.

EXERCISE: Show that an effective procedure can be regarded as a data structure. Hint: Both are finite.

The usual implementation of a semantic network or frame is based on the LISP notion of a property list; that is a list of named values attached to an atom. The slots are named and may contain lists of values and also have other *facets*. The usual facets are AKO, IS-A, Demons (IF-NEEDED) and Default values. Some writers distinguish between generic frames and call them flavours and specific ones related to objects. Objects may be thought of as entities in the sense used above, or as stereotypes of actions, objects or events, or as manipulable entities that can receive messages and take action depending on the contents of each message and the state of the database. A whole style of programming, 'object oriented programming', has grown up around this latter concept and is likely to prove important in knowledge engineering. The IS-A slots allow property inheritance through an either breadth-first or depth-first search through more abstract frames to fill a value in. If the demon facet is filled then its procedure can be fired to fill in a value, and if all else fails the value can be set to the default.

Consider a fairly simple frame like the one for a dog.

Frame: Dog
IsA: Mammal, pet, best-friend (if human)
Legs: Number; up to four
Name: String; Default Rover
Licensed: Y/N; If needed call search records; default N
Method of exercise: Call weather-for-a-walk routine; default 'walk in park'
Food: String list; default Meaty Hunks + Bonio
Temper:Fuzzy ; default 'bark worse than bite'
Probability of needing vet in a year: 0.50 (based on insurance stats)

Now the frame for a specific dog, the one next door.

Frame:Bran
IsA: Dog
Owner:String;Value = Peggy
Breed:String;Value = Jack Russell
etc.

Uncertainty about how to fill these frames, i.e. reach an internal representation or understanding of a dog or of Bran, arises in several ways. Most dogs have four legs, but occasionally legs are lost in accidents or deformed puppies are born. Do we call a stump a leg? When is the weather too bad to go for a walk? What is the probability (and the possibility) of being bitten? Thus, all sorts of techniques must be available. The other thing to note, and it is this which really separates frames from relations, is that we can go on adding attributes as new information arises. We can also change the type of an attribute by altering its length: Dogs might become a special case of FOOD if we use the frame in some contexts, or new dog foods might come on the market resulting in the list of foods growing longer. Thus, the records are variable length in two senses: the values can be lists of indeterminate length and the number of slots may change dynamically.

Frames have the feature known as property inheritance. This determines that lower level frames inherit the same slots (at least) as all higher level ones, and their defaults. Slots may contain or point to triggers leading to the possibility of event or data driven processing. We shall be giving an example of the application of this in Chapter 10.

In connection with databases, Stonebraker has recently introduced [234] an extension to the IGRES language which enables it to handle triggers, and forward and backward chaining. The remarkable thing about this is that only two new words need be added to the language to accomplish this. The use of ALWAYS turns INGRES commands into triggers and the DEMAND command has the effect of a 'lazily evaluated' trigger. The latter means that the relational model must be extended in the sense that the values of a relation may be derived rather than stored in the relation. This gives an alternative approach to that of frames, but only in a limited sense. It does however reinforce our view that these two technologies are growing closer, and may one day merge.

For future reference, let us define a *table* to be a relation-through-time. An *extensional frame* is then a subset of an infinite dimensional Cartesian product. An *intensional frame* is a 'presheaf' of extensional frames; i.e. it varies with time and may have infinitely many null values. For the definition and mathematics of presheaves the reader is referred to the end of Chapter 6. The notions of intension and extension are explained very fully in Date [53].

3.4.1   Fuzzy frames

This section assumes some familiarity with fuzzy sets. Although this is not fully covered until Chapters 5 and 6, we feel strongly that this is the right place for the inclusion of this material. Readers may wish to return to this section after reading Chapter 5 and the relevant portions of 6.

What we have said above about the problems of applying general frames to special cases leads us naturally to the notion of fuzzy frames and fuzzy inheritance. If we consider for a moment the Dog frame and the Bone frame and we have recorded somewhere in the structure the fact that dogs enjoy bones, then we are naturally led to the question of how much a particular dog likes bones. Bran inherits the general property of liking bones but only does so to a certain extent. The inheritance is therefore a partial one. Computational mechanisms are required to control and propagate this inheritance.

Therefore we need to relax the two fundamental requirements of a relational database management system for the purpose in hand; that is the requirements that the relations be finite dimensional and that the entries in each attribute be atomic. An example may usefully be drawn from Quantum Mechanics, wherein the eigenfunctions of the wave equation represent its decomposition into 'measurables'. We do not know *a priori* how many of these measurables there might be, but it is reasonable to presume there are very many indeed. Because of this, it makes sense to assume that there are potentially an unlimited number. To cope with this assumption Quantum theorists work in infinite dimensional vector spaces – Hilbert space. What we are proposing for frames is essentially the same generalization applied to the relational model. Relations occur in finite Cartesian products and frames in infinite ones; i.e. in Hilbert space. In some sense this is to do with not knowing how many of the available dimensions in a particular problem are going to be discernible. Also we do not, in practical situations, know in advance which of the available attributes will be useful.

We can combine the two extensions of the notion of relation in the manner of a pushout in the category of categories as shown in Fig. 3.10 (although we make this statement without any pretence of rigour, since we haven't defined the arrows or functors).

Thus, we assert, the fundamental mathematics exists which makes possible the rigorous development of a theory of fuzzy frames. The practical consequences of this are that it provides a very neat way to express knowledge where partial property inheritance is involved, and as we have seen in the previous chapter

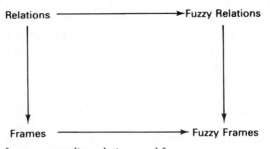

Fig. 3.10 Fuzzy frames generalize relations and frames

appropriate knowledge representation is one of the key prerequisites for successful knowledge engineering. Furthermore, fuzzy frames represent a profound extension of the relational data model, including as they do the advantages of fuzzy relations (discussed above) and the logical power of frames.

To explain the mechanics of fuzzy frames it is preferable to use an example, rather than to develop the formal mathematics. In doing so we will introduce a syntax similar to that used in LEONARDO III [263].

Consider the following (toy) problem. You are faced with the selection of estimating the safety implications following on the purchase of various leisure items. Frames give us a way of representing knowledge about and data concerning objects or concepts. The most natural way to analyse (remembering that we are thinking of building a computerized advisor here) the problem is to list the objects involved. Suppose they include a dinghy and a hang-glider. These objects are types of more general objects, and have associated with them various properties. We can represent our knowledge in the seven frames below. In each case we annotate them with explanation of the syntactic convention.

F1   *Possession*
      IsA   :Object
      Cost   ;undefined [fuzz]
      Necessity   :undefined [fuzz]
      Utility   :high[fuzz]
      Safety   :high [fuzz]

Here the IsA slot points to another frame, in this case the most general one possible. This is a fuzzy frame in two respects. First, the degree of property inheritance from the frame(s) in the IsA slot may be specified as a number between 0 and 1 in square brackets after the name. In this case no value is given and the default value of [1.00] is assumed. Secondly, the other slots may contain fuzzy sets (vectors of truth values) as values. The bracketed expressions indicate the type of the value; either [fuzz], [real] or [text]. The fuzzy sets used in the Possession frame may be represented as shown in Fig. 3.11.

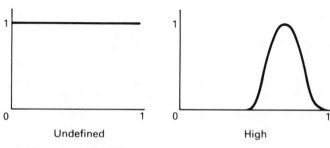

               Undefined   High

Fig. 3.11   (a) The fuzzy set undefined
            (b) The fuzzy set high

F2	*Vehicle*		F3	*Toy*	
	IsA	:Possession		IsA	:Possession
	Necessity	:high		Necessity	:low
	Safety	:high		Safety	:undefined
	Utility	:high		Utility	:high
	Cost	:high		Cost	:low

The Toy frame will inherit the value 'high' for Safety, since the slot contains 'undefined'; the uniform fuzzy set on the interval scale. The other slots are unaltered. In certain applications, such as database ones, it may be preferable to allow inheritance into even those slots which contain defined values. In such a case the inheritance mechanism is modified in such a way that the intersection (minimum) of the fuzzy sets in the parent and child is taken. This corresponds to what we choose to designate the *Fuzzy Closed World Assumption.* That is, if the values assigned to slots represent immutable knowledge about the state of the world and the constraints it imposes, then we would not wish to permit a contradictory reassignment that ignored the influence of the value in a parent. Graham and Jones [260] take this discussion further in looking at the problems of conflict resolution in the context of fuzzy inheritance.

F4	*Borrowed object*		F5	*Dangerous object*	
	IsA	:Possession [0.5]		IsA	:Object
				Safety	:minimal

Here we have the sad situation where a borrowed object, such as a book, may pass from *meum* to *tuum* without the transition being too noticeable. Thus only 0.5 of the property may be inherited. The mechanism is that the fuzzy sets are truncated at the 0.5 level. Two new fuzzy sets have been introduced, so we give their definition pictorially, as before. As we have pointed out, those readers not already familiar with fuzzy sets may wish to read Chapters 5 and 6 at this point and return to this section later. The next section of this chapter may, however, be safely proceeded with.

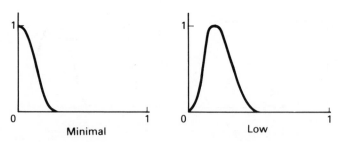

Fig. 3.12   (a) The fuzzy set minimal
                (b) The fuzzy set low

Now we come to the frames describing the most specific items in the scheme shown in Fig. 3.12.

F6 *Dinghy*
  IsA   :Vehicle [0.4],
            Toy [0.6],
            Dangerous object [0.1]
  Draft   :3 [real]
  Safety   :undefined
  Cost   :undefined

F7 *Hang-glider*
  IsA   :Vehicle [0.05],
            Toy [0.9],
            Dangerous object [0.9],
            Borrowed object,
  Safety   :undefined
  Cost   :undefined

We now have to understand how the undefined slots in these lowest level frames may be filled. Notice that we have a non-fuzzy slot for Draft, and multiple inheritance from higher levels. Let us look at the Safety slot of Dinghy first.

Since a dinghy is a vehicle the slot inherits 'high', but as this is only true to the extent 0.4 the fuzzy set is truncated at this level. It also inherits the value 'minimal' from Dangerous-object, but only to degree 0.1. These fuzzy sets are combined with the union operator as shown in Fig. 3.13. If this were the final result of some reasoning process the resultant fuzzy set would be defuzzified (in this case with the mean-of-maxima operation) to give a truth or possibility value for the term 'safe'. Alternatively linguistic approximation could be applied to return a word corresponding to a normal, convex fuzzy set approximating the returned value. In different applications the moments defuzzification method may be applied. This is a control decision in the same category as the fuzzy closed world assumption. The diagram also shows the fuzzy set for the dinghy's cost.

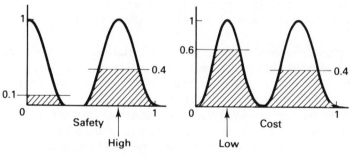

Fig. 3.13 Consequent fuzzy sets for dinghy

The case of the safety slot of Hang-glider is a little more interesting. Figure 3.14 illustrates the text. Here, the Safety slot inherits the union of the fuzzy set minimal from Dangerous-object and high from both vehicle and possession (via Borrowed-object [0.5]). Applying the operation of union or disjunction to these three fuzzy sets – we of course exclude 'undefined' from this process – to represent the view

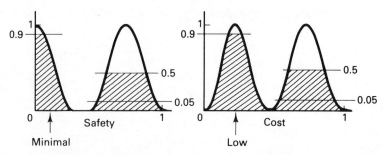

Fig. 3.14   Consequent fuzzy sets for hang-glider

that IsA attributes are *alternative* viewpoints from which the object may be viewed, we arrive at a resultant fuzzy set. Defuzzification then gives the value 0 (or its linguistic approximation 'minimal').

Thus the system is able to deduce correctly that a hang-glider is a very dangerous toy. Notice however that the truncation of high actually occurs at 0.5 rather than 0.05, coming as it does from the Borrowed-object–Possession route. The apparently counter-intuitive nature of this result – which, incidentally only has noticeable consequences under the moments rule – is due to the incompleteness of our example semantic model. Clearly, the reason we have adopted the view that a hang-glider is only a vehicle to a small extent is that one usually thinks of a vehicle as a safe-ish means of getting from A to B and, indeed, back again. This is not independent from our assumptions about dangerous objects. We consider this point further in [260]. Currently, the topic of design criteria for fuzzy semantic models is undergoing research, but remains only partially solved. What is required is analogous to the theory of normal forms presented earlier in this chapter. Another research topic is the design of query languages for fuzzy frame systems.

We have thus presented, via a simple example, the basic theory of fuzzy frames and explained its logic of inheritance. The material on fuzzy logic presented in the remainder of this book is mostly concerned with its use in production systems.

Logic is a much abused word. In Chapter 6 we shall have a great deal to say about it. Here, we merely wish to point out how we use the word in this book. For us, logic is a part of the theory of knowledge, of epistemology. It is that part concerned with what have often been called the laws of thought. Now, there is nothing in that definition which restricts logic to the positivist, instrumental logic criticized by, for example, Weizenbaum in [236]. Nor does it necessarily refer to current mathematical logic, which clearly has a very restricted domain of applicability compared to the range of human concerns. In a recent article, Leith [237] points out that attempts to computerize the law with PROLOG are doomed to failure because of the complexity of the legal decision making process. In doing so he attacks logic as a means of understanding. We feel that his arrows are aimed at the wrong target though; it is not logic that is at fault but the restricted, unreal mathematical logic of the first-order predicate calculus that is the vulnerable target. If thought obeys laws at all, and much human effort is invested in this assumption, then there must be a set of logical systems which describe them. We will see later that Intuitionist (in other words Materialist) logic does admit a mathematical formulation which overcomes many of the objections of Leith, Weizenbaum and others. The logic of Russell and Whitehead is not the same as the logic of Aristotle or of Hegel. The principle difference is that positivist logic cannot deal with contradiction, except in very circuitous ways, and in this it is fundamentally flawed as a method of dealing with human reason. Our advocacy of fuzzy frames is predicated on the assumption that the underlying logic will be found in category theory and intuitionism; it will be higher order and fuzzy and admit infinitary truth objects. Thus perhaps the critics of artificial intelligence will be able to focus their attention on its real shortcomings instead of the chimera of 'logic'. The real problem with artificial intelligence is its misuse for inhuman ends and not the particular tools used, or misused, by individual researchers. We return to some of these points in Chapter 6.

We now leave the speculative issues related to fuzzy frames for a topic which has attracted considerable attention recently.

3.5 INFERENCE AND DATABASE ACCESS METHODS

The data dictionary in a relational database system has the profound effect of decoupling the programs which access the database and the data. Thus the addition of a new attribute to a relation does not mean that all the programs which refer to that relation must be modified. The other profound effect of the relational model (in its complete form at least) is the way attention is directed to referential integrity. The dictionary stores the names and attributes of all relations together with various extra information on authorizations and validation. In theory, although not in most current implementations, it also stores the integrity rules. At a minimum this involves storing whether the relationship between two relations is one-to-many or one-to-one and into or onto. Of course it would be extremely wasteful to store all such relationships. Many-to-many relationships are only stored implicitly via the existence of two one-to-many relationships, sometimes invoking a dummy relationship. However, the relation model has no inferencing capabilities on these relationships. For example, in the functional dependency diagram shown in Fig. 3.15 (taken from Addis [3]) there is no explicit statement of what the relationship between ORDERFORMS and PARTS is.

In fact it is many-to-many and neither into nor onto, but the database does not store this explicitly and it may be a complex matter to determine such information. Therefore, one role of inferencing in databases is to allow such implicit facts to be determined as and when required. It is relatively straightforward to encode integrity checks in a logic programming language like PROLOG whose interpreter can then resolve implicit references by backtracking.

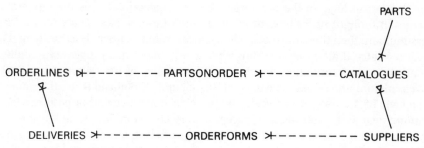

Fig. 3.15   Data semantics

This is one of the reasons why several database suppliers have been building PROLOG interfaces to their products. This kind of inference is important in applications such as parts assembly databases. If we store the fact that a bicycle consists of a frame, handlebars, gears and two wheels, and we further store that a wheel has a rim, spokes, a hub and a tyre, then we can infer that a bike uses spokes, although this is not made explicit.

Another task of database inference is to determine contextual information when a query is made. For example if we ask: 'Find the names of all employees located in London' we could translate into SQL as follows.

```
SELECT NAME

FROM EMPLOYEES

WHERE LOCATION='LONDON'
```

Usually, we might wish to assume, employees in the same department work in the same place. If the database is in normal form we can then produce a more efficient query by using this fact to factor out redundant information. The query would then become:

```
SELECT NAME

FROM EMPLOYEES

WHERE DEPTNO=

     SELECT DEPTNO

     FROM DEPARTMENTS

     WHERE LOCATION='LONDON'
```

In a database without any inferential capability the user must make this route explicit in the way the query is formulated: 'Find the names of all employees who work in departments located in London'. The 'hidden join' problem is the problem of inferring the joins that must be performed even when they are not stated explicitly. This kind of database inference overlaps with the problem of natural language queries which we turn to in what follows. Systems such as INGRES include query optimizers which address this problem. It is the existence of query optimization techniques that allows relational products to compete, in terms of efficiency, with conventional network implementations. Very often the underlying physical database is a network database, and advanced software, including some techniques with their origin in the AI labs, decides on how to navigate the database to solve each query.

Currently, a huge amount of research is going on into the relationship between databases and knowledge-based systems. Brodie and Mylopoulos [234] contains a wealth of material and is highly recommended to those wanting a glimpse of the state of the art and of likely future directions. Among the problems covered, which we have not the space or inclination to cover here, are the questions of how to manage large knowledge bases in big systems and questions of efficient implementation.

3.6 COMMUNICATING WITH DATABASES IN NATURAL LANGUAGE

In the period since 1975 there has been a phenomenal increase in the number of papers published and general interest in the topic of computer understanding of natural language. Very recently we have witnessed the emergence of commercially available products which (almost) realize the ideal in the very limited context of database enquiry. A typical such product is INTELLECT which provides a front end to such products as FOCUS, DB2(SQL) and ADABAS. INTELLECT is based on the earlier ROBOT system of Harris, and uses the data dictionary to impose contextual restrictions on its grammar.

INTELLECT uses four types of knowledge and data to analyse sentences: two lexicons, a grammar based on an augmented transition network (ATN), the data dictionary and the data in the database itself. The lexicons are split into two to assist in tailoring the interpreter to a specific implementation. One contains common English words such as 'what' or 'for', and the other words specific to the application in hand. We should explain briefly the notion of an ATN before describing INTELLECT any further.

The earliest attempts to describe formally the syntactic structure of language were generally based on production rules. Thus, the fact that a sentence could be decomposed into a noun phrase and a verb phrase gives rise to a typical production. Backward chaining can be applied to sets of such rules to achieve a parse. This method turned out to be somewhat cumbersome and it was found beneficial to compile the rules into a 'transition network' which can be represented in tabular form. In fact this is just a finite state automaton. The network represents the different ways to get from a sentence to a valid parse. These networks can be *augmented* by allowing flags to be set as the parsing proceeds. The effect is that the networks can have a hierarchical structure which permits large networks to 'call' more specialized ones. To recognize (or *accept* in

Automatonese) a sentence, the parser moves along the links of the network trying to find recursively an example of the concept specified by the link it has reached. For example, to analyse the sentence 'Cheap electrical stores buy more stock' an ATN parser would start with its network for sentences

Noun phrase   Verb phrase

Startstate1 ——————→ State2 ——————→ Endstate

and then call the 'noun phrase' network and start by searching the lexicon for a determiner corresponding to the first word in the sentence 'Cheap'.

Determiner   Adjective   Prepositional
Proper noun   phrase
Adjective   Noun

Startstate ——————→ State2 ——————→Endstate
Jump

It would fail, so it proceeds to the next path and identifies the word as a proper noun. Its occurrence as an adjective in the lexicon gives rise to ambiguity which must be resolved later. Then the next word is processed, and so on.

To get a feel for how INTELLECT works, and especially how it resolves ambiguities, consider the following dialogue.

```
.How many cooks are in the company?

YOUR REQUEST IS AMBIGUOUS TO ME. DO YOU WANT:

  1): CURRENT JOB TITLE = COOK.

  2): LAST NAME = COOK.

PLEASE ENTER THE NUMBER OF THE INTERPRETATION YOU INTENDED

.2

PARAPHRASE: COUNT THE EMPLOYEES WITH LAST NAME = COOK.

ANSWER:    1

NEXT REQUEST

.Give me a spreadsheet of the percent of total salary in each department

PARAPHRASE: PRINT A CALC PERCENTAGE OF THE TOTAL ANNUAL SALARY IN EACH

  DEPARTMENT OF ALL EMPLOYEES.

     <A report is printed>

.Show it in a piechart

(Etc.)
```

The system has dealt with the ambiguity of 'cook' and will deal with the elliptical 'it' in the last sentence by referring back to what it has last performed.

It is worth noting however that most sentences will be equally well processed by INTELLECT if they are reversed. This can result in some highly amusing dialogues.

Sowa [193] sums up the case for attempting to use English and other human languages to communicate with computer systems as follows.

> 'Menus are good for selecting options, but they are awkward for expressing relationships. Mathematical equations are good for relationships, but they cannot express commands. Programming languages issue commands, but they cannot ask questions. Query languages ask questions, but they cannot give explanations. Only natural languages can serve all the functions of human communication within a common, flexible framework.'

Whilst agreeing with this statement in general, we must add that for some purposes natural language can be exceedingly cumbersome. That is why mathematical notations, for example, have been developed. Furthermore, Sowa does not mention that most characteristic feature of discourse in natural language: its ability to deal with incompletely and inexactly expressed concepts and to resolve and assimilate contradiction.

In some cases a formal language, which need not be difficult to learn if it is close to natural language, can be more concise without being harder to understand. Sowa cites, by way of example, the following three enquiries on a personnel database.

(1) From the skills inventory, get me the name, employee number, department, and years in service of the engineers with knowledge of German located in the New York area.
(2) List name, employee, no., dept., and service years for engineers in New York who know German.
(3)
```
SELECT NAME, EMPNBR, DEPT, SEVYRS

FROM SKILFILE

WHERE    JOBCODE = 'ENG'

         AND SKILCODE = 'GERMAN'

         AND LOC = 'NY'.
```

The last construct is a query expressed in SQL and is not difficult to understand, providing that you know the name of the attributes and relations in the database. The first expression on the other hand requires this knowledge also, but is long and unwieldy. It is also ambiguous, but the parser we envisage would probably not detect the possibility of a language or a piece of knowledge being located in

New York. It is the second sentence which, being both shorter and less explicit about the provenance of the data, we would like to be able to use. To interpret such sentences a knowledge-based system is required to understand familiar abbreviations such as 'no.' and to have knowledge of the database structure: the context. This is the classical problem of the relationship between syntax, semantics and pragmatics. This problem remains to this day an unsolved one, but several systems have emerged which approximate a partial solution.

Workers in both database theory and AI have made contributions in the area of natural language computing. Codd produced a system called RENDEZVOUS which combines a subset of English with a menu approach. PROSPECTOR exploits partitioned Bayesian networks to support an English-like dialogue with the user. This approach is also apparent in Sacerdoti's LADDER system, which accepts queries on a distributed database about naval logistics. LADDER would transform the query

What ships faster than the Kennedy are within 500 miles of Naples?

into four questions:

Find speed of Kennedy
Find location of Naples?
Find ships with distance to Naples LE 500
Find ships found with speed faster than Kennedy

We have already had occasion to mention the main issues in natural language understanding, syntax, semantics and pragmatics. The last two are intimately connected with the analysis of anaphora; that is, making references implicitly where only the context can determine the meaning. Anaphora occurs in two principal ways, most notably reference and substitution. Anaphoric reference occurs when pronouns (or even pro-verbs and pro-adjectives) are used in place of explicit descriptive phrases. It also occurs in the use of general noun phrases which can be restricted to more definite references by referring to some earlier event. Anaphoric substitution occurs when an earlier phrase can be substituted directly for the anaphor and as ellipsis, where there is not even a phrase to indicate that something should be substituted. An example taken from LADDER illustrates this:

```
What is the length of the Constellation?

(LENGTH 1072 FEET)

of the Nautilus?

TRYING ELLIPSIS: WHAT IS THE LENGTH OF THE NAUTILUS

(LENGTH 319 FEET)

displacement?

TRYING ELLIPSIS: WHAT IS THE DISPLACEMENT OF THE NAUTILUS

(STANDARD-DISPLACEMENT 4040 TONS)
```

Winograd's experimental SHRDLU system [210, 252] for understanding sentences about the blocks world uses a simple heuristic to deal with noun substitution, as follows:

(1) Look for a noun phrase which contrasts with the substitute. Change the meaning of the referent to accommodate the new adjective. For example, if the sentence was 'The green block supports a *big* blue pyramid and a *little* one', then the adjective phrase 'little blue' can be applied to pyramid.
(2) If no contrasts can be found, substitute the most recent noun phrase that contains a head noun.

Wallace [204] has a system, QPROC, for querying ICL's IDMS databases. QPROC is written in PROLOG. It is admitted that this leads to an implementation too slow for many practical purposes, and this seems to be a common problem with natural language systems. INTELLECT and LADDER, according to published figures, seem to be encouraging exceptions.

The difference between natural and formal languages amounts to three major distinctions. Words in natural language are intrinsically vague and defy formal definition. Natural language is inherently ambiguous and understanding depends on astronomical quantities of contextual information. Lastly, the interpretation is pragmatic and teleological; it depends on the objectives of both speaker and listener and their models of each other. Computer assisted training packages developed at Logica recognize this by incorporating a student model [35]. The functional aspects of natural language processing can be taken to consist of two tasks: converting the natural language into a high-level formal language and executing the formal statements. The second task is better understood, and computer scientists have an armoury of techniques for parsing formal statements. This leads us to the belief that the first task should be minimized by the use of a formal language as close to the original as possible. Zadeh's PRUF [214] uses fuzzy logic in an attempt to achieve this end and can be regarded as treating the first of the three distinctions mentioned above. The second, ambiguity, is dealt with by search and the use of contextual bindings via a data dictionary. As yet very little is understood about pragmatics, and we suspect little development will occur until a new generation of computers with processing power several orders of magnitude greater becomes available. That the ability to deal with anaphoric reference is a desirable characteristic of human languages can be adduced to the brevity it permits in communication. It is hardly surprising that speech should avail itself of all the computational power of the human brain to use abbreviated forms such as anaphors whenever possible. For this reason, some authors have claimed that real natural language systems will require an almost complete array of the capabilities of human intelligence to succeed.

Schank's conceptual dependency theory, which we dealt with in Chapter 2, has been applied to story understanding but little has so far been published on recent attempts to apply it to database enquiry. The strong relationships exposed in this chapter between frames (or scripts) and relational database theory seem to be beckoning researchers in that direction.

For the immediate future, we think that the most benefit will be obtained from the development of high level 'English like' *formal* languages. Fuzzy logic provides a tractable and computationally efficient vehicle for progress in this direction, but the advances represented by systems such as INTELLECT in parsing sentences and dealing with anaphora will also be very important in such new languages.

3.7 SUMMARY

This chapter has surveyed the theory of logical database design, and introduced fuzzy relations and their applications. We showed how relations could be regarded as a special case of frames and, combining these themes, how fuzzy frames could be developed as a means of overcoming many current problems in knowledge engineering. The view that relations are important leads to the incorporation of knowledge engineering within the corpus of conventional software engineering with the obvious advantages when it comes to building large and complex real systems as compared with the toy problems of much artificial intelligence research.

After a brief discussion of the importance of artificial intelligence inference methods in database access we turned to a survey of progress in the application of natural language processing to database enquiry.

3.8 FURTHER READING

On the basic database material there are no better references than Date [53] and Ullman [202]. Martin [140], although a little outdated now, provides another good source with much useful material on the physical implementation and software issues. Kroenke [124] is again very out of date but is very readable and is especially good on the management issues.

Addis [3] comes close in his concerns to the theme of this chapter.

On the relationship between databases and logic programming we recommend Clocksin and Mellish [47]. Bobrow and Winograd [25] is worth reading in the context of frames on which there is a mine of readable and useful material in Brachman and Levesque [34].

The question of the relation between data and knowledge-based systems is covered by Brodie and Mylopoulos [234], but this is a set of conference proceedings and not all the papers are readily accessible to the non-specialist reader.

Sowa [193] is an important source for the material on natural language and much else, and Wallace [204] provides a good, if a little tedious, survey.

Part three
Uncertainty

4

Uncertainty

> 'Modern-day computers are amazing pieces of
> equipment, but most amazing of all are the
> uncertain grounds on account of which we
> attach any validity to their output'
>
> *Structured Programming*, E. Dijkstra *et al.*

4.1 THE SOURCES AND KINDS OF UNCERTAINTY

4.1.1 Introduction

The proper representation and management of uncertainty is inextricably bound
up with the development of knowledge-based systems for execution on a
computer.

To arrive at a decision in the presence of absolute certainty with respect to all
the relevant facts and considerations is a luxury rarely afforded to human beings.
Assumptions must be made about data values which are not available, about
events which may or may not have occurred, and about consequences likely to
flow from a given decision. Many of these assumptions may be made
unconsciously or subconsciously. Some may be made explicitly, with whatever
degree of justification may be adduced. Mathematics may be prayed in aid of some
assumptions made on statistical bases. Otherwise, rules of thumb and accrued
experience serve as a guide.

In this chapter, we examine some of the main methods which have been
proposed and utilized in representing and managing uncertainty in computer-
based knowledge engineering projects.

The sources and kinds of uncertainty may be, at a first approximation, classified
as follows:

random event;
experimental error;
uncertainty in judgement;
lack of evidence;
lack of certainty in evidence;

In this book, we are concerned with the analysis of a decision making process whereby a course of action is selected from a range of possibilities in the presence of uncertainty with regard to the pertinent data, and knowledge is used to combat the uncertainty in arriving at the 'best' decision.

By the phrase 'a course of action' we mean both the selection of a physical action, and the assignment of a value to some consequent variable based on current antecedent information.

The decision-making process can be defined as a set of applicable rules of the form

IF D IS D_x THEN A IS A_y

where the D are data points in some N-dimensional data space, and the A are actions in some one-dimensional action space.

Thus

$$D_x = \{D_1, D_2, \ldots, D_n\}.$$

A number of kinds of uncertainty afflict our estimates of the components D_i of D_N.

(a) *Instrumental error*

We may define the dimension D_i to be a real numeric dimension, but be unable to measure D_i with an adequate degree of precision. This is, of course, the standard situation in scientific measurement, and is managed on the assumption that errors of observation are normally distributed about the true value of the observed variable.

Here the 'rule' would be a function

$$A = F(D_i) \qquad i \in \{1, \ldots, n\}$$

and statistical techniques allow us to induce the expected error in A given the estimates of the errors in the D_i.

(b) *Conceptual error*

The dimension D_i may not be real-valued. Its definition may be linguistic, and the possible data values will then have to be selected from a set of linguistic descriptors. For example, in a determination of a patient's clinical symptoms, the degree of pain present can only be described in terms such as 'slight pain', 'severe pain', 'very severe pain' and so on.

4.1.2   Sources of uncertainty in knowledge-based systems

There is no positive, exact definition possible for either a knowledge-based system or an expert system. Every attempt to give one is doomed to either triviality or is so all-encompassing as to be useless. For example, one definition has been proposed by Zadeh (in a public lecture) as follows. 'An expert system is a machine for reducing uncertainty.' This is certainly an attribute possessed by every expert system worth the name, but must include many systems which we would not want to so call, such as the act of tossing a coin to choose a course of action, or a system to compute the $n + 1$th decimal place of π where n is the highest one ever computed. On the other hand, medical expert systems certainly have this character. Other definitions, such as 'a system which simulates the behaviour of a human expert', have the aspect of triviality and are not exclusive to what we want to call an expert system; a payroll system replaces experts in some senses. The same applies to the definition of a knowledge-based system. It is difficult to conceive a computer system which is not based on knowledge of some sort; payroll systems include plenty of knowledge about tax rates, possible classes of deductions, etc. The point is the way in which the knowledge is represented. In most payroll systems the representation is procedural, probably in the form of COBOL programs. If we were to shift our ground slightly and insist that a knowledge-based system was based on rules, then what would we do about systems based on frames? Or if the definition were to encompass only non-procedural representations of any type, we might still have some concern about frame systems with procedural attachment. Chapter 2 has taken up the details of all the different ways of representing knowledge in computer systems. Our concern here is with uncertainty. If we accept that an informal definition based on some list of attributes is acceptable, then Zadeh's 'definition' does have some useful consequences.

We take a broader view however. Not only expert, but many knowledge-based and all decision support systems have the character of uncertainty reduction machines. Chapter 8 explores the decision support aspects of this in more detail. In this chapter we shall not only explore various theories of uncertainty, but also make the point that the various methods of handling uncertainty explicitly in computer systems are all important. The whole of the book is an exploration of this theme. The chief methods available at present, in practical systems, are summarized in Fig. 4.1.

The definition of an expert system depends in an intimate way on how we think

---

A decision support system is a machine for reducing uncertainty:

- Statistics and probability
- 'What if' and targeting
- Verbal descriptions
- Fuzzy sets
- Non monotonic logic

Fig. 4.1 Some methods of handling uncertainty

of an expert. From the point of view of systems that reduce uncertainty an operational definition of an expert might be 'a person who can answer a question which no-one else has an answer to' or 'someone who cannot afford to say "I don't know"'. We expect our doctor to answer positively, and would soon go elsewhere otherwise. The result of a visit to the doctor should be that our level of uncertainty is reduced. The danger inherent in this is that human experts tend to err on the side of certainty, perhaps in order to maintain a dubious credibility. This is a serious danger for computer-based expert systems. Imagine an expert system to control a nuclear power plant which was *certain* it hadn't made a mistake. Thus the need arises in a very profound sense for expert systems to handle uncertainty.

If we think of an expert system as consisting of a data base, knowledge base, a knowledge application system and some method of interacting with the real world, then we might classify the sources of uncertainty in these four dimensions.

Partial, vague or incomplete data contribute to uncertainty, leading to the need for complex inference strategies involving multiple chains of reasoning. Some authors, such as Bonissone and Brown [240], treat incompleteness separately from uncertainty. This has obvious operational utility, but, while incompleteness has its own sources, the end result is always uncertainty. For completeness, the sources of incompleteness (no pun intended) are: estimates of the outcome of future events, failure to record past events precisely or pertinently enough and the impossibility of knowing the intentions of other actors or the internal operations of natural processes. Sometimes the cost of obtaining data is the critical factor, but this does not change the principle. Much of the uncertainty in inferential behaviour may be attributed to incompleteness in the data or in the knowledge bases.

The knowledge base can be subject to uncertainty for the following reasons. It may be the case that the experts on the subject disagree or are just plain wrong. It can be incomplete, so that there are exceptions to rules and the rules do not cover the state space. It can be expressed with a degree of precision, or granularity, which is not appropriate to the problem at hand. It can be too shallow, so that causal links are not explicated as in cases where we reason by correlation; if you have red spots then you are suffering from measles. It can be merely very difficult to express in the available representation language(s) for several reasons. Lastly, it may be the sheer size of the knowledge base that causes the uncertainty.

In the knowledge application system we are dealing, in some sense to be made precise in Chapter 6, with logic. The kinds of uncertainty present can be classified as follows:

variation in the degree of belief;
variation in the degree of likelihood;
variation in the degree of possibility or necessity;
variation in the degree of precision;
variation in the extent to which a proposition holds;

variation in the degree of truth or provability of a proposition;
variation in the degree of the mandate for performing some action;
variation in the degree of compulsion or duty;
variation in the degree of relevance;
the existence of exceptions.

First generation expert systems have, typically, dealt only with likelihood via probability theory or belief and extent via various *ad hoc* methods. To this day many of these lvariants are beyond our ability to deal with. However, modal logics have for some time contributed to the study of belief and possibility, fuzzy logic has provided means for dealing with imprecision, extent and possibility and, more recently, nonmonotonic logic has offered hope for the treatment of exceptions. The key point is that there is no *a priori* reason to expect that the mathematics of these different kinds of uncertainty should be the same. For example, the conjunction of two uncertain facts may be represented by taking the minimal certainty (possibility) or the product (probability). No-one has yet solved the general problem of how to conjoin uncertain propositions which partake in more than one kind of uncertainty. The solution to this problem may well mark the beginning of a study of genuine artificial intelligence.

The natural world is the ultimate source of all uncertainty. In the present context the chief sources are as follows:

unreliable sources of data and information;
the abundance of irrelevant data;
the imprecision of natural language and sensory apparatus;
lack of understanding;
faulty sensory equipment;
conflicting or complementary sources of facts;
hidden variables producing apparent randomness;
the energy required to obtain certain data.

These types may arrive singly or in groups, whether data is collected manually or automatically.

The classification given so far has arisen from attempts to justify various forms of possibilitic or fuzzy reasoning, in the face of a strong position within the expert systems community that such things are 'unrigorous', unnecessary or can be dealt with in other ways. However, such concerns as we have expressed predate even the development of fuzzy set theory. For, in 1961 we find Professor Shackle [241] expressing concern about the foundations of economics and decision theory:

' . . . in analysing decision, the use of a distributional uncertainty variable, that is, probability, becomes in principle inappropriate and must give way to a non-distributional uncertainty variable such as possibility, understood as discriminable in some manner into degrees; for example, by being identified with potential surprise.'

Even before this Keynes in 1921 [242] had pointed out the need to complement probability with other notions such as that of weight of evidence:

> 'new evidence will sometimes decrease the probability of an argument, but it will always increase its "weight".'

It is only since 1965 that we have had even the possibility (sic) of a unified approach to forms of uncertainty other than probability. The more cynical among us could go further, and point out that the Kolmogorov foundations for statistics are shot through with logical holes. For example, take the foundational notion of a point event. If statistics is a subject concerned with aggregate phenomena how can it make any sense to argue always and entirely from points and individuals. Surely, the lesson of cybernetics is that this is a foolish procedure. Lawvere has suggested, informally, ways round this problem using category theoretic methods, but, so far as we know, no-one has taken up the cudgels.

Having made an attempt to classify the sources of uncertainty it is incumbent upon us to make some attempt to state how these problems may be overcome. Much of the rest of this work is devoted to precisely this question. Here, we will only take up a few of the more pressing issues.

4.1.3   Techniques for handling uncertainty

As we have said already, nonmonotonic logic, truth maintenance systems or default reasoning may be useful in dealing with incompleteness or exceptions (see Chapter 6). They also have application to dealing with faulty sensors and to the problem of knowledge base size through the mechanism of qualifying conclusions. If the experts disagree we have various options: weighting their views, doing experiments and learning or building self-organizing controllers.

Conflicting or complementary sources might be dealt with using the theory of 'endorsements' due to Cohen [243]. Fuzzy methods, as we will see often in this book, can be used to deal with imprecise or linguistic data.

All the methods which have been proposed for dealing with uncertainty in computer systems fall into two broad classes; non-numerical methods such as endorsements, high granularity symbol manipulation and nonmonotonic logic; and various numerical methods. All of these inference techniques have a 'truth bearing item' which is used to qualify propositions and which is propagated through the inferences made. Let us have a critical look at some of these methods.

In systems based on Bayesian probability inference is predicated on the formula:

$$\text{Prob}\{X \text{ is } A\} = \frac{\text{Prob}\{Y \text{ is } B \mid X \text{ is } A\}\text{Prob}\{X \text{ is } A\}}{\text{Prob}\{Y \text{ is } B\}}$$

The problems with this approach are that this formula is not commutative, that it depends on global assumptions of the independence of evidential variables, that the hypotheses are assumed to be exhaustive and exclusive and that a qualified conclusion has no clear semantic interpretation. These all contribute to making dialogue with the system difficult and unnatural. For example, it is easy to confuse asking 'How sure are you that the sparking plugs are dirty?' with 'How dirty are the plugs?'. Thus, the answer 'don't know' becomes ambiguous, and enormous effort to insert a context will be required.

The Shafer–Dempster theory of evidence does permit users to be ignorant in a slightly clearer manner. Evidence supporting and denying hypotheses is stated explicitly and data are represented at the appropriate level of granularity. However, it relies on the same global assumptions of independence as the Bayesian approach and it is difficult to trace the propagation of evidence.

Fuzzy reasoning, on the other hand, makes no global assumptions about the independence, exhaustiveness or exclusiveness of evidence. That is not to say it is without weaknesses from the system builder's viewpoint. There is no explicit statement of the reasons for supporting or refuting hypotheses, and it is difficult to trace the propagation of uncertainty unless a fairly elaborate system is constructed with this aim in mind.

Cohen's theory of endorsements is based on the idea that accumulation of evidence can, under certain conditions, lead to false conclusions. It is a heuristic approach which uses context-dependent rules to define how 'endorsements' may be continued, added or removed. Consider, as an example, the following statements:

(1) Sixth formers tend to run fast.
(2) Young people over 15 tend to run fast.
(3) A lot of fast runners were born in 1971.
(4) Young people over 16 are likely to be in the sixth form.
(5) Sharon is 16 and at school.

We might deduce from these fact as follows:

(6) Sharon might run fast.   (2 and 5)
(7) Sharon might be in the sixth form.   (4 and 5)
(8) Sharon is likely to run fast.   (1 and 6 and 7)

Clearly, 8 is highly dubious on any criterion of common sense. We need to be very careful, thus, when accumulating evidence. Cohen's theory does have the advantage that it requires no independence assumptions and the reasoning may be easily traced. However, there is no provision for dealing with weight of evidence and we cannot represent ignorance or contradiction readily. This is a problem with all theories that offer no second-order measure of uncertainty such as ranges of values.

As far as knowledge-based systems are concerned, a good mechanism for representing uncertainty ought to have the following properties.

- Consistent and natural semantics.
- An appropriate level of granularity as required.

- It should allow appropriate assumptions about independence.
- An intelligent, meaningful dialogue and knowledge representation manager.
- Easy and intelligible tracing of aggregation and propagation of uncertainty.
- It should store the reasons for its support for or arrival at hypotheses.
- Second-order measures of uncertainty.
- It must be able to resolve conflict.
- For large or real-time knowledge-based systems, heuristic control strategies must be possible.
- Cognitive emulation of how experts handle uncertainty may be desirable in some cases and should be possible.
- Its logic should be context dependent.

At this point it is appropriate to remark on granularity: RULES ARE SUMMARIES. In other words the chunking of knowledge represents abstraction, and often this is how human experts reduce or eliminate uncertainty. This is very like the idea of dispositions – implicit quantifiers – which we will encounter later in Chapter 6. This point is reinforced by the fact that many of the most successful expert systems avoid all explicit or numerical representations of uncertainty by using solely linguistic labels. Experienced experts often insist that they use a rule of thumb that assigns linguistic labels to ranges of numerical input. We have encountered this with, for example, insurance assessors and computer capacity planners. The former insist that 'a low standard of insulation' is an exact term to them. The latter tell us that 'a high multi-programming level' occurs *exactly* when a certain numerical threshold is past. Discontinuities in the output are avoided by specifying enough such labels. Thus a simple and important method of handling uncertainty is the assignment of linguistic labels at an appropriate level of granularity. The determination of this level is a problem in knowledge elicitation; and not always a trivial one.

Such simple methods, while not always appropriate, should not be dismissed out of hand. In financial models, for example, rerunning the model under a range of different assumptions – sensitivity analysis – is an important method of reducing uncertainty. Just because no deep issues in cognitive psychology are raised does not mean we can ignore it in knowledge engineering.

Expert systems will have to be made accountable. Uncertainty must be handled appropriately with a good mix of strategies. Getting it wrong, even slightly, could lead to legal action in some cases.

4.2 PROBABILISTIC REPRESENTATIONS

The first source of uncertainty to be examined is that associated essentially with randomness – the estimation of the likelihood of a given event occurring out of a possible set of events which can be enumerated.

Probability was first studied in the seventeenth century by Pascal and Fermat, in the context of gambling. The Chevalier de Mere, in the fashion of the time, was wont to dispose of his share of the proceeds of the gabelle across the gaming table. He did rather well betting on the occurrence of a single six in four tosses of a cubical die, and then took a bath betting on the occurrence of a double six in twenty-four tosses of two cubical dice. Pascal remarked that he possessed 'très bon esprit', but 'il n'est pas géomètre'.

It is pleasing to see, given the present-day focus on the management of uncertainty in the highly practical context of developing effective knowledge-based systems, that the earliest research into what is now the highly abstracted science of statistics occurred in such a pragmatic context.

Given a specified (and artificial) game with a randomized element, such as dice, cards or lotteries, what is the correct division of the stakes between banker and player to permit the player to define a winning strategy? This was the motivation behind the development of classical probability theory. The artificial nature of the problems studied during the development of the theory allowed three significant axioms to be employed.

Firstly, we as a player will state in advance a rule to which we will adhere during an endless succession of unchanging games. Secondly, the game itself (the pack of cards, roulette wheel or whatever) remains unchanging during this succession of games. And thirdly, implicit in the game is a 'true' randomizing element (whatever that might mean).

The Chevalier's domestic economy was sustained through his belief that one six is likely to occur in four throws by the arithmetic that

- not throwing a six in one throw of the die will occur $5/6$ of the time;
- not throwing a six in four throws will occur in $(5/6)^4$ of the population of four throws of the die;
- and thus throwing a six in four throws of the die will occur in $[1 - (5/6)^4] = 0.518$ of the population of four throws of the die. The odds are more favourable than not.

His undoing lay in the fact that not throwing a double six in a throw of two dice has the probability $35/36$, and that therefore the probability of throwing a double six in twenty-four throws of two dice is $[1 - (35/36)^{24}] = 0.491$ which is more unlikely than likely.

The application of the empirical science of probability to life assurance came very quickly thereafter. The problems of operating in the real world on the basis of the initial axioms were seen clear. Equitable based their life premiums on the 'Northampton Life Table', a compilation of life expectancies based on baptismal records at Northampton. This was a good choice. The compilation was grossly biased by the assumption that people were baptised as babies, which, at least in Northampton in the eighteenth century, was nowhere near the case. The massively understated life expectancies which resulted in very profitably high insurance premiums caused Equitable to flourish. The then current government based its retirement annuities on the same tables and thus lost its shirt. See Price [173].

The lesson to be learnt is that the edifice of statistical decision theory is based on the assumptions that there is

- a valid hypothesis that experimental data are complete and unbiased;
- and the mechanisms generating the experimental data continue in force on an unchanged basis.

4.3 BAYESIAN REPRESENTATIONS

As we saw in the previous section, decision making under classical probability theory rests on three postulates:

- there is a value which may be assigned in advance to the probability of an event;
- decisions will adhere consistently to a rule stated in advance, irrespective of accruing experience;
- events themselves are the result of a randomizing process.

To believe that this is an effective way to go forward in the real world is to place some exacting demands on our credulity. We are in effect saying that we have perfect knowledge of objective reality, with the sole exception being the precise outcome (from a well specified set of alternatives) of one or more randomized events.

In fact our knowledge of objective reality is rarely complete at any interesting decision point. We work on the basis of reasonable hypotheses for those facets of reality which are not known with precision, and these hypotheses are constantly updated in the light of new information received. This information may arise fortuitously, or it may be the result of a purposeful experiment or test carried out to gather these further data.

We are dealing here with the concept of 'inverse probability' – the likelihood of an event having a given cause, rather than a cause giving rise to a given event. The thing which is being measured is the change in a state of mind, rather than any change in an objective state. Thus given some degree of uncertainty concerning reality, we make some hypotheses, and assign to each hypothesis an initial likelihood, called the 'prior probability' of the hypothesis. We then perform some test, and on the basis of the outcome, revise our probabilities associated with each hypothesis. The revised probabilities are called the posterior probabilities. They may then be used as the prior probabilities for some further test, provided only that the further test is measuring some parameter truly independent of the measurement taken in the first (or any previous) test.

As we shall see, the virtue of the Bayesian approach is that we are allowed to assign subjective prior probabilities to our hypotheses in situations where incomplete knowledge does not allow us to compute these probabilities on any arithmetic or mechanistic basis.

Central to Bayes's thesis is the 'Principle of Insufficient Reason'. This states that in assigning our prior probabilities to alternative hypotheses, we are free to assign equal probabilities to each, in the absence of any 'Sufficient Reason' to the contrary. The ice is rather thin hereabouts; and the more enthusiastic proponents of the usage of Bayesian probability theory for all purposes, who cheerfully cast stones at the so-called *ad hoc* nature of other formalisms for uncertainty management, rarely seem to base their case on this component of the argument.

We have to make a 'closed world' assumption that all possibilities may be covered by a finite set of mutually exclusive and independent hypotheses. These are Hypotheses *Hi*, $i = 1, n$. Associated with each hypothesis is a prior probability $Pr(i)$, assigned on the basis of our knowledge of the universe. This is shown in Table 4.1.

Table 4.1

Hypothesis	A priori probabilities
H1	Pr (H1)
H2	Pr (H2)
.	.
.	.
Hn	Pr (Hn)

A test may be carried out (or fortuitous information gathered) and the result of the test is an event E_j, where $j = 1, m$, and where the E_j are again a mutually exclusive and all-encompassing set of events.

The conditional probabilities of the events based on the assumption that each of the hypotheses in turn is true may be summarized as in Table 4.2. Here

$$Pr(Ej : Hi) = \text{Probability of Event } j \text{ if Hypothesis } i \text{ is true}$$

Table 4.2

Hypothesis	Events		
	E1	E2	Em
H1	Pr(E1 : H1)	Pr(E2 : H1)	Pr(Em : H1)
H2	Pr(E1 : H2)	Pr(E2 : H2)	Pr(Em : H2)
.	.	.	.
.	.	.	.
Hn	Pr(E1 : Hn)	Pr(E2 : Hn)	Pr(Em : Hn)

We should note that

$$\sum_{i=1}^{n} Pr(Hi) = 1$$

and

$$\sum_{j=1}^{m} \Pr(Ej : Hi) = 1$$

The overall probability of obtaining the event *Ej* is defined as

$$\Pr(Ej) = \sum_{i=1}^{n} \Pr(Hi) * \Pr(Ej : Hi)$$

Bayes's Theorem now states that the posterior probability of hypothesis *Hi* given the observation of event *Ej* is

$$\Pr(Hi : Ej) = \Pr(Hi) * \frac{\Pr(Ej : Hi)}{\Pr(Ej)}$$

or in other words, the revised probability in the hypothesis is the prior probability, multiplied by the ratio of the conditional probability of event occurring given the hypothesis as true to the overall probability of the event occurring.

The mechanics of carrying out this process on an arithmetic basis were first enunciated by the Rev. Thomas Bayes, an eighteenth century non-conformist minister. His paper, *Essay towards solving a problem in the Doctrine of Chance*, was published posthumously in 1763 by the Royal Society, having been communicated and edited by the Rev. Richard Price, another dissenting divine.

Consider how the arithmetic works in the following example experiment. We will place into a bag four balls – either three white and one black; or three black and one white. You are to figure out which we have done, and you are allowed to experiment by taking a ball from the bag, checking its colour, and replacing it.

The hypotheses are:

3 white and 1 black: Hypothesis A
3 black and 1 white: Hypothesis B

and in order to allow us to use the principle of insufficient reason with a good conscience, we will volunteer to select our action based on the toss of a coin.

Therefore the prior probabilities of Hypotheses A and B are both exactly 0.50.

You perform a test by drawing a ball, which may turn out to be either white or black. These are events *E1* and *E2*. The matrix of conditional probabilities is shown in Table 4.3.

Table 4.3

Hypothesis		Events	
Name	Prior	E1	E2
A	0.50	0.75	0.25
B	0.50	0.25	0.75

Assume event $E1$ (white ball drawn) occurs. We can now apply Bayes's Theorem to develop the posterior probabilities for hypotheses A and B.

$$Pr(A:E1) = 0.50 * \frac{0.75}{0.50} = 0.75$$

$$Pr(B:E1) = 0.50 * \frac{0.25}{0.50} = 0.25$$

The revised probabilities of events $E1$ and $E2$ occurring in a repeat of the test are

$$Pr(E1) = 0.75 * 0.75 + 0.25 * 0.25 = 0.625$$

and

$$Pr(E2) = 0.25 * 0.75 + 0.75 * 0.25 = 0.375$$

Because repeated trials in this experiment are independent, you are free to repeat the test. Suppose you once again draw a white ball. The new posterior probabilities are

$$Pr(A:E1) = 0.75 * \frac{0.75}{0.625} = 0.90$$

$$Pr(B:E1) = 0.25 * \frac{0.25}{0.375} = 0.10$$

It's starting to look rather as if Hypothesis A may be true. However, notice particularly that it is your degree of belief in the trueness of A which is increasing. The objective reality is that there was originally, and still is, an exact $50:50$ chance that hypothesis A reflects what really occurred.

Succeeding tests which again drew white balls would increase the posterior probability asymptotically towards one, but would never reach it. The method can never arrive at absolute arithmetic certainty, but can only reach arbitrarily close, until some (again subjective) threshold is exceeded at which you are content to treat the hypothesis as verified.

If we consider this experiment in the light of classical probabilities, we see that the same results precisely may be obtained. On random selection with replacement, given a population of three white balls and one black, the probability of two consecutive whites being drawn is

$$3/4 * 3/4 = 9/16$$

and in a population of three black and one white is

$$1/4 * 1/4 = 1/16$$

The probability of one hypothesis is nine times the other, as with the Bayesian approach.

The key point of the Bayesian approach, then, is not that its results differ from classical theory in situations where both approaches may be taken; but rather that the principle of insufficient reason allows us to form *a priori* probabilities for hypotheses in situations where detailed knowledge does not allow us to establish strict mechanically based odds.

EXERCISE: evaluate how your conclusions based upon the Bayesian approach, using the principle of insufficient reason, would differ from those based upon the classical probabilistic approach if I were to select my action in the example above based upon the strategy 'If I throw a six with a dice, put three white balls and one black into the bag; else put three black balls and one white', and you had:

  (a) no information as to how I selected my action, and
  (b) three white balls were selected consecutively.

Bayesian statistics were used in the development of what may be regarded as the very first expert system, created at Bletchley Park near London during the Second World War. The Government Communications Headquarters (GCHQ) were located at Bletchley, with the task of cracking enciphered German transmissions, and in particular the highly encrypted Enigma signals. Manual methods were clearly insufficient to cope with the vast flow of signal intelligence on a timely basis.

> 'Looking at the cipher traffic, an experienced hand might say that such and such a thing "seemed likely", but now that mass production was the objective, it was necessary to make vague, intuitive judgements into something explicit and mechanical'. (Hodges [98] page 196.)

A. M. Turing, who was based at Bletchley during the War, turned his attention to the use of Bayes's Rule to provide this mechanization, and was the first to present the method in terms of odds rather than probabilities.

Probabilities and Odds are related by the formulae

$$\text{Odds} = \frac{\text{Probability}}{(1 - \text{Probability})}$$

and

$$\text{Probability} = \frac{\text{Odds}}{(1 + \text{Odds})}$$

Rearrangement of terms in Bayes's Theorem then yields the formula

$$\text{Odds}(Hi : Ej) = \text{Odds}(Hi) * \frac{\Pr(Ej : Hi)}{(1 - \Pr(Ej : Hi))}$$

where the denominator of the ratio can also be expressed as $\Pr(Ej : \sim Hi)$ the probability of observing the event Ej given the falsity of hypothesis Hi. This ratio is sometimes referred to as the Likelihood Ratio. The advantage of using odds is just that the simplification in the formula for updating the odds allows the logarithms of the odds and the likelihood ratio to be added, i.e.

$$\text{Log(Odds . posterior)} = \text{Log(Odds . prior)} + \text{Log(Likelihood Ratio)}$$

which, in the absence of a computer, is a simpler procedure.

Turing proposed the term 'ban' to represent these logarithmic odds, with the term 'deciban' (analogous to decibel) representing 'about the smallest change in weight of evidence that is directly perceptible to human intuition'.

The likelihood ratio is also sometimes referred to as the Logical Sufficiency factor *LS*. If

$$\Pr(Ej:Hi) \gg \Pr(Ej: \sim Hi),$$

then

$$LS \gg 1$$

In other words, if the conditional probability of observing Event *j* if Hypothesis *i* is true is very much greater than the conditional probability of observing the same event if the hypothesis is false, making *LS* very much greater than unity, we can say that the occurrence of the event very strongly confirms the hypothesis, and may be regarded itself as sufficient evidence to believe the hypothesis.

Analogously, we can define the Logical Necessity factor *LN* as

$$LN = \frac{\Pr(\sim Ej:Hi)}{\Pr(\sim Ej:\bar{H}i)}$$

Here, if the conditional probability of not observing the Event *j* if Hypothesis *i* is true is very much less than the conditional probability of not observing the event if the hypothesis is not true, *LN* will be very much less than one.

The event may then be regarded as necessary evidence for us to believe in the hypothesis, and its absence may make the hypothesis so unlikely as to be discounted.

It is sometimes said that the Logical Sufficiency and Logical Necessity factors and their associated items of evidence define in some absolute sense the conditions which supply sufficient or necessary evidence for some hypothesis to be held. This is not the case. The accrual of evidence weighed on an arithmetic basis can never reach either zero or unity with respect to a hypothesis. In a practical context, some threshold arbitrarily close to either bound may be reached, but the decision as to where this threshold should lie is a subjective one. If you toss a coin a hundred times and it comes down heads every time, your initial hypothesis that the coin was unbiased is now very hard to sustain, since the probability of the sequence is $(1/(2^{100}))$. This is a small number, but it is not zero. This is the purist's approach, of course, since few people's threshold of incredulity would not have been breached by the witnessing of such an event. It does, however, serve to underline the pragmatic (and *ipso facto* non-mathematical) approach which we all take in relating observed occurrences in the real world to the provable statements which mathematics can provide to sustain our beliefs.

Logical Sufficiency and Logical Necessity factors are sometimes used as the starting point for assembling information for a knowledge base. For example, if a car will not start, one possibility is that the battery is flat. In the absence of any other data, we might assign a prior probability of 0.25 to this hypothesis. However, if the engine turns over vigorously, we could rule out the hypothesis that the battery was flat. In a rule-like format, this might be expressed

IF engine IS turning_vigorously THEN battery IS ok
$\{LS = 100 \; LN = = 0.0001 \; Prior = 0.25\}$

The Prior Odds are $1/3$. If the engine does indeed turn vigorously, the Posterior Odds are $1/3 * 100 = 33.3$ and the Posterior Probability is $33.3/34.3 = 0.97$. For practical purposes, we might choose to regard the hypothesis that the battery was okay as proven. Equally, if the engine does not turn, the Posterior Odds are $1/3 * 0.0001 = 0.000033$ and the Posterior Probability is $0.000033/1,000033 = 0.0000032$, which for practical purposes says that the battery must be flat.

This short cut of eliciting the Logical Sufficiency and Necessity factors can enable draft systems of rules to be set up more easily than by going through the formal process of elaborating the set of hypotheses exhaustively with their associated prior probabilities, and then generating the full matrix of conditional probabilities.

However, the danger should be clear; there is no longer any guarantee that the true conditional probabilities of the closed set of events obtainable under all tests will sum to unity for each of the hypotheses. The mathematical underpinnings of the method are being eroded. Since the objective of developing a knowledge base is to provide a tool of practical utility, this may not matter. The ability to rank order a set of hypotheses and pick the relatively most likely can be valuable. But clearly a knowledge base built on this empirical approach must likewise be validated by extensive empirical testing.

Another practical problem in the development of Bayesian networks is the requirement that all tests performed should be independent. To the extent that tests are not independent, we are double counting evidence. Weight of evidence will then misleadingly accrue to some hypotheses. There is no good way around this. If we had enough detailed knowledge of objective reality to be absolutely sure that there was no correlation at all between any of the variables in our universe of tests, we would be in a state of perfect knowledge, and tools for the management of uncertainty would be redundant.

Philosophically, we are unlikely to be in this state of grace, but more proximately, the volume and detail of data that such a state would imply would rule out the mechanical implementation of the system in any technology we could foresee.

Our problems are compounded in the practical arena by the difficulty of ascertaining whether or not a given event has in fact occurred. In a mechanical implementation of a Bayesian network, a human agent will be despatched to report on the result of a test. Sometimes the test will allow only yes/no answers; 'Is the ball white or black?', would be the question associated with the example given above. More frequently in real situations, there may be some degree of truth in the result of the test *vis-à-vis* the question, or some degree of uncertainty in the mind of the respondent as to the correct answer.

Practical systems often follow the example of PROSPECTOR, and allow the user to place the answer along some continuum. The question may be phrased 'On a scale from -5 to $+5$, how sure are you that the engine oil is dirty?', where $+5$ implies 'definitely dirty' and -5 implies 'definitely not dirty'.

Zero on this scale implies 'not known' or 'no evidence'. (1) would imply somewhere between 'don't know' and 'yes'; (2) somewhere further towards 'yes' than (1); and so forth. On a rather *ad hoc* basis, the general approach taken has been to interpolate positive responses linearly between unity and the Logical Sufficiency to provide a revised factor for generating the posterior probabilities; and likewise to interpolate linearly between zero and the Logical Necessity factor for negative responses. For a response of zero, simply set the posterior equal to the prior probability. This is a pragmatic approach, which indubitably leads to functioning systems, and therefore has some degree of validity. However, there is little mathematical justification for the approach, and neither is there any discrimination between the various possible sources of uncertainty leading to the zero response implying 'don't know' or 'no evidence'.

This is an issue in dimensionality. The agent's response of '0' may imply

- a complete lack of comprehension of the question;
- a physical problem in obtaining the reading requested;
- an expert's view that the reading was mid-way between 'yes' and 'no';
- the presence of too much noise to allow measurement of the parameter requested.

Currently demonstrated systems have not tackled the issue of discriminating between these and other sources of uncertainty underlying the agent's lack of usable input. Engineering considerations make it clear that the increase in dimensionality needed to elucidate the precise reasons for this lack of input is similar to that needed to comprehend full natural language input. Cracking that particular problem is a task that in other than exceptionally limited closed worlds has not seriously been addressed. It is no criticism of demonstrated knowledge-based systems that this larger problem has not yet been subsumed into the effective solution of more tractable tasks where the compromises in the gathering of evidence are clear.

4.4   CERTAINTY FACTORS

An alternative method of weighting the aggregation of evidence in favour of some *a priori* hypothesis is the use of certainty factors. This technique is originally due to Shortliffe, [186] and was developed under the aegis of the Stanford Heuristic Programming Project in the early 1970s.

The context was the development of computer-based medical consultation systems, and in particular the MYCIN project, which was concerned with replicating a consultant in antimicrobial therapy.

The basic thesis is that there is at any point in time a certainty factor *CF* associated with any given *a priori* hypothesis. This factor ranges in value from -1

representing the statement 'believed to be wholly untrue' to $+1$ representing the statement 'believed to be wholly true'.

There is no assumption that N mutually exclusive hypotheses cover the universe of discourse, nor that $\Sigma_i CF(i) = 1$, either initially or later. Thus the method is not in any sense statistical in its origins or bases.

The certainty factor itself is computed as the difference between two measures; the current measure of belief MB and the current measure of disbelief MD:

$$CF(H:E) = MB(H:E) - MD(H:E)$$

for each hypothesis H given evidence E.

The belief and disbelief measures both range from 0 to 1.

Critical to the use of certainty factors is the method of updating belief in hypotheses as evidence accrues. The formula used by Shortliffe is

$$MB(H:E1, E2) = MB(H:E1) + \{MB(H:E2) * [1 - MB(H:E1)]\}$$

which effectively states that the belief in hypothesis H after evidence $E2$ is increased by the weight of the evidence associated with $E2$ proportionately to the current degree of belief.

This formula has a number of pragmatic attractions:

- it is symmetric with respect to the accrual of evidence from different sources. It does not matter whether we discover evidence $E1$ or $E2$ first.
- it is cumulative asymptotically to certainty, or to put it another way, linear with respect to the logarithm of additional evidence. This accords both with intuition and in a general sense with the mathematics of information theory.

The relationship between evidence and a hypothesis in MYCIN (and succeeding MYCIN-like systems) is expressed in terms of rules. Each rule has associated with it a 'Tally Factor' which represents the innate credibility of the rule itself.

Thus we might have rules which said

IF engine IS not_turning THEN battery IS flat $(T\ 0.6)$
IF horn IS not_blowing THEN battery IS flat $(T\ 0.9)$

Evaluating these rules in either order, and assuming both pieces of evidence turn out to be present, gives us an accrued belief in the hypothesis of a flat battery of 0.96.

However, there may be a weight of belief associated with the antecedent clause – for example, the engine might be turning, but not very vigorously. The weight of belief in the hypothesis is obtained by multiplying the weight of belief in the antecedent by the credibility (or tally factor) of the rule. Thus if the evidence 'engine is not turning' had a degree of belief of 0.5, the evidence accruing to the hypothesis 'battery is flat' from the application of the first rule would be $0.5 * 0.6 = 0.30$.

Rules may be expressed with multiple antededent clauses

IF *a* IS *b* AND *c* IS *d* THEN *x* IS *y* (*T* 0.*n*)
IF *a* IS *b*   OR *c* IS *d* THEN *x* IS *y* (*T* 0.*n*)

The operations or conjunction and disjunction ('and' and 'or') are imple-mented as minimum and maximum operations respectively. The basic thinking here is that if one piece of evidence AND another are required to satisfy the antecedent condition of a rule, the conservative and safe approach is to define the weight of evidence for the antecedent as being equal to the smaller of the two available values. Correspondingly, if one piece of evidence OR another is required to satisfy the antecedent, we are free to take the higher of the two weights as representing the evidence available. (As we shall see, this is essentially the mechanism used in fuzzy set theory as well.)

As noted above, one of the key research thrusts in the MYCIN project was to develop a methodology for eliciting rules and knowledge from acknowledged experts in the domain with which the experts could feel comfortable. In a sense, this requirement took precedence over formal mathematical justification for the methods employed, and since the evaluation of the completed system depended essentially on empirical validation by comparison of test cases with the results obtained by human experts, this approach is not necessarily to be criticized.

But there are traps for the unwary in this representation of uncertainty. Consider the compound rule

IF   engine IS not_turning
AND   horn   IS not_blowing
THEN battery IS flat   (*T* ?)

and compare it with the same essential knowledge represented in two separate rules above. What should the credibility of the rule, represented here by a question mark, be?

If 'engine is not turning' has evidence 0.7 and 'horn is not blowing' has evidence 0.3, use of the two separate rules will lead to a belief in the battery being flat of

$$(0.7 * 0.6) + (0.3 * 0.9) * (1 - 0.7 * 0.6) = 0.58$$

Using the compound rule, the truth of the antecedent to the rule is minimum $(0.7, 0.3) = 0.3$, and the belief in the hypothesis of 'flat battery' is $0.3 * ?$.

If we require the two representations to deliver the same belief in the hypothesis of flat battery, it seems that the credibility of the compound rule must be 1.93, in order for the identity $0.3 * 1.93 = 0.58$ to be true. Since, by our definition of terms, the credibility cannot exceed 1.0, the maximum belief derived from the compound rule can only be 0.3, compared with 0.58 when the rules are separate.

What is one to make of this? The approach taken is based on the need to ease the problem of knowledge elicitation from the expert. The expert might provide the information in either of the two ways portrayed, and why not – to someone (rightly) unconcerned with the arithmetic of aggregating evidence mechanically, there may be no surface difference between the knowledge provided in either format. Since it is the responsibility of the expert to provide the tally factors for the rules, it is hard to see how such an expert can consistently provide 'correct' factors when the grouping of the evidence in different ways generates such variegated results.

In the presentation of certainty factors, Shortliffe [186] suggests a link between certainty factors and Bayesian Probabilities. A perhaps more rigorous basis for the use of certainty factors has been provided by the Shafer–Dempster theory of evidence [244]. Shortliffe asserts that the link may be expressed in the following formula:

$$Cf(H:E) = \frac{Pr(H:E) - Pr(H)}{Pr(H)}$$

saying that the certainty associated with the Hypothesis H after accruing evidence E is a function in the change in probability proportionate to the previous probability.

The utility of this approach is, once again, purely pragmatic. It lies in the elicitation of knowledge from the domain expert. Duda and Reboh [223] describe the point well; people have little intuitive relationship to the prior or posterior probabilities (or odds) associated with a hypothesis, but are more comfortable in explaining their change in state of certainty in a hypothesis following the accrual of some evidence E.

Thus the above formula, suitably re-arranged, permits propagation of posterior probabilities through an inference net based on conversationally elicited views of certainty or confidence, whilst at least doffing a hat to mathematical rigour.

The hat-doffing may fail to charm the purist. Equally, the purist may fail to charm the engineer in the absence of the purist's provision of an alternatively effective procedure for replicating the very visible success of the engineer's pragmatically based systems.

4.5 FUZZY SETS

Fuzzy sets as a concept were introduced by Zadeh in 1965 [238], although analogous concepts were treated on a mathematical basis a hundred years ago by Poincaré in relation to imprecision in vision (see Poston [169]).

The key thrust of fuzzy sets theory, and the associated logic of approximate reasoning, is to deal with the common sense logic and concept representation available to all of us, but in a framework more directly analogous to our natural forms of human reasoning.

Bertrand Russell stated in 1923 that

'All traditional logic habitually assumes that precise symbols are being employed. It is therefore not applicable to this terrestrial life, but only to an imagined celestial existence.'

Formal, symbolic, or classical logic, may be used to represent natural language statements. For example, the statement

Some child laughed

may be represented as

$\exists X \{CHILD(X) \wedge LAUGHED(X)\}$

which may be read as

There exists an entity X such that X is a child and X laughed.

The notational conventions and manipulative capabilities of symbolic logic will be covered in Chapter 6, and need not detain us here. The point to note for the moment is that the original expression, a simple sentence with a subject and a verb, has been transliterated into a complex sentence with three pronouns and a conjunction. This is a way of representing the original statement; it is less clear that it is a good model of the thinking process that led to the utterance.

In this chapter, we have been dealing principally with the degree of belief associated with a hypothesis covering some known set of facts, and it will be consistent to introduce the basic ideas of fuzzy sets in the same way.

The key thing to note is that instead of assigning a numeric value to the degree of belief in a hypothesis, in fuzzy sets we assign a linguistic value. Thus a hypothesis may be considered 'possible', 'unlikely', 'highly_probable', 'certain' and so on; these words are fuzzy sets. They represent the fundamental imprecision which is associated with the formation of concepts. The two rules which we used earlier could be phrased in the fuzzy sets paradigm.

IF engine IS not_turning THEN flat_battery IS possible
IF horn   IS not_blowing THEN flat-battery IS probable

where possible and probable in this case are linguistic fuzzy sets, as illustrated in Fig. 4.2. The other thing to note is that these concepts need have nothing to do with mathematical notions of probability or possibility – they are merely labels – provided, that is, that their ordinal relationship (and their behaviour under certain linguistic transformations) corresponds to that found in ordinary speech.

As we will see in the next chapter, using fuzzy sets in this way allows us to represent uncertain knowledge with linguistic labels but still retain the possibility of combining the weights of individual utterances and propagating degrees of truth (or belief, or possibility or what have you) through a decision tree or inference network.

Since the whole of the next chapter is devoted to this subject, we will not dwell any further on fuzzy sets at this point. The interested reader may like to look ahead before continuing this chapter.

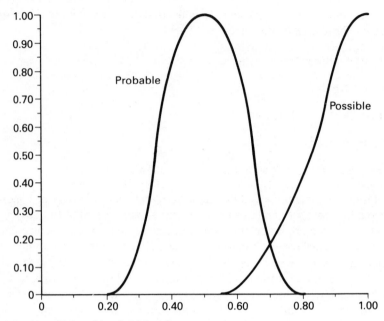

Fig. 4.2   'Possible' and 'probable' as fuzzy sets

4.6   UNCERTAINTY AND KNOWLEDGE ENGINEERING SOFTWARE

This section takes a critical look at the various existing types of knowledge engineering products available; languages, shells and toolkits. From their strengths and weaknesses is derived a set of attributes of an idealized delivery vehicle which will be required if knowledge-based systems are going to address the problems of business successfully. The derivation also takes account of the needs of a number of commercial applications. Considerable attention is paid to uncertainty management, reflecting the view that many of the weaknesses in current products derive therefrom.

We conclude that knowledge-based systems, if they are to model a sensible range of problems, will have to form part of a more general software milieu and include a number of specific features which are described. The list of desirable features which knowledge engineering products should have is annotated with estimates of the difficulties in implementation and time-scales. Throughout this section the central role of uncertainty management is emphasized.

During the first half of the 1980s, many commercial organizations have begun to implement knowledge-based computer systems using a wide variety of approaches. Many of the techniques derive from nearly thirty years of research and development in artificial intelligence, but, equally, the business problems which are being attacked involve computational problems for which other techniques have been developed. These techniques include simulation modelling, database management, fourth generation languages, decision theory and methods for improving the human–machine interaction, such as object oriented programming, menu technology and so forth. What is missing, for the emergent activity of knowledge engineering, are truly high-level development environments which couple all these developments with the techniques of non-procedural programming and knowledge representation schemata: in other words, couple conventional technologies with those to be found in the current generation of AI workstations and expert systems software products.

4.6.1 AI programming languages, shells and environments

Most of our readers will, we suspect, be familiar with the controversy which rages over the relative benefits of expert system shells, AI workstations and so-called AI languages. At one extreme we have the gloomy view that if anything is to be achieved at all it will require a lifetime of dedication to write the system in some arcane programming language, and at the other the view promulgated by some authorities that an expert systems project is only worthwhile if it can be accomplished in a matter of weeks in which case a shell will do the job quite adequately. Either of these extreme views misses the point that there exists a spectrum of worthwhile applications, differing in complexity, potential payback and not least in the tools and skills required for their development. In our view therefore, the truth lies somewhere between these extremes, and it is that one should choose the most appropriate tool for the job. This wisdom however does not guarantee to us that appropriate tools are available 'off the shelf' nor does it tell us how to specify the features indicated by a particular task or project. At a minimum, a knowledge engineering project designer must ask the following questions before embarking on software procurement:

- What knowledge representation formalisms are needed?
- What control strategies should be supported?
- What logics are involved?
- Which methods of handling uncertainty, if any, should be catered for?
- What is the role of procedural programming, database technology and advanced interfaces?

The first question is probably the most important. Many authors consider that artificial intelligence is chiefly concerned with search and efficient strategies for its accomplishment. However, although this is a perfectly valid point of view as far as theory is concerned, the key unsolved problems tend to be those relating to the representation of knowledge. The logic programming movement, on the other hand, ducks this issue by and large by making the tacit assumption that the first-order predicate calculus is a representational formalism which, in some sense, underpins all others. Only in certain centres are various deviant logics considered relevant: fuzzy logic, nonmonotonic logic, equational logic, etc. Let us consider briefly the wealth of knowledge about knowledge representation before moving on to consider different logics, uncertainty management techniques and methods for embedding knowledge engineering systems in conventional computer programs.

Amid much confusion about terminology, the notion of using frames to represent object knowledge has received wide acceptance in AI circles. We consider semantic networks, scripts, units, objects, schemata, and so on to derive principally from the same justification and therefore not to merit separate consideration here. For details see Chapter 2. While the notion of a frame is a generalization of a relation (within the meaning of database theory) permitting variable numbers of attributes, higher order notions of what is 'atomic' and inheritance, it gives an exceedingly powerful way of representing symbolically knowledge about entities. The logic programming school too has given us powerful methods for dealing with data relationships based on the first-order predicate calculus. The merits of production systems are also widely recognized. It is necessary however to recognize that there is a school of thought in AI and, indeed, knowledge engineering which cleaves strongly to the thesis that their subject is about (and only about) symbol manipulation. Numbers are only special sorts of symbols, and procedures are irrelevant. Cognitive science lends support to the thesis, since numbers and their manipulation are a learned skill, no less than history, which can direct us to civilizations of extent and grandeur which were almost wholly ignorant of the concept of algorithm, if not in some sense of number. But we do not live at such a historic conjuncture, and computation is so fundamental to the productive process on which our society is based and the exchange process which regulates it that knowledge representation through the vehicle of procedural, effective computation fits very naturally into the mental furniture of experts in many fields.

We hold the view that almost any knowledge-based application will require, at a minimum, the capability of executing fragments of procedural code as the consequent of a fired rule or slot of an accessed object, and that an appropriate vehicle for such system development must provide an intrinsic language in its set of tools for the instantiation of such procedures. Later we will look at the justification for this view in commercial experience. Access to external procedures, written shall we say in C, are equally important for two reasons: efficiency and expediency. Genuinely computationally intensive procedures will gain by being written in a language which compiles efficient native code on the host machine, and existing subroutine libraries may provide proven code which it is more expedient to use than to rewrite.

While not wishing to minimize the achievements of logic programming in any way, it is necessary to remark on the apparent obsession with first-order theories that it has inherited from conventional (i.e. late nineteenth and early twentieth century) symbolic logic. It has been said that expert systems which use uncertainty are merely 'concealing knowledge which could be made explicit'. We observe that many of the problems of uncertainty management derive from attempts to remain first order. Also any attempt to expose, in a complete form, knowledge about a subject smacks slightly of mysticism. After all if we knew everything about the universe we wouldn't need the probabilistic contrivances of the quantum theory to explain it. While some expert systems dealt with knowledge which is sufficiently granular to admit a representation which does not involve the propagation of uncertainty, many will concern relative knowledge of a complex *Ding an sich* (thing-in-itself) which eludes absolute knowledge. The point to be made here is that first-order theories are intrinsically incapable of representing uncertainty in a natural manner. For an exposition of the arguments and an explanation of terms see Chapter 6. While it has been shown that frames can be regarded as a first-order notion, here too it is an intensely unnatural way of viewing them.

Knowledge representation in logic needs a computational form of higher-order logic, just as a frame or network description language will be the better for including higher-order types. Notwithstanding this type of development, it seems to us that every real commercial application we have been involved with has been presented in such a way that a whole range of representation techniques have been involved. This is precisely because real problems involve knowledge about objects, events, procedures, relations and performance; not just one. Existing AI products focus on one or two methods of representation. Possibly this results from the academic origin of many products where purity rather than pragmatism is the issue. Commercial applications require products which mix and match knowledge representation techniques even if pure theory is occasionally compromised. This is an urgent issue, and we cannot afford to wait for the theoreticians to sort out the problems with higher-order systems. To argue further we need to take a definite view on what an expert system is, and we have given such a view earlier in this chapter.

Clearly, many applications can be built using only deterministic logic; that is, propositions are known to be *true* or *false*. Sometimes this is said to be extended to tri-state logic where *true*, *false* or *unknown* are acceptable responses to a query, but this in fact obfuscates the essential binary nature of the choices available. Unless specific information is provided in the knowledge base to handle the *unknown* condition, paths through the equivalent rule-base will be selected which simply ignore an object whose value is set to *unknown*. The solution derived will still depend on true/false conditions attached to the potential values of some subset of objects within the scope of the system, or depend on the proposition that 'A is unknown is true'. The practical impact of this is that the result delivered by the system will be of the form; the solution is *X*. Also, explanations generated cannot explore the impact of the unknown on the answer in any meaningful manner. On the other hand, a system which can cope with uncertainty will be able to deliver a solution of the form: the answer may be *X*, or *Y* or *Z*; and right now I would call the expectations 85%, 75% and 15% respectively. And explain how this was derived.

If the nature of the problem demands that multiple plausible answers in the above form should be delivered routinely, then the system must, in the first place, be able to manage uncertainty and, in the second, have some inbuilt rationale to justify whichever method of management has been selected.

The end user, busy at a task, uninterested in mathematical, philosophical or cognitive subtleties, will nevertheless have an instinctive feeling (in appropriate cases) that an answer of the above form is reasonable, or at least more reasonable than a crisp response. The fact that the numbers associated with the options are unnormalized will be of no concern. The issues of whether these should be regarded as probabilities, possibilities, weights or whatever are unlikely to prepossess the user's mind. The researcher and, it is to be hoped, the vendor of application vehicles is obliged to take a more austere view. If there is no rigorous mathematical justification for whatever approach has been taken to uncertainty management, at least this should be stated in the health warning.

Having made a strong case for knowledge engineering tools to include a variety of techniques for uncertainty management, it must also be said that many knowledge engineering applications preclude the delivery of uncertainty measures attached to the advice they give. For example, take two perfectly normal expert systems which assist in matching products to a client's needs. The first example is an advisor on the most suitable electrical appliance to meet some set of constraints and requirements. An answer which is delivered in the form: 'I am 67% certain that you should buy a Hoover model ABC123' will be treated with great scepticism by the consumer. A positive exact answer is required. The second example involves a system for selecting the most appropriate investment fund for an individual. In this case the customer *expects* an answer hedged with uncertainty, because that is exactly what a human advisor would provide. Our software tools ought to be broad enough to encompass both approaches.

Another point to be made about the use of uncertainty measures in the first-generation expert systems tools, especially shells, is that designers are often tempted to hide knowledge inside the numbers representing uncertainty. In other words, the uncertainty consists in the knowledge engineer not knowing enough about the expert's knowledge. The only way to avoid this danger is to be aware that it exists, and to use uncertainty methods cautiously and only when necessary or appropriate. Only future practical systems will let us know if there is a general theory of what is appropriate. At present we have to rely on arguments based on common sense as in the examples discussed in this paragraph.

As we have already said, expert systems will have to be made accountable, so that uncertainty must be handled appropriately with a good mix of strategies. To make this possible knowledge engineering tools must provide a range of ways of propagating uncertainty which can be applied under procedural or logic-based control during problem solving within expert systems. So far very few offer more than one method.

In an ideal world, a theory of uncertainty management would allow a canonical form of the nature of uncertainty to handle the above, and other, representations of uncertainty as facets of an encompassing theory. This area is undergoing active development by researchers such as Bonissone, Brown, Mamdani, Yager and others. At present however, it is clear that the various formalisms for describing and computing with uncertainty remain diverse, and will have a tendency to remain so while researchers adopt entrenched, mutually exclusive and mutually antagonistic postures, failing to recognize thereby that the future of knowledge engineering rests on delivered commercially viable systems, as well as or rather than on research for its own sake. The present state of the art therefore demands that an application vehicle be able to provide, as disjoint tools, the range of facilities currently known to have solved problems in practice – Bayesian networks, certainty factor models, fuzzy set based models and deterministic rules.

This, of course, pushes the choice of the appropriate method down to the application builder, as opposed to the vehicle builder. Re-enter the knowledge engineer, and arise the recognition that there are two distinct levels of expert system building: that involving and that excluding uncertainty management; and that the most significant contribution of the knowledge engineer is the definition of the level at which an application sits, and the selection of the knowledge representation, uncertainty management and inference techniques to be used at each level.

Two major types of productivity aid, beyond mere programming languages, are now beginning to emerge as commercial products; expert system shells at the lower end of the market and sophisticated special-purpose hardware carrying software to enhance knowledge-based system development at the top end. These latter environments are usually based on hardware optimized for a symbol manipulation language such as LISP or PROLOG or sometimes several. On top of these languages are added context sensitive editors, graphics, object oriented features such as icons, knowledge representation languages and usually some form of built-in inference method. Typical such systems are LOOPS, KEE and ART. The idea is to speed system development by providing many of the more commonly used programs and tools and enough raw computer power to quickly build prototypes which might ultimately run on some other machine. The idea is similar to the one behind fourth generation languages, where program generation is facilitated by exploiting common data processing patterns. If all else fails, these systems give access to the basic languages so that flexibility is not sacrificed; code can be hacked out in LISP, POP11 or C as a last resort. Also programmers can add their own tools to the environment. One problem with the early systems, apart from high cost, is that it is not always easy to run systems written in LISP or suchlike on conventional machines at the required speeds. New hardware developments are gradually overcoming this problem. A more serious problem is the lack of more conventional tools: database management, modelling and reporting software, and effective network communication facilities.

The other kind of product is the shell. The early expert systems such as MYCIN, DENDRAL and PROSPECTOR contained very narrow specific knowledge about the subject matter of medicine, mass spectrography and geology. It was realized very quickly that it could be useful to excise this knowledge leaving the 'shell' of the inference mechanism and add some means for easily plugging in new knowledge. Thus the shell based on MYCIN (EMYCIN for 'empty MYCIN') could be used to build an expert system in another domain without the overhead of building a knowledge application system. Unfortunately, it was soon found that the inference methods required varied significantly from one domain to another, and that a shell which was good at diagnosing faults in machinery couldn't be used for a system to tune that machinery or to control it. Ignoring the fact that the systems on which the shells were based were not without problems – MYCIN could not be turned into a training aid for doctors because it contained no knowledge *about* its reasoning – attempts to build really flexible shells have generally failed. We believe that the solution is to be found in a study of decision support software. What is required is a set of tools, of which shells could form a component, at reasonable cost to aid system development on conventional hardware. Let us look at some of the better established products.

At the low end of the market there are a number of products which will run on micro-computers. AL/X, SAVOIR, ERS, ENVISAGE, CRYSTAL and EXPERT EDGE are all broadly based on the Bayesian network approach of PROSPECTOR, while M1 and T1 Personal Consultant are based on the approach in MYCIN or EMYCIN. Other products such as Xi and KES provide basic forward and backward reasoning mechanisms but have no means of expressing uncertainty other than by the granularity of the terms used. All these systems come equipped with a fixed inference strategy and allow knowledge to be entered in rule form. They have found a number of applications, principally in domains similar to the PROSPECTOR and MYCIN archetypes, such as fault diagnosis and classification of data. Very recently a new generation of shells has begun to emerge. These offer extended knowledge representations (e.g. rules and frames – ESP Frames, Leonardo I, Emes), extended procedural capabilities (e.g. Crystal, Leonardo II) and/or a variety of uncertainty mechanisms (e.g. Leonardo III). This is an encouraging development, but still most shells fit the above description.

The more elaborate environments such as ART (Automated Reasoning Tool), KEE (Knowledge Engineering Environment), KnowledgeCraft and LOOPS typically provide support for LISP and fairly flexible built-in control strategies together with more complex knowledge representation methods as well as production rules, for example, frames. Inference is still not under rule control but the degree of flexibility is much greater and a wide range of applications have been tackled. The price to be paid for the additional flexibility is that systems do take longer to build and the systems are, of course, much more expensive. The fact that these systems tend to run on specialized hardware means that there is a problem in delivering applications to end users; either the application must be rewritten for a conventional machine or there is a task in persuading the users to invest in a new type of workstation. Surprisingly perhaps, uncertainty management in such systems usually has to be entirely hand crafted and is often very difficult indeed.

What is missing from these products has to be considered on two levels. The purchaser of a low-cost shell does not expect to get all the power of an advanced programming environment. Something that will address a specific problem or aid learning about the technology will often suffice. At the other extreme the AI workstation buyer expects to have to code the inference strategy by hand to some extent. But what both classes of user are coming to expect from their machines in almost every area *except* AI is there should be easy graphics, database enquiry, spreadsheet facilities, code generation, etc. By analogy, expert system builders have the right to expect that AI environments contain a set of usable modules which can be chosen according to the application in hand. To some extent this already exists: shells now often contain a means of choosing between forward and backward chaining search, and workstation products usually offer at least two knowledge representation methods in addition to several search regimes. The big weaknesses are in precisely the areas of modelling (procedural programming) and uncertainty handling where one is lucky if any built-in methods exist. This is why this section has concentrated so heavily on these two issues. We recognize the importance of what has been done in other areas, but we also believe that suppliers will not need so much prompting to enhance, say, the range of representation methods. We suspect that entrenched positions in the knowledge engineering community are partially responsible and our purpose is to argue against these.

AI techniques were, until quite recently, applied to 'toy domains' or microworlds such as the blocks world. There, the main requirement was that some important computational or cognitive principle could be uncovered by studying the behaviour of the programs written. The requirements of commercial applications are, of course, quite different, and the business goals of maximizing profits or shareholder wealth and so on lead naturally to specific *technical* demands on developmental systems. For example, an end product should result and the cost should be lower than the anticipated benefits. In a nutshell, there should be as little risk as possible in relation to potential returns.

First we must ask what the crucial technical demands of commercial systems are. We can best do this by looking at some existing systems and a few systems which have been projected. Our recent experience with network maintenance systems has shown that the bulk of the functionality and usefulness of such systems is provided by conventional computer science techniques. The expert system component is to do with fault diagnosis and advice on office procedures in the main, but this is a tiny part of the overall problem of recording fault reports, providing management statistics, locating nodes and spare parts in the inventory, assigning labour and so on. DEC's XCON system, renowned by now for its cost effectiveness is largely procedural code written in BLISS-32. The quality of that code must be held to contribute significantly to its success. Our feeling is that the existing tools match up very poorly to the problems faced by system developers in this respect.

4.6.2 Knowledge acquisition issues

Much has been written about the so-called 'knowledge engineering bottle-neck'. That is to say it is widely believed that the main stumbling block in the construction of knowledge-based systems is that of eliciting expert knowledge from humans. This may have been true for the early, university-based, expert systems in fields such as medical diagnosis or chemistry, but in commercial applications the type of knowledge is typically less esoteric; in some cases it is downright simple. For example, the knowledge in the system to control a cement kiln is pure rule of thumb and in many financial systems the same is true. Thus we believe that the bottle-neck problem is largely a myth handed down as part of the early tradition of artificial intelligence. In a commercial context it seems that the main obstacle is not knowledge acquisition but software development, as is the case with conventional development using fourth-generation techniques. Experience at Logica on the ARIES project has certainly provided some evidence to support this view so far. The fire risk system knowledge elicitation was performed on target and any small delays that did occur were more concerned with the procurement of suitable hardware and software so that the knowledge acquired could be mapped onto a working prototype. Some other Logica projects are also object lessons which could be said to confirm this view, although this is not the place to review them in detail. Saying that knowledge acquisition is not the main bottle-neck in system development is not to minimize its problems. These are many. For a survey of techniques to assist in knowledge acquisition see [208]. Our point is that the real bottle-neck is in passing from a preliminary paper model to operational code with enough functionality to be usable by ordinary folk without Ph.Ds in computer science.

We characterize this problem as the software milieu bottle-neck. The obstructions are chiefly caused by inadequate freedom in representing knowledge, uncertainty and inference inherent in the task domain, and also by the tendency for extant knowledge-engineering tools to ignore many of the concerns of conventional computing: array processing, help messages, ease of documentation, screen generation, database integrity, modularity, call interfaces, etc.

To illustrate the second of these two points take, for example, a typical simple fault diagnosis problem. Such a problem, according to conventional wisdom, ought to be ideal for a KBS, but in practice fault diagnosis is done in a complex business environment where other requirements exist and sometimes predominate. In the case we are thinking of the requirement was to automate the management of customer fault reports for a videotext system. No one with any experience of building simple expert systems needs to be told how simple a matter it is to take an expert system shell and automate a small decision tree which encodes cause and effect related to hardware and network faults based on a dialogue with the complainant. The requirements of management in this case went much further. Response times of about a second were essential, the development was time and cost critical, fault reports and responses had to be logged and management statistics produced, a local area network which connected several 'helpers' and a large customer and hardware details database, and financial models had to use the system's output and in turn contributed to the database. Thus the expert system was the simplest problem, the hard part was to embed it in the whole complex of conventional systems which were being engineered.

To illustrate the first set of problems is harder, but it is not difficult to see that human problem solvers rely on a vast range of representations and are likely to switch between them during problem solving. A knowledge engineer contemplating the purchase of an expensive knowledge engineering environment has to wonder whether the representations it comes equipped with will be adequate or will have to possess a degree of prescience that we have not experienced. Descending into low-level LISP is an expensive and time consuming option, to be avoided where possible, not to mention the cost of re-educating the development staff. Thus we have argued above for more flexible tools based on the most profound advances in artificial intelligence.

The foregoing considerations lead to the programmatic part of this chapter. We present this programme to stimulate discussion in the expert systems community.

4.6.3 A programme for knowledge engineering software development

We conclude from the above discussion that knowledge-based systems, if they are to model a sensible range of problems, will have to form part of a more general software milieu and include many of the features listed below. Some of these could be implemented immediately, some are already on their way to the market and some involve research issues of varying complexity. We have attempted to indicate which category each feature falls into, together with an estimate of the number of years it will take to bring each feature out in a commercial product.

(1) Extended non-procedural logic programming to include, on top of first-order logic, the following as and when required:

(a) Higher-order types.

This is definitely a research issue, but the Alvey project on new logic programming languages may suggest some results. Principally, a project for the pure mathematicians and computer scientists. 15–25 years until a new language incorporates these ideas.

(b) The logic of equality (equational logic).

SRI have already produced a language on this basis but research issues still exist. 10–20 years or perhaps a solution integral with resolution of the preceding issue.

(c) Function application and composition.

LISP does it. What is required is integration with logic and procedural methods. Two years.

(d) Multivalent truth objects.

The theory is sound enough to permit immediate implementation, but some issues are unresolved. One year for implementations based on fuzzy sets and up to 25 years for a topos theoretic solution.

(e) Additional logical operators (as in e.g. non-monotonic or modal logic).

We will see default reasoning facilities in workstation products in the next year, but the research problems remain unsolved.

(2) A range of knowledge representation formalisms with means to form new ones by composition and links to the logical language. These should include:
  (a) networks,
  (b) productions,
  (c) procedures,
  (d) relations,
  (e) frames.
This already exists partly in AI tools. We expect steady improvement over the next ten years.

(3) A range of flexible inference and control methods with object-oriented features and directed at the range of knowledge representations and logics. This too already exists partly in AI tools. We expect steady improvement over the next five or six years.

(4) A complete procedural recursive programming language with good typing properties and a rich syntax. The procedural and non-procedural languages should be able to call each other. There is no obstacle to doing this now. The only question is why it hasn't been done. Next year?

(5) A range of induction and automated learning methods. At present learning algorithms tend to exist in separate products. Integration into AI tools by 1990 at the latest. There are still some research issues however.

(6) A relational database and retrieval languages based on algebra and calculus. The announcement of Oracle and KEE on the IBM PC/RT addresses this problem.

(7) High-quality report and graphical output presentation. AI environments have it to a degree. Shells need it within a year. The functionality, in this respect, of the IBM Personal System 2 (PS2) range may be a precursor of such developments.

(8) Optional modules to handle:
  (a) natural language parsing;
  (b) physical device descriptions (as in e.g. image processing);
  (c) program generation.
Aside from the long-term research issue in natural language understanding (50 years hence?) this should become normal within three years or so.

(9) Hardware independence: the ability to execute on desktop, mid-range and mainframe machines as appropriate, and to operate in a network environment. This depends on hardware developments, but a move to writing tools in C is already occurring, indicating that suppliers are already responding to the problem.

(10) A language able to sustain high execution speeds. Once again a hardware issue unless LISP and PROLOG are abandoned. In the case of shells expect to see something within a year.

(11) Embeddability: the ability for a developed system to be called via a high-level

set of procedural invocations from a larger host system. This is already a property of some systems. Shells should sport it within two years.

(12) Multiple options for the management of uncertainty, including Bayesian networks, certainty factor models, fuzzy models as well as deterministic and nonmonotonic logic. Products will begin to appear within the next year but until the outstanding research issues are addressed improvements will still be possible.

Our time estimates are tentative and slightly optimistic if anything. The key question is not the provision of any one of the items on our 'wish list', but the emergence of products which provide several of them in an integrated form. This, in itself, may take longer due to the constraints imposed by there being a single developer of such a product. The enormous investment required means that success is predicated on commercial success with *existing* technology. The other side of the coin is that such success will occur with higher frequency as tools gradually acquire more functionality along the lines suggested here. The process has a general circular form – better products, more success stories, more investment, better products, . . .

In order to satisfy the requirements of knowledge engineers in respect of software products, commercial software suppliers have to be brought to an understanding of the needs of knowledge engineering in a commercial environment. We have to engage in propaganda and agitation with a view to convincing them that their financial success is not incompatible with the aims of our science. Before we can do this we have to achieve a unity among the contradictory views of the various schools of thought within knowledge engineering and artificial intelligence.

4.7 SUMMARY

In the last two chapters we dealt with knowledge and data representation, the first subject of our sonata. This chapter has begun the study of the second of the three major dimensions of knowledge-based systems, uncertainty management. The third dimension, inference or reasoning methods, will be dealt with later.

We analysed the sources and kinds of uncertainty and showed that no one mathematical technique was capable of dealing with them all. We then discussed probabilistic representation, the representation of evidence by certainty factors and, very briefly, introduced fuzzy sets.

We concluded by looking at the management of uncertainty in current expert systems software. This was extended into an analysis of the deficiencies of knowledge engineering tools in general and some suggestions as to how the situation can be remedied and what users may reasonably expect in the future.

This chapter has stated the general theme of this work. The next chapter makes an explicit statement of its second subject, fuzzy set theory.

4.8   FURTHER READING

There is very little in the readily available literature which we can recommend here. Most of our source material is scattered through the academic journals or various edited volumes. Goodman and Nguyen [77] provide a large but, alas, almost totally incomprehensible coverage. Dubois and Prade [59] and Zimmermann [222] and our next chapter cover Fuzzy Set Theory at various levels of detail and difficulty. Shafer [244] and Buchanan and Shortliffe [245] give the material on certainty factors, and details on Bayesian probabilities can be found in Small [190], Forsyth [69] and Duda and Hart *et al.* [223]. Prade [171] provides a concise summary of alternative options and certain aspects of the material discussed above is also explored by Jones in [108] and [263].

5

Fuzzy set theory

'This is called the vague and uncertain.
Approach it and you will not see its head;
Follow behind it and you will not see its rear.'

Tao Te Ching, Lao Tzu

5.1 HISTORICAL REMARKS

Fuzzy set theory was defined in its present form by Lotfi Zadeh in his seminal paper in *Information and Control* in 1965 [238]. In fact the idea of using fuzzy mathematical structures had occurred to Poincaré in the nineteenth century in the context of visual perception, but this was not developed until Zeeman and Poston took up the idea in the early 1970s [169]. Their 'fuzzy geometry' bears little formal relation to Zadeh's theory. It did find some applications in Quantum Theory, but in comparison to the huge number of applications of the theory of Zadeh it was poorly received. This latter has been applied in engineering, business, psychology and even in such abstruse areas as semiotics. It has been used to solve many practical problems from product pricing to the automatic control of a cement kiln. Hitachi, in Tokyo, have even produced a fuzzily controlled passenger train. Thus in a matter of twenty years a totally new piece of mathematics has had considerable practical impact on the world we live in. And yet, we still hear claims that fuzzy sets is 'bad mathematics', 'not rigorous', and the like. There is not space in a work of this nature to discuss why this should be. We will content ourselves with an exposition, and leave readers to form their own opinions.

Zadeh's original motivation came from attempts to construct numerical controllers for complex electronic equipment. This was recognized as a difficult problem because, partly due to the law of requisite variety [228], as the controlled equipment became complex the controller became so even more rapidly. So much so that the controllers were either ineffectual or so complex as to defy the understanding of their designers. Zadeh formulated this in his Principle of Incompatibility:

'As the complexity of a system increases, our ability to make precise and yet significant statements about its behaviour diminishes until a threshold is reached beyond which precision and significance (or relevance) become almost mutually exclusive characteristics.'

The way round this contradiction, according to fuzzy set theory, is to represent vague, imprecise human knowledge directly rather than mediating with some artificial representation such as a precise formula. In the context of automatic control, it turns out that a human operator formulates a control policy as 'when the gauge shows hot, I have to turn this knob down a little bit' rather than as 'when the temperature increases beyond 98.4 the input is reduced by 2.3%'.
We will see in this chapter how such a regime can be realized.

Recent developments in fuzzy set theory are its introduction into knowledge engineering, cognitive psychology and various engineering applications. Fuzzy expert systems exist in such diverse fields as medicine and earthquake forecasting. A whole branch of mathematics has grown up around the idea that any mathematical structure may be fuzzified (the extension principle is covered in the next chapter) so that we now have Fuzzy Topology, Fuzzy Groups and so on as serious fields of mathematical endeavour. Perhaps the most exciting recent development is the work of Nowakowska [247] in *Cognitive Sciences*, where fuzzy sets and the theory of stochastic processes together are used to provide a mathematical foundation for a theory of objective and subjective time, events, and much of social science and semiology.

In this book we will focus on knowledge engineering applications however. To facilitate this we proceed first to an elementary exposition, to be followed by a more terse version giving most of the basic mathematics which we feel will be useful in this context.

5.2   INFORMAL DEVELOPMENT

> 'But the next day one of his followers said to him, "O Perfect One, why do you do this thing, for though we find joy in it, we know not the celestial reason nor the correspondency of it."
> And Sabbah answered:
> "I will tell you first what I do; I will tell you the reasons afterward." '
> *The Perfect One*, Laurence Housman

5.2.1   Basic definitions

The concept of a 'Fuzzy Set' turns out to be a very easy and intuitively natural idea for most people to grasp. Now this in itself is interesting. Many of the fundamental concepts underlying classical set theory, and the discipline of mathematical logic, turn out to be extremely counter-intuitive. For this reason, courses in logic and set theory appear in the syllabuses of universities. They are seen to be difficult topics, worthy of formal study, rather than being part of the assumed mental furniture of the informed twentieth century adult. And it is certainly true that many intelligent people find that the courses are challenging, mind-expanding, difficult or (say it in a whisper) downright boring.

Set Theory and Formal Logic are alternate paradigms of the way in which mathematicians seek to bring structure and order to models of the real universe. It is in many ways the very formality which this entails which lies at the heart of the conceptual difficulties encountered by the student of these disciplines.

In this section, we will introduce the idea of fuzzy sets theory in a completely non-mathematical and informal manner. The formal treatment will be covered in the next section of this chapter, and in Chapter 6.

Consider first what we mean by a *set*. A set is defined by its members. Thus we may consider, for example, the set of all members of your family. All the members of your family have the property in common that they are related to you. This common property is sufficient to allow us to identify whether any given person is, or is not, a member of that set. Another set might be formed by the members of a golf club. Again, any individual either is or is not a member of the club, and the club membership roll serves to define the set. A person is either a member of the 'Boondoggle Golf Club' or is not. Nice and crisp – crystal clear.

All of classical set theory is based on this 'premise' that any given entity can readily be identified as being a member of a given set or not. And, of course, in much of the real world, this premise is quite true – you really can tell if someone is a member of your club by the membership roll.

But consider the set of people who are 'golfers'. Is any given person a 'golfer' or 'not a golfer'? This immediately begs the question – 'What do you mean by a "golfer"?' Do you mean someone who is a member of a golf club? (Many people are competent golfers but don't currently hold a membership.) So is skill at the game the defining feature? (Many people who pay their annual dues feel well entitled to call themselves golfers, even if their activities on the course appear more like those of grave-diggers to an unbiased observer.) Perhaps someone who is a member of a golf club and has a handicap of 16 or less? (Try explaining that to someone who's worked hard to get their handicap down to 17.) Perhaps . . . but the point is clear; there are many definitions of what is meant by the word 'golfer', and many equally valid views on whether a given individual is or is not to be regarded as a golfer.

The boundary of the set named 'golfer' is not a crisp one. There is no universally agreed predicate which will unambiguously separate all of humanity into 'golfers' and 'not golfers'. But there is nonetheless some cohesion in the term. Quite clearly there are people who are under the most generous definition 'not golfers' – never even visited a golf course, never picked up a golf club, don't know the basics of the game . . . ; and other people (Jack Nicklaus, Tom Watson . . .) who most clearly fall into the most restrictive definition of the set. Thus the set does exist; it is only its boundary which is imprecise – which is 'fuzzy'.

And this is the intuitive definition of a fuzzy set. It is a set where the boundary is not clear; or where the predicate whereby we can test whether some entity is a member of the set cannot return a guaranteed value of 'true' or 'false'. It is a set where some of its members have a membership which is less than complete.

In classical set theory, the Venn diagram, named after the nineteenth century mathematician John Venn, is frequently used to provide a graphical representation of several sets. (The diagram was originally used a century previously by Euler, and more properly should be called by its original name – Euler Circles.) A set is represented by a closed figure of arbitrary shape. The visual representation allows us to see conveniently the relationships amongst a number of sets – whether, for example, there are any entities which are members of several sets, or only of one.

In Fig. 5.1 we see a Venn diagram. It represents the two sets 'members of my family' and 'members of the Boondoggle Golf Club'. There is no overlap between the two sets. No member of my family is a member of the golf club, and equally no member of the golf club is a member of my family. (It is not known whether the members of my family or the members of the golf club have the greater reason to feel satisfied about this state of affairs.)

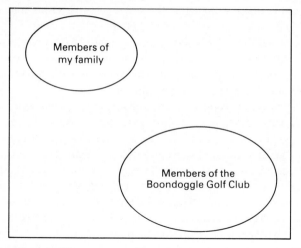

Fig. 5.1   Venn diagram (1)

Another Venn diagram in Fig. 5.2 shows us three sets: the members of the Boondoggle Golf Club; people with a golf handicap of less than 5; and people with a golf handicap of more than 20.

Some people with a handicap of less than 5 are not members of the club, and some people are; and correspondingly for people with a handicap greater than 20. The overlapping areas of the sets represent those people falling into two (or more) sets. Thus we can see that no-one has a handicap which is both less than 5 and more than 20. [Exercise: does everyone in the Boondoggle Golf Club hold a handicap?] The overlapping areas are called, rather reasonably, the *intersection* of sets. An object which falls into the intersection of two sets is a member of one of

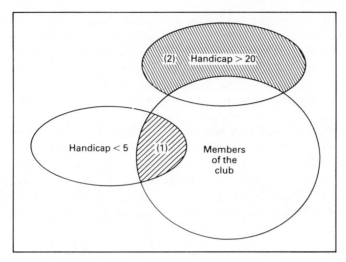

Fig. 5.2   Venn diagram (2)

the sets AND a member of the other set. So the area labelled (1) in the diagram represents those people who are 'members of the Boondoggle Golf Club AND have a handicap of 5 or less'. Note carefully that this area of intersection is now a defined entity in its own right; there is a predicate which tells us whether some object is in it or not; and thus it is itself a set.

If we are interested in sets, and then the areas of intersection of two sets, we should also consider the areas covered by two sets taken together. This is termed the *union* of two sets. It represents the set of objects which are in one of the sets OR in the other. Like the intersection of two or more sets, the union of two or more sets is a set in its own right. Thus in our diagram, we can see the set of people who have a handicap of less than 5, OR who are a member of the Boondoggle Golf Club, OR have a handicap of more than 20: the line around the outside of the three circles. The test which determines the membership of a set is called the predicate of set membership.

While we are looking at these Venn diagrams, we should consider those objects which are *not* in some set. Clearly, they are the objects which do not fall within the figure representing the set. This too is a set. It is termed the *complement* of the initial set. Thus in Fig. 5.2 the area labelled (2) represents those people who are NOT members of the Boondoggle Golf Club AND who do have a handicap of more than 20. This definition of NOT explains why we have an outer box around the diagram. In the absence of the outer box, we would have no limit to the area delimited by the definition. The box in this case represents 'all people in the world'. In general, the name of the box is the 'universe of discourse' in which we are operating. It is the universal set, from which all the elements that enter our discussion are drawn.

The sets we have used in the examples have the property of being 'discrete'.

Thus they have a countable number of members. Another type of set is called 'continuous'. In continuous sets, the candidate objects which may be members of the set may take values drawn from a continuous domain, rather than a discretized domain. Very frequently, the continuous domain is the 'Real Line'; the set of real numbers from minus infinity to plus infinity.

When dealing with continuous sets, it is convenient to use an alternative representation to the Venn diagram. We can use a 'truth diagram'. Figure 5.3 illustrates the sets of numbers 'between 8 and 12 inclusive' and 'between 10 and 16 inclusive'. The horizontal axis of the diagram is the domain, or 'universe of discourse' of the sets. The vertical axis represents the 'degree of membership' of any set defined over the universe of discourse for each point in the universe. Quite arbitrarily, the limits of the degree of membership are selected to be zero, indicating non-membership; and unity, representing membership.

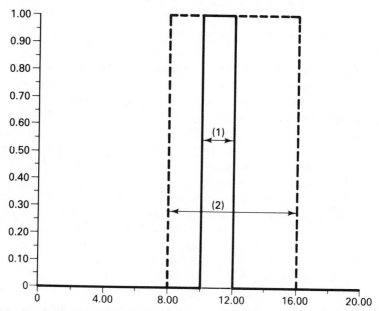

Fig. 5.3   Truth diagram of two sets

The diagram indicates pictorially the results of the operations of union and intersection carried out on sets. The area marked (1) illustrates those numbers 'between 8 and 12 AND between 10 and 16'; in other words the numbers between 10 and 12. Likewise, the area labelled (2) illustrates the numbers 'between 8 and 12 OR between 10 and 16'. Numerically, the grade of membership of any number in any set is either 0 or 1. Another way of saying this is to notice that the numbers zero and one themselves form a discrete set (0, 1), and that membership of any set must be selected from this set of values.

We can use these truth diagrams now to introduce graphically the idea of a 'fuzzy set'. Consider the set called 'small numbers'. 'Small' is a word we use in our everyday vocabulary, and of which we clearly have a good understanding. It is in the nature of this informal real-world understanding of the word that there is no precise boundary to its scope of correct usage. Thus any sort of representation like Fig. 5.4 is a poor representation of what we mean by the word small, although it follows the precepts of classical set theory.

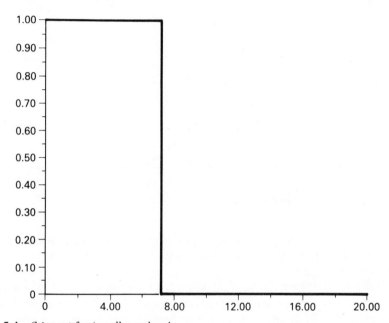

Fig. 5.4   Crisp set for 'small numbers'

In the diagram, the suggestion is that any number less than 7.456 is in the set of small numbers; and any number larger is not. Thus 7.455 is a small number; and 7.457 is not a small number. The completely spurious precision of this boundary is quite clear; and the boundary itself is the transition between complete membership and complete non-membership of the set.

If we could just relax this requirement that there is an instant transition from membership to non-membership, we could draw a figure like Fig. 5.5 to represent the concept 'small numbers'. Here, only the number zero has complete membership of the set 'small numbers'. As we move along the axis of the diagram, the membership levels decrease, until when we reach 15, there is no level of membership left.

Of course, there is an implicit assumption in both the classical and fuzzy definition of the set 'small numbers' that the universe of discourse is consonant with the problem under examination. The distances which are regarded as small

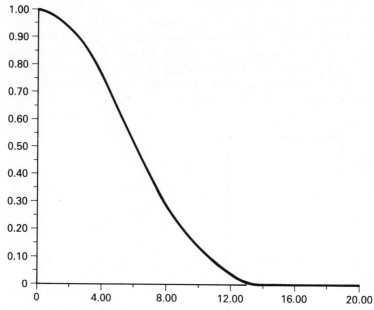

Fig. 5.5 Fuzzy set for 'small numbers'

in astronomy are not those which are regarded as small in quantum mechanics. Thus the selection of the universe of discourse is closely tied to the context in which we are operating.

The informal definition of a fuzzy set is simply a set whose members may possess a grade of membership at any level between complete membership and complete non-membership, or in terms of our truth diagram, between zero and one.

The reason that this definition of a set is, in many ways, more intuitively appealing to the non-mathematician lies in the fact that such fuzzy sets represent many of our normal linguistic concepts more reasonably than a classical set. Such ideas as 'small numbers', 'expensive restaurants', 'tall buildings' and so on do not fit well into the classical set-theoretic paradigm. Most of the qualifiers that we use in ordinary conversation do not have crisp boundaries to their region of applicability.

And thus there is an intuitive correspondence between our natural linguistic qualifiers (or adjectives) and fuzzy sets.

An immediate comment to be made on the grade of membership shown in Fig. 5.5 is 'what degree of reliance is to be placed on the grade of membership shown at each point in the domain?' Is the line shown some absolute definition of the concept 'small numbers', and if so, where do we look for the definition? Clearly, it is not absolute. The definition of the grade of membership is subjective, and furthermore is likely to be context dependent. The fuzzy set 'tall buildings' will have a different connotation in Manhattan compared with a residential suburb, and even in a given context, different individuals will have a different view as to its shape and boundaries. To that degree, a fuzzy set is an approximation to reality. But then, any objective model is to some degree an approximation to reality, and in instances where fuzziness in concept is legitimately recognized, a fuzzy set is likely to provide a better approximation than a classical set.

As you will see later, methods exist to extend the concept of a fuzzy set to cater for the further imprecision in assigning the grade of membership at each point. We can regard the grade of membership as a fuzzy set in itself, as in Zadeh's concept of an 'ultra-fuzzy set'. Or we can regard the grade of membership as the expected value of a probability distribution, as in Norwich and Turksen's concept of a 'stochastic fuzzy set' [84]. But for the present we will assume that the grade of membership is a scalar value at each point in the domain.

5.2.2 Combining fuzzy sets

What we shall do now is to examine the ideas of union, intersection and complementation as applied to fuzzy sets. In Fig. 5.6 we illustrate two sets: the set of 'small numbers' and the set of 'numbers near 10'. By analogy with Fig. 5.3 we can define the intersection of the sets (the set of 'small numbers AND numbers near 10') as the area in the overlap between the two sets. This is the area labelled (1) in Fig. 5.6.

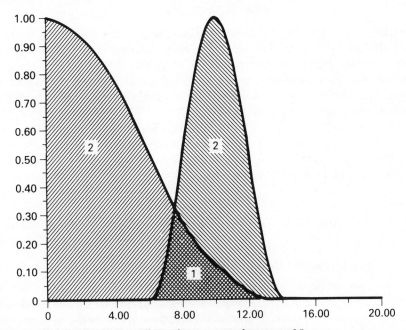

Fig. 5.6   Two fuzzy sets: * small numbers, + numbers near 10

Notice that the greatest grade of membership of this set is less than one. For example, the number 10 has complete membership in the set 'numbers near 10', but a membership of only 0.12 in the set 'small numbers'. We can interpret this verbally by remarking that, given our definitions, there is no number for which it is completely true that it is both 'small' and 'near 10'; and for numbers that have some grade of membership in both of these sets, we will assign the smallest, the most restrictive, grade of membership to the intersection.

Is there a convenient arithmetic formula to describe this intersection? Clearly, what we are doing is taking the arithmetic minimum of the two candidate grades of membership.

Thus we can write down a formula for the intersection of two fuzzy sets A and B as

$$\mu(A \text{ AND } B) = \min\{\mu(A, \mu(B)\}$$

where the symbol μ ('mu', the Greek lowercase m) stands for the grade of membership of a set.

In a like manner, the union of the two fuzzy sets 'small numbers' and 'numbers near 10' is the area under one of the curves, or the other, or both. This is shown in Fig. 5.6 as the area labelled (2). For numbers that are in one set OR the other, we assign the maximum, the least restrictive, value to the grade of membership.

Thus arithmetically, the formula for the union of two fuzzy sets can be expressed as

$$\mu(A \text{ OR } B) = \max\{\mu(a), \mu(b)\}$$

At this stage, it is useful to consider applying these formulae to the classical sets illustrated in Fig. 5.3. In these sets, the grades of membership are of course restricted to values selected from the set $\{0, 1\}$. Applying these formulae to these classical sets yields the identical sets for the union and intersection. Thus in the special case of fuzzy sets with a 'zero degree of fuzziness', the arithmetic of fuzzy sets theory reduces to the classical case.

This allows us to consider the problem of complementation of fuzzy sets. In the classical case, membership of a set implies a grade of membership of unity; non-membership a grade of membership of zero. Generalizing this, we can define the complement of a fuzzy set to be defined as

$$\mu(\text{NOT } A) = \{1 - \mu(A)\}$$

which again reduces to the classical case in the event of a zero degree of fuzziness.

5.2.3 Fuzzy production rules and inference

We turn now to the general concepts of inference, implication and deduction. Formally, these are in fact importantly different concepts, which are explored in detail in Chapters 3, 6 and 7. But informally, they are regarded as pretty well interchangeable ideas, all related to the recognized fact that if we know one thing to be true, we can often assert that something else must therefore be true. This is the sense in which we shall deal with implication and inference in this chapter.

For example, if we look at a kettle, and see that steam is coming out of the nozzle, then we can deduce that the water inside the kettle is boiling. We could write this down as a rule:

IF kettle is steaming THEN water is boiling

The rule has a structure:

IF ⟨something⟩ THEN ⟨something else⟩

The ⟨something⟩ associated with the IF is termed the 'antecedent clause' of the rule. The ⟨something else⟩ associated with the THEN is termed the 'consequent clause'. And if the antecedent clause can be shown to be true, then we regard the consequent clause as true. (This is really a condensed version of the formal reasoning method known as Modus Ponens, to which we shall return in Chapters 6 and 7.)

We are blurring the lines at the moment between Logic and Set Theory. Strictly, any set theory is a model of some underlying logic (and again this will be explored in Chapter 6); but more informally, we can regard a set theoretic description and a propositional description of the same state of affairs as being interchangeable for our current purposes.

Consider the rule:

IF the traffic light is green THEN the traffic may cross

The antecedent clause 'the traffic light is green' can be regarded as a logical proposition which is either true or false. Equivalently, it can be regarded as a set theoretic statement which concerns itself with whether or not the traffic light is included in the 'set of green traffic lights'. The sets of traffic lights of various colours are, of course, classical or crisp sets, with membership levels of zero or one. Consider now a rule involving fuzzy sets.

IF the weather is hot THEN the beach will be crowded

Using our set theory model, the antecedent clause is addressing the question 'does today lie in the set of hot days?' The 'set of hot days' is clearly a fuzzy set. There is no universally agreed temperature at which the weather suddenly comes to be regarded as hot. And equally the concept 'the beach will be crowded' is associated with the fuzzy set 'crowded beach'.

In the crisp case, our informal rule of inference said that if the antecedent clause was true, then so was the consequent. In the fuzzy case, we say that if the antecedent clause is true *to some degree* then the consequent clause can be true *to no more than the same degree*. Thus in any given instance of application of a fuzzy rule, we assess the degree of membership of the object under consideration to the fuzzy set in the antecedent clause. Figure 5.7 illustrates a possible fuzzy set representing the concept 'hot weather'.

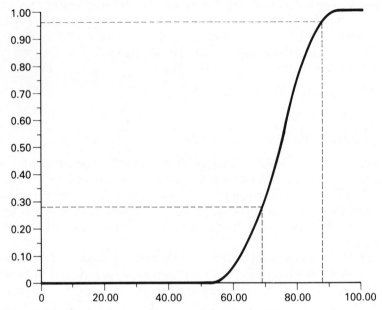

Fig. 5.7   Truth that 'weather is hot': * hot weather

We have marked on the figure the degree of membership of the set of days when the temperature is 50, 70 and 90 degrees Fahrenheit. Figure 5.8 shows a possible fuzzy set representing the concept 'crowded beaches', with these truth levels indicated.

The interpretation of these levels is that if the temperature is 70 degrees, the area marked (1) and cross-hatched represents, as a fuzzy set, the degree of likely crowd on the beach. If the temperature is 90 degrees, the area labelled (2) and singly-hatched represents the likely degree of crowding. (What if the temperature is 50 degrees?)

The areas outlined by the truncated fuzzy sets at these various levels give us a feeling of 'rightness'. All they are saying is that the hotter the weather, the more crowded the beach will be, and representing this idea in a pictorial fashion. There is more 'weight' on the crowded end of the picture, and a greater degree of truth in the statement that the beach is crowded. Simply looking at the diagram confirms to us the information that we introduced to the system with our initial rule. But we are dealing with the usage of fuzzy sets as a component of a decision support system. Clearly, the rule we have adduced is part of our personal decision support system concerning whether or not we go to the beach today. Presumably, at some high level of crowding, we will decide to give the beach a miss, even if the weather is very hot indeed. Our decision is a crisp, indeed a binary one: we either go to the beach or not. How can we develop an algorithm (a recipe) which will determine our decision on an automated basis from the shape of the fuzzy set generated by

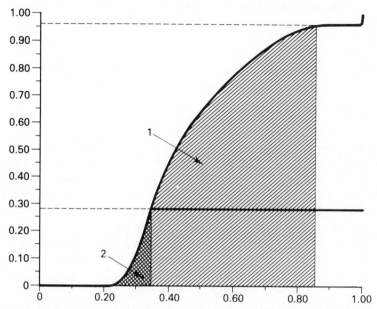

Fig. 5.8 Fuzzy set at various truth levels: * crowded beach

the application of our rule? We need to represent this complex object, a fuzzy set, by a single value – by a scalar – which can then be tested against some threshold value along our scale of 'crowdedness'.

There are a number of approaches we could take. One is to say that it is reasonable to take the maximum degree of truth in the consequent fuzzy set, and to read off from the diagram the corresponding value of the variable 'crowding'.

This is not the only way in which we can manipulate the consequent fuzzy set. Later in this section, we shall discuss other methods, and contrast their areas of applicability. The important thing to focus on at this stage is that we have now produced an arithmetic mechanism which allows us to set up a fuzzy rule, to apply it to some measured situation, and then to derive an output or forecast value from the consequent part of the rule.

Let us turn now to a larger example, involving several rules, and serving to illustrate not only the arithmetic processes of using fuzzy sets in practice, but the method of setting up a problem description for either manual or computerized solution.

Consider how one might describe the system one uses to regulate the temperature of a domestic shower. We can assume that the temperature is adjusted by a single mixer tap, so the flow can be considered constant, and the control variable is the ratio of the hot to the cold water input. The state variable, used to describe the current state of the system, is the perceived temperature of the water arriving on the skin – the 'water temperature'.

The first thing to do is to develop the 'term set' of descriptors or qualifiers used to describe the perceived temperature of the water. As a first attempt, perhaps the list

- 'freezing'
- 'cold'
- 'just right'
- 'hot'
- 'scalding'

represents the discrimination one has on the water temperature variable.

Next, we define the fuzzy sets to represent each of these qualifiers. The scale and extent of the domain must be selected. One obvious candidate scale is the actual temperature in degrees Celsius. But do we in fact know the temperature of the water at which we find it comfortable to shower? Few people take a thermometer into the shower with them, so we may be better off to create an arbitrary subjective scale, ranging for convenience from say 0 to 100 along some 'psychological continuum'. It is just coincidence that in this case the boundaries of the domain are the same as the boundaries of the domain of scientific temperatures of liquid water. The qualifiers 'freezing' and 'scalding' are used in their colloquial rather than scientific senses. Zero on the scale should be taken to mean 'all cold water and no hot' and likewise one hundred to mean 'all hot water and no cold'.

Figure 5.9 shows a set of definitions for the five selected qualifiers.

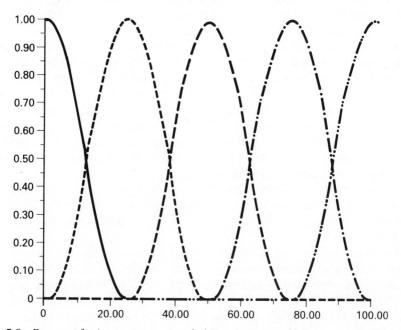

Fig. 5.9   Fuzzy set for 'water temperature': * Freezing, = scalding, + cold, $ just right, − hot

Table 5.1   Fuzzy set definitions

T	(1)	(2)	(3)	(4)	(5)
0	1.00	0.00	0.00	0.00	0.00
5	0.92	0.08	0.00	0.00	0.00
10	0.68	0.32	0.00	0.00	0.00
15	0.32	0.68	0.00	0.00	0.00
20	0.08	0.92	0.00	0.00	0.00
25	0.00	1.00	0.00	0.00	0.00
30	0.00	0.92	0.08	0.00	0.00
35	0.00	0.68	0.32	0.00	0.00
40	0.00	0.32	0.68	0.00	0.00
45	0.00	0.08	0.92	0.00	0.00
50	0.00	0.00	1.00	0.00	0.00
55	0.00	0.00	0.92	0.08	0.00
60	0.00	0.00	0.68	0.32	0.00
65	0.00	0.00	0.32	0.68	0.00
70	0.00	0.00	0.08	0.92	0.00
75	0.00	0.00	0.00	1.00	0.00
80	0.00	0.00	0.00	0.92	0.08
85	0.00	0.00	0.00	0.68	0.32
90	0.00	0.00	0.00	0.32	0.68
95	0.00	0.00	0.00	0.08	0.92
100	0.00	0.00	0.00	0.00	1.00

(1) 'freezing'
(2) 'cold'
(3) 'just right'
(4) 'hot'
(5) 'scalding'

In tabular form, they can be represented as shown in Table 5.1, which is a useful representation for us to 'hand-calculate' our way through this example.

In a similar manner, we now need to set up the descriptors for our control variable. First, select the variable; then define its domain and scale; generate the term set; and define the fuzzy sets for each term.

Suppose we select 'adjustment to the mixer' as our control variable, with the term set

– 'much more cold'
– 'more cold'
– 'leave alone'
– 'more hot'
– 'much more hot'.

In a scientific sense, the control variable might be parameterized by degrees of rotation of the mixer tap. But then even fewer people take a protractor into the shower with them than do a thermometer, so perhaps an arbitrary scale from − 2 to + 2 might be preferred. So our definitions of the control variable term set might be as shown in Fig. 5.10.

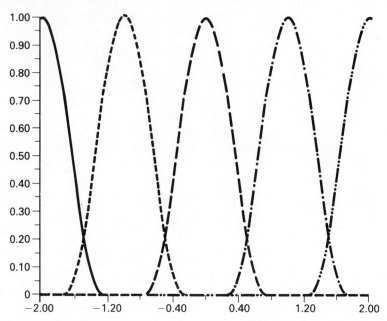

Fig. 5.10 Fuzzy sets for 'adjustment to mixer': * much more cold, = much more hot, + more cold, $ leave alone, − more hot

We are now ready to draw up the set of rules which will generate the control action. They would seem to be pretty straightforward:

R1:   IF   'water temperature' IS 'freezing'
        THEN   'adjustment to the mixer' IS 'much more hot'

R2:   IF   'water temperature' IS 'cold'
        THEN   'adjustment to the mixer' IS 'more hot'

R3:   IF   'water temperature' IS 'just right'
        THEN   'adjustment to the mixer' IS 'leave alone'

R4:   IF   'water temperature' IS 'hot'
        THEN   'adjustment to the mixer' IS 'more cold'

R5:   IF   'water temperature' IS 'scalding'
        THEN   'adjustment to the mixer' IS 'much more cold'

Notice that there is one rule for each of the descriptors in the term set of the state variable. We would expect that; there would be little point in defining a term if we never planned to use it to any purpose. Of course, this is something to bear in mind very clearly when we come to more practical examples in Chapter 10. In general, we will expect to generate a rule for every combination of terms in the term sets of all our state variables. If we have five variables, each with five possible fuzzy states, we have to expect to create $5^5 = 3125$ rules, unless we can confidently state that some areas of the state space are unreachable – in other words that some combinations of the control variables are implausible in practice. We shall return to this topic at some length in Chapter 10. In the meantime, consider the problems you would face with ten variables each adopting one of ten possible fuzzy values; what would be a necessary approach to make the problem computationally feasible?

Anyway, back under the shower, how do we use these rules? We sample the temperature of the water, possibly using a specially designed organic thermocouple like 'a hand'. This gives us a value for the state variable, which is actually going to be fuzzy. You would describe it verbally, perhaps using one of our existing term set, such as 'freezing', 'cold' or 'just right'. More likely it would be intermediate between some of our term set: 'a little bit colder than just right, but not really cold'. We can process this fuzzy set in conjunction with our set of rules, but arithmetically it will be simpler to select a point in our state domain as representative of the peak of this perceived fuzzy set. Perhaps the value 40 on our 0–100 scale can be used to represent the phrase used above. We shall return to the case where we wish to describe the state as a fuzzy set later in this section.

We now look at each rule in turn (and every rule exhaustively), testing the truth of the antecedent proposition (the IF clause) with respect to our state variable value. The truth can be determined from Table 5.1 or graphically from Fig. 5.9. A summary of the antecedent truths is shown in Table 5.2.

Table 5.2   Antecedent truth values

Rule	Antecedent	Truth
R1	'Water is freezing'	0.00
R2	'Water is cold'	0.32
R3	'Water is just right'	0.68
R4	'Water is hot'	0.00
R5	'Water is scalding'	0.00

There is some non-zero truth in the propositions that the temperature is 'cold', and that it is 'just right': rules R2 and R3. There is no truth in the antecedent propositions of rules R1, R4 or R5. Thus rules R2 and R3 will make a contribution to our control action, and now become the focus of our attention.

Intuitively, we decided earlier that the consequent part of a rule could be no more true than its antecedent component. So we can modify Fig. 5.10 by reducing, or truncating, the fuzzy sets covering the domain of the control variable according to the truth of the corresponding antecedents in the rules in which they feature. Figure 5.11 shows the resultant fuzzy sets.

The two rules R2 and R3 which have contributed to the outcome are seen clearly. It is helpful to picture all the rules as having contributed some evidence: it just happens that rules R1, R4 and R5 have 'contributed at the zero level'. This rather convoluted way of looking at things will be helpful when we return to a more formal discussion of inferencing methods in Chapter 7.

So now, in this rather simple way, we have generated a solution to our control problem. There is some evidence that the 'adjustment to the mixer' ought to be 'more hot' water; and rather more evidence that the course of action should be to 'leave alone'. Intuitively, this seems right. The temperature was somewhat low, so some sort of increase seems to be indicated.

It is important to emphasize that the control action to be taken IS fully represented by the output fuzzy set shown in Fig. 5.11. What we have to do now is to translate this fuzzy set into an executable control action.

Two methods are available: 'arithmetic defuzzification' and 'linguistic approximation'. The idea of linguistic approximation is due to Esragh and Mamdani [254] and is aimed at translating the consequent fuzzy set into a verbal phrase describing the control action. The algorithm to achieve this is described and discussed in Section 5.2 and for the present we shall simply remark that the consequent control action can be described as 'leave alone or more hot'.

Arithmetic defuzzification aims instead at extracting a single scalar value from

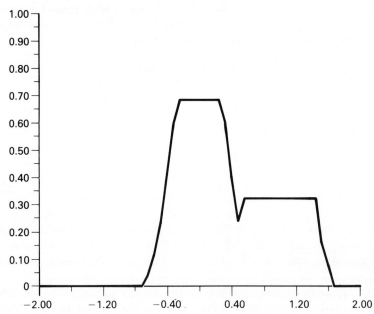

Fig. 5.11 Consequent fuzzy set: * consequent fuzzy set with state variable of 40

the consequent fuzzy set, which most accurately represents the fuzzy set, and thus becomes the prescriptive control action. (This is the most frequently employed approach in the computerized applications of fuzzy sets.) Essentially, we have to address the question of which scalar most 'properly' represents the fuzzy set. There are two obvious candidates: one is the point in the domain at which the maximum truth value of the fuzzy set is to be found ('the maximum method'); the other is the point in the domain at which a line perpendicular to the axis would pass through the centre of area of the fuzzy set ('the moments method').

In general, these will generate different prescriptive control actions. Figure 5.12 illustrates the two solutions provide in the current case. Under the maximum rule, a value of 0.00 units is prescribed; under the moments rule, a value of +0.32. Which is to be preferred?

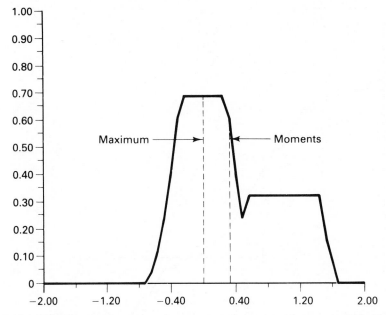

Fig. 5.12   Defuzzification operators: * consequent fuzzy set with state variable of 40

There is no absolute or theoretically grounded method of making a selection. We are trying to characterize a complex object by a single scalar, and the selection of the appropriate method is essentially empirical. It turns out that the appropriate rule to use is governed essentially by the nature of the application problem, and the expected pattern of desirable control actions. The key point is that the use of the maximum rule will lead to discontinuities in the control space, induced by marginal continuous changes to the state variables. The plateau of some truncated fuzzy set will represent the maximum truth of the consequent fuzzy set at some point in the state space, and the point in the control domain at which this maximum occurs will remain constant over quite wide variations in the state variables, until suddenly some other fuzzy set will generate the maximum truth. At this point, the value of the prescribed control variable will switch instantaneously to some new value. One particular rule from the rule set is dominant at any point, and for a range of values around that point. On the other hand, the moments rule 'weighs the evidence' from all the fuzzy sets in the control space, and provides a continuous response to variations in the state space. Figure 5.13 illustrates the control behaviour of our (very simple) model as the perceived temperature ranges through its state space from 16 to 85, using both the maximum and moments rules. Which method should we use in this case?

For continuous control problems of this kind, it seems clear that the moments rule is more appropriate. However, for applications of the decision analysis kind,

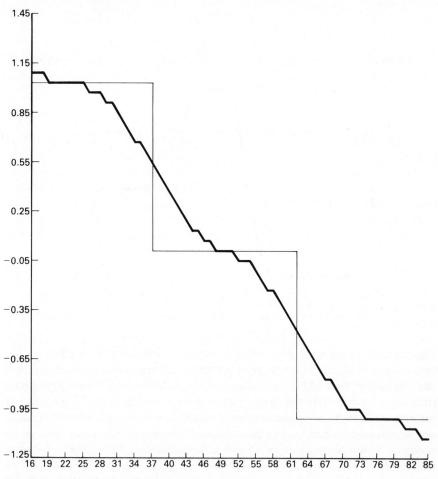

Fig. 5.13 Defuzzification operators

where the prescribed action is one of selection between a set of discrete alternatives, the maximum method will generally be preferable.

So, using in this case the moments rule, we see that the generated action is to increase the temperature by taking the control action of turning the mixer tap +0.32 units.

EXERCISES:

1. Qualitatively, what will be the effect of redefining the control term set to contain: (a) fewer qualifiers; (b) more qualifiers; (c) qualifiers with a higher degree of overlap?

2. Consider varying the state term set in the same way as in exercise 1.

3. What governs the appropriate density of the two term sets, and what are the trade-offs?

5.3 FORMAL DEVELOPMENT

5.3.1 Basic definitions

Having by now grasped some intuition about the naturalness and perhaps the utility of representing uncertain knowledge with fuzzy sets, we now proceed to a more detailed exposition. The next chapter will explore further into the connections with mathematics and introduce generalizations of the definitions to be introduced here. This section is concerned with the basic mathematical machinery necessary to understand the application of fuzzy sets to knowledge engineering and the construction of fuzzy languages for computation. Mathematical rigour is not our prime preoccupation. The intention is merely to lay bare enough of the mathematical machinery to enable readers to understand the operation and construction of fuzzy computer programs.

We start with the definition of the most usual version of fuzzy set theory based on ordinary set theory which, from now on, we assume is familiar to the reader.

A fuzzy set is a function μ from a set A, called its *domain*, to the unit interval $I = [0, 1]$; that is

$$\mu : A \to I.$$

μ is also said to be a fuzzy subset of A. The function on A which assigns to every point of A the value 1 can be identified with A itself, so that we need not ever consider ordinary sets except insofar as they are special cases of fuzzy sets. The set consisting of the points of A for which μ has a non-zero value is called the *support* of μ. We can also identify μ with its graph by considering it to consist of the set of ordered pairs $\{(a, \mu(a)): a \in A\}$. Such graphs should be familiar from the preceding section. For any $a \in A$, $\mu(a)$ is called the *grade of membership* of a in A. Thus a fuzzy set is the generalization of a set where an element can be a member of a set *to some degree*. This degree can be interpreted as a truth value (in fuzzy logic), as the possibility that a certain predicate corresponding to the domain applies to a given element, or in a number of other ways.

Two fuzzy sets, μ and λ, are said to be equal if they share the same domain and

$\mu(a) = \lambda(a)$ for all a. A fuzzy set is *normal* if its grade of membership attains the value 1 at at least one point of its domain. It is *regular* if it only has one peak; i.e. if $a < b < c$ then $\mu(a) > \mu(b) \Rightarrow \mu(b) \geqslant \mu(c)$.

We define the union, intersection and complementation operations in this theory as follows.

Let $\mu : A \rightarrow I$ and $\lambda : B \rightarrow I$. Then their union $\mu \cup \lambda$, and intersection $\mu \cap \lambda$ are given by

$\mu \cup \lambda : A \times B \rightarrow I$, $\mu \cap \lambda : A \times B \rightarrow I$,
$\mu \cup \lambda(a) = \max(\mu(a), \lambda(a))$, and
$\mu \cap \lambda(a) = \min(\mu(a), \lambda(a))$ for all $a \in A \cup B$.

The complement of μ, NOT(μ), is given by the function $\text{NOT}(\mu)(a) = 1 - \mu(a)$ on the same domain.

These operations are illustrated in Fig. 5.14. They are not the only ones to have been used but are the ones most appropriate for possibility theory and knowledge engineering applications. The reasons for this are discussed in more detail below. Note that the intersection of two normal fuzzy sets need not be normal.

These definitions complete the analogy with set theory. However fuzzy set theory has a much richer structure and we now introduce some additional operations which have application in approximate reasoning and computer languages with simulated imprecise reasoning.

The additional operations are often called *hedges*, and we will see their application very shortly. The four hedges we consider are called concentration, dilation, normalization and intensification.

Before introducing the formal definitions, let us pause to consider a fuzzy set in a new light. We can identify the domain of a fuzzy set with a *linguistic variable*. Suppose A is a set of people's heights then a value of this variable might be 'tall', 'average' or 'short'. A is a subset of the real line and these values – the term set – may be represented by the fuzzy sets illustrated in Fig. 5.15. In this way A is said to be a linguistic variable with values in the term set as completed to include all linguistic modifications of terms.

In ordinary language we can extend any such set of terms by using adverbial or adjectival qualifiers such as very, slightly, rather and so on. Thus we speak of a person being very tall or rather short. The usual way of defining the fuzzy set 'very tall' given 'tall' is by squaring all the grades of membership of tall. In the same way 'fairly tall' can be obtained by taking the square root. This is illustrated in Fig. 5.16.

These definitions are not the only ones available, but they have been shown experimentally [95] to correspond to normal usage fairly well. Formally the concentration of a fuzzy set μ is given by

$$\text{Conc}(\mu)(a) = \mu^2(a)$$

Its dilation is given by

$$\text{Dil}(\mu)(a) = \mu^{0.5}(a)$$

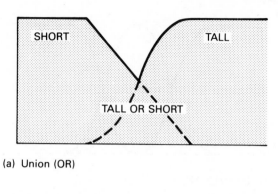

(a) Union (OR)

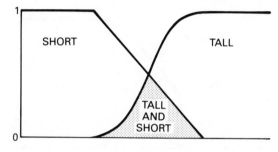

(b) Intersection (AND)

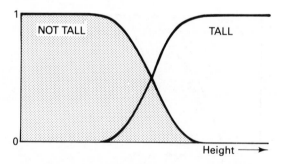

(c) Complementation (NOT)

Fig. 5.14   Fuzzy set operators: − the maximum method, * the moments method

These are examples of power hedges with powers 2 and 0.5. Other powers may be used to strengthen or weaken the effect of particular words. For example, if very is defined by squaring the membership grades then extremely might require that they be cubed. In general this will depend on the application in mind. An alternative method of defining the concentration and dilation hedges is to see a shift operation. Figure 5.17 gives an example.

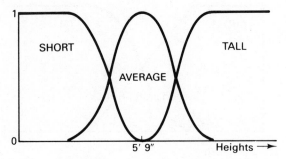

Fig. 5.15   Term set for men's height

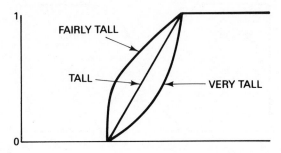

Fig. 5.16   Power hedges: $\mu_{\text{very tall}}(x) = \mu_{\text{tall}}^2(x)$, $\mu_{\text{fairly tall}}(x) = \mu_{\text{tall}}^{0.5}(x)$

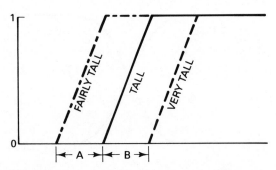

Fig. 5.17   Shift hedges: $\mu_{\text{very tall}}(x) = \mu_{\text{tall}}^2(x - A)$, $\mu_{\text{fairly tall}}(x) = \mu_{\text{tall}}^{0.5}(x + B)$

The normalization (Norm) and intensification (Int) operations are defined as follows.

$$\text{Norm}(\mu)\,(a) = \mu(a)/\max(\mu(a))$$

$$\text{Int}(\mu)\,(a) = \begin{cases} 2\mu^2(a) & \text{for } 0 \leqslant \mu(a) \leqslant 0.5 \\ 1 - 2(1 - \mu(a))^2 & \text{for } 0.5 < \mu(a) \leqslant 1 \end{cases}$$

These are illustrated in Fig. 5.18.

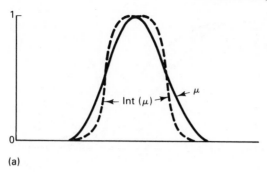

(a)

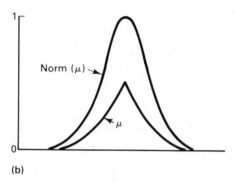

(b)

Fig. 5.18   (a) Intensification, (b) Normalization

The completion of the term set of a linguistic variable is obtained by applying combinations of all the operators we have met so far. Thus, for example, if we start with the terms 'tall', 'average' and 'short' over the variable 'men's heights in Madrid in 1658' then the completion must include terms such as 'not very tall', 'tall or average', 'very very very tall', 'short but not very short', and so on. Note here that we have had to be very precise about the domain of discourse. Tall buildings and tall men have very different ranges, and the notion of a tall person varies with time, sex and provenance. Note also that we have identified 'and' (which is taken to mean the same as 'but') with intersection and 'or' with union. Thus we are now moving from fuzzy set theory to a form of fuzzy logic, in this case the form known as Approximate Reasoning. We shall move happily to and fro between the two to exploit the geometric intuition of the set theory and the linguistic clarity of the logic. Rest assured that mathematics guarantees us that this is valid procedure – technically the set theory is a 'model' of the logic; a concept to be explicated in the next chapter.

As an example let us examine the construction of a term which we might wish to label 'moderately short' and which is equal to 'short but not very short'. In Fig. 5.19 we show the steps necessary to construct this term. First we construct

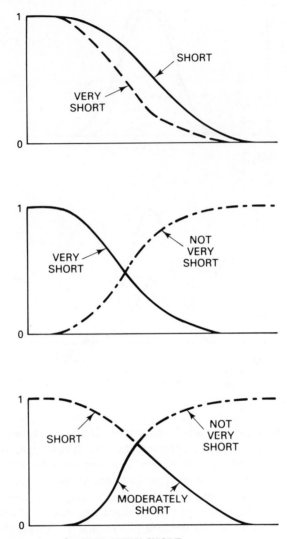

Fig. 5.19   Construction of MODERATELY SHORT

'very short' by squaring all the points of 'short', now take away from 1 to get 'not very short', which is a mirror image of 'very short'. Lastly, take the maximum with the original 'short' term to apply the 'but' = 'and' operation. The resultant term must then be normalized, since it is a requirement in most applications that term sets are normal; the reason being that terms can then be assumed to apply with equal weight in arguments.

5.3.2   Fuzzy numbers

Up to now we have dealt with fuzzy sets which express predicates like 'tall'. In most applications there is also the need to deal with numeric values. Fortunately there is a well developed theory of fuzzy numbers which we can exploit.

The simplest case occurs when we wish to say that a price is 'about 7' or is 'high'. Hedges can be defined to fuzzify numeric input values. Thus 'about 7' might be defined as the fuzzy subset of the real line given by:

$$\text{'about 7' } (x) = \begin{cases} x-6 & \text{if } 6 < x \leqslant 7 \\ -x+8 & \text{if } 7 \leqslant x < 8 \\ 0 & \text{otherwise} \end{cases}$$

This is only one possibility. In general a fuzzy number is any normal, regular fuzzy subset of the real line $\mathscr{R}$. Figure 5.20 shows the difference between regular and irregular fuzzy sets.

Operations of addition, multiplication, etc. have been defined on fuzzy numbers. The details may be found in Zimmermann [222] or Dubois and Prade [59]. Since we shall not use any of these operations in this chapter this need not detain us. The definitions are given where they are required in the next chapter, when we come to the treatment of fuzzy quantifiers.

5.3.3   Fuzzy relations and Approximate Reasoning

We have been dealing exclusively with examples where we have combined fuzzy sets over the same domain, or where the intersection of domains is not empty. What happens when we wish to apply two or more incomparable predicates such as 'tall' and 'heavy'? The answer is that we must introduce the notion of a fuzzy relation.

A (binary) fuzzy relation between two sets A and B is a fuzzy subset of their Cartesian product; which is defined as the set of all ordered pairs of elements from A and B. For example if $A = B = \{1, 2, 3, 4\}$ then the fuzzy relation 'a is much larger than b' might be expressed by the following matrix.

	x			
y	1	2	3	4
1	0	0.1	0.4	0.9
2	0	0	0	0.2
3	0	0	0	0
4	0	0	0	0

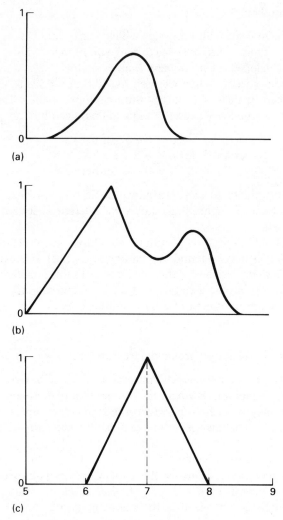

Fig. 5.20 (a) Non-normal, regular (b) normal, irregular (c) Fuzzy number, normal, regular

The union, intersection and the other operations on fuzzy sets can be extended to fuzzy relations. This is very easy because fuzzy relations are just fuzzy sets on product domains, therefore the max, min, $1 - \mu$ definitions go through more or less unaltered. More importantly, we may define the composition of two fuzzy relations $\mu : A \times B \rightarrow I$ and $\lambda : B \times C \rightarrow I$ as follows. Denote this composite relation by $\lambda \circ \mu$. Then define

$$\lambda \circ \mu(a, b) = \mathrm{Sup}_B \mathrm{Min} \{ \mu(a, b'), \lambda(b', c) \}$$

where Sup stands for the continuous analogue of the Maximum operator (Supremum). This operation may either be understood geometrically, as we shall see in a moment, or by analogy to the usual matrix multiplication operation where addition and multiplication have been replaced by max and min respectively. For example let us compose two discrete relations

μ	b_1	b_2	b_3	b_4	b_5
a_1	0.1	0.2	0	1	0.7
a_2	0.3	0.5	0	0.2	1
a_3	0.8	0	1	0.4	0.3

and

λ	c_1	c_2	c_3	c_4
b_1	0.9	0	0.3	0.4
b_2	0.2	1	0.8	0
b_3	0.8	0	0.7	1
b_4	0.4	0.2	0.3	0
b_5	0	1	0	0.8

to give

$\lambda \circ \mu$	c_1	c_2	c_3	c_4
a_1	0.4	0.7	0.3	0.7
a_2	0.3	1	0.5	0.8
a_3	0.8	0.3	0.7	1

The first value, 0.4, is obtained as follows.

Max(Min(0.1, 0.9), Min(0.2, 0.2), Min(0, 0.8), Min(1, 0.4), Min(0.7, 0))
= Max(0.1, 0.2, 0, 0.4, 0) = 0.4

EXERCISE: Verify the remainder of the computation of $\lambda \circ \mu$.

The compositional rule of inference is based on this definition of the composition of relations. This rule makes it possible to design computational languages for the manipulation of sets of fuzzy production rules. The properties of the Sup–Min composition make it possible to perform both forward and backward chaining on the rules in a way which very closely reflects the process of natural reasoning. Thus the application of fuzzy set theory to practical knowledge engineering problems goes far beyond the arithmetic of min and max as found in many expert system shells and indeed in the theory of certainty factors which we introduced in Chapter 4. For the description of forward and backward chaining inference strategies see Chapter 7.

To develop the corresponding geometrical intuition, let us now return to a more serious version of the shower control problem we met in the last section.

First let us state some more complicated rules as elicited from the human operator of the shower. The objective here is to either have a refreshingly cold or stimulatingly hot shower, but to avoid medium temperatures and water so hot that it would scald or damage the user.

> If water is COLD then decrease about 1 unit.
> If water is COOL then increase about 1 unit.
> If water is WARM then increase about 2 units.
> If water is HOT then decrease about 1 unit.

To process these fuzzy productions we must first establish the term sets for the input and output linguistic variables. Figure 5.21 shows how these have been defined over numerical ranges representing the water temperatures and the possible changes to the temperature control tap.

The rules may be represented in the product of these two ranges as shown in Fig. 5.22. Each rule is represented by a fuzzy set which is the Sup–Min composition of the antecedent and consequent clauses. They are then combined using the maximum operator to indicate an implicit OR standing between each of the rules. The next step is to read a measurement of the shower temperature and use this to 'slice through' the aggregated rule to give an output fuzzy set. This is shown by the hatched area in Fig. 5.23.

This output fuzzy set represents the truth or possibility that a given change to the controller will satisfy the rules. To transform this information into an actual change in the controller it is necessary to defuzzify. As we have seen, there are two methods available, either taking the centre of moments (the centre of gravity of a cardboard cut-out of the shaded area) or the arithmetic mean of the maxima of the resultant fuzzy set. In fact other methods are available, but as they have little practical consequence we will not consider them here. The end product is a numerical value on the 'change to input' scale. We must now use a method known as linguistic approximation to return to a member of the original term set. This is done by choosing the term which is 'most true' at the given value. In the case illustrated this is 'increase by 1 unit' for both methods of defuzzification. In general the results may differ and it has been found that for continuous control applications the 'moments' method gives better, more stable, results as the output tends to change continuously with the input. In decision making applications the

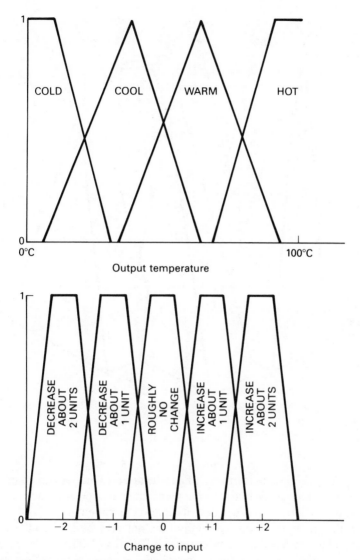

Fig. 5.21   Fuzzy sets for shower control problem

maximum method is usually better, as we have seen earlier and we will see again in examples in subsequent chapters.

In this example the input was an actual temperature. If we think of knowledge engineering examples where the input might be a linguistic term, such as COOL, we would have had to use linguistic approximation to defuzzify the input also. This is done merely by taking the maximum (or centre of moments) of the fuzzy

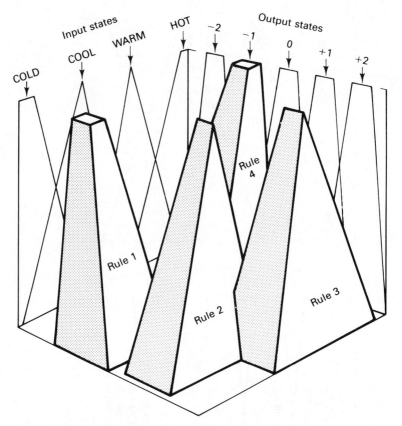

Fig. 5.22 Extension of the rules

set representing the selected term or its hedged variant. Thus we can imagine a set of rules concerning stock market prices and their movements, and an expert system where traders are asked to describe market sentiment as 'bullish', 'bearish' or 'neutral'. The input in this case might be 'not very bullish' and the output something like 'a reversal in the price trend is HIGHLY LIKELY'. The lesson to be learnt here is that fuzzy set theory provides a means whereby linguistically expressed, vague terms may be supplied to a system which can convert them into a rational numeric form, perform complex inferences with the propagation of uncertainty levels through the inference network, and finally convert the answer back to an anodyne linguistic form. Furthermore, the Sup–Min rule ensures great computational efficiency during this process compared, say, to probability theory, and allows the manipulation of evidence (or possibilities).

What we have been looking at is the mathematical basis of Zadeh's theory of Approximate Reasoning. This theory starts with the notion of a linguistic variable as we have described it, including its term set, hedges and domain, then adds

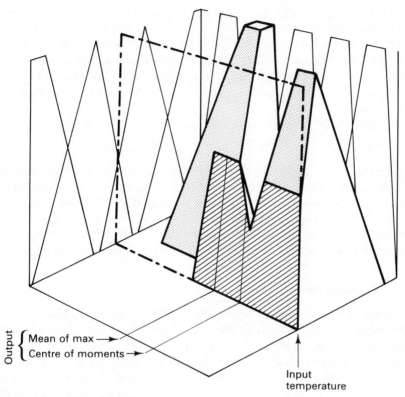

Fig. 5.23   The output fuzzy set

various additional items of structure, such as rules of inference, truth functional modification and quantifiers.

The rule of inference used in the above is known as Fuzzy Modus Ponens and allows us to handle inferences of the following form in either forward or backward chaining mode. (For an explanation of these terms see Chapters 6 and 7.) Thus:

The tomato is very red
If a tomato is red then the tomato is ripe

together allow us to infer

The tomato is very ripe

This is achieved, in Approximate Reasoning, precisely as described in the example on the shower above.

Interestingly, the study of uncertainty has led us directly to the study of inference. The most controversial issue in Approximate Reasoning is that of truth functional modification. This allows us to use rules of the form:

IF A IS TRUE THAN B IS NOT VERY TRUE

The methods of reasoning are as described above but many logicians object to taking liberties with TRUE in this way. Haack for example regards the whole idea of a truth value, other than TRUE or FALSE, as 'barbaric' and many logicians have criticized the notion of VERY TRUE as being without meaning. Even fuzzy set theorists have had their doubts. Tong and Efstathiou [198] argue that truth functional modification is redundant in that the statements under consideration rarely involve truth as such, but usually some form of confidence level. Thus we could rephrase the example above to read

IF A IS BELIEVABLE THEN B IS NOT VERY BELIEVABLE

or some such. They also argue that the problems arise because different kinds of uncertainty are often confused. In practice the solution is to be aware that the word 'true' may have a meaning quite separate from that assigned to it by logicians and philosophers, to remain steadfastly aware of exactly how it is being used, to be clear about exactly which of the many kinds of uncertainty are being manipulated (see Chapter 4) and lastly to avoid the term TRUE if at all possible.

5.3.4 Choosing the right combination operators

We have concentrated on the standard forms of the operations of fuzzy set theory so far. It is worth mentioning that there have been alternative suggestions for the operations of union, intersection, composition, etc. One of the early justifications for the ones we have given was that Bellman and Giertz were able to construct a set of plausible axioms from which these operations could be derived – for details see [222] or [59]. However all sets of axioms may be questioned as to plausibility, and in fact other fuzzy logics (or set theories) have been found to be better for specific applications. There are two major systems other than the one we have dealt with:

(1) Intersection or conjunction is defined by the product operation given by $\mu \cap \lambda(a) = \mu(a) * \lambda(a)$; and union disjunction by the probabilistic sum, so that $\mu \cup \lambda = \mu(a) + \lambda(a) - \mu(a) * \lambda(a)$.
(2) Intersection or conjunction is defined by the bold intersection operation $\mu \cap \lambda = \max(0, \mu(a) + \lambda(a) - 1)$; and union or disjunction by the bold union, $\mu \cup \lambda = \min(1, \mu(a) + \lambda(a))$.

All these systems give rise to suitable lattice structures on the set of fuzzy subsets of a set. Very few systems with a different complement (or negation) operation have been proposed.

Zimmermann [222] suggests the following criteria for the selection of a suitable fuzzy logic for an application.

(1) Axiomatic strength. This refers to the possibility of deducing the operators from a minimal, plausible set of axioms.
(2) Empirical fit. Empirical testing must always be used to validate the results of a fuzzy model, and one of the variables is the choice of operators.

(3) Adaptability. Some operators (none mentioned here) admit of parametrization to fit a specific problem.
(4) Numerical efficiency. Generally, parametrizable operations require more computation than the ones given in this section. Of these the max–min is the most efficient.
(5) Compensation. With the max–min logic the degree to which an element belongs to the intersection is not affected by the degree to which it belongs to both of the contributing fuzzy sets. This may be important in some applications where 'weightings' are important. The product operator is compensatory in this sense. It satisfies the property that if $\mu \hat{\ } \lambda(a) = k$ for some a, then there exist different μ' and λ' such that $\mu' \hat{\ } \lambda'(a') = k$.
(6) Range of compensation. If one uses a convex combination of max and min operators, compensation could occur in the range between min and max. With the product operator this is extended to the range $]0, 1[$. The larger this range the better.
(7) Aggregation behaviour. When many combinations are involved the truth values of the resultant fuzzy set tend to get smaller and smaller. The more slowly this happens the better, but on no account should the truth increase.
(8) Required type of measurement scale. The type of scale on which membership functions are constructed can be a nominal, interval, ratio or absolute scale. Different operators may require different scale types; e.g. min is admissible for ordinal information while product is usually not.

These useful criteria are intended to help in selecting operators for applications. We might also begin to see the desirability of a software product which left these choices open for the user or system designer.

The most important points here, in our belief, are numbers 1, 2, 4 and 7. In nearly every practical application in knowledge engineering, the max–min logic is the appropriate one. However, much work needs to be done to fully validate this bold statement. Certainly, in control problems some other logics have already proved their superiority. There may even be applications where it is necessary to switch dynamically from one set of operators to another. Clearly, this will require great understanding and discipline, and should not be undertaken lightly.

5.3.5 Measures of fuzziness: entropy and information

How fuzzy is a fuzzy set? How much information does one contain? These are the questions we attempt to answer in this subsection. We are concerned with 'fuzzy measures' which is a branch of fuzzy mathematics devoted to exploring the foundations of possibility theory by following the analogy with theoretical probability. This is dealt with in the next section. The reader interested in the details is referred to [222] or [59].

Before we can tell how much information a fuzzy set contains, we must first have a measure of information. Consider first the storage of the symbols for the letters of the alphabet in a digital computer. Such a machine may be regarded as a set of registers which may be 'on' or 'off'; corresponding to two numerical symbols 1 and 0. How many registers are required to store 26 letters, 10 digits, minimal punctuation, say '. , :' and a symbol representing a space; 40 characters in all? With one register we can only distinguish two states, with two registers we have $2^2 = 4$ possibilities; i.e. 00 01 10 11. In general with n registers the 'variety' available is 2^n. Thus, since the lowest power of two greater than 40 is $2^6 = 64$, six registers must be set aside to store a symbol from our restricted alphabet. Modern computers in fact use at least eight registers, telegraph or telex code used five. The amount of information which can be transmitted to us by such a single set of registers, or word, depends on its size. A single register word can only send one message (if we agree on the code in advance); so that if we have agreed that if the register contains 0 the situation is normal but that a 1 means the building is on fire, then no information concerning flood could ever be conveyed. In other words one register can send one 'bit' of information. Two registers can send three messages, but it is convenient to represent the quantity of information on a logarithmic scale, so, taking logs to the base 2, we say that the two registers can carry two bits of information. The logarithmic scale is necessary to make the measure independent of the number of states the registers might take in a more general case. The amount of information that can be sent with our word in a time corresponding to n changes of state is therefore $n\log_2(S)$, where S is the number of states that each register can take.

The notion of information is closely related to a classical notion in statistical mechanics; that of entropy. Just as the amount of information in a system is a measure of its degree of organization, so the entropy of a system is a measure of its degree of disorganization. The one is simply the negative of the other. For the background to these ideas see Wiener [229] or Ross-Ashby [228]. The notion of entropy is closely related to the idea that states can occur with varying degrees of probability. Thus if we have a system in which any one of n events may occur with probabilities $p_1, p_2, \ldots p_n$, where their sum is 1 of course, then the entropy H of the system is given by

$$H = -\sum_{i=1}^{n} p_i \log(p_i)$$

which is just the negative of the information carrying capability of that system.

Returning to the question of how to measure the degree of fuzziness of a fuzzy set, De Luca and Termini have suggested (see [59]) that such a measurement function should satisfy the following, rather natural conditions. Given a set X, let $P(X)$ denote its set of fuzzy subsets and let $d : P(X) \rightarrow [0, \infty]$ be the measurement function. The conditions are:

(1) $d(\mu) = 0$ iff μ is a crisp set
(2) $d(\mu)$ has a unique maximal value for the fuzzy set: $\mu(x) = 0.5$ for all $x \in X$
(3) $d(\mu) \geqslant d(\lambda)$ iff $\mu(x) \geqslant 0.5 \Rightarrow \lambda(x) \geqslant \mu(x)$ and $\mu(x) \leqslant 0.5 \Rightarrow \lambda(x) \leqslant \mu(x)$
(4) $d(\mu) = d(\text{Not}\mu)$

In words, crisp sets are not fuzzy at all, the most fuzzy subset is always half true, intensified fuzzy sets are less fuzzy and a set is as fuzzy as its complement.

Now suppose d is defined as follows for any fuzzy subset μ of X and any $x \in X$.

$$d(\mu) = H(\mu) + H(\text{Not}\mu), \text{ where}$$

$$H(\mu) = -K \sum_{i=1}^{n} \mu(x_i) \log(\mu(x_i))$$

where n is the number of elements in the support of μ and K is a positive constant. In the continuous case the limit of this expression gives the obvious definite integral. The quantity $d(\mu)$ is called the *entropy* of the fuzzy set μ. The expression may be simplified by substituting the Shannon function S, defined by

$$S(x) = -x\log(x) - (1-x)\log(1-x))$$

to give the entropy as

$$d(\mu) = K \sum_{i=1}^{n} S(\mu(x))$$

THEOREM

The entropy function satisfies the De Luca–Termini conditions.

PROOF

(1) If $\mu(x) = 1$ then $\log(\mu(x)) = 0$, otherwise $\mu(x) = 0$ (since μ is crisp). Hence the product expression $\mu(x)\log(\mu(x))$ is zero for all x.
(2) By differentiation, the maximum value of S occurs when $\mu(x)$ is a constant.
(3) This is left as an exercise to the reader.
(4) This is obvious from the definition and the commutativity of addition.

EXERCISES:

(1) Prove that $d(\mu) \geqslant d(\text{Int}(\mu))$.
(2) Which is fuzzier; μ or its normalization?
(3) Compare the entropies of the following hedges with a base fuzzy set. VERY, FAIRLY (power versions), VERY, FAIRLY (shift versions).
(4) This is a hard exercise. What additional axioms are required to fully characterize the entropy as a measure of fuzziness?

Several other measures have been proposed which satisfy the above conditions. One of the most useful is due to Yager and uses the idea of a Hamming distance; see [222]. However the systems theoretic implications of entropy make it an attractive metric. Interesting questions arise about the entropy of fuzzy systems as they evolve autonomously in time.

The next concept to exercise us concerns degrees of fuzziness also. However, this time we ask about the fuzziness of the structure of the notion of a fuzzy set itself. An *ultrafuzzy* set is one whose membership values are themselves fuzzy sets. In other words, given sets X and Y, an ultrafuzzy set is a function

$$\mu : X \to \tilde{P}(Y)$$

where $\tilde{P}(Y)$ denotes the set of fuzzy sets on Y. When $Y = X$ these are called level-2 fuzzy sets, and when $Y = I = [0, 1]$ we speak of type-2 fuzzy sets. These definitions can be generalized recursively to type-m and level-m fuzzy sets.

It is possible to define generalizations of the set-theoretic operations we have already met to ultrafuzzy sets, although it is not altogether straightforward. For details see [59] or [222].

The application of ultrafuzzy sets concerns the notion of fuzzy functions between sets; functions such as inclusion or those representing the passage of time are particularly important. In general, the fuzzification of mathematical concepts in this way is performed by utilizing the Extension Principle which we will meet in the next chapter. So far they have had little relevance in knowledge engineering, so we now return to practical issues for the remainder of this chapter.

5.3.6   Possibility theory, probability and certainty measures

In this section we compare fuzzy logic in the guise of possibility theory with the theory of probability, with which it is often confused. We also show that fuzzy measures incorporate and generalize various other theories of uncertainty. In particular we consider Shafer's belief functions [244] and Shackle's consonant belief functions [241]. This provides a justification for the use of fuzzy logic in expert systems.

In classical probability theory, the addition of probabilities in the continuous case depends on the development of a theory of integration in which limits are freely interchangeable with integrals (infinite sums), and this in turn depends on the development of a measure theory. A probability measure is a function π from σ-algebra (generally thought of as the power set of some set) $P(X)$ to $[0, 1]$, satisfying the following properties:

(PM1) $\pi(X) = 1$
(PM2) For every disjoint sequence of sets A_i in $P(X)$

$$\pi\left(\bigcup_{i \in N} A_i\right) = \sum_{i=1}^{\infty} \pi(A_i)$$

N is the set of natural numbers. Clearly $\pi(\varnothing) = 0$.

If we relax the additivity condition, we can define a *fuzzy measure* as a function satisfying the following conditions:

(FM1) $\pi(\varnothing) = 0; \pi(X) = 1$
(FM2) $\forall\ A, B \in P(X)$, if $A \subseteq B$ then $\pi(A) \leqslant \pi(B)$ \hfill (monotonicity)
(FM3) If $\forall\ i \in N$, $A_i \in P(X)$ and $\{A_{ij}\}$ is a monotonic sequence $\{A_1 \subseteq A_2 \subseteq \ldots \subseteq A_n \subseteq \ldots)$
then

$$\lim_{i \to \infty} \pi(A_i) = \pi\left(\lim_{i \to \infty} A_i\right)$$

\hfill (continuity)

A probability measure is then just a special case of a fuzzy measure.

A *belief function* is a measure on X for which

(BF1) $\pi(\emptyset)=0$; $\pi(X)=1$; $A\in P(X)$ $0\leqslant\pi(A)\leqslant 1$;
(BF2) $\forall A_i\in P(X)$ we have

$$\pi(A_1\cup A_2\cup\ldots\cup A_n)\geqslant\sum_{i=1}^n\pi(A_i)-\sum_{i<j}\pi(A_i\cap A_j)$$
$$+\cdots+(-1)^{n+1}\pi(A_1\cap A_2\cap\ldots\cap A_n)$$

$\pi(A)$ is interpreted as the degree of belief that an element belongs to A. Since $\pi(A)+\pi(\text{not}A)\leqslant 1$, a lack of belief in $x\in A$ does not necessarily imply a stronger belief in $x\in\text{not}A$. A probability measure is a belief function, and a belief function is a fuzzy measure. Belief functions are discussed by Shafer [244].

Shackle [241] defines a special case of a belief function called a *consonant belief function* where $\pi(A)$ is to be interpreted as the degree to which one may be surprised to find that $x\in A$. The conditions are:

(CB1) $\pi(\emptyset)=0$; $\pi(X)=1$;
(CB2) $\pi(A\cap B)=\min(\pi(A),\pi(B))$.

A further specialization of consonant belief functions are *certainty measures*, which satisfy:

(CM1) $\exists C\subseteq X$ such that $\pi(A)=1$ if $A\supseteq C$ and $\pi(A)=0$ otherwise.

Shafer and Dempster introduced *plausibility measures* which are measures satisfying:

(PM1) $\pi(\emptyset)=0$; $\pi(X)=1$.
(PM2) $\forall A_i\subseteq X$

$$\pi(A_1\cap A_2\cap\ldots\cap A_n)\geqslant\sum_{i=1}^n\pi(A_i)-\sum_{i<j}\pi(A_i\cup A_j)$$
$$+\cdots+(-1)^{n+1}\pi(A_1\cup A_2\cup\ldots\cup A_n)$$

The belief functions found in MYCIN, EMYCIN and IBM's ESE shell are similar, but not identical, to the above. In particular they range over the interval $[-1,1]$ rather than $[0,1]$. Also they admit no calculus of distributions as do all the measures presented in this section.

Lastly we define *possibility measures*, due originally to Zadeh, as measures for which:

(PS1) $\pi(\emptyset)=0$; $\pi(X)=1$;
(PS2) For any family $\{A_i\}$ of subsets of X, $\pi(\bigcup_i A_i)=\sup_i\pi(A_i)$.

A possibility measure with certain additional conditions can be made into a belief function. A possibility measure on finite X is a plausibility measure, which in turn is a fuzzy measure.

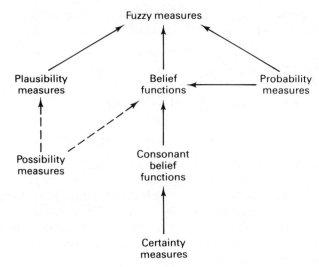

Fig. 5.24   Uncertainty measures

Figure 5.24 summarizes the relationships between the measures we have introduced. For proofs of the relationships see Dubois and Prade [59]. The dotted lines indicate that extra conditions are required for the 'is-a' link to hold.

A possibility measure can be constructed from a normal fuzzy set by setting $\pi(A) = \sup_{x \in A} \mu(x)$. The reverse process is also usually possible. Thus we can interpret fuzzy set theory as a theory of possibility, and indeed see its place among other theories of uncertainty. Dubois and Prade point out that, by analogy with modal logic (see Chapter 6) we can interpret a consonant belief function as the dual notion of a *necessity measure*.

Using fuzzy measures it is possible to develop a theory of integration (due to Sugeno), conditional possibilities and the analogue of Bayes's Theorem. This has not yet, to our knowledge been applied in expert systems. Yager [249] has introduced the idea of possibilistic production systems, and given a heuristic to minimize the cost of developing the search tree in find a goal.

Let us now turn to the comparison of possibility theory with probability theory. Zadeh put it like this in 1977.

> 'Intuitively, possibility relates to our perception of the degree of feasibility or ease of attainment whereas probability is associated with a degree of likelihood, belief, frequency or proportion.'

That is, possibility focuses on the imprecision of perception and language. Also, some event can simultaneously have a low probability and a high possibility (but not *vice versa*). For example, it is very possible that I can stop typing now and make a cup of tea, but since I have just had one it is very unlikely.

The primitive notion in probability and statistics is that of an event. Nowakowska [247] introduces a complex theory of events based both on fuzzy sets theory and on the theory of stochastic processes. She points out that, especially in the social sciences, an event is a change in some fragment of the world which may be perceived as fuzzy, such as an opinion or attitude. Her theory of subjective and objective time shows that humans may perceive the precedence even of crisp events differently from time to time. Thus probability theory alone is inadequate for the explication of events. The mathematical models she proposes have application in cognitive psychology and in semiotics, but have not yet been thoroughly tested experimentally. However, this work does show clearly the interpenetration that is possible between the two subjects and their complementary nature.

Given some predicate p, the possibility that an element x satisfies p may be expressed as a fuzzy set μ. Outside the support of μ, x cannot be p. In this way any fuzzy set induces a possibility distribution on the values of the predicate. For an example, let p be 'Simon is young', where young is a fuzzy set. The fuzzy restriction implied by 'young' acts as an elastic constraint on the values which may be assumed by the underlying variable. We can now translate the expression into a possibility distribution:

$$\pi(\text{Age}(\text{Simon})) = \text{'young'}.$$

We give one of the classic examples (taken in this case from Zimmermann [222]) to finally distinguish a probability from a possibility distribution. Consider the statement 'Hans ate x eggs for breakfast'. We associate both kinds of distribution with the variable x as follows:

n	1	2	3	4	5	6	7	8	9	10
$\pi_x(n)$	1	1	1	1	0.8	0.6	0.4	0.2	0.1	0
$P_x(n)$	0.1	0.8	0.1	0	0	0	0	0	0	0

where $\pi_x(n)$ represents the possibility that the statement might be true and $P_x(n)$ represents its probability of being true. The probability distribution could have been determined by observing Hans at breakfast on a large number of occasions, say 100. The corresponding experiment to determine the possibility distribution is less humane, since it involves stuffing poor old Hans full to the point of illness and finally mortality, but only on one occasion for each integer. Thus probability and possibility give totally different results.

The application of the foregoing in knowledge-based systems is that fuzzy set theory provides a sound mathematical basis for modelling various kinds of uncertainty. No independence assumptions are required and the calculus is highly computationally efficient when it comes to propagating uncertainty through inference nets. Other methods of handling uncertainty are not excluded but should be mixed in with great care.

5.4 SUMMARY

This chapter introduced the basic ideas of fuzzy sets and their mathematical underpinnings. After a few historical remarks and an informal, heuristic introduction, we introduced the most widespread version of fuzzy set theory based on min and max operations. Other systems were briefly mentioned and evaluated. It was shown how fuzzy relations and the compositional rule of inference could be used to build fuzzy production systems.

The entropy of a fuzzy set was introduced as a means of measuring fuzziness and ultrafuzzy sets were mentioned.

Next we discussed the relationships between various theories of uncertainty and compared, in particular, possibility and probability theory.

In the next chapter we will look at, *inter alia*, fuzzy logic in more detail.

5.5 FURTHER READING

Textbooks on fuzzy set theory are fairly scarce. Dubois and Prade [59] is undoubtedly the most comprehensive available. Zimmermann [222] is more elementary and is packed with worked examples. We have drawn on these books in the production of this chapter and therefore they are the most natural choices for further reading. Another invaluable source of knowledge of current developments in fuzzy mathematics is the journal *Fuzzy Sets and Systems*.

More specialized interests will be catered for by Schmucker [250] which applies fuzzy set theory to risk analysis and to the building of expert systems in that field, Nowakowska [247] which constructs fuzzy models of cognitive processes and Kandel and Lee which treats of applications to switching and automata theory. For a more general view readers may find Negoita [157] of interest.

Various commercially available computer systems exist which utilize fuzzy logic. It is worthwhile examining their documentation if it can be obtained. The FLOPS system is described in Buckley *et al.* [248] as well as in documentation available from the authors. ICL Knowledge Engineering, in Manchester, can supply information on REVEAL, and Creative Logic Ltd, at Brunel Science Park, Uxbridge, produce the LEONARDO product. Many other product vendors claim to incorporate fuzzy logic, but this usually refers to the use of certainty factors or Bayesian probabilities.

Zadeh's most significant papers on Fuzzy Set theory and related issues have been, most usefully, collected together in a single volume [146] which is highly recommended to anyone with an interest in the subject. Particularly pertinent papers by Zadeh for our coverage in this book are [215, 216, 255]. Norwich and Turksen's work [164] on stochastic fuzziness shows how probability and possibility theory can interact usefully.

Part four
Decision

6

Classical, non-standard and fuzzy logics

'There foam'd rebellious logic, gagg'd and bound'
Game of Logic, Lewis Carroll

6.1 HISTORICAL INTRODUCTION

'Philosophy misses an advantage enjoyed by the other sciences. It cannot like them rest the existence of its objects on the natural admissions of consciousness, nor can it assume that its method of cognition, either for starting or for continuing, is one already accepted.'

So says Hegel in the 'lesser' Logic [92]. Hegel, of course, placed logic at the root of philosophy and would, we are sure, have agreed that the above statement applied to it especially.

Logic begins, in the Western world at least, with Herakleitos of Ephesos (c. 500 BC) whose conception of the natural order as an organic unity of mind and matter presupposes a distinctive mode of reasoning, which for him was part of the semi-mystical *logos*. Herakleitos's views are strongly paralleled in the works of Lao-Tsu (c. 500 BC), in the *I Ching* or classic of changes and much of early Confucian thought. Both traditions are concerned with the whole of life: man as well as nature, being as well as thought.

His views were emphatically rejected by his contemporary, Parmenides of Elea, who asserted that, contrary to the evidence of the senses, the universe must be immutable – *ex nihil, nihil fit*. The logical dilemma this implied was first addressed by the atomicists, Leucippus and Democritus, who assigned a reality to the concept of 'not being'. The Elean view culminated a hundred years later with the founding by Zeno of the anti-Pythagorean school of Sophists.

Plato, who owed a debt to the reasoning of both Herakleitos and Parmenides, can, arguably, be said to be the founder of formal logic in that he was the first to consider logic as an 'autonomous science with the task of ascertaining the supreme principles of affirmative and negative propositions' [195]. In other words Plato was the first to abstract the laws of thought from the concrete wholeness of nature in a systematic manner. His pupil Aristotle is usually credited with this because of his development of the syllogism, and it was this abstraction that made further developments possible. Aristotle noticed that certain abstract rules were involved in argument that was considered to possess either truth or practical efficacy. The famous syllogism:

All men are mortal.
Socrates is a man.
Hence, Socrates is mortal.

is an example of one such general principle of reasoning which applies not only to Socrates and to men, but to many propositions about the objects of the world and their properties.

During the Dark Ages from the sack of Alexandria to the early Renaissance, the Graeco-Roman traditions of logic were kept alive principally in the writings of Boethius (d. AD 524). The teaching of the seven 'liberal arts' was divided into the quadrivium of arithmetic, geometry, astronomy and music, and the trivium of grammar, rhetoric and logic. Number was held to govern both proportion and the transition from 'non-being' to 'being', and took precedence over logic. The emergence of 'scholastic teaching' in the twelfth century, following Abelard and Thomas Aquinas, reversed the priority and placed logic first among the arts. Hugo of St. Victor said it 'provides a means of distinguishing between modes of argument and the trains of reasoning themselves' [130]. As always, there was a vigorously held opposing view: Roger Bacon, clinging to the Ptolemaic synthesis, continued to give pride of place amongst the arts to mathematics.

But, in general, up to the nineteenth century logic was principally considered as a branch of philosophy. The medieval Scholastics used logic to prove the existence of God. Kant under the influence of the anti-clerical ideas of the French Revolution extended Aristotle's categories both to end the influence of Scholasticism and to provide deeper insights into the structure of perceptions, thus laying the foundations with Locke and Hume for much of what passes today as the scientific method; i.e., modern Empiricism. The influence of Kant on modern logicians such as W. V. Quine is still very strong. Just as Kant countered the repressive traditions of the schoolmen, Hegel found Kant's separation of man from nature (the Thing-in-itself or *Ding an sich*) and rigid timeless categories equally oppressive, and in one way returned us full circle to the views of the Pre-Socratic Greeks. In a sense, Hegel's work on logic, including in this the classification of all syllogisms and its application to the categories of Nature, sums up all previous development of logic in the West and East. However, many felt that logic was a completed science; there was nothing left to do.

New developments in logic had to wait for the intervention of mathematicians who were seeking answers to their own esoteric problems. Leibnitz had earlier dreamed of a symbolic calculus which could encompass all mathematical knowledge, but it is now generally accepted that the founders of modern formal logic were Boole (whose contribution became Set Theory), De Morgan, and

Jevons the economist who was responsible for the ideas of marginal utility theory. In 1879 Gottlob Frege published his *Begriffsschrift* which is truly the start of modern logic in that it introduced the propositional calculus and quantifiers in a form that while dissimilar to modern notations is recognizable. Frege (pronounced fray-ger) was the first person to abstract logic and treat it as entirely separate from mathematics. Development then proceeded apace. The list of significant contributors is too long to give here but includes such names as Peano, Cantor, Russell, Brouwer, Heyting, Kolmogorov and Gödel. For a survey of mathematical logic the reader is directed to reference [93] whose introductions and preface give an excellent history up to 1931.

Mathematical logic moved away from many of the concerns of philosophy in this period. It was concerned, like mathematics, with abstract objects and structures, but also with the language used to describe these objects, their definition and the logical rules the language obeys. Because of this restricted and highly abstract context it was possible to work in a world where propositions need only be interpreted as 'true' or 'false'. Aristotle's classical laws of identity ($A = A$), contradiction, and the excluded middle came into their inheritance; the objects of logic were fixed and immutable. If a statement was not false then it must be true and if a false conclusion resulted from a sound argument then at least one premise (although this does not tell us which one) must be false. Russell himself pointed out that this related little to the world of men and affairs.

But, at least for the purposes of mathematicians, formal logic was thought to be adequate and complete.

Unfortunately, many philosophers and scientists, impressed by the elegance and success of the theory and under the influence of the prevailing Kantian or Neo-Kantian views, began to apply formal logic to arguments about natural science and language. The poverty of theory in many of the social and human sciences may be directly attributed to this misapplication of logic. Nowhere was the damage so apparent as in the new science of political economy wherein the followers (in some cases the epigones) of Petty, Smith and Ricardo worked with the immutable categories of Land, Labour, Capital, and Rent as though they were fixed by natural law rather than constantly determined by history. With this in view it is perhaps less surprising to see men like Jevons and Keynes active in both areas. Furthermore, as the nineteenth century progressed mathematicians were themselves beginning to find intractable problems with these systems of formal logic, and it is at this point that we begin to observe serious schisms in the mathematical community culminating, in our view, with the split between Brouwer and Hilbert or between Constructivism/Intuitionism and Formalism.

On the one hand Russell found that if severe restrictions were not imposed on the type of objects one could discuss, one came up against the same kind of paradoxes which had bedevilled the ancient Greeks, such as: the set of all sets is both a set and not a set. The ever practical Greeks had eventually shrugged their shoulders and learned to live with the paradoxes; otherwise perhaps we would not have all learned 'fractions' in school – a two thousand year old hangover from the lack of a notation to handle incommensurables. This particular paradox and other problems in the foundations of Analysis led to the development of the theory of types and higher-order logics.

The paradoxes of mathematics, both those which led the Greeks to abandon certain lines of research and the modern ones which have had the opposite effect, are all essentially concerned with the problem of infinity. Marx, in his *Mathematical Manuscripts* [251], draws attention to the inadequacy of the notion of limit found in both Newton and Leibnitz. Not until D'Alembert and Cantor did this notion begin to be clarified. In the idea of a limit we have a most vivid illustration of the tension between absolute and relative truth which appears to be behind many controversies in theoretical physics [233].

On the other hand, Brouwer showed that the use of the principle of the excluded middle in certain arguments led to problems and this led to the birth of the Intuitionist school of mathematics, which questions not only the Aristotelian laws but also the applicability of two-valued interpretations of logical calculuses and the very notion of proof. Finally (or at least finally for the time being), Gödel put the last nail in the coffin of the Hilbert Programme, which aimed to base all of mathematics on first-order logic, by publishing his two famous incompleteness theorems.

Since then we have witnessed the development of a large number of extensions to and deviations from standard logic, many of which are surveyed and discussed in this chapter. In particular we focus on the development of Fuzzy Logics and various other non-standard logics which have applications in Artificial Intelligence. This is an area of research wherein the subject matter (models of human reasoning) is not so conveniently abstract as to allow the use of purely two-valued, first-order logic. In fact, some researchers in AI are beginning, perhaps unconsciously, to echo the words of Hegel at the head of this section; the study of the human mind cannot rest on logics already fixed and accepted [189]. Its richness requires the use of many logical formalisms and some formalisms that logicians might not call logic at all. This seems to be related in some way to Gödel's theorem which might be very loosely paraphrased by saying: however good a logical system is, there is always something which it cannot quite manage to do!

For us logic is the analysis of all human methods of purposeful thought and rational practice. No single formal system of logic as yet encompasses this broad definition, but then no single theory can explain human intelligence either.

Logic, if defined as the science of the process of thinking, is concerned with the process of cognition. This remark has two interesting consequences for students of artificial intelligence. First, the so-called cognitive movement in psychology is seen to be profoundly important. Knowledge must be seen as a *process*. Secondly, the study of epistemology is raised to a new level of practical significance for logic itself. We know of no modern philosopher who has addressed these problems in a unified manner. In fact the only reference which makes these points in any clear way is [232].

The remainder of this chapter will deal with the logics which are of use in the study of Artificial Intelligence and especially with the theory of Approximate Reasoning and Fuzzy Logics. We will not burden the reader with any more history, but instead caution the reader to look for the inner contradictions and the path of development of each theory; in that sense our treatment is an essentially historical one. We look at connections between the various logical systems dealt with and briefly mention some of the links with computer science which have been noted of late. Lastly, we introduce some mathematical constructions which are important to logic and which might in the future provide a genuine unification of the theory. These sections (principally 6.6) may be omitted at first reading. We have tried to write with the general reader in mind, but the dictates of space sometimes mean that they may be difficult for the reader who is not, as mathematicians arrogantly put it, mathematically mature. The references at the end of the section will provide all the background required.

6.2 CLASSICAL FIRST-ORDER LOGIC

This section introduces the notion of a model in the sense used by formal logicians and attempts to give some intuitive feel for what it means to say that a theory is 'first order'.

The building blocks of first order logic are the connectives $\wedge$ (and), $\vee$ (or), $\neg$ (not), $\Rightarrow$ (implies), the equality symbol $=$, the quantifiers $\forall$ (for all), $\exists$ (there exists) and a sequence of variables $a, b, c, d, \ldots, a_1, b_1, c_1, \ldots$. We allow also pairs of brackets to help the formulae remain legible.

The phrase 'first order' indicates that to apply the logic to a particular topic we will have to supply some additional non-logical symbols. For example, to apply the logic to Set Theory we have to introduce the membership relation symbol $\in$ (belongs to). In general, we would introduce a set of relation symbols, function symbols and constant symbols.

In first-order logic the quantifiers can be applied only to the elements of the domain of discourse; e.g. in set theory to the elements but not to sets themselves. Second-order logic allows us to quantify over sets and some functions, third-order lets in sets of functions, and so on.

The other thing that needs to be said in relation to first-order systems is that some mathematical theories and objects can be axiomatized with a finite set of first-order axioms but others (for example the notion of a torsion free group) need an infinite list of first-order axioms to characterize them. Yet other theories admit no first-order axiomatization at all. In particular the familiar axioms which characterize the real number system $\mathscr{R}$ are not first order and it can be shown that there is no such set of axioms. The Archimedean axiom for example states that

$$\forall x \exists n (x \leqslant n)$$

This is not first order because the existential quantifier ranges over the real natural numbers and not over the elements of an arbitrary model. We will be more precise about models shortly. As an example of a first-order sentence consider the following statement from algebra

$$\forall x \forall y \forall z \qquad (x + (y + z) = (x + y) + z) \qquad (1)$$

This sentence is first order because x, y and z and for that matter $+$ are arbitrary symbols of an abstract language. Throughout the remainder of this chapter the reader should be alert for higher-order sentences and try to get a feel for what looks like a first-order statement on sight, as it were.

Thus, we have the notion of a formal language chosen to suit some particular purpose. A *model* of this language is an assignment to each variable and constant of the language some abstract object, usually an element of a set, M which takes relation symbols to relations in the Cartesian product of that set

$$M^n = M \times M \times M \times M \times \ldots \times M$$

and function symbols to functions

$$M^n \rightarrow M.$$

The next idea we will need is that of a *free* variable, that is a variable not within the scope of any quantifier in some given expression. For example, in the formula

$$x + y = 0 \qquad (2)$$

x and y are free whereas in

$$\exists y (x + y = 0) \qquad (3)$$

only x is free, and in

$$\forall x (\exists y (x + y = 0)) \qquad (4)$$

both x and y are *bound*. A *first-order sentence* is a formula without any free variables. A *formula* is any expression constructed from the atomic formulae of the language L using quantifiers and the propositional connectives. An *atomic formula* is an expression constructed from the terms of L using a relation symbol (including $=$), where the *terms* are those expressions constructed from the variables and constant using function symbols. We will not bother here to formalize the definition of free variables, since the intuitive notion will be sufficient for our purposes in this book. The interested reader is recommended the excellent exposition of Barwise [19] for further details.

We will need the notion of an *assignment* of L in a model M; that is a function g from the variables of L into M. It is then possible to extend this notion to all the terms of L. We can now say whether the assignment g *satisfies* the formula ϕ in the model M.

This is written as

$$M \models_g \phi$$

a notation distantly deriving from Frege's original paper [93].

We think of g as semantically interpreting the meaning of the syntactic expression in the world given by M. For example, if M is the world of integers (arithmetic with whole numbers) then formula (4) above *means* 'every number corresponds to a negative one with the same magnitude' whereas in L itself the plus sign has no meaning, it is merely a symbol. If ϕ is a sentence then the truth or falsity of

$$M \models_g \phi$$

is totally independent of the particular g chosen and we write $M \models \phi$ and say that M is a *model* of ϕ. M is a model of a set Φ of sentences if $M \models \phi$ for all $\phi \in \Phi$. Later we are going to need to know that a class of models for a language L is *elementary* if there is a finite set of first-order sentences of L such that every member in the class is a model of Φ.

6.2.2 Propositional and predicate calculus

It is customary to split first-order logic into two parts; the first part deals with the connectives:

$$\wedge, \vee, \neg \text{ and } \Rightarrow$$

and is called propositional logic. The other, harder, part deals with quantification and equality, and is called predicate logic.

If we pose ourselves the question of how the truth or falsity of a propositional formula depends on the truth or falsity of its component atomic formulae, then it is natural to ask whether there are any formulae whose truth is independent of the values of their components; are there any tautologies?

We now introduce two new symbols t and f to be thought of as representing 'true' and 'false'. A *valuation* for a set of formulae P is a function v from P to the set $\{t, f\}$. By induction, we only need to define v on the atomic formulae and note the rules obeyed by the connectives; e.g.

$$v(\neg p) = f \text{ if } v(p) = t$$
$$v(\neg p) = t \text{ if } v(p) = f$$

Rather than write down all these conditions it is easier to represent them in a *truth table* as follows.

p	q	$\neg p$	$p \wedge q$	$p \vee p$	$p \Rightarrow q$
t	t	f	t	t	t
t	f	f	f	t	f
f	t	t	f	t	t
f	f	t	f	f	t

The method of truth tables gives a computational mechanism for determining the truth of any formula which we will explain by illustration. Let us for example express Aristotle's law of contradiction as

$$\neg\,(p \wedge \neg\, q)$$

and expand its truth table as follows.

p	$\neg\,p$	$p \wedge \neg\, q$	$\neg\,(p \wedge \neg\, p)$
t	f	f	t
f	t	f	t

First we work from right to left by breaking down the proposition and then left to right using the basic truth tables for the connectives to propagate the truths for every possible combination of t and f for the prime constituents (p in this case). To make the method clear let us now analyse the proposition

$$(\neg\,(p \wedge \neg\, q) \wedge q) \Rightarrow p$$

p	q	$\neg\,q$	$p \wedge \neg\, q$	$\neg\,(p \wedge \neg\, q)$	$\neg\,(p \wedge \neg\, q) \wedge q$	$(\neg\,(p \wedge \neg\, q) \wedge q) \Rightarrow p$
t	t	f	f	t	t	t
t	f	t	t	f	f	t
f	t	f	f	t	t	f
f	f	t	f	t	f	t

In this case the proposition is true unless p is false and q is true (simultaneously). The alert reader will have noticed that the law of contradiction is a tautology of the propositional calculus: i.e. it is always true regardless of the value of p and q.

EXERCISES

Using the method of truth tables prove that the following are tautologies:

1. $p \vee \neg\, p$ (law of the excluded middle)
2. $\neg\,\neg\,)p \Leftrightarrow p$ (law of double negation)
3. $\neg\,(p \wedge q) \Leftrightarrow (\neg\, p \vee \neg\, q)$
                 (de Morgan's laws)
   $\neg\,(p \vee q) \Leftrightarrow (\neg\, p \wedge \neg\, q)$
4. $(((p \Rightarrow q) \Rightarrow r) \wedge (\neg\, r \Rightarrow q)) \Rightarrow (p \Rightarrow r)$

Hint: You can argue your way out of doing the second part of 3 with a little thought.

We say that a set of formulae A is *consistent* if there is a *valuation*

$$v : A \rightarrow \{t, f\}$$

such that $v(p) = t$ for all $p \in A$. It can be shown [19] that for any model M, any set of sentences true in M is consistent.

The next question we ask is 'What is a proof?' To answer this one we give a definition of a *formal system* as a language L, and set of *axioms* which latter must include all tautologies, all formulae of the form

$$\forall x\phi(x)\Rightarrow\phi(t) \quad \text{and} \quad \phi(x)\Rightarrow\exists x\phi(x)$$

along with some axioms for equality which we will not need to state explicitly here. We also need some *rules of inference.* The simplest of the ones we choose is called, somewhat obscurely, *Modus Ponens*:

$$\frac{(\phi\Rightarrow\psi),\ \phi}{\psi}$$

read as "from 'phi implies psi' and 'phi' we infer 'psi'". This rule will be referred to in more detail in the chapter on Inference Methods along with a more informal treatment of some others. We also have the rules of generalization or introduction: If x is bound in ψ then

$$\frac{\phi\Rightarrow\psi(x)}{\phi\Rightarrow\forall y\psi(y)},\quad \frac{\psi(x)\Rightarrow\phi}{\exists y\psi(y)\Rightarrow\phi}.$$

For a good reliable introduction to a more general concept of formal systems see [99]. In some contexts a formal system is referred to as a Post Production System after Post [98]. We have already met production systems in Chapter 2 when we discussed knowledge-based systems.

A small warning at this point. It is easy for us to confuse inference with implication because of our habits of natural language. This should be strenuously avoided here where implication represents a relation between symbols and inference is a 'higher level' relation between statements. Formal logicians have to learn some of the blind rule-following stupidity of machines to retain this separation even if they remain geniuses in other respects.

A *proof* of ϕ from a set of axioms A in a formal system is a finite sequence $\phi_1,\ \phi_2,\ \dots,\ \phi_{n-1},\ \phi_n$ of formulae such that $\phi_n=\phi$ and each of which is an axiom or follows from a lower numbered axiom by one of the three rules of inference. If it is provable we write

$$A\vdash\phi$$

As we have indicated there are other ways of constructing formal systems than the one given here. In Chapter 7 we will look more closely at the whole area of inference methods and rules of inference with an eye on the possibilities for computer automated reasoning. In particular the reader should be aware of the other possible inference rules known as *Modus Tollens* and the Resolution Principle:

Modus Tollens	Resolution
$p\Rightarrow q$	$p\vee q$
$\neg q$	$p\Rightarrow r$
$\neg p$	$q\vee r$

EXERCISE

Write down the definition of a formal system and proof where Resolution replaces *Modus Ponens*. Are there any advantages or disadvantages? For a discussion of the answer to this exercise see [82].

We now state two important results without proof, referring the reader to [19] or [148] for details and to [99] for explanation of the proofs.

(a) *Gödel's Completeness Theorem*

$$A \models \phi \text{ if and only if } A \vdash \phi$$

Recall from 6.2 that $A \models \phi$ means that ϕ is true in all models of A. Thus the theorem may be read: 'ϕ is true in all models of A precisely when ϕ is a theorem of A'.

(b) *Compactness Theorem*

If A is any set of first-order axioms then if every finite subset A' of A has a model, then A has a model.

The word compact here will not mean much unless you know that it is borrowed from another branch of mathematics, Topology, where a formally similar theorem is related to the idea of functions being bounded in some sense.

(c) *The Gödel Incompleteness Theorems*

These are:
(1) Let T be a formal theory containing arithmetic. Then there is a sentence ϕ which asserts its own unprovability and is such that
  (i) If T is consistent, ϕ is unprovable;
  (ii) If T is ω-consistent, then ϕ is unprovable.
(2) Let T be a consistent formal theory containing arithmetic. Then the sentence
     'T is consistent'
   is unprovable.

Remark on notation and abuse of language:
In the jargon used by mathematicians the phrase 'if and only if' is the equivalent of 'implies and is implied by'. Mathematicians are traditionally lazy (why look for elegant proofs otherwise?) so they usually write just iff. If you see 'iff' in this book it is not a spelling mistake iff the proofreaders were not mathematicians. We have warned already about confusing ⇒ with inference and yet we sometimes still write ⇔ for iff, although we will try not to do so in this chapter. A very famous but, in fact, non-existent French mathematician dubbed this behaviour *abus de langage*. We nevertheless hope the reader does not find our language abusive!

Although we quote the theorem in its classical form for completeness, ω-consistency need not concern us here. The interested reader can look at Smorynski [191].

The key point is that Hilbert's programme, to show that mathematical systems which used abstract, non-constructive (i.e. infinite) methods could be justified by purely finite methods, is overthrown. How can one prove the consistency of the richer, abstract, system when T cannot even prove its own consistency?

We have seen in this very brief introduction to classical logic, therefore, that it is not a topic without serious problems and paradoxes arising from its first-order nature. We will soon turn to other problems arising from its being two-valued.

The only point that remains in our discussion of classical logic is to examine its relation to set theory. It is this relationship which gives rise to the term Boolean Logic which we shall use from now on since 'classical' is really the wrong word. After all, the Greeks and Romans would have been horrified by the restricted formalities we have described.

The reader has already had an introduction to set theory in the previous chapter and will understand terms like union and intersection and can draw a Venn diagram if pressed. References taking the reader from the very beginning of the subject to well beyond what is set out here are [185], and [137].

The formal theory of sets includes the membership relation symbol in the language and a number of axioms. The actual choice of axioms is the subject of a debate which we shall not enter, nor shall we list all the axioms. We merely give an important example of such an axiom. The Power Set axiom allows us to form the set of all subsets of any given set. It states

$$\exists p \forall y (y \in p \Leftrightarrow \forall z (z \in x \Rightarrow z \in y))$$

or in a more anodyne and familiar terminology

$$\{y : y \subseteq x\} \text{ exists and is a set}$$

EXERCISE

Recalling our earlier remarks about abstract symbols such as y and p, consider why x is free in the above formulae and explain how the notation $\{\ :\ \}$ is connected with quantification.

Set theory is a model for the first-order predicate calculus but it is not elementary; there is no finite set of first-order axioms [111]. Lawvere [127] has shown however that there is an elementary higher order model. We will return to this model in our discussion of category theory. Because of the intimate relation between logic and its model in set theory we often confuse the two from now on. For instance, if we have a proposition such as 'x is a man' we will confuse this with the set of all men. Another useful equivalent is the characteristic function of a set X which is the function $\chi : X \to \{0, 1\}$ given by

$$\chi(x) = 1 \text{ iff } x \in X$$

We have now returned to the problem of truth as soon as we think of the symbols

0 and 1 as standing in place of t and f. Every set is uniquely determined by its characteristic function. For example the set $\{x \in \mathcal{R} : 0 \leqslant x \leqslant 4)$ can be represented by the graph of its characteristic function.

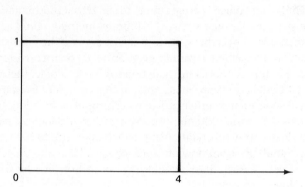

Fig. 6.1   Numbers less than 4

It is important to note that the power set of any set has the structure of a Boolean lattice and thus (by the Stone Representation Theorem [107]) a Boolean algebra. This gives us a powerful algebraic technique for handling the tautologies of logic. We give some definitions to make this clearer.

A partially ordered set or *poset* is a set X together with a partial order relation $\subseteq$ such that $\forall\ x,\ y,\ z \in X$ we have

(PO1) $x \subseteq x$ Reflexivity
(PO2)   If $x \subseteq y$ and $y \subseteq x$ then $x = y$ Antisymmetry
(PO3)   If $x \subseteq y$ and $y \subseteq z$ then $x \subseteq z$ Transitivity

In any poset we define the *meet* of x and y:

$$x \wedge y = \{z \in X : z \subseteq x \text{ and } z \subseteq y)$$

the *join*:

$$x \vee y = \{y \in X : z \subseteq x \text{ or } z \subseteq y\}$$

and the *complement* of x:

$$\neg x = \{y \in X : x \wedge y = 0 \text{ and } x \vee y = 1\}$$

where 0 and 1 are respectively the meet and join of all elements of X.

A *Boolean lattice* is a poset with 0 and 1 satisfying

$x \wedge x = x$ $x \vee x = x$
$x \wedge y = y \wedge x$ $x \vee y = y \vee x$
$x \wedge (y \wedge z) = (x \wedge y) \wedge z$ $x \vee (y \vee z) = (x \vee y) \vee z$
$x \wedge (x \vee y) = x \vee (x \wedge y) = x$
$x \subseteq y$ iff $x \wedge y = x$

$$x \subseteq y \text{ iff } x \vee y = y$$
$$x \wedge (y \vee z) = (x \wedge y) \vee (x \wedge z)$$
$$x \vee (y \wedge z) = (x \vee y) \wedge (x \vee z)$$
$$x \wedge \neg x = 0 \qquad\qquad x \vee \neg x = 1$$
$$\neg \neg x = x$$
$$\neg (x \wedge y) = \neg x \vee \neg y \qquad\qquad \neg (x \vee y) = \neg x \wedge \neg y$$
$$\text{and if } x \subseteq z \text{ then } x \vee (y \wedge z) = (x \vee y) \wedge z$$

EXERCISES

(1) Verify that the set of subsets of a set forms a Boolean lattice.
(2) Prove the tautologies of propositional calculus given in the earlier exercise using the above equations in place of the method of truth tables. Hint: ⇒ corresponds to ⊇.
(3) Show that if 0 and 1 exist then they are unique.

6.3 EXTENSIONS TO BOOLEAN LOGIC

Returning now to truth tables, let us examine the ways in which we can combine two propositional variables p and q. It is clear that there are exactly 16 possible truth tables for binary connections as follows

p	q	F A L S E	∧			E X C L ∨	$\Rightarrow_1$						$\Rightarrow_2$		T R U E
0	0	0	0	0	0	0	0	0	0	1	1	1	1	1	1	1	1
0	1	0	0	0	0	1	1	1	1	0	0	0	0	1	1	1	1
1	0	0	0	1	1	0	0	1	1	0	0	1	1	0	0	1	1
1	1	0	1	0	1	0	1	0	1	0	1	0	1	0	1	0	1

It is relatively simple to identify the ones corresponding to our intuitive ideas of the meaning of AND, inclusive and exclusive OR, NOT, TRUE and FALSE. Choosing an implication table is somewhat harder. If we choose 1101 ($\Rightarrow_2$) this looks like implies (and in fact is what we use) but has the curious property that if p is false then $p \Rightarrow q$ is true regardless of the truth value of q. So that 'the moon is made of green cheese' logically implies (in the propositional calculus) that 'zero is greater than one'. This is known as material implication and clearly is useless for handling contingent statements. Another choice might well be 1001 ($\Rightarrow_1$) which might be designated exclusive implication (Exercise: Why?). The difficulty here is that if p is false then we really do not have much information about q unless we

174 *Classical, non-standard and fuzzy logics*

already have settled on the appropriate truth tables. This is further a result of the fact that the word true is too general. Something can be necessarily true or possibly true. This observation led to the development of modal logics which include unary operators L (it is necessarily true that) and M (it is possibly true that) in the formal language. To interpret L and M however, truth tables are not sufficient. We need to extend our notion of model so that it includes a set P of 'possible worlds' and relate them formally to the function and relation symbols. This done, we can interpret Lp as valid if p is true in every possible world and Mp as valid if p is true in some possible world. We also need extra axioms:

$$Lp \Rightarrow p$$
$$L(p \Rightarrow q) \Rightarrow (Lp \Rightarrow Lq)$$

and extra inference rules such as

$$\frac{p}{Lp}$$

There are, in fact, several systems of modal logic referred to by such charming designations as T, S4 and S5. For an introduction to these see Zeman [220] or Haack [86].

There has been great disagreement over modal logics, some of it stemming from Aristotle's works on truth [97] and much from modern logical considerations. Russell, for example, insisted that the truth of a proposition could not admit any modality and that only propositional functions could have such properties. However, we have shown that the classical or Boolean methods are inadequate in some respects and modal logic is only one of the techniques which have been invented to overcome their shortcomings.

It turns out that modal logic has practical application. If our possible worlds are taken to represent the possible states of the store of an abstract computer we can develop a programming language based on modal logic, just as many conventional languages are based on Boolean logic. For a brief discussion of one such language see Turner [201].

It should be noted that modal logic and other extended logics involving extra operators are not truth-functional: i.e. the truth value of a formula cannot be derived solely from the truth values of its prime constituents.

There is however a totally different (perhaps complementary) way out of the dilemmas of Boolean logic. Modal logic is essentially a syntactic extension, bringing new symbols to the language. We can however retain the syntactic apparatus and extend the semantics. The easiest way to conceive of this is to allow the truth tables to take values other than 0 and 1 (or t and f if you prefer). The least perturbation, one would expect, should arise from the addition of one extra truth value. The problem then is how to interpret this extra symbol; is it 'unknown', 'half true', 'unprovable' or something else? Another problem relates to whether it is commensurate with the accepted notions of true and false.

Lukasiewitz [135] was concerned with contingent statements about the future.

This is related to Aristotle's refutation of the Master Argument of Diodorus which leads to Fatalism if we accept such statements as true or false. The argument is intimately related to the whole question of modality as is pointed out by Hintikka [97]. Such statements are given the value i, for indeterminate, but i can be interpreted in many ways as is discussed in Haack [86].

Compare Lukasiewitz's truth tables for three-valued logic

p	$\neg p$	$p \wedge q$	t	f	i	$p \vee q$	t	f	i	$p \Rightarrow q$	t	f	i
t	f	t	t	f	i	t	t	t	t	t	t	f	i
f	t	f	f	f	f	f	t	f	i	f	t	t	t
i	i	i	i	f	i	i	t	i	i	i	t	i	t

with those of two-valued logic written in this different layout:

p	$\neg p$	$p \wedge q$	t	f	$p \vee q$	t	f	$p \Rightarrow q$	t	f
t	f	t	t	f	t	t	t	t	t	f
f	t	f	f	f	f	t	f	f	t	t

It will be seen that the tables are identical for the two input values t and f.

The quantifiers can be viewed as infinite conjunction and disjunction and receive an interpretation in this way.

$$\forall x p(x) = \bigwedge_{x \in X} p(x) = \begin{cases} t \text{ if every } p(x) = t \\ f \text{ if some } p(x) = f \\ i \text{ otherwise} \end{cases}$$

$$\exists x p(x) = \bigvee_{x \in X} p(x) = \begin{cases} t \text{ if some } p(x) = t \\ f \text{ if some } p(x) = f \\ i \text{ otherwise} \end{cases}$$

where X is the set of variables of the language.

Other systems of three-valued logic due to Kleene [114] and Bochvar [26] exist with different truth tables and have a different interpretation for the third value as 'undecided' and 'meaningless' respectively.

It is particularly interesting that all these logics have a different implication operator. The attentive reader will recall that in the case of two-valued logic there were only 16 truth tables and even then it was hard to choose the correct one for implication. Now the choice becomes harder still because there are $(3^3)^3 = 19\,683$ possibilities. This, of course, makes it easier for the logic to represent richer forms of reality, but the mathematics gets correspondingly harder; as we have seen there are several interpretations for the third value. It is tempting to introduce fourth and fifth values or more. This further explodes the number of truth tables to the extent that we must look for other, usually algebraic, means of verifying truisms. The natural conclusion of this exposure to temptation is to introduce infinite valued logic.

Before moving on, let us try to see a common pattern in the two and three place truth tables. A little inspection and thought will show that if we replace t and f with 0 and 1 and i with the numerical value 0.5 we can say that

$$v(p \wedge q) = \min(v(p), v(q))$$

in the case of both Boolean and Lukasiewitz logics, where v is the valuation function.

Similarly we observe

$$v(p \vee q) = \max(v(p), v(q))$$
$$v(\neg p) = 1 - v(p)$$

Taking $\neg p \vee q$ as the definition of $\Rightarrow$ gives us the machinery to construct truth tables for all finite and infinite valued logics of the Lukasiewitz type. To do this we merely take the above formulae as the definitions of the truth tables.

Readers should recognize these formulae from earlier chapters on fuzzy sets theory. In fact fuzzy sets provide a model for these logics just as set theory models Boolean logic, and this is what we discuss next.

6.4 FUZZY LOGIC AND APPROXIMATE REASONING

6.4.1 The extension principle

In ordinary set theory we can combine a sequence of sets $A_1, A_2, \ldots, A_n$ to form a new set called their Cartesian product and denoted by

$$A_1 + A_2 \times \cdots \times A_n \qquad \text{or} \qquad \prod_{i=1}^{n} A_i$$

This is defined as the set of ordered sets or n-tuples consisting of one member of each of the original sets (the projections). More formally, we define

$$\prod_{i=1}^{n} A_i = \{(a_1, a_2, \ldots, a_n) : a_i \in A_i\}$$

It is useful to develop some geometrical intuition to think about Cartesian products. The usual way to do this is to restrict attention to two or three sets which are pictured as line segments. So, if A and B are two straight line segments the product is a rectangular segment of the plane and a typical ordered pair (a, b) is a point (Fig. 6.2). In the case of three sets A, B and C we get a cuboid (Fig. 6.3).

If geometrical intuition is helpful in set theory then it is even more so with fuzzy

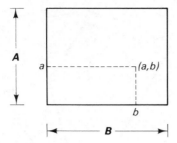

Fig. 6.2   Cartesian product of two dimensions

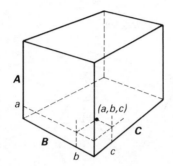

Fig. 6.3   3D-product

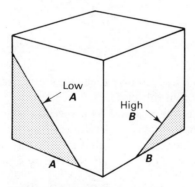

Fig. 6.4   Fuzzy subsets of different domains

set theory. Let us explore how to visualize the product of two fuzzy sets. In Fig. 6.4 we have shown two fuzzy subsets of *A* and *B* by drawing their membership functions as graphs on the walls of a cube.

Now we want to 'extend' these graphs throughout the Cartesian product of *A* and *B*. This clearly will produce two fuzzy subsets of $A \times B$ pictured in Fig. 6.5. The diagram also shows their union by the heavy line. How can we combine these two subsets to give a reasonable generalization of intersection in the Cartesian

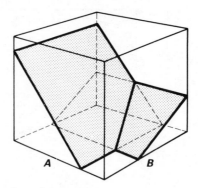

Fig. 6.5   The extension of two fuzzy sets

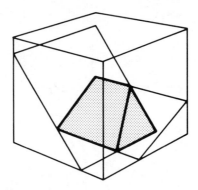

Fig. 6.6   The product of fuzzy sets

product? One obvious way is to take their minimum over $A \times B$. This gives the shape shown in Fig. 6.6 in this case.

This construction can be regarded as a special case of a general method of fuzzifying standard mathematical operations. This method is known as the extension principle. In general it says that given a function $f : \prod X_i \to Y$ we can induce a fuzzified version of f whose values are fuzzy subsets B of Y such that

$$\mu_B(y) = \sup_{\substack{x \in X \\ y = f(x)}} [\min(\mu_{A_i}(x_i))]$$

for fuzzy subsets A_i of X_i. In the above example we effectively fuzzified the function $\wedge : A \times B \to A \times B$. The sup is redundant since $y = x$. Readers should check this for themselves. It turns out (Gaines [139]) that the Lukasiewitz logic we have considered is precisely the 'extension' in this sense of the propositional calculus. We can now use the extension principle to introduce quantifiers as follows.

$$v(\forall x p(x)) = \inf_x(v(p(x)))$$
$$v(\exists x p(x)) = \sup_x(v(p(x)))$$

where x is a member of the underlying set. The implication operator is given by

$$v(p \Rightarrow q) = \min(1, 1 - v(p) + v(q))$$

as opposed to the operation which arises from our earlier definition of $\neg p \vee q$; that is $v(p \Rightarrow q) = \min(1 - p, q)$.

The nice thing about this implication is that it corresponds to the notion of the inclusion of fuzzy subsets introduced in Chapter 5.

We now demonstrate methods of proof for the tautologies of this logic by considering the excluded middle law $p \vee \neg p = 1$. This fails, since if $v(p) = 0.5$ then

$$
\begin{aligned}
v(p \vee \neg p) &= \max(v(p), v(\neg p)) \\
&= \max(v(p), 1 - v(p)) \\
&= \max(0.5, 0.5) = 0.5 \neq 1
\end{aligned}
$$

On the other hand we *do* have

$$v(\neg \neg p) = 1 - v(\neg p) = 1 - 1 + v(p) = v(p)$$

so that the law of double negation is a tautology.

EXERCISES

(1) Prove the analogues of De Morgan's laws:

$$
\begin{aligned}
v(\neg (p \wedge q)) &= v(\neg p \neg q) \\
v(\neg (p \vee q)) &= v(\neg p \neg q)
\end{aligned}
$$

(2) Disprove $p \wedge \neg p = 0$

6.4.2   Rules of inference

Inference rules are required for a formal system of fuzzy logic. One approach here is to apply the extension principle to fuzzify the usual rules of inference such as *modus tollens* or reduction. We can fuzzify *modus ponens* as follows. If we have p and $p \Rightarrow q$ as theorems the valuation of theorem q is given by

$$v(q) = \min(v(p), v(p \Rightarrow q)) = \min(v(p), 1 - v(p) + v(q))$$

which could be interpreted as: 'If we have evidence for p and evidence that p implies q then q can be asserted at least as strongly as p unless we doubt the implication, in which case we can assert q with strength $v(p) + v(p \Rightarrow q) \leqslant 1$.

Clearly, $v(p) + v(p \Rightarrow q)$ has to be greater than 1 to make any inference at all. This interpretation will be useful in a succeeding chapter when we come to consider fuzzy backwards chaining in expert systems.

The next question we must answer is how this logic interprets as a set theory. The fuzzy set theory described in Chapter 5 with primitive operations of union (max), intersection (min), complementation $(1 - x)$ and inclusion is a model for this logic. Of course, we wish to introduce operations corresponding to hedges and this is quite easy. For example we can introduce an operator S into the language such that if p is a formula then so is $S(p)$ (read 'strongly p'). We then need a rule of inference:

$$\frac{S(p)}{p}$$

$S(p)$ could be defined as $v(S(p)) = (v(p))^2$

Probably, in any computer implementation, one would want to introduce a whole family of such hedge operators and inference rules to go with them.

In fact, the logic we have presented here is not the only candidate with a suitable set theoretic model. Other logics and models are useful in certain contexts. They correspond, basically, to different interpretations of uncertainty. For example the notions of bold union and intersection, corresponding to the definitions

$$v(p \wedge q) = \max(0, v(p) + v(q) - 1)$$
$$v(p \vee q) = \min(1, v(p) + 1 - v(q))$$

have been used for certain applications. For a complete discussion see Dubois and Prade [59]. The interesting point, in our view, is that all the operations suggested so far are examples of general mathematical constructions known as t-norms and t-conorms. Because of all the different kinds of uncertainty in the real world our logic should perhaps allow us to switch logical systems but, to avoid total *laissez faire*, restrict us to using t-norms for 'and'. We will return to these points later in this and other chapters. Meanwhile here are the formal definitions.

A t-norm (short for triangular norm) is a binary operator T on the unit interval (or in full generality on any suitable lattice) such that:

$$T(0, 0) = 0; \quad T(1, x) = T(x, 1) = x;$$
$$T(x, y) = T(y, x);$$
$$T(T(x, y), z) = T(x, T(y, z));$$

For all w, x, y, z satisfying $w \leqslant y$, $x \leqslant z T(w, x) \leqslant T(y, z)$

The definition of a conorm is obtained from the above by changing $\leqslant$ for $\geqslant$ and 0 for 1, in other words a conorm is a norm in the dual lattice. The most important consequence of the definition is that every t-norm is bounded above by the t-norm by taking minima. In fact there is a lower bound also, given by

$$T(x, y) = \begin{cases} x \text{ if } y = 1 \\ y \text{ if } x = 1 \\ 0 \text{ otherwise} \end{cases}$$

Dually, every conorm is bounded below by maximum.

The importance of this result should be obvious. It says that when combining uncertain statements with a fuzzy logic using max and min this is in some sense the limiting case, a view which is important when interpreting fuzzy set theory as a theory of *possibility* as opposed to using probabilistic combinators such as $x + y + xy$ which are not at the limit.

6.4.3 Approximate reasoning

Zadeh's theory of Approximate Reasoning (AR) uses and extends fuzzy logic in an attempt to reason with uncertainty in a way which captures much of the richness of natural language and natural reasoning. The extent to which it succeeds is still a matter of debate as we shall see later. His aim was to formalize such statements as:

Peter is rich.
Ian is not very poor.
If Peter is poor and Ian is precise then they should write on vagueness.
Most men are mortal and some are philosophers.
That 'Fuzzy Sets are fun' is very true.

The locution 'very true' in the last sentence is problematic in the context of the fuzzy logic so far presented because *true* is itself a fuzzy set. Up to now our truth values have been ordinary numbers. Such statements, Zadeh claims, require that we bring to bear on them a fuzzy-valued logic. For example, in the statement

'Ian is poor' is very true.

poor is a fuzzy subset of the linguistic variable *wealths* and *true* is a fuzzy number (i.e. a fuzzy subset of the unit interval) hedged by *very*. In the worst case we might write

'This sentence is fairly false' is very true.

and end up with a horrible contradiction. As usual in logic any attempt at self reference is problematical, but with the approximate interpretation of truth the above construction has at least syntactic credibility. 'This sentence is false' is neither true nor false in the usual sense, but if it is 'half true' and 'true' is given the meaning of 'provable' then the contradiction begins to lose some of its force.

Let us now have a look at Zadeh's theory in more detail. We start with the base fuzzy logic already described and rules for representing complex sentences such as 'If John is fairly tall and not very rich or about average age then John is normal' given representations for their constituent parts. Zadeh presents four types of rule to do this:

(1) Composition rules
   Given 'X is A and Y is B' we construct the fuzzy relation in the Cartesian product of the linguistic variables of A and B corresponding to the operation involved; *and, or*, etc. See Fig 6.5 and 6.6.
(2) Modification rules
   Given 'X is hA' where h is a hedge we construct a new fuzzy subset by applying a power operation, a shift or one of the standard hedges such as *not*. See Fig. 6.7.
(3) Quantification rules
   Consider the sentence 'qX is A' which might be 'most people are hungry'. q is a

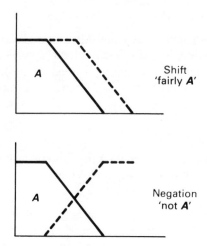

Fig. 6.7 Hedge

fuzzy quantifier such as *most, some, several,* etc. expressed as a proportion or a percentage or as a fuzzy number. Then the proportion of X's that are A is a fuzzy subset of the unit interval. The fuzzy subset of a given fuzzy set which are A is computed by multiplication with q.

(4) Qualification rules

Here, we want to represent the sentence "'X is A' is τ" where τ could be *true, likely, possible* or what have you.

There is still a great deal of controversy surrounding truth functional modification whether in the form of truth, probability or possibility qualification. The theory has been criticized from a philosophical point of view by Haack [86] and from a more pragmatic standpoint by Tong and Efstathiou [198]. Their criticisms may be summarized by the view that *true* is an absolute rather than a relative predicate like *tall* and therefore cannot be qualified, and furthermore that in normal language the hedged forms of *true* are related in a highly vague manner and are not susceptible to formal treatment. Also there are some mathematical problems such as lack of closure under logical operations. Schwartz [182] has recently pointed out that using an interval logic can remedy many of the defects of the theory.

The present authors' view is that for most practical purposes both the qualification and quantification rules may be dispensed with. Quantification can be dealt with implicitly as we will see in the section on REVEAL. Our reason for abstaining from truth functional modification, apart from its computational complexity, is principally that we do not believe that it is the main role of fuzzy set theorists to attempt models of natural language. Although this is undoubtedly a useful line of research, from a practical or computer science point of view we are a long way from achieving models of 'commonsense reasoning' or understanding free form human speech. All fuzzy methods can do is provide a formal model which is *close* to natural reasoning. To illustrate this point we will now attempt to analyse one implementation of fuzzy logic from a formal point of view.

The REVEAL policy language permits statements of the following forms.

1. ⟨Assert1⟩
2. IF ⟨Assert2⟩ THEN ⟨Assert1⟩

where ⟨**Assert1**⟩ is of the forms '*S* is *T*' or '*X* is *A*' and ⟨**Assert2**⟩ can be a combination of such expressions using AND and OR. Here *S* and *T* are string variables, *X* is numeric and *A* is a fuzzy set or *qualifier*. *A* may be an expression combining several pre-defined fuzzy sets. Also the numeric variable may be an expression evaluating to a number. So we have assertions and production rules. For example the following are assertions.

```
HT.OF.JOHN IS NOT VERY TALL

PRICE IS LOW

SWITCH IS 'ON'

STRING(7) IS STRING(150)
```

Stating several assertions it is as if a conjunction stood between them:

```
PRICE IS LOW AND SWITCH IS 'ON' AND ....
```

Rules are processed after assertions and treated as if a disjunction stood between them. Chapter 8 gives a worked example, but here we treat of the formal aspects only. Compare the syntax of REVEAL in the following example with that of a logic programming language like PROLOG.

```
HT.OF.JOHN IS TALL

IF PRICE IS LOW THEN DEMAND IS INCREASED
```

In PROLOG:

```
tall(Johns_height)

increased(Demand) :- low(Price)
```

Apart from the way in which PROLOG subsumes the fuzziness into the predicate descriptors the syntax is formally identical.

The input to a policy is restricted to a single value of each numeric or string variable addressed. This is a genuine restriction since we cannot pass an entire fuzzy set to the policy as we can in the general theory. Whether this is a restriction in practice is an entirely different question and one we will not take up here. A policy consisting of assertions needs no input. The output can be either a fuzzy set or a numerical or string variable. Which it is depends on the inference rules in force at run time; the 'mean of maxima' or 'moments' introduced in Chapter 5.

Kowalski [122] defines a logic program as a set of Horn clause procedures. A Horn clause is exactly what has been described above when stating the REVEAL syntax except that the atoms can be fuzzy relations. We hope that the presentation of fuzzy logic given above will make it clear that this can be regarded as logic programming every bit as much as PROLOG. However, there is no guarantee that only first-order logic is involved (more on this later) and no provision as yet for dealing with 'goals' but this is not a problem in principle.

6.4.4   Possibility and fuzzy modal logics

Traditionally, modal logic deals with the categories of possibility and necessity. Since one of the most prevalent interpretations of fuzzy logic is as the logic of possibility, it is natural to ask what the fuzzy extensions of the classical modal logics are. Lakoff [125] and Schotch [181] have defined fuzzy modal operators based on the idea of possible worlds. We know, however, of no practical applications of this work. Possibility is usually dealt with in a manner analogous to probability by fuzzy set theorists following the lead of Zadeh [238].

We will not discuss possibility in detail in this chapter since it was dealt with adequately for practical purposes in Chapter 5. Suffice it to say that there are various probability logics in existence just as there are several possibility logics as we have seen.

6.5   OTHER LOGICS FOR EXPERT SYSTEMS

6.5.1   Nonmonotonic logics and fuzzy quantifiers

Haack [86] has pointed out that deviant logics, i.e. those which depart from classical first-order systems, can deviate in only two fundamental ways. Either they can relax the requirement that statements can be only 'true' or 'false' in which case the results are usually truth functional; examples are fuzzy logic, intuitionistic logic, Lukasiewitz logic. Or, they can admit new operators, such as L and M in modal logic. Nonmonotonic logics are of the latter kind and are about as far away from truth functionality as you can get, and very weird in other ways too. What are they and why have they been introduced? It is this question we will try to answer in this section.

Most logical systems are 'monotonic' (which means one-directional: increasing or decreasing) in the sense that adding more axioms will always increase the number of theorems provable. In nonmonotonic logic we find, to the contrary, that some theorems may be lost when an axiom is added to the system. To motivate this odd idea consider being informed that 'Woody is a bird'. Since we know that most birds can fly, we might well assume that Woody can fly. When, later, someone tells us that Woody is an ostrich we have to revise our belief in Woody's aeronautical prowess; most ostriches can't fly. This is the kind of inferential behaviour which motivated the work of McDermott and Doyle [145].

Nonmonotonic logic is thus introduced for the very practical purpose of dealing with a form of uncertainty in reasoning processes; as with fuzzy or probabilistic methods the truth of statements is in doubt. Nonmonotonic logic is intended to apply specifically to situations where the initial information is incomplete and where this is irremediably the case. There are several formulations of nonmonotonic logic, all, it seems, arising from different intuitive motivations. We will deal with them in turn.

McDermott and Doyle [145] introduce an operator M which may be interpreted as 'is consistent', 'is possible' or 'whose negation is unprovable'. So that in the example given above we would write:

$$(\forall x)[[\text{Bird}(x) \wedge M\text{Fly}(x)] \Rightarrow \text{Fly}(x)]$$
$$\underline{\text{Bird(Woody)}}$$
$$\text{Fly(Woody)}$$

since it is not possible to derive $\neg$ Fly(Woody); from which MFly(Woody) follows by a new inference rule called, rather unpleasantly, 'possibilitation'.

There is a dangerous scent of self-reference in this approach, since provability is a property of the whole system in which M resides, so that we are proving a theorem on the basis that we already know what the provable theorems of the system are. The entailment relation is usually written as in nonmonotonic logic. The difficulties with nonmonotonic logics revolve mainly around finding an adequate notion of proof. In this system proof is defined in terms of certain conditions being satisfied. In classical first-order logic we have

$$\text{Th}(A) = \text{Th}(\text{Th}(A))$$

where Th means 'the theorems of the system derivable from'. This is called, for reasons which should be obvious, a 'fixed point theorem'; the theorems of classical logic are all fixed points. Now let S be a set of sentences to be regarded as premises. Define an operator NM_A such that

$$NM_A(S) = \text{Th}(A \cup A_{s_A}(A))$$

where

$$A_{s_A} = \{Mp : \neg\, p \in S\} - \text{Th}(A)$$

that is, the set of 'possible' theorems which are not false and not provable.

For S to be a fixed point we require that $S = \text{Th}(A \cup A_{s_A}(S))$ where A is conceived as classical logic plus the operator M. Various fixed point theorems may now be proven.

The concept of fixed points makes it possible to define various notions of provability of varying strengths. For example a proposition is *arguable* if it occurs in some fixed point of A. We illustrate the relationships between these various definitions in Fig. 6.8.

Let us look at the theories generated by certain sets of sentences. The set

$$T1 = \{Mp \Rightarrow \neg\, q,\ Mq \Rightarrow \neg\, p\}$$

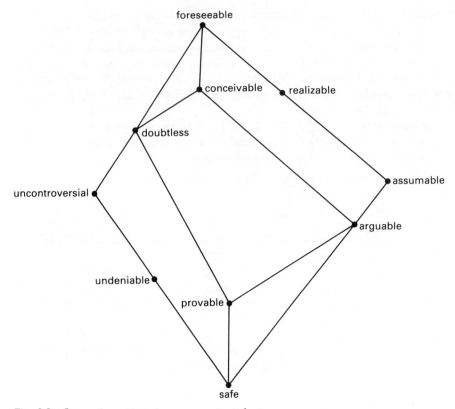

Fig. 6.8   Semantic motions in nonmonotonic logic

gives rise to a theory with two fixed points in which both p and q cannot be simultaneously proven. In fact, one contains $\neg p$ and Mq and the other has $\neg q$ and Mp as theorems. If T2 = $\{Mp \Rightarrow \neg p\}$ then T2 has no fixed points and so is an inconsistent theory, but T2 has a sub-theory given by T3 = $\{Mp \Rightarrow \neg p, \neg p\}$ which is consistent. It is this sort of peculiarity which gives rise to the need to introduce all those different notions of provability. But the problems don't end there. Consider the theory obtained from T4 = $\{Mp \Rightarrow q, \neg q\}$. It is inconsistent because its fixed points must include $\neg Mp$ (from the axioms) and must also include Mp (since $\neg p$ is not among the fixed points, so that Mp is in the assumptions). Adding $\neg p$ as an axiom will make this into a consistent theory. The point to notice here is that all the usual logistic ideas go haywire. Also in nonmonotonic logic there is not necessarily any relationship between the operator M and its dual L. L is usually given by $\neg M \neg$, and interpreted as necessity or, in Moore [153], 'belief'. The theory given by $\{Mp, \neg p\}$ is consistent, which is very hard to interpret unless you interpret M to be a modal operator. This leads to an attempt to base nonmonotonic logic on some system of modal logic such as T, S4 or S5 mentioned earlier in this chapter. This remedies the lack of explicit rules of inference for M and allows the development of a reasonable model theory. We state without proof the following theorems.

THEOREM

All closed instances of the modal axioms are derivable in nonmonotonic logic and are necessary, no matter what other axioms are present.

THEOREM (Completeness)

p is true in all modal models (T, S4, S5) of A iff Ap (in the respective model theory).

The most plausible candidate for the base logic turns out to be S5. However it turns out that the system actually collapses into S5 itself.

THEOREM (McDermott)

If $A \vdash_{S5} p$ then $A \vdash_{S5} p$

In this approach fixed points might be interpreted as 'possible views of the world'. Consider, for example, a robot exploring some micro-world and modifying its database according to what it discovers on its travels but required to make predictions and form plans of action. If we hang on to the modal idea and try S4 we still have problems. For example, in S4 $Mp \Rightarrow p$ is a theorem but, if $T5 = \{LMp \Rightarrow \neg p\}$ then T5 is consistent in S4 but not in nonmonotonic S4.

Moore [163] has suggested that one reason for all the difficulties is that McDermott and Doyle confuse two separate issues of nonmonotonic reasoning: those of default reasoning and autoepistemic reasoning. Default reasoning is the drawing of plausible conclusions from partial evidence in the absence of evidence to the contrary. The example about birds is of this type. Autoepistemic reasoning is reasoning about one's own knowledge or belief. However, we have already pointed out the self-referential consequences of this interpretation, and further we believe that it is the practical problem of default reasoning that is of most interest.

A more restrained approach to nonmonotonic logic is taken by Reiter [176] who merely adds an operator M and defines the notion of a default: an expression of the form

$$\frac{A(x) : M\beta_1(x), \ldots, M\beta_n(x)}{w(x)}$$

where $x = (x_1 \ldots x_k)$ and A and the βs are formulae whose free variables are chosen from among the x_is. For example, in the schema

$$\frac{\text{Bird}(x) : M\text{Fly}(x)}{\text{Fly}(x)}$$

we assert that if x is a bird and it is consistent to assume that x can fly then we can infer that x can fly. Reiter is concerned with the closed world assumption of

188 *Classical, non-standard and fuzzy logics*

database theory (see Chapter 3) and with the so-called frame problem. The closed world default may be stated as

$$\frac{:M \neg p(x)}{\neg p(x)}$$

which is to say that if x is an individual and $p(x)$ cannot be deduced, then $\neg p(x)$ may be inferred. Notice that this is exactly what happens if, in PROLOG, failure is taken to be negation. The frame problem, in AI, is the problem of determining which aspects of a situation remain unchanged under certain changes of state. For example, when one enters a room one does not need to check whether one's clothing is still on in normal circumstances. Abstraction from the invariant features of a situation is what makes problem solving possible. In first-order representations it is necessary to represent this knowledge of invariants quite explicitly in clauses of the form

Height(john,afternoon) = Height(john,morning)

It is interesting to note that the additional positive knowledge required in the frame problem is paralleled by the addition of negative knowledge in the first-order representation of the closed-world problem; a sort of duality exists. Reiter proposes a frame default to formalize the kind of reasoning found in STRIPS [176] as follows:

$$\frac{:M \neg p(x, f(x, s))}{p(x, f(x, s))}$$

The problems with default logics are that the order in which theorems are deduced can affect what the theorems are, and that they may not have the 'extension property'; $A \vdash p$ and $A \subset A'$ imply that $A' \vdash p$. Reiter defines the closed extension of a theory inductively and shows that a closed normal default theory always has an extension theory which is 'semi-monotonic'; that is to say that adding defaults will not cancel theorems. To some extent this is an attempt to overcome the problems with the McDermott and Doyle formulation which seems to us a little more practical than Moore's. In practice, according to Reiter, computational treatments must have a heuristic element (an inference engine). Proof methods are based on a top-down default method which puts the system in such a state as to be able to use a technique such as resolution in the later stages of mechanical proof procedures. The objective here is to eliminate defaults and show that the original set is consistent. However, there is no general way to achieve this in logical systems, so that we must have some heuristics. The question remains as to whether this merely ducks the problem.

Another approach is that of McCarthy [143] which restricts nonmonotonic logic to deal with more specific problems. He introduces 'circumscription' as a 'rule of conjecture that can be used along with the rules of inference of first-order logic'. The difference is that circumscription only holds if the propositions are positively demonstrable. This is not remarkable if we note that the intuitive basis is in the frame problem, or a special case of it called the qualification problem which may best be understood from an example: if someone asks you the way to the pub and you reply that you could go via Beijing, they must point out that they want a short route. If you then say tunnel through that hill another qualification will be forthcoming if they haven't launched a physical attack by now. The problem is how to avoid this (to us) unnecessary qualification. We know some objects in a given class and we have some ways of generating more. We jump to the conclusion that this gives every object in the class; we *circumscribe* the class to consist of the objects we know how to generate.

If A is a first-order sentence containing $p(x)$, Φ is a predicate expression and we write $A(\Phi)$ for the result of replacing every occurrence of p in A by Φ, then define the circumscription of p in $A(p)$ to be the sentence schema

$$[A(\Phi) \wedge (\forall x) [\Phi(x) \Rightarrow p(x)]] \Rightarrow [\forall x] [p(x) \Rightarrow \Phi(x)].$$

An example may be found in the blocks world [252].

If A is the sentence

is_block(a) $\wedge$ is_block(b) $\wedge$ is_block(c)

and Φ is $(x = a \vee x = b \vee x = c)$ the circumscription of is_block in A yields

$$(\forall x) [\text{is\_block}((x) \Rightarrow [x = a \vee x = b \vee x = c]]$$

Another example is the induction schema for the natural numbers, which is the circumscription of nat ($=$ is_a_natural_number) in the sentence

$$\text{nat}(0) \wedge (\forall x) [\text{nat}(x) \Rightarrow \text{nat}(x+1)].$$

As usual, circumscription has a model theory the principle result of which is

THEOREM

All models minimal in a predicate p contain the circumscription of p.

where a model of A is minimal in p if as few as possible tuples x satisfy the predicate p.

Circumscription is more general than the usual notions of default reasoning, since all statements can be proven. However there do seem to be genuine problems. The biggest one concerns its practical usefulness. It is difficult to see how it could be applied in any real computer system. It is not a genuine nonmonotonic logic since it extends first-order logic. McCarthy's use of the term 'rule of conjecture' raises the question of truth values at the meta-level. If a sentence may be unproven, proven or conjectured, then surely we have at least three truth values and are being led inexorably towards a multivalent or fuzzy logic.

Truth maintenance systems have been studied by McAllester. These systems keep track of the predecessors and the methods of derivation for every conclusion reached. If a contradiction is encountered it tries to find an initial assumption which accounts for it and retracts that assumption.

The most complicated version of nonmonotonic logic to appear to date is that of Bossu and Siegal [31] who also are concerned with the closed world assumption in database applications. This paper is fairly remote from any practical application which we can think of. As with all the systems we have looked at this one permits reasoning without having to prove the axioms or assumptions. This can be useful and it does arise in real world examples, but the computational problems are vast and especially so with the more elaborate systems.

All the systems of nonmonotonic logic we have considered so far have been based on classical logic with two truth values and two quantifiers. We now consider systems which attack the same basic problems on the basis of intuitionistic logic (see the next sub-section for details) and fuzzy logic. It has been argued that a correct formulation of a problem will avoid the need for nonmonotonic reasoning and that arguments based on probability will suffice.

Gabbay proposes a semantic model based on the idea of 'sets through time', H-sets (which we expound further in Section 6.6) or states of knowledge. To each atomic formula at a given 'time' assign a point of $\{0, 1\}$ in such a way that if the value 1 (true) is attained then it persists for later times. This can be extended recursively to all propositional formulae. There is also an operator M interpreted as 'could become true later' satisfying:

$$Mp \vee \neg p$$
$$\neg Mp \Leftrightarrow \neg p$$
$$(Mp \Rightarrow q) \Leftrightarrow ((\neg p \vee q)$$
$$(Mp \Rightarrow \neg q) \Leftrightarrow \neg q$$

The following inferences are valid in this logic

$$\frac{\neg Mp}{\neg p} \qquad \frac{M(p \wedge q)}{Mp}$$

as we would hope, and the theory generated by $\{Mp, \neg p\}$ is no longer inconsistent.

Also he introduces a nonmonotonic inference rule which is the transitive closure of Reiter's default rule and is quite similar. The details are given in Turner [201]. This logic is both fairly strong and more intuitively appealing than any we have considered so far in our opinion. It also ties in well with fuzzy logic and major currents in modern mathematics as we shall see later. The notion of proof and the underlying semantics are based on intuitionistic logic to which we turn in the next section.

Zadeh's extension of fuzzy logic to include fuzzy quantifiers also has some of the aspects of a nonmonotonic logic [217]. His way of dealing with the problem of Woody the ostrich is to notice that the statement 'Birds can fly' is a *disposition*; that is, a statement in which there is an implicit fuzzy quantifier. Thus the disposition may be transformed into the proposition 'Most birds can fly'. The semantic meaning of a proposition, in this approach, is represented as a procedure which tests, scores and aggregates the elastic constraints induced by the proposition. A series of inference rules are introduced to permit reasoning with dispositions.

Suppose we start with the disposition 'Birds can fly' and restore the suppressed quantifier to give 'Q_1 birds can fly', where Q_1 is a fuzzy number representing 'most' as a proportion of 1. If we also have the proposition 'Q_2 flying birds have feathers' we may infer that at least $Q_1 \otimes Q_2$ birds have feathers, where $\otimes$ is the product of fuzzy numbers [59]. In general this 'chaining syllogism is expressed by

$B \subseteq A$

Q_1 A are B
Q_2 B are C
$$\overline{\geqslant (Q_1 \otimes Q_2) \; A \text{ are } C}$$

which is a special case of the 'intersection/product' rule:

Q_1 A are B
Q_2 (A and B) are C
$$\overline{(Q_1 \otimes Q_2) \; A \text{ are } (B \text{ and } C)}$$

We also have the 'consequent conjunction' rule:

Q_1 A are B
Q_2 A are C
$$\overline{Q_3 \; A \text{ are } (B \text{ and } C)}$$

where Q_3 is the fuzzy number or interval defined in fuzzy arithmetic by:

$$0 \otimes (Q_1 \oplus Q_2 \ominus 1) \leqslant Q_3 \leqslant Q_1 \otimes Q_2$$

and where

$$\wedge, \; \vee, \; \oplus, \; \ominus$$

represent min, max, addition and subtraction respectively.

Other such syllogisms are discussed in Zadeh [218].

This approach is a fairly new one and is not without problems. How are the dispositions to be transformed without an extensive database of explanations? The product syllogism gives a rule of minimal inference only which is analogous to necessity. Possibilistic inference is harder. As far as we know no-one has solved the problems of completeness or consistency for this logic. However, when combined with theories of fuzzy probability, it does hold out some hope of providing a less problematical way of dealing with default reasoning on a computer because everything is made explicit in the formal language in a concise manner. After all, when we assert that birds can fly we really cannot defend the assertion in that exact form, whereas 'most birds can fly' is eminently defensible.

We shall see later that there is an intimate connection between fuzzy logic and intuitionism. It is still an unsolved problem whether the fuzzy quantification of Zadeh can be unified with quantification in a category of 'sets through time' (a topos).

Doyle [57] draws a distinction between what he calls imprecise reasoning (fuzzy logic) and nonmonotonic reasoning on the basis of their abilities to deal with incomplete information. In the latter, the incompleteness is exact and judgements are binary. Approximation only enters when the set of beliefs is regarded globally. In the logics of uncertainty such as Zadeh's, the incompleteness is inexact; the statements are themselves vague. He further suggests that the two approaches are orthogonal and looks forward to a combined approach. This question revolves round the interpretation of the latent quantifier in 'Birds fly'. Do we know 'exactly' that all birds can fly until we come across a penguin, or do we know in advance that the statement is imprecise. We would claim that the latter is obviously the case. However, the exact amount of imprecision is definitely open to question; we cannot assume that we know with precision the possibility, or indeed the probability, of any given bird being able to fly.

We would assert quite strongly that there is a sort of duality between approaches using fuzzy quantifiers and nonmonotonic logics. It appears that similar problems can be solved by both approaches but we would suggest that any computer system attempting to combine the two would be a very dangerous enterprise indeed. Much more work needs to be done before this duality theory can be developed.

6.5.2   Intuitionist logic and topological models

The usual model for classical logic is set theory and, in particular, negation is interpreted as complementation. This provides a useful intuitive feel for the consequences of negation because we can draw a Venn diagram to guide our proofs of tautologies such as the laws of the excluded middle and double negation; $\neg\neg\,)p=p$.

To see this consider Fig. 6.9.

The area labelled A inside the circle represents any proposition (or set). Its negation is the area labelled B, outside the circle but within the square representing our current universe of discourse. The double negation is just all the points not in B, or in other words A.

This nice scheme seems to make the theorem obvious, but to see just how much we depend on our model suppose now that we only recognize *open* subsets of the universe, that is the sets without their boundaries. Now, the complement of A is the largest open set disjoint from A and this may, in general, be smaller than the set theoretic complement which is a closed set. In the illustration we use a useful convention due to E. Kronheimer to denote open sets: a hook drawn over the boundary indicates which side of the boundary the open set lies by the convention that the open ends of the hook lies in the open set. (See Fig. 6.10.)

It can now be seen that the double complement of A need not be equal to A, it

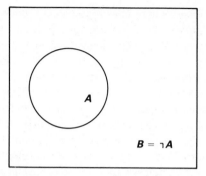

Fig. 6.9   Complement in set theory

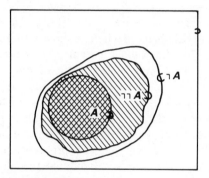

Fig. 6.10   Intuitionistic complement

must merely be a larger open set. We will not prove this here since it is not relevant to our aims. The proof is a simple exercise in the pathology of General Topology. Hint: Consider a space with just three points.

We will, nevertheless, need to recall the definition of a topological space very briefly. The interested reader is referred to Kelley [239] for details and the best definition of a topologist we have yet come across: 'a topologist is a man who doesn't know the difference between a doughnut and a coffee cup'.

A topological space is a set equipped with a notion of some of its points being 'as close together as you like'. This is equivalent to defining which subsets (the open ones) do not contain their boundary points. So we specify a subset of the set of subsets (the power set) and require that it is closed under finite intersection and arbitrary union operations. For a few pathological cases it is necessary to require that the empty set and the whole space are open.

A fuzzy topology for X is a family T of fuzzy subsets of X such that:

(A) $\varnothing,\ X \in T$

(B) $A,\ B \in T \Rightarrow A \wedge B \in T$

(C) $[(\forall i \in I) A_i \in T] \Rightarrow \bigvee_{i \in I} A_i \in T$

Our interest in these objects here is as topological models of logical systems. It turns out that, as we have hinted, they are appropriate to models of intuitionistic logic just as set theory models classical logic. Looked at in this light we maintain that there is nothing so very special about classical logic since topological intuitions are just as (un)natural as set theoretic ones.

Intuitionism takes a strong philosophical position within mathematics. For an intuitionist, semantics is identified with proof theory; so that the intension of $p \wedge q$ is that we have a proof of p and a proof of q and similarly for the other connectives. Quantification may only take place over a defined domain, thus we say 'for all x in X' rather than just 'for any x'. In more general treatments quantification takes place over functions as we shall see later (Section 6.6). Lastly the proofs referred to must be constructive, which is actually not a very clearly defined term (see Troelstra [199]) but for our purposes may be regarded as meaning that proofs must proceed in finite steps and abjure *reductio ad absurdum*. Thus Brouwer denied the validity of the hairy ball theorem when he showed that the only proof possible was by contradiction. (The hairy ball theorem assures us we all have a crown in our hair: Every vector field on a sphere has a singularity.) One formation of constructive mathematics is particularly relevant to the development of knowledge-based systems. This is the theory of types due to Martin-Löf which is described briefly in Turner [201].

In this approach we identify types with propositions or, in the model, with sets or the objects of a suitable category. The set of proofs of a proposition p is referred to as $O(p)$ the set of objects of type p. We then make the following identifications:

$$O(A \vee B) \Leftrightarrow O(A) + O(B)$$
$$O(A \wedge B) \Leftrightarrow O(A) \times O(B)$$
$$O(A \Rightarrow B) \Leftrightarrow O(A) \Rightarrow O(B)$$
$$O(\exists x A(x)) \Leftrightarrow (\Sigma c \in C) O(A(c))$$
$$O(\forall x A(x)) \Leftrightarrow (\Pi c \in C) O(A(c))$$

As with the Church–Curry lambda calculus the basic operations are function abstraction and application, but the language differs in not being type free which has some important consequences for computational applications. As with Zadeh's theory of quantifiers the semantics of type is provided by giving a rule of computation called evaluation. The statements of type theory,

A is a type
$A = B$
$a \in A$ (a is an object of type A)
$a = b$ in type A

can have different interpretations in set theory, proof theory or the theory of computation. For example, the third statement above could stand for:

a is an element of A
a is a proof of A
or a is a procedure to compute A.

If we interpret A as a specification of a task and a as a program to carry it out then we can, following Martin-Löf, define a functional programming language and associated specification language and a formal means of deriving programs from their specification. We will later discuss how fuzzy set theory can be embedded in intuitionistic logic. These developments taken together make it possible, in principle, to create a new programming language which combines a powerful functional programming language capable of handling uncertainty and intrinsically associated with a declarative specification language and a means of proving that programs meet their specification.

6.5.3   Temporal, intensional, equational and other logics

There are as many logical systems possible as there are categories in our thinking. We will deal briefly here with a few that have shown promise for applications in artificial intelligence or knowledge-based programming.

Temporal or tense logic deals with the logic of locutions which involve time as explicated by tenses in natural language. For example, in normal discourse if Simon is alive, we can infer that Simon will have lived unless, of course, Simon is an immortal. There seems to be no way to express this in predicate logic thus the need arises to find a suitable solution to the problem. Several suggestions have been advanced. We can use a many-sorted logic in which variables are intrinsically classified into 'sorts' such as instants, events, actions and so forth. We can merely shrug off the problem and satisfy ourselves with the sets through time interpretation of intuitionism, thus getting away from the problems of natural language by formalizing the way verbs are handled. For most decision support applications this latter seems to us to be the correct approach. However, if natural language is the object of study, a genuine temporal logic may be called for.

In temporal logic the truth value of a statement may vary with time. To model this we introduce temporal operators F, P, G and H to be interpreted as

> will be true in the future
> was true once
> will become permanently true from now
> has been true up to now

The following relations hold among these operators and serve to define two in terms of the others.

$$Gp \Leftrightarrow \neg F \neg p$$
$$Hp \Leftrightarrow \neg P \neg p$$

It is also necessary to define a relation of temporal precedence which is at least transitive and usually has other conditions to remove the possibility of multiple pasts (or futures) existing, and guarantee that time is continuous and has no beginning (or end). There are various systems of temporal logic which vary according to the conditions imposed on this relation. All of them contain the tautologies of predicate calculus and the sentences generated by the following axiom schemata.

$$G(p\Rightarrow q)\Rightarrow(Gp\Rightarrow Gq)$$
$$H(p\Rightarrow q)\Rightarrow(Hp\Rightarrow Hq)$$
$$p\Rightarrow HFp$$
$$p\Rightarrow GPp$$

The rules of inference are *modus ponens* and two which only apply to axioms:

$$\frac{a}{Ga} \quad \frac{a}{Ha}$$

Allen [6] has applied temporal logic to reasoning about a database of historical data and makes claims for his system's computational efficiency. He employs a many-sorted calculus with the sorts: properties, time intervals, events and so on. Temporal relations of overlap, meeting, starting, finishing, preceding, during and equality are used and represented as a network. An important point is that time is represented as a set of intervals rather than as a set of points, leading to a higher level of chunking (see Chapter 2) and allowing reasoning to ignore irrelevant facts and eliminate the need for dealing with fuzzy dates to represent relative knowledge.

Haack [86] surveys earlier developments in tense logic due to Prior and Quine. She also gives a classification of non-standard logics to include those with additional operators (modal, tense, deontic, epistemic, preference, imperative and erotetic), those with different notions of truth values and inductive logics. Epistemic logic adds the operators K and B meaning 'knows that' and 'believes that' respectively. Deontic logic is the logic of duty and has operators for 'it ought to be the case that' and 'it is permitted that'. Formally, these schemes will not be very different from modal logic although the rules of inference and the theorems will be different. So far, these logics have found little application in artificial intelligence, but Sloman [189] has suggested that many knowledge represen-tation formalisms are required for knowledge-based systems; a view with which we strongly concur. Thus, we can expect to see such techniques being used in the future. Already, Zadeh has made an attempt [217] to deal with some aspects of imperative logic through the use of fuzzy quantifiers and this promises an alternative path to that of pure imperative logic. Luc Steels has suggested that AI will need to consider what he calls intensional logic. That is, the logic of meaning as opposed to the logic of reference (extension). To explain this idea, when we talk about Bach we mean a certain individual who is the referent or extension in the world of the atom 'Bach'. However, if we speak of the composer of the Musical Offering, then the extension, Bach, does not fully capture the meaning of the description; since we can imagine a world in which someone else wrote that work. In place of semantic assignments, intensional logic assigns a function which will compute the extension when required. Steels's team at Brussels have developed a system called KRS which uses intensional logic to unify several knowledge representation formalisms within one system.

Jackson [103] has applied a form of epistemic logic based on game theory to advice-giving expert systems. In this application, we are modelling experts who have to reason about their client's belief as well as their own. Jackson describes a representation language which includes syntactic, semantic and pragmatic aspects. The semantics is derived from Hintikka's semantics for two-valued games. He claims that this approach obviates much of the need for nonmonotonic logics.

One very exciting recent development is the interest in computer theorem proving using equational logic, which has led to the development of the new logic programming language EQLOG by Goguen and Meseguer [76]. EQLOG unifies Horn clause first-order predicate logic with functional programming (see the next section). It is based on the smallest logic containing both Horn clauses and equality. Functions are computed by term rewriting and predicates by unification (up to equality) and backtracking. There is a completeness theorem for this system, and appears to give more than systems like POPLOG which merely bring languages like PROLOG and LISP together without offering anything extra. Also the language can be made to support an object-oriented programming style with strong typing and inheritance. Equational logic is a system wherein the axioms are given in terms of rules of substitution. We will deal with functional programming and Horn clause logic in the following section.

6.5.4 Functional and logic programming

In this section we look at the connections between computer programming languages and logical formalisms. Distinctions are often made between applicative, assignment, functional, imperative and declarative programming and procedural and non-procedural languages. We here explain these distinctions and offer some definitions of terminology which will be useful later. Secondly, we shall explain the connection between the language LISP and the λ-calculus, and between PROLOG and first-order predicate logic.

Conventional programs work by assigning values to variables which represent storage locations in memory. Any prior value stored in that location is overwritten and lost forever unless steps have been taken previously. Applicative languages such as LISP do not use this destructive assignment process, and thus, in some ways, are closer to the way human information processing proceeds. In practice this means that the processor has to periodically do some 'garbage collection' to get rid of values no longer required in order to save on storage. Another common feature is 'lazy evaluation' whereby values are not computed until a function requires them. Such languages are based on function application and composition and depend on a logical system known as λ-calculus which we will describe below. Applicative programming becomes functional programming when it maintains 'referential transparency', which is to say that every expression or variable has the same value within a given scope; all variables are local. This implies that we can always substitute an expression with one of equal value without altering the value of the whole expression. This property is useful in theorem proving and database enquiry where rewriting expressions and substitution are fundamental operations.

A procedural language instructs a computer *how* to carry out a particular task. A non-procedural one tells it only *what* to do. Consider the following database enquiry which asks how many employees are working in each department, and in those groups, what the total and average salaries are.

```
SELECT DNAME, JOB, SUM(SAL), COUNT(*), AVG(SAL)

FROM   EMPLOYEES, DEPARTMENTS

WHERE  EMPLOYEES.DEPTNO = DEPARTMENTS.DEPTNO

GROUP BY DNAME, JOB
```

This query in fact produces correct output but the results need not concern us here. The language is SQL. Notice that nowhere is the computer told how to answer the question. This would involve obtaining a list of employees. sorting it by department and job and then computing the count and average and total salaries. Finally, department name must be substituted for department number in the output. That would be a fairly complicated procedure involving reading records and saving intermediate results at each stage. The non-procedural language SQL, based on relational calculus which we covered in Chapter 3, makes all this unnecessary. In actual implementations of SQL, as might be found in the ORACLE product for example, there are built in functions which introduce an element of procedurality. In other words purity is a rare boon. The term declarative is a slightly more general one, because it includes purely descriptive languages. It is more to do with the way data or knowledge is represented than with any particular programming paradigm. This was looked at from a slightly different angle in Chapter 2. The opposite of a declarative language is usually referred to as an imperative one, but this usage is falling back under the onslaught of the snappier but less euphonic 'non-procedural'. The language PROLOG also has a declarative and non-procedural style; however we will see later that it is far from being a non-procedural language although its rules are stated in a mostly declarative style. Let us now turn to the logics which make such languages possible.

The λ-calculus originated in the 1930s and was principally due to Alonzo Church. His original motivation was to provide a foundation for all of mathematics based on rules; that is, the idea of a function being a process of passing from argument to value rather than Dirichlet's more modern notion of functions as graphs (subsets of relations). It is possible to think of such functions or rules as being given by natural language sentences applied to arguments (also expressed in words), or as computer programs which may be applied to other computer programs or structures. In both cases the language is *type free*, which is to say that there is no distinction between the sort of objects which constitute a function and those which can be its possible arguments. In particular, a function can be applied to itself. The axiom of foundation makes this impossible in ordinary set theory and the logic which it models. Church's original theory was shown to be inconsistent by the discovery of the Kleene–Rosser paradox, but he managed to salvage a consistent subtheory which forms the basis of current research and of a number of programming languages, the most prominent of which has been LISP which originated in about 1956 [144].

In LISP, which stands for LISt Processing, as with the λ-calculus there is no distinction between program and data, both of which are expressed as hierarchically structured lists.

The λ-calculus represents a class of partial functions defined on the integers which turn out to be the recursive functions, and these are equivalent to the Turing computable functions. Based on this equivalence the Church–Turing hypothesis states that the ordinary, intuitive notion of a function that can be computed by a terminating algorithm is equivalent to the notion of a recursive function. Thus the interest of computer scientists in this subject is not surprising. Church soon discovered that the λ-calculus was undecidable. The problem concerned whether the terms of the λ-calculus have a normal form; in the language of Turing machines these are functions which have no unpleasant infinite loops, and are equivalent to Turing's 'satisfactory' machines.

In order to achieve completeness Church introduced the abstraction operator λ which lets us create or 'abstract' a function from terms of the language. Thus, $(\lambda x M)a$ is the function which is equal to the result of substituting a for all occurrences of x and applying the function M. For example, we can make a function of one argument as follows:

$$g = (\lambda x 2 * x + 3)$$

So that $g(1) = 5$, $g(2) = 7$, $g(3) = 9$, and so on. Additionally, the λ-calculus supports an operation based on a term which takes the values 'true' and 'false' which permits conditional expressions to be included in function definitions. For example,

$$g = (\lambda x \text{ if } x > 5 \text{ then } f(x) \text{ else } -f(x))$$

Function abstraction and application are the primitive operations of this logic. The operator λ extends the type of the language in a universal way which is analogous to the way that introducing inverse elements x^{-1} extends the language of elementary group theory, or negative numbers extend that of integer arithmetic. However, Curry showed that λ is not absolutely necessary although it is intuitively appealing in a mathematical context. Modern dialects of LISP have begun increasingly to drop the explicit lambda notation, but it is still implicitly present as is apparent from the care that has to be taken with variable bindings in difficult programs.

Formally, the language is defined as follows: The alphabet consists of variables x, y, z, . . . together with symbols for reduction $\rightarrow$, equality $=$ and abstraction. The terms are defined recursively as follows:

Variables are terms
Application of two terms yields a term
If M is a term and x is a variable the $(\lambda x M)$ is a term

The well-formed formulae are defined by saying that if M and N are terms, $M \rightarrow N$ and $M = N$ are formulae. The reduction, equality and abstraction operators are defined by requiring that they satisfy certain axiom schemes. For details see Barendregt [18].

A variable is *free* if it is not in the scope of a λx and *bound* otherwise. In this way λ is analogous to the universal quantifier $\forall$ of predicate logic or the definite integral of school calculus.

As with the other logics we have considered there is a model theory which may be expressed in terms of combinatory algebra or lattices. A graphic theoretic model has been proposed by Plotkin [18] which comes close to the concerns of LISP programmers. The model theory contains the usual fixed point theorems.

FIXED POINT THEOREM

For every term M there exists a term F such that $\vdash_\lambda MF = F$.

In fact there is a systematic construction for the fixed points. Let $Y = \lambda f (\lambda x f(xx))\, (\lambda x f(xx))$. Then it may be shown that $\downarrow Yf = f(Yf)$. Y is known as the 'paradoxical combinator'.

The existence of a Gödel type self-referential sentence makes it possible to prove incompleteness by a diagonal argument as with classical logic.

All of the many dialects of the LISP language rest on the λ-calculus. LISP is in some ways a very low-level language resting on very few primitives which can be thought of as specifying a virtual machine. The most fundamental primitives are CAR, CDR (pronounced coo'der), ATOM and LAMBDA (or PROG). The only primitive data type is the list. A list consists of a head and a tail (physically a pointer to the head of another list). CAR returns the head as an atom and CDR the tail as a list. Atoms refer to values in store and are the raw material from which lists are built. CONS constructs new lists by adding a new head to a list. There are in addition several control structures and arithmetic and relational operators. Like C and PASCAL, LISP is a recursive language. To give the reader the general flavour of LISP we present below the algorithm which solves the problem of the towers of Hanoi in LISP and in C for comparison.

The problem may be succinctly described by the following story. Once upon a time, in Hanoi, there was a monastery. The monks had been set the task, by the Buddha, of transferring the 64 golden discs stacked on a tower, or pole, to a nearby one. Fortunately for them there was a spare tower nearby, for the discs were fragile and would break if a large one were placed atop a small. Legend says that when they have completed the task the world will end. Certainly, at one move per second the minimum time to complete the task is longer than the whole history of the universe up until now. So perhaps the legend is true.

First, Fig. 6.11 shows the algorithm in C. Note the role that recursion plays in the routine; the 'hanoi' procedure calls itself with altered parameters. This is often a convenient way to express algorithms that arise in problem solving.

```
/* Towers of Hanoi in C.
*/
#include stdio.h
main ()
{
  extern int nd;          /* declaration - global integers */
  char a,b,c;             /* declaration - strings */
  printf("\nTowers of Hanoi benchmark\nHow many discs ? ");
  scanf("%d",&nd);        /* enter number of discs */
  a='A';b='B';c='C';      /* name the poles */
    hanoi(nd,&a,&b,&c);   /* call hanoi procedure */
  printf("\nProcessing complete.");
}                         /* end main routine*/


int hanoi(nd,t1,t2,t3)    /* hanoi procedure defn */
char *t1,*t2;             /* simulate call by reference */
{
  if(nd<1) return;        /* you can't play with no discs left */
    hanoi(nd-1,t1,t3,t2); /* call hanoi with one less disc - case 1 */
    printf("\nMove from tower %c to tower %c",*t1,*t2);
    hanoi(nd-1,t3,t2,t1); /* call hanoi with one less disc - case 2 */
  return nd;
}
#include ?stdio.lib?
```

Fig. 6.11   Towers of Hanoi in C

Now for the COMMON LISP version shown in Fig. 6.12.

```
(DEFUN HANOI (N)                ; Define the function with parameter N

    (TRANSFER 'A 'B 'C N))

(DEFUN MOVE-DISC (FROM TO)      ; Define printing instruction

    (LIST (LIST 'MOVE 'DISC 'FROM FROM 'TO TO)))

(DEFUN TRANSFER (FROM TO SPARE NUMBER)

    (COND ((EQUAL NUMBER 1) (MOVE-DISC FROM TO))  ; conditional branch

        ( T (APPEND (TRANSFER FROM            ; case 1

                        SPARE

                        TO

                        (SUB1 NUMBER))   ; number - 1

                (MOVE-DISC FROM TO)      ; case 2

            (TRANSFER SPARE

                TO

                FROM

                (SUB1 NUMBER))))))
```

Fig. 6.12 Towers of Hanoi in LISP

To bring out the role of λ abstraction and the primitives more clearly we show a slightly different method expressed in another LISP dialect in Fig. 6.13. Also we illustrate the starting and finishing position output from a routine enhanced with some elementary graphics.

```
HANOI:

    (LAMBDA (Disklist A B C)

        (IF Disklist THEN

            (PROG ()

                (HANOI (CDR Disklist) A B C)

                (PRINT (LIST 'MOVE (CAR Disklist) 'FROM A 'TO B))

                (HANOI (CDR Disclist) C B A))))
```

Fig. 6.13 Towers of Hanoi in LISP dialect

Note the very deeply nested parentheses. This is one of the things that LISP users most commonly complain about. It is often very difficult to see clearly what is going on in a program through all the brackets. This is compounded because LISP is actually a very *low* level language. To be useful in the context of high productivity knowledge engineering environments, it is necessary to have a very extensive library of functions written in advance to make the language higher level. Some of the advanced environments discussed in later chapters are of this type.

For further details of programming in LISP the reader is referred to Winston and Horn [211].

Just as LISP is based on the λ-calculus, so PROLOG is based on the first-order predicate calculus; but there are some important differences in the analogy. In particular, PROLOG is a far more declarative language than LISP.

As another example of the use of recursive programming to solve the problem afflicting the monks of Hanoi, we include the rendition of the algorithm in the LEONARDO system, as exemplifying procedural coding style within an expert system shell. This algorithm is shown in Fig. 6.14.

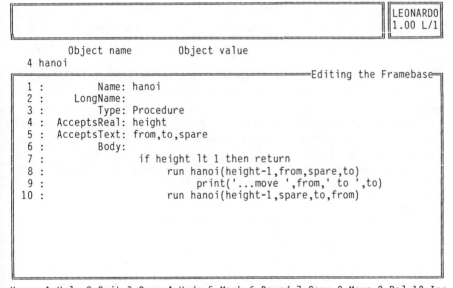

```
                                                          LEONARDO
                                                          1.00 L/1

           Object name          Object value
     4 hanoi
                                                   ═Editing the Framebase═
      1 :         Name: hanoi
      2 :     LongName:
      3 :         Type: Procedure
      4 : AcceptsReal: height
      5 : AcceptsText: from,to,spare
      6 :         Body:
      7 :                   if height lt 1 then return
      8 :                       run hanoi(height-1,from,spare,to)
      9 :                           print('...move ',from,' to ',to)
     10 :                       run hanoi(height-1,spare,to,from)




Keys: 1 Help 2 Quit 3 Comm 4 Undo 5 Mark 6 Bound 7 Copy 8 Move 9 Del 10 Ins
```

Fig. 6.14   Towers of Hanoi in LEONARDO

One of the important motivating applications in the development of PROLOG was automatic theorem proving. It was the discovery by Robinson [177] in 1965 of the resolution principle which began to make this feasible on computers. There are two problems to be overcome when using this inference rule. Firstly, suitable pairs of propositions must be chosen for resolution. Secondly, it is usually necessary to make some substitutions. For example, if we have selected the propositions $A \lor V$ and $\neg C \lor D$ then only after some substitutions are we able to replace A and C by some common proposition A' as resolution requires. The computational process which does this is called 'unification' and is a sort of run-time type checking. It works by searching the database for a match for the variables under consideration. For details of this process see Bundy [37]. The various search strategies which overcome the possible combinatorial explosion of proof trees are covered, albeit briefly, in Chapter 7. The other key development in logic which contributed to the development of PROLOG and other logic programming languages was the discovery that in the determination of the values of recursive functions using a theorem prover it suffices to work with clauses of a certain restricted type: the Horn clauses. These are clauses with at most one unnegated literal. For example

$$q \lor \neg p1 \lor \neg p2 \lor \neg p3 \lor \neg p4$$

is a Horn clause. It is equivalent to

$$p1 \land p2 \land p3 \land p4 \Rightarrow q.$$

So, an equivalent formulation is that the Horn clauses represent rules with only one consequent. Formally, a 'clause' is an expression of the form

$$A_1 \land \ldots \land A_n \Rightarrow B_1 \lor \ldots \lor B_m$$

PROLOG represents its clause 'backwards'. As with most programming languages, the best way to understand them is through examples. One is shown in Fig. 6.15.

The first line may be read as saying: the predicate hanoi is true of the variable N *provided that* the predicate move is true of its arguments. The next line stops backtracking when the number of discs reaches zero, and the other move clause says that move is true provided that *all* the following predicates are satisifed. The

```
-------------------------------------------
hanoi(N) :- move(N,left,centre,right).

move(0,_,_,_) :- !.

move(N,A,B,C) :-

     M is N-1,

     move(M,A,B,C),

     inform(A,B),

     move(M,C,B,A).

inform(X,Y) :- write([move,from,X,to,Y]),nl.
-------------------------------------------
```

Fig. 6.15   Towers of Hanoi in PROLOG

last line merely defines a message function. The backtracking mechanism will be explained in Chapter 7.

PROLOG predicates can be interpreted as relations, which makes the language particularly suitable for database enquiry. We have already discussed this a little in Chapter 3. Viewing a set of Horn clauses as a database, leads us to ask about the semantics of the logical operators, and in particular of negation. When the Prolog interpreter answers a user's query with 'No' it is indicating not that the fact is untrue but that the backtracking has failed to find a true instance in the database. The identification of negation with failure is equivalent to the closed world assumption which we discussed in Section 6.5.1. In cases where we would not wish to make the assumption that the database contains all relevant knowledge this can result in grave problems. Clarke [45] defines the *completion* of the database on this basis: If a proposition is unprovable in the database then its negation is a theorem. Flannagan [67] points out that the assumption that this is a statement about the *completeness* of the (theory of the) database is incorrect, since it only asserts that the negation is *consistent* with the theory. Kowalski [122] gives an example which is used by both authors to support their arguments. This consists of the database

Bob teaches Maths
Bob teaches History

which is equivalent to

Bob teaches X if $X =$ Maths or $X =$ History.

The argument then revolves around whether, in order to assert that

not(Bob teaches Logic)

it is necessary to assume that the if is an iff, or whether the mere consistency of the last clause is sufficient. The practical issue is less arcane. If we have a personnel database in a properly run company and we ask to see the salespeople working the northern territory then we expect to see them all. On the other hand, and this is often the case in knowledge-based systems involving uncertainty, if our database is a compendium of knowledge, such as an encyclopaedia, which may be incomplete or inexact, the situation is quite different. Here the first-order approach of PROLOG has to give way to either nonmonotonic approaches or, dually, to a fuzzy approach.

In Chapter 2 we gave an example of a small PROLOG program in the domain of Anthropology. Careful readers will have noted that it asserts that Dad is married to Mum but not the reverse. A little thought will show that if we included the rule (commutativity of marriage) that states:

x married-to y if y married-to x

then the problem would be solved. Sadly, a loop results. After studying backtracking in Chapter 7 the reason should become apparent.

EXERCISE. Consider to what extent the above mentioned problem is a weakness of PROLOG or the result of a poor implementation of the interpreter.

Another difficulty with PROLOG is the trouble it takes to deal with counterfactuals or hypothetical (subjunctive) assertions. Gabbay and Reyle [74] give the following example of a difficult case, based on the controversial British Nationality Act.

IF (X was born in the UK) AND
(if father-of (X) were alive at time t then father-of(X) would be a citizen at time t) AND etc.

They propose an extension to PROLOG, called N-PROLOG, which overcomes the problem by introducing hypothetical implication into the language. Another recent development which can be viewed as an extension to PROLOG is EQLOG, which unifies Horn clause programming with functional programming by introducing equational logic. Goguen and Meseguer [76] claim convincingly that EQLOG has operationally complete semantics, strong typing, user definable abstract data types and parametric modules. This is one of the most promising developments but remains at an experimental stage at the time of writing.

The declarative style in which facts and rules are expressed and the strong relation with logic has tempted some authorities to refer to PROLOG as a non-procedural language and a 'logic programming' language. It is neither, although it approximates both. The order in which the clauses are written, while not affecting the output, can gravely affect the time taken and the side effects produced (such as dialogue) during processing. The existence of the operator ! known as 'cut' which can affect backtracking is about as procedural a device as you can get. Lastly, predicates such as 'assert' and 'retract' are implicitly higher-order constructs which take PROLOG out of the orbit of the first-order predicate calculus. For details of the language see Clocksin and Mellish [47], and for a discussion of logic programming and PROLOG see Kowalski [122]. The next section takes a more critical look in this respect and in terms of the difficulty of handling uncertainty with such languages. The amount of mathematical machinery we have to use may deter some readers, but the section may be safely omitted at a first reading.

The application of logic programming to build an expert adviser on the British Nationality Act has been criticized by Leith [237] on the grounds that there can be no 'clear rules' in law. This is itself a controversial point in jurisprudence. The difficulty in practice is that judges interpret the law on the basis of a vast amount of social and political data which are not part of the written law. The computer programs however assume a closed world. This, of course, is a criticism which can be extended to most computer systems. Leith fails, we feel, to do justice to the notion of logic however. First-order, crisp logic is not the only logic available (as he assumes) and the closed world assumption is not the only one possible. The arguments presented in this chapter may be of direct relevance to this debate.

Note to the reader

The next section is included to support some of the positions advanced in this book. However, it does, necessarily, assume quite a deal of mathematical knowledge. We suggest that some readers will want to skip or flick through it very quickly. Doing this will not compromise the reader's understanding of the remainder of the text which, from here on, comes down to a much more practical and non-mathematical level.

****

6.6 FUZZY LOGIC AND CATEGORY THEORY

6.6.1 Historical remarks

In this section we turn to some rather difficult mathematical concepts. Our objective is to suggest that a certain mathematical point of view may assist computer scientists in achieving systems which adequately reflect at least part of the richness of human reasoning. The less mathematically inclined reader may safely omit this section, although we have made some attempt to explain the concepts involved in such a way as to be accessible to non-mathematicians.

Several papers appeared during the early 1980s discussing the connections between fuzzy sets theory and the theory of elementary toposes (or topoi for some authors) [40, 63, 155, 167, 168]. The latter theory is particularly attractive for several reasons. Firstly, it unites two previously distinct branches of mathematical thought: Algebraic Geometry and Logic, thus bringing geometrical intuition into the tool kit of the logician. Secondly, it is known that if one thinks of a topos as a (relativized) foundation for mathematics, then many of the well known constructions of ordinary mathematics are available, and especially those of the predicate calculus. In fact, it has been said [197] that toposes provide a constructive internal form of higher-order logic.

One current area of interest to fuzzy set theorists is quantification, which has been investigated by Zadeh [217]. The subject seems to be not without its problems. If it were known that the 'fuzzy world' were a topos then we would not only know that the crisp quantifiers lived in that world, but would have an explicit, essentially algebraic, construction of them, and a guarantee of good behaviour.

Lastly, toposes implicitly generalize logic in the sense of Intuitionism. That is to say we lose the classical law of the excluded middle (as indeed we want to) and only Kolmogorov's generalized law of negation holds [72, 121]. Even so, it is known that toposes provide an adequate axiomatization for 'set theory' [50].

Historically, there are several general points to be made. One is that Goguen [75] investigated the axioms required for a category of fuzzy sets following, very much, the work of Lawvere [128] which led the latter to discover the topos notion. It is clear that a similar process of generalization was at work in the sense that both a topos and a category of fuzzy sets have, except in the trivial case, a many-valued truth object. Also, both the fuzzy sets community and workers in sheaf theory (which was the geometric progenitor of toposes) were interested in representing concepts with their abstract constructions. The question was (and is) how to specify the common ground between the two approaches.

Eytan [63] claimed that a certain category whose objects were fuzzy sets was not only a topos but a Grothendieck or 'French' topos; which is a stronger condition. Unfortunately, not all the proofs appear in the paper and it is not easy to follow the reasoning. However, many of the constructions described are extremly interesting and, we daresay, useful.

Carrega [40] claimed exactly the opposite. The interesting point is that, at about the same time that Carrega's paper appeared so did one by Pitts [167] which also asserts that the category in question is not a topos. The present authors' reading of each paper indicated, at first, that while asserting the same result they could be mutually contradictory. The points of detail necessary to resolve this seem to have escaped attention except that in a so far unpublished paper by Eytan one rather elegant and perhaps obvious solution has been proposed [64]. Furthermore, Pitts' asides are profound and lead to some, we believe, fruitful lines of investigation for those of us who wish to use fuzzy reasoning in knowledge engineering applications. In fact, most of the intuition behind this work came from a purely practical involvement with REVEAL. This section will introduce the basic mathematical notions and explain the relevance of this work for the future of knowledge engineering. It is loosely based on a paper by Graham [79].

6.6.2 Category theory

The notion of category arises when we observe that the various kinds of function useful in mathematics are all important precisely because they preserve 'structure' in some sense. This is best seen from some examples. Consider Table 6.1.

Table 6.1

Objects	Morphisms	Structure
Sets	Functions	Points
Groups	Homomorphisms	Multiplication
Vector spaces	Linear mappings	Linearity
Topological spaces	Continuous functions	Nearness
Metric spaces	Metric functions	Distance
Affine spaces	Affine mappings	Straightness
Fuzzy (Tolerance) spaces (Poston [169])	Fuzmic maps	Indistinguishability
Sets	Relations	?
Categories	Functors	Associativity
Fuzzy sets	?	?

Thus, we talk about the objects and (interchangeably) the maps, morphisms or arrows of a category. The arrows must compose associatively and there must be an identity arrow for each object. When we think of the 'higher order' notion of the category of categories the idea of functor arises as the correct notion of structure-preserving arrow. Functors can have various additional properties related to the preservation of structure in addition to associativity and identities. For example, a Cartesian closed category is one which permits the construction of all limit and colimit constructions: products (Cartesian), kernels, sums (direct), co-kernels, intersections, unions, etc., all form examples of the latter. Also, we must be able to form function spaces or 'power set' objects. These have a lattice structure which can be viewed as the structure of a category where a map exists exactly when there is an inclusion in the power set.

The other interesting definition relating to functors arises when we have two *adjoint* functors:

$$F$$
$$A \quad G \quad B$$

for which there are bijections

$$f: \mathrm{Hom}_B(Fa, b) \cong \mathrm{Hom}_A(a, Gb) \text{ for all objects } a, b$$

satisfying a naturality condition. For details see MacLane [136].

The most important example in our present context is the exponential adjointness relation between the product and power set functors, for which we introduce the notation:

$$\frac{X \longrightarrow Y^A}{A \times X \longrightarrow Y}$$

6.6.3   Lattices, Heyting algebras, locales and frames

A Heyting algebra H is the generalization of a Boolean algebra (or lattice) appropriate to Intuitionistic logics (see [52]). It is a Cartesian closed (small) category in which for all objects A, B

$$B^A \cup A^B$$

has at most one point. We could also define a Heyting algebra as a partially ordered set $(H, \wedge, \vee)$ such that

$1 \wedge x = x$	;	$0 \vee x = x$	;
$x \wedge x = x$	;	$x \vee x = x$	;
$x \wedge y = y \wedge x$	;	$x \vee y = y \vee x$	;
$x \wedge (y \wedge z) = (x \wedge y) \wedge z$	;	$x \vee (y \vee z) = (x \vee y) \vee z$	;
$x \wedge (y \vee z) = x = (x \wedge y) \vee x$			

Negation or compliment can be defined as $\neg x$ iff $x \rightarrow 0$ where $x \rightarrow y$ denotes the largest element whose intersection with x is dominated by y.

Note that we do *not* have either $\neg \neg x = x$ or $x \vee \neg x = 1$ although we do have $x \wedge \neg x = 0$ in general; this distinguishes Heyting from Boolean algebras. An example is the lattice of open sets of a topological space. This example gives rise to the so-called topological models of logic.

We now proceed to the definitions of internal categories, frames and locales. We wish to regard complete Heyting algebras as generalized topological spaces. This is because when we later come to consider toposes as generalized categories of sheaves over a space the natural way to do this is to regard the base space as a lattice. However from a category theoretic point of view we will also require a definition of morphisms, and the natural definition of homomorphism for Heyting algebras does not preserve implication (containment). For this reason we introduce the category of frames whose objects are complete Heyting algebras but whose arrows are functions preserving finite meets and arbitrary joins and which satisfy

$$x \wedge \mathbf{V}Y = \{x \wedge y : y \in Y\} \text{ (Infinite distribution)}$$

Note that this notion of frame has absolutely no connection with the frames of Chapter 2 nor with the frame problem. Frames form a much more convenient category to work in than do Heyting algebras since it is algebraic and generalizes a geometric notion. The category of Locales has the same objects, complete Heyting algebras, but its arrows go in the opposite direction. These arrows are usually referred to as 'continuous maps'. If Ω is the functor which takes a topological space to its lattice of open subsets, then assigning to each locale A its set of points (maps from $\{0, 1\}$ to A) is a functor right adjoint to Ω.

So far we have defined categories as if they were primitive concepts, but have noticed that some of the notions we can define in the category of sets turn out to have the properties of categories themselves. We refer to such entities as category objects or internal categories. Examples are lattices, Heyting algebras, locales, etc. These have a dual nature as structures within (Sets) and as categories in their own right. To exploit and generalize this and other properties of the category of sets we turn to a newer notion.

6.6.4 Toposes

Another special kind of category is an elementary topos; that is a Cartesian closed category with a subobject classifier. The latter condition says that there exists a unique map $1 \rightarrow H$ (called 'true') such that for all subobjects $A' \rightarrow A$ there is a unique characteristic function f such that the system shown in Fig. 6.16 is a pullback.

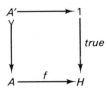

Fig. 6.16 Subobject classifier

An example in the category of sets and functions is a topos with classifier $\{0, 1\} = 2$.

The other motivating examples arose in the context of algebraic geometry, the work of Alexander Grothendieck [83] being of particular significance. All categories of sheaves over a 'site' (a generalization of a topological space) turn out to be toposes. It turns out that H has the structure of a frame.

There are now many generalizations/extensions of the notion of topos in circulation; logos, etc.

It is worthwhile noting at this point that while the classical logical laws of the excluded middle and double negation fail in the way indicated above in a Heyting algebra and, *a fortiori*, a topos, the situation in fuzzy logic is slightly different. The double negation law holds and the middle is not excluded for a different reason; namely

$$x \wedge \neg x \neq 0$$
$$x \vee \neg x \neq 1$$

We conjecture that this indicates that the restriction of generality in passing from toposes to fuzzy sets is of value precisely because of these properties, and that attempts to fuzzify equality (see Section 6.6.6) may be counter-productive in seeking too great a generality.

An alternative approach which may prove profitable is to dispense with the Heyting algebra structure and concentrate on the structure of the lattice of fuzzy subsets. Negoita and Ralescu [158] describe this as a Morgan algebra. Now, it is known that given any algebraic theory we can construct a topos with exactly the logical properties required to prove the 'theorems' of that theory. The authors are indebted to Christopher Mulvey for pointing out the existence of this method. It seems natural to speculate that the topos constructed from the theory of Morgan algebras would be worthy of study. Arbib and Manes [11], Negoita and Ralescu [158] and Eytan [63] discuss the use of monads to construct 'fuzzy theories' in an arbitrary category, but this seems to be essentially different from what is proposed here. The key technology here seems to be the theory of Locales, discussed in Johnstone [107]. Johnstone also [106] takes a view on the controversial subject of the correct plural of topos which we adhere to here. He points out that people don't carry their hot drinks around in 'thermoi'; which is why we have tried to use 'toposes' consistently herein.

It is well known [50, 72, 117, 127] that in any topos we can construct the operations of the predicate calculus as follows.

(1) true: $1 \to H$
(2) false: $1 \to H$ classifies $0 \to 1$
(3) and: $H \times H \to H$ classifies $(t, f) : 1 \to H \times H$
(4) $\Rightarrow$: $H \times H \to H$ is classified by the equalizer of 'and' with the projection
(5) not: $H \to H$ arises as the composite of $(1, \text{false})$ with $\Rightarrow$
(6) or: $H \times H \to H$ is the composition of (not, not) with 'and' followed not; which agrees with our usual definition.

This gives the Heyting algebra structure on H. In category theoretic terms we say that H is a Cartesian closed category. To construct the quantifiers is a little harder; briefly it is known that we can construct the so-called doctrinal diagram [117] for any topos E as shown in Fig. 6.17.

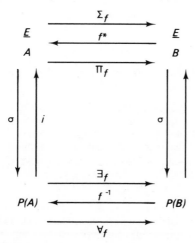

Fig. 6.17 Doctrinal diagram

Internalizing, we can represent this as

$$\exists_f : H^A \to H^B \forall_f : H^A \to H^B$$

Other useful constructions are:

$$\{.\} : A \to H^A \qquad \text{singleton}$$
$$\Delta : A \to A \times A \qquad \text{diagonal}$$

Freyd [72] explains how this may be extended to the full first-order calculus, introducing a formal language and its interpretation in a topos, and the associated model theory.

This very brief sketch is supposed to convey two ideas. One is that once you have a topos you have an adequate framework for first-order logic. The second is harder to justify from what has actually been written here, and is the notion that a topos has a dual nature. There is a contradiction between the 'internal' and 'external' aspects of a topos. For example, the treatment of power 'sets'. This arises as a corollary of the point of view that adjoint functors lie at the heart of all mathematics; see [136].

6.6.5   Presheaves and sheaves – generalized Flou sets

Fourman [71] defines a presheaf to be a contravariant functor F from the category of a base space (a lattice) X to (Sets); i.e.

$$\rho_U^V : F(V) \to F(U) \qquad \text{if } U \subseteq V$$

and

$$\rho_U^W = \rho_U^V \rho_V^W$$

A sheaf is a presheaf such that:

(F1) $\rho_{U_i}^U(s') = \rho_{U_i}(s'') \forall i \in I \Rightarrow s' = s''$

(F2) $\rho_{U_i \cap U_j}^{U_i}(s) = \rho_{U_i \cap U_j}^{U_j}(s) \Rightarrow \exists s \in F(U)$

is such that $\rho_{U_i}^U(s) = s_i \qquad \forall i \in I$

where $\{U_{ij}\}$ is a family of objects in X, and

$$U = \bigcup_I U_i$$

$$s', s'' \in F(U); \qquad s_i \in F(U_i)$$

Consider a fuzzy set $m : X \to I$ where I is the unit interval $[0, 1]$ and X is any set. Define the level sets of m as follows:

$$A_i = \{x \in X : m(x) \geqslant i\} \qquad \text{where } i \in I$$

The A_i form a family of sets indexed by I. Denote the union of this family by A.

Now, I may be regarded as a lattice or as a category where the objects are the downward segments of I and the arrows are defined as follows: If $a \leqslant b$ then the map

$$\alpha_b^a : [0, a] \to [0, b]$$

is given by inclusion.

Clearly, composition is well defined and there are identities. So we have a category, in fact, a complete distributive lattice; also referred to as I by 'abus'.

Notice that each map in I gives rise to a corresponding inclusion map of level sets

$$t_i^j : A_j \to A_i$$

given by $t_i^j(a) = a$, since if $a \in A_j$ then $\boldsymbol{m}(a) \geqslant j \geqslant i$.

We can represent the situation diagrammatically by:

$$[0, 0] \to \cdots \to [0, i] \to [0, j] \to [0, k] \to \cdots \to [0, 1]$$
$$A_0 \quad \leftarrow \cdots \leftarrow A_i \quad \leftarrow A_j \quad \leftarrow A_k \quad \leftarrow \cdots \leftarrow A_1$$

Clearly the process just described gives rise to a contravariant functor from I to the category of sets. It is easy to prove that it is a presheaf. So every fuzzy set gives rise to a presheaf. This seems to be a generalization of the well known Flou sets. [Exercise to the reader: Try to show these objects are sheaves.]

Of course, not every presheaf of sets of this form gives rise to fuzzy set. This is easy to see by considering the mushroom shaped graph in Fig. 6.18 and looking at the level sets thereof.

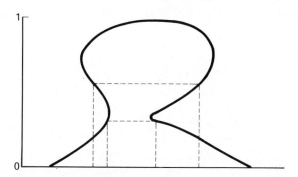

Fig. 6.18 A pathological presheaf

We can construct an internal notion of a sheaf in any topos. We proceed as follows. A closure operator is a map $j : H \to H$ such that $j^2 = j$ and which preserves *and* $: H \times H \to H$ and *true*: $1 \to H$. For example (*not, not*) is a closure operator. This generalizes the notion of a Grothendieck topology. Switching emphasis, if B' is a subobject of B then denote by $cl(B')$ the result of applying (B, j).

B' is said to be j-dense if $cl(B') = B$.

A is a j-sheaf if for all j-dense B' in B we have that $(B, A) \to (B', A)$ is an isomorphism.

We also define

$$H_j \xrightarrow{\hspace{3cm}} H \underset{\longrightarrow}{\overset{\longrightarrow}{\quad 1, j \quad}} H$$

as an equalizer and note that H_j and H are sheaves. The full subcategory of j-sheaves is a topos with classifier H_j.

6.6.6 Categories of fuzzy sets

A fuzzy set is a map $m:A \to H$. We want to extend this notion to a category by a suitable definition of fuzzy mappings. The obvious definition is that produced originally by Goguen [75] where maps are 'simplifications'; i.e.

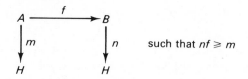

such that $nf \geq m$

Note the relation with increased knowledge, clarification or simplification. There is about this concept something reminiscent of entropy.

This category fails to be a topos because it is impossible to make it satisfy the subobject classifier condition unless $H = \{0, 1\}$. This is proven by Carrega [40] although the present author had proved it independently.

Another definition of map, introduced by Eytan [63], is as follows. A map is given by a relation

$$f : A \times B \to H$$

satisfying:

$$
\begin{array}{ll}
f(a, b) \leqslant m(a) & \forall a \in A,\ \forall b \in B \\
f(a, b) \leqslant n(b) & \forall a \in A,\ \forall b \in B \\
m(a) \leqslant \sup_B f(a, b) & \forall a \in A \\
f(a, b) \text{ and } f(a, b') \leqslant \delta(b, b') & \forall a A,\ \forall b,\ b' \in B
\end{array}
$$

where δ is the Kronecker delta.

Carrega claims that this category is equivalent to a generalization of Goguen's category. Certainly, the requirement that H is a chain is unnecessarily restrictive, and the only example which can be found giving rise to a chain is the algebra generated by the down segments of the interval $[0, 1]$ – the classical case! For example, consider any power set.

Pitts, on the other hand, proves that Eytan's category is embedded in the category of H-sets, known to be equivalent to a category of sheaves and thus to a topos. He then shows that Fuz-H is a topos only in the case where H is Boolean. Now in a topos this means that H is isomorphic to $1 + 1$ where 1 is the terminal object. However, in general, the global sections (points) of $1 + 1$ can be an arbitrary complete Boolean algebra [197]. The question then arises as to whether H has only two sections in this case.

If the latter were true, it would prove [50] that Fuz-H was a model of (Sets).

It may be useful here to summarize the definitions of H-sets and subconstant objects thereof, the latter being identified by Pitts with fuzzy sets.

An H valued set or H-set is a relation $[\![. , .]\!] : A \times B \to H$ satisfying conditions of symmetry and transitivity. Mappings of H-sets may be defined also; see [167].

Subconstant objects are defined as subobjects of the form:

$$\delta(i, i') = \begin{cases} 1 & \text{if } i = i' \\ 0 & \text{otherwise} \end{cases}$$

The picture in Fig. 6.19 may help.

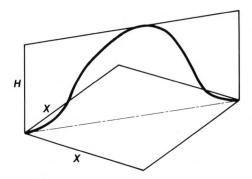

Fig. 6.19 Subconstant objects

This raises a whole series of interesting problems:

(1) Can we indeed show that H has two sections exactly? This involves some explicit constructions in H-Set.
(2) Some of our problems arise from the choice of $1-p$ as the valuation of not. Are there any other candidates?
(3) Is another definition going to be useful in practical contexts? This is likely to be the case where we are using linguistic approximation to describe temporal negation, wherein phenomena repeat themselves in enriched forms after double negation.
(4) Is it possible to sidestep these problems by a totally different choice of the morphisms? This seems unlikely and leads naturally to the idea of abandoning fuzzy for intuitionist logic as far as programming is concerned, but the latter is so much harder to work with.
(5) Which of the constructions which we have in H-Set can be carried over to the full subcategory of subconstant objects; i.e. the fuzzy sets? Assuming that all the interesting cases have H non-Boolean (this we assert is going to be the case) then we still know that Fuz-H is a full subcategory of a topos. Now, the finite sets form a full subcategory of Sets, and we can do many useful things with only finite sets. Think of computers for instance! Of course, finite sets form a topos but that only weakens the argument slightly. How will the logical constructions – not, and, or, $\exists_f$, $\forall_f$ – in the surrounding topos look when we consider their application in the subcategory? Clearly, the most immediate problem is again negation, but ignoring this for the present what do the constructions of the quantifiers induce? It would be interesting to explore the bearing of these constructions on Zadeh's theories of fuzzy quantification [217].
(6) Can we introduce the fuzzification of equality by working with a 'fuzzy valued' logic; i.e. by treating the value 'true' as an object in the function space $I \to I$? Some of these questions are answered in an unpublished paper by Eytan [64]. His solution of the problem pointed out by Pitts is to revise the definition of maps in Fuz-H so the intuitionistic version of the Kronecker delta is used. This relation is given by:

$$\delta_e(i, j) = 1$$
$$\delta_e(i, j) = \delta_e(j, i)$$
$$\delta_e(i, j) \wedge \delta_e(j, k) \leqslant \delta_e(i, k)$$
$$\delta_e(i_1, j_1) \wedge \ldots \wedge \delta_e(i_n, j_n) \wedge r(_1, \ldots, i_n) \leqslant r(j_1, \ldots, j_n)$$

for all relations $r : Xx \ldots xX \rightarrow H$. Eytan proves that with this definition of arrows the category Fuz-H is actually equivalent to (H-sets) and is therefore a topos of sheaves. This corresponds well to the idea that the semantics of fuzzy logic is that of stages of knowledge and leads to the possibility (as yet unrealized) of a unification of multivalent with nonmonotonic logic through this kind of semantics. Further evidence that this point of view is the correct one comes from the work of Hohle [101] who proves the remarkable fact that the internalization of the ordinary notion of topological space to H-Set is equivalent to the notion of fuzzy topological space due to Lowen [134]. He has also shown that subgroup objects in H-Set are the fuzzy groups of Rosenfeld. He points out, interestingly, that fuzzy set theory can be viewed from two different philosophical points of view: intuitionistic or positivist. The internal logic of H-Set is intuitionistic whereas in ordinary fuzzy sets theory the logic is the Lukasiewitz–Tarski system we have dealt with earlier in this chapter. This begins to settle the point about using $1 - x$ as negation. However, Hohle also points to the lack of closure of the positivist system which some people might find disturbing.

6.6.7   What kinds of logic are suited to fuzzy set theory?

Several multivalent and fuzzy logics are surveyed in Dubois and Prade [59] and some have been dealt with in this chapter. The most interesting from a practical point of view is Zadeh's Approximate Reasoning. See Section 6.4.

If we accept the view that quantifiers are required in our logic then Zadeh's theory is doubly attractive, but there are a number of yet unsolved problems related to completeness, consistency and so on. Also there is the nagging doubt that a fuzzy quantifier such as 'some' is really no more than an ordinary quantifier qualified by a possibility (which is the approach adopted in REVEAL [109]). It is tempting to look to topos theory for the answer to some of these problems, either by generalizing the notion of topos (especially the notion of subobject classifier) or by extending fuzzy set theory in the way suggested by Pitts. The latter's most profound 'aside' was that one should expect to have to fuzzify equality as well as membership.

In Approximate Reasoning [59, 190] when we say that 'A is *true*', we usually think of the diagonal set as representing truth; not, notice, the 'equal-to-one-everywhere' fuzzy set. For that reason if we were trying to find a subobject classifier we *might* proceed as follows.

Classifying a subobject means answering the question: 'Is it true that A is in B' or equivalent. If we work with the (lattice generated by the) unit interval I, it is tempting to

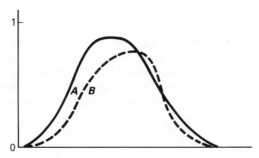

Fig. 6.20   'Nearly contained' subsets

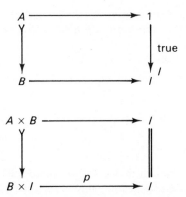

choose I for the truth object, but this means that the function true : $1 \rightarrow I$ picks out a particular value (down segment) as value. However, we assert that this may, at least, hamstring our intuition; being a subobject cannot be dealt with so 'crisply'.

Consider for example two fuzzy subsets of the same domain as shown in Fig. 6.20. There is clearly a sense in which we might wish to say that B is (nearly) a subset of A, or $A \subseteq B$ is true. In topos jargon our subobject classifier true : $1 \rightarrow I$ has to assign a value in the function space (I, I). So we want a pullback of the form shown in Fig. 6.20. Taking adjoints we get the system shown in Fig. 6.21 where p takes $(b, m(b))$ to the degree to which $b, m(b)$ is in the subobject. This presentation is deliberately informal, it is intended to stimulate rather than inform. We have not looked at the details, but this approach does offer some hope of meeting the requirement of 'fuzzifying equality'.

6.6.8   Problems of knowledge representation

Knowledge engineers face many problems, not least of which are those associated with extracting knowledge from human beings who do not always express themselves in frames, semantic networks, production rules and the other formalisms dealt with in Chapter 2. Mapping human knowledge into a convenient structure requires much of the engineer as well as of the formalism used. The idea behind Logic Programming is that if the knowledge can be written down as a series of clauses such as

> All men are mortal,
> Socrates is a man

or

> $x \in MEN \Rightarrow x \in \wedge MORTALS,$
> Socrates $\in MEN$

then some inference rules can be methodically applied to produce valid conclusions, such as the mortality of certain philosophers. There are, of course, many ways in which the rules of inference can be applied, but the choice of strategy is chiefly a matter of economy. The choice of 'backtracking' in the PROLOG language is an example of such a method (see Chapter 7). What is more interesting is the logical properties of the clauses and the rules of inference themselves. From an intuitionist point of view these represent knowledge about the practice of reasoning with concepts.

Proponents of logic programming assert that the first-order predicate calculus is good at, if not the only way of [123]), representing knowledge. The defects in this position can be intuited from a list of examples:

(1) Modal thinking
(2) Problem solving by geometric intuition
(3) Deontic thinking
(4) Epistemic thinking
(5) Meta-thinking
       etc. . . .
(*n*) Non-Boolean thinking.

All these modes of thought are current and all are indispensible, and they are either not, or are badly, addressed by logic representations. Perhaps we can see this most easily by asking the computer logicians questions about semantics and pragmatics. Also, anyone familiar with PROLOG will be aware of the difficulties in representing uncertainty and of dealing with rule contention and 'symbiosis'; by which we mean the situation where two rules are useful together but not in isolation. Our own experience indicates the power of such an approach [109, 190].

As an example consider the following REVEAL program (to be considered again in Chapter 8).

1. **THE SELLING PRICE SHOULD BE LOW**
2. **THE SELLING PRICE SHOULD BE ABOUT 2*DIRECT . COST**
3. **IF THE COMPETITION PRICE IS NOT VERY HIGH THEN OUR SELLING PRICE SHOULD BE NEAR THE COMPETITION**

This illustrates a situation where statements 1 and 2 evidently contradict each other and, less obviously perhaps, one where the removal of these 'fuzzy constraints' (in the sense of Bellman and Zadeh [24]) renders rule 3 meaningless. It is the totality of the three statements which has meaning. The power of Approximate Reasoning in this case is its ability to automatically resolve the contradictions and continue to make the inference of a value for SELLING which is optimal in some sense. Thus, two of the key problems faced by knowledge engineers are addressed simultaneously: how to represent uncertainty and how, given the constraint of a production system, to deal with rule contention. These points will be explored further in the two following chapters.

To assert that Approximate Reasoning or its instantiation in REVEAL is Logic Programming is not our intention, but we do maintain that there are similarities which, if exploited, will lead to the goal we seek. Kowalski [122] is aware of the desirability of handling higher-order constructs, and of course in real life the language does have higher-order statements. Because of the informal way in which we express knowledge, often using second-order formulations, it would certainly be more convenient to allow such constructions in the formal system. The topos theoretic approach promises much in this respect, just as fuzzy methods offer much in terms of representing concepts and knowledge about concepts. Baldwin's FPROLOG is certainly a step in the right direction [15].

We are often confronted with scepticism about the logical soundness of the fuzzy approach, even where its efficacy is accepted. Thus the need arises to search for a profound level of justification for fuzzy logic which will, at a minimum, allow fuzzy logic to enjoy the apotheosis of classical logic; i.e. its situation within the foundations of mathematics. It should also extend the latter to deal with uncertainty and non-Boolean forms of reasoning.

The theory of elementary toposes provides a ready-made answer. Therefore it is attractive to site fuzzy theories in this context if possible.

Our last point is a philosophical one. Intuitionism in mathematics opposes itself to Formalism. Formalists fail to understand that axioms arise from our practice in nature and are not arbitrary constructions of pure thought. The historical connection of formal logic with Kantianism and its latter day derivatives – Empiricism, Pragmatism, Positivism, etc. – is therefore no accident; a poor substitute for scientific thought when we are attempting to build that hardest of all models, a model of human reasoning. Topos theory is, so far as we are aware, the only foundational formalism that comes near to combining the richness of the Heraclitean dialectic with the power of a rigorous foundational discipline.

The research proposed in this section is therefore of importance to knowledge engineers, mathematicians and philosophers alike.

"Πάντα ρεῖ, οὐδὲν μέναι"*.
            Herakleitos

6.7 SUMMARY

This chapter has concerned itself with the means by which decisions and judgements are reached, in general and in particular under uncertainty. We have introduced a vast amount of mathematical apparatus, from formal logic to abstract algebra. Starting with classical logic, we showed how it was possible to use the inbuilt contradictions to develop various logics of uncertainty. We discussed their use in building knowledge-based systems. Lastly we introduced the reader to a research area in fuzzy mathematics: the attempt to unite intuitionist logic and fuzzy set theory.

6.8 FURTHER READING

The seminal work on modern formal logic is of course Boole [29]. Bundy's book [37] on mathematical theorem proving is most enlightening and pertinent to the connection between artificial intelligence and the subject matter of formal logic. For the basic category theory we recommend MacLane [136] and Johnstone [106]. For a basic but classical text on logic programming there is no better than Kowalski [122] or Clark and Tarnlund [46]. Barwise [18] is an excellent survey of modern mathematical logic whilst its relationship to linguistics is very clearly discussed in Alwood *et al.* [1], and to philosophy in Ayer [13]. Some of the material of this chapter is further developed in Turner [201]. Fuzzy logic is covered well in Dubois and Prade [59] although it is fairly difficult to read, if comprehensive. An easier introduction seems not to exist, the closest being Zimmermann [222].

The historical section at the opening of this chapter assumes a great deal of

---

*All is flux, nothing remains stationary.

background. This and other remarks in this chapter are supported *inter alia* by references [94, 166, 195, 196].

The mathematical material in Section 6.6 again assumes a lot of background. Relevant further reading to supply such a background is to be found in [88, 96, 126, 159, 174, 205].

Several papers in Gupta and Sanchez [85] provide good introductory material on fuzzy sets, while Kickert [113] deals with the relationship of fuzzy sets and decision making from an operations research standpoint.

A non-formal introductuion to some of the mathematical concepts is given in Beckman [20], and Burge [38].

7

Inference methods

'He'd run in debt by disputation,
And pay with ratiocination.'
Hudibras, Samuel Butler

7.1 INTRODUCTION

We now come to the other principal component in a knowledge-based system, the knowledge application system or, as it is often called, the inference engine. Given that knowledge is stored in a computer in some convenient representation or representations, the system will require facilities for navigating through and manipulating the knowledge if anything is to be achieved at all. In this section we deal with the various techniques that have been used, paying particular attention to the treatment of uncertainty.

One subject is only given scanty treatment; that is, the subject of tree searching. This is so extensively and well covered in the existing literature that we felt it necessary only to briefly mention each strategy and give the appropriate references. The best general references are Addis [3], Nilsson [163] and Winston [210].

Inference in the usual logical sense is the process of drawing valid conclusions from premises. In our wider sense it is any computational mechanism whereby stored knowledge can be applied to data and information structures to arrive at conclusions which are to be plausible rather than valid in the strict logical sense. This, of course, poses problems in relation to how to judge whether the conclusions are reasonable, and how to represent knowledge about how to test conclusions and how to evaluate plausibility. Thus we see again, as in the last chapter, that knowledge representation and inference are inextricably bound together. In the next section we turn to logic once more to begin our investigation of systems for knowledge application.

7.2 INFERENCE METHODS AND LOGIC

7.2.1 Rules of inference: crisp and fuzzy

In Chapter 6 we introduced the idea of rules of inference in a formal system. In this chapter we return to this idea at a much more informal level, based partly on the approach of McCawley [253]. Recall that a formal system comes equipped with the connectives

$\wedge$ (and), $\vee$ (or), $\neg$ (not), $\Rightarrow$ (implies), $\Leftrightarrow$ (iff) and (sometimes) $=$

and with (at least) two quantification symbols

$\forall$ and $\exists$.

The primitive symbols are usually taken to include only *and*, *or*, *implies* and *not*. These symbols can be used together with propositions to make up sentences, and these are valid sentences when they follow by specified rules of inference from a few selected sentences called axioms. The rules of inference we will use here fall into two classes called rules of introduction and rules of elimination. The introduction rule for *and* says that, for example, if the sentences:

Ronald is American
Margaret is English
Helmut is German

are all true, then we may infer that the sentence:

Ronald is American and Margaret is English and Helmut is German

is also true. The corresponding elimination rule says that if the previous sentence is true then we may infer that any one of the earlier three holds. We may state the rules more succinctly as follows.

$\wedge$ introduction

p
q
r
$\overline{}$
$p \wedge q \wedge r$

$\wedge$ elimination

$\overline{p \wedge q \wedge r}$
p

Similarly, we can state rules for the other connectives and the quantifiers.

$\vee$ introduction

$\overline{p}$
$p \vee q \vee r$

$\vee$ elimination

$\overline{p \vee q \vee r}$
one of p, q, r

The rules of $\neg$ introduction and elimination are known as *reductio ad absurdum* and 'the law of the excluded middle' respectively. They are not valid in all logical systems. For the purposes of reasoning one of the most interesting rules is $\Rightarrow$ elimination which is also known as *modus ponens*:

$p \Rightarrow q$ (*Modus ponens*, $\Rightarrow$ elimination)
$\underline{p}$
q

This rule sanctions inferences of the form:

If Socrates is a man, then he is mortal
Socrates is a man
   Therefore
Socrates is mortal.

$\Rightarrow$ introduction sanctions the following type of argument:

Whoever committed the murder left by the window.
Anyone leaving by the window would have mud on his boots.
If the butler committed the murder, then he left by the window.
Therefore he has mud on his boots.
So, if the butler did it he has muddy boots.

This just says that implication is transitive;

$p \Rightarrow q$ ($\Rightarrow$ introduction)

$\underline{q \Rightarrow r}$

$p \Rightarrow r$

Now the rules for the quantifiers.

$\forall$ introduction (generalization) $\forall$ elimination

$\underline{p}$ $(\forall x : q(x))p(x)$

$(\forall x)p(x)$ $\underline{q(a)}$

                                       $p(a)$

$\exists$ introduction

$\underline{p(a)}$

$(\exists x)p(x)$

EXERCISE: Try to write down the rule of $\exists$ elimination.

Returning to *modus ponens* as a model of reasoning *forwards* from premises to conclusion, we can put the case as follows. From a fact p and a rule $p \Rightarrow q$ we may deduce a new fact q with certainty. Two other rules of inference which follow from those given above are *modus tollens* and the resolution principle which latter is the basis of automatic theorem proving systems [177]:

Modus tollens   Resolution

$p \Rightarrow q$ $p \vee q$

$\underline{\neg q}$ $\underline{\neg q \vee r}$

$\neg p$ $p \vee r$

Modus tollens is clearly a very different kettle of fish from *modus ponens*; we are reasoning *backwards* from the falsity of a conclusion to the falsity of the premise. *Modus tollens* is much harder for humans to understand and compute with although it is similar to a lot of problem-solving behaviour, as we will see later. For example, suppose p = 'It is raining' and q = 'It is cloudy', then the two kinds of inference are exemplified by:

If it is raining then we know it must be cloudy.
If it is not cloudy then we know it can't be raining.

In the latter case we are implicitly invoking the rule of *modus tollens* on the implication 'if raining then cloudy'.

One or two words of caution are appropriate at this point. The reader should beware of confusing inference with implication; to say that the proposition $p \Rightarrow q$ is true is to assign it a truth value, whereas to infer the truth of q from that of p and $p \Rightarrow q$ is to assign a truth value to the proposition q. The importance of this distinction becomes especially clear when we notice that the implication operator in most logical systems is not the causal implication of common-sense reasoning. Thus the following assignments of truth values to sentences in classical logic are quite consistent even though they fly in the face of common-sense.

The moon is made of green cheese	false
Neil Armstrong was the first man on the moon	true
H. G. Wells was the first man on the moon	false
The moon is made of green cheese implies that Neil Armstrong was the first man on the moon	true
The moon is made of green cheese implies that H. G. Wells was the first man on the moon	true

To see this is the case refer to the truth table for $\Rightarrow$ given in Section 6.3. This notion of implication is known as material implication. In some modal logics the implication is closer to our usual idea.

Up to now we have assumed that the value of propositions can be only either true or false. In the case of most practical reasoning, uncertainty is involved. There are cases where it is difficult to decide whether the adjective 'cloudy' is exactly true. For example if the cloud cover is exactly 55% then are we to say it is insufficiently cloudy to imply rain or not? The extension principle (see Chapter 6) allows us to fuzzify both *modus ponens* and *tollens*. Suppose that $p =$ 'it is raining' is true to the extent 0.7, then the minimum degree of truth we would wish to assign to $q =$ 'it is cloudy' is 0.7. However, if we only know the implication $p \Rightarrow q$ to the extent 0.5 then our confidence in the conclusion is further diminished to a number which depends on the way in which the uncertainty is to be interpreted, or the fuzzy logic in use. If we are dealing with probability the value would be $0.5 \times 0.7 = 0.35$. If possibility then $\min(0.5, 0.7) = 0.5$. It is easier to see what fuzzy *modus ponens* does if we consider not just individual truth values, but the entire fuzzy sets underlying them. To see this suppose 'raining' is a fuzzy set defined on the variable 'inches of rain per unit time' and given by the vector $p = [0\ 0.4\ 0.7\ 0.9\ 1]$ and that cloudy is similarly defined over 'percentage of cloud cover' by $q = [0\ 0.3\ 0.7\ 1]$. Then the fuzzy relation describing $p \Rightarrow q$, using the sup-min composition described in the preceding chapter, is

$$\begin{bmatrix} 0 & 0.3 & 0.7 & 1 \\ 0 & 0.3 & 0.7 & 0.9 \\ 0 & 0.3 & 0.7 & 0.7 \\ 0 & 0.3 & 0.4 & 0.4 \\ 0 & 0 & 0 & 0 \end{bmatrix}$$

From this, given a value for p we can infer a fuzzy set for q. The procedure is known as fuzzy *modus ponens*.

It is usual in practical applications to require that the answer is a single truth value rather than a fuzzy set, and we have seen in Chapter 5 how the fuzzy implication rule can be chosen from either the mean of the maxima or the centre of moments of the resultant fuzzy set. We must, however, point out that the implication function given above ($\neg$ ext(p) $\vee$ ext(q)) is not the only one possible. For example, the minimum of the extensions is appropriate in some applications.

Fuzzy *modus tollens* can be operated in the same way, but working this out in detail is left as an exercise to the reader, since it has not been much in evidence in applications so far. The reasons for this will become clearer when we come to consider fuzzy backward chaining later in this chapter.

7.2.2 Forward and backward chaining

Up to now in this chapter we have only considered the problem of how to infer the truth value of one proposition from another using a rule of inference in just one step. Clearly however, there will be occasions when such inferences (or proofs) will involve long chains of reasoning using the rules of inference and some initial suppositions (or axioms). We now turn to the generalizations of *modus ponens* and *modus tollens* which feature strongly in all expert systems.

To fix ideas we will consider an expert system whose knowledge is represented in the form of production rules and whose domain is the truth of abstract propositions; $A, B, C, \ldots$ The knowledge base is as follows.

Rule 1: A and B and C implies D
Rule 2: D and F implies G
Rule 3: E implies F
Rule 4: F implies B
Rule 5: B implies C
Rule 6: G implies H
Rule 7: I implies J
Rule 8: A and F implies H

To start with, let us assume that a two-valued logic and *modus ponens* are available, and that the expert system has been asked whether proposition H is true given that propositions *A* and *F* are true. We will show that the system may approach the problem in at least two quite distinct ways. Let us also assume for the present that the computer stores these rules on a sequential device such as magnetic tape, so that it must access the rules in order unless it rewinds to rule 1.

The assumption is that *A* and *F* are true. If we apply all the rules to this database the only rules that fire are 5 and 8 and the firing of rule 8 assigns the value true to *H*, which is what we were after. Suppose now that rule 8 is excised from the knowledge base. Can we still prove *H*? This time only rule 5 fires, so we have to rewind and apply the rules again to have any chance of proving the target proposition. Below we show what happens to the truth values in the database on successive applications of the rules 1 to 7.

	Iteration number							
	0	1	2	3	4	5	6	7
A	T	T	T	T	T	T	T	T
B		T	T	T	T	T	T	T
C			T	T	T	T	T	T
D				T	T	T	T	T
E								
F	T	T	T	T	T	T	T	T
G					T	T	T	T
H						T	T	T
I								
J								

So, *H* is proven after five iterations. Note, in passing, that further iterations do not succeed in proving any further propositions in this particular case. Since we are considering a computer strategy, we need to program some means by which the machine is to know when to stop applying rules. From the above example there are two methods: either 'stop when *H* becomes true' or 'stop when the database ceases to change on rule application'. Which one of these two we select depends on the system's purpose, for one interesting side effect of the latter procedure is that we have proven the proposition *B*, *C*, *D* and *G* and, were we later to need to know their truth values, we need do no more computation. On the other hand, if this is not an important consideration we might have proved *H* long before we can prove everything else.

It should be noted that we have assumed that the rules are applied 'in parallel', which is to say that in any one iteration every rule fires on the basis that the data are as they were at the beginning of the cycle. This is not necessary, but we would warn of the confusion which would result from the alternative in any practical applications; a knowledge-based, and thus essentially declarative system, should not be dependent of the order in which the rules are entered, stored or processed unless there is some very good reason for forcing modularity on the rules.

These two strategies are both known as *forward chaining* or *data directed* reasoning, because they begin with the data known and apply *modus ponens* successively to find out what results are implied. In expert systems, this strategy is particularly appropriate in situations where data are expensive to collect but potentially few in quantity. Typical domains are financial planning, process control, the configuration of complex systems and system tuning.

In the example given, the antecedents and consequents of the rules are all of the same type: propositions in some logical system. However, this need not be the case. For example, in industrial control applications the inputs might be measurements but the output control actions. In that case it does not make sense to add these incommensurables together in the database. Variations on forward chaining now include: 'pass through the rules until a single rule fires then act'; 'pass through all the rules once and then act'.

There is a completely different way we could have set about proving H, and that is to start with the desired goal 'H is true' and attempt to find evidence for this to be the case. This is *backward chaining* or *goal directed* inference. It is usual when the only thing we need to do is prove H and are not interested in the value of other propositions.

Backwards chaining arises typically in situations where the quantity of data is potentially very large and where some specific characteristic of the system under consideration is of interest. Most typical are various problems of diagnosis, such as medical diagnosis (MYCIN) or fault finding in electrical or mechanical equipment. It must be said however that fault diagnosis is usually regarded as a forward chaining problem, and most commercial systems take this view in terms of the syntax they offer for this type of problem. With this proviso, most expert system shells are based on some form of backward chaining. Many of them involve backward chaining under uncertainty, and we will deal with two varieties of this in Section 7.5 of this chapter.

Returning to our original eight rules, the system is asked to find a rule which proves H. The only candidate rules are 6 and 8, but 6 is encountered first. At this point we establish a new subgoal of proving that G is true, for if we can do this then it would follow that H were true by *modus ponens*. Our next subgoal will be to prove that D and F are true. Recall that we have told the system that A and F are true, so it is only necessary to prove D (by $\wedge$ – introduction). The whole proof proceeds as follows.

Trying to prove H
Try rule 6
Trying to prove G

Try rule 2
F is true, trying to prove D
Try rule 1
A is true, trying to prove B
Try rule 4
It works, B is true
Backtrack to trying rule 1
Trying to prove C
Try rule 5, it works, C is true
Apply rule 1, D is true
Apply rule 2, G is true
Apply rule 6, H is true

The observant reader will have noticed that we could have proved H in one step from rule 8. The point is that rule 8 was not reached and the system could not know in advance that it was going to be quicker to explore that rule than rule 6. On the other hand if the original line of exploration had failed (suppose rule 4 was deleted) then the system would have had to backtrack and try rule 8. Figure 7.1 illustrates the proof strategy, with the upward arrows denoting implication and all branches designating an 'and' combinator.

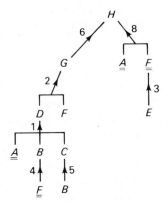

Fig. 7.1   Backward chaining through an AND tree

It is these considerations that lead to viewing backward chaining as a strategy for search through trees built in some solution space. The strategy we have described is usually called depth-first search in that context. In the next section we look at alternative strategies.

Barr and Feigenbaum [16] point out that most problems may be represented either by search for points in a state space, by reduction to simpler subproblems or by game trees. The point which emerges quite quickly is that all these representations are formally equivalent insofar as methods of search are concerned, even if they are not always equally convenient in terms of efficiency of search. The problem of mechanically choosing a convenient representation is still a long way from being solved. Here we will assume that a representation has been chosen and that the problem is to search for a solution (or solutions) only.

7.2.3 Mixed strategies and tree search

We have introduced two fundamental forms of inference, forward and backward chaining. In practice most reasoning is a mixture of at least these two. Given some initial assumption, we infer a conclusion by reasoning forwards and then apply backward chaining to find other data which confirm these conclusions. This process of abduction will be dealt with further in the next section. Alternatively, we start with a goal, backward chain to some plausible reason and then forward chain to exploit the consequences of this new datum. Both these methods can be represented as a search through a branching network or tree, and trees may be searched in a number of ways. We turn briefly now to some of the available methods. The subject of tree search is so well covered in the existing literature that we will not attempt exhaustive descriptions of every technique, but try to give the general idea for each one with a view to giving some intuition as to when a particular technique is likely to be appropriate to a problem.

Methods of searching trees may be conveniently divided into blind search and informed search. The latter is often called heuristic or intelligent search. The two basic methods of blind search are called depth-first and breadth-first search. Depth-first search corresponds to what we did in the example given in the preceding section. It is important however not to totally confuse backward chaining with depth-first search. The terms backward and forward chaining refer to the relationship between goals and data, whereas a depth-first search may be applied to either and refers only to the solution strategy. It is convenient sometimes to blur the distinction and think of depth-first search as the 'usual' way of doing backward chaining. The following diagrams illustrate the difference between depth- and breadth-first search of a state tree. We have used the same tree as in the previous section (Fig. 7.1). Depth-first search proceeds broadly as follows. Look for the left-most (or first) node beneath the goal node (or initial data in the case of forward chaining) and check if it is terminal (i.e. proven or a goal), if not establish it on a list of subgoals outstanding. Start again with the node reached as goal. Once there are no lower level nodes then, providing the current node is not terminal, go back to the last subgoal on the outstanding list and take the next route of descent to the right. If the tree has an AND/OR structure, as in our example, then success indicates going back to the last AND node, while failure indicates a return to the last outstanding OR node. Since we do not know in advance how deep the search may go only to find a failure or dead end before backtracking, it is sometimes convenient to place a restriction on the maximum depth of any one exploration. In fact the search may go on forever with infinite trees, in which case the only course is to set a limit. This is called a depth bound. The danger, of course, is that the required solution may be one step below the

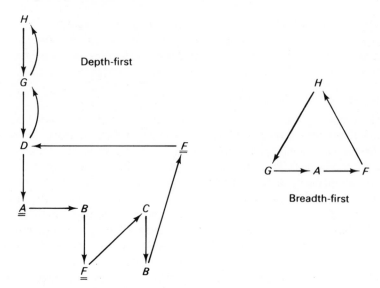

Fig. 7.2   Search strategies

bound level. There are two principal methods of implementation for this kind of search, although it can be shown that the logical systems on which they are based are formally equivalent. In languages like PROLOG which depend on the idea of pattern matching the implementation technique is called 'backtracking' and is as we have described except that explored paths are explicitly deleted and blocked and variable bindings undone at that stage, whenever failure is encountered. Backtracking accounts for much of the declarative nature of the PROLOG language since it is relatively transparent to the user. The other method, prevalent in lower level languages like LISP and PASCAL is known as recursive descent. In this case the route recording has to be hand crafted and the garbage collection done later (in most LISPs automatically). Recursive algorithms need to beware of one subtlety: if, in the above example, we were to have had rules of the form $A{\Rightarrow}B$ and $B{\Rightarrow}A$, then there is every possibility that the search could continue forever in a loop. This must be explicitly checked.

Breadth-first search expands all the nodes immediately below the initial node. Then, working from left to right, expands all these nodes until a solution is reached or the tree is completely expanded. This procedure has one striking advantage over the depth-first method; it guarantees that the shortest solution is found, if it exists. On the other hand, breadth-first search in large solution spaces can lead to huge computational costs; the so-called combinatorial explosion. This is because the cost of expanding the nodes at any level is typically the square of that on the previous level. In some cases it is appropriate to assign costs (other than computational costs) to each link of the tree. A good example is the 'travelling saleman' problem, which is essentially the problem of how to optimize the delivery route of a vehicle which must visit a number of sites once and only once on its tour. The generalized cost in that case is a linear combination of distance, time, fuel and risk costs. In a tree with costs both depth- and breadth-first techniques may be used but will be modified to expand the nodes with lowest cost first. Clearly, if an optimal solution is required breadth-first search will tend to be better.

Combining the ideas of forward and backward chaining with that of breadth-first search leads to the notion of bidirectional search. In this, a goal is expanded backwards and the initial data expanded forwards until the two trees being built can be joined, leading to a complete path. This can sometimes be much more efficient than other blind strategies. The problem we mentioned in the last section of how to avoid blind alleys or unnecessarily long searches can be dealt with in a number of ways. In our current example, we might choose, during a depth-first search, to expand those nodes with the smallest number of clauses in the antecedent. As it happens, this is the wrong strategy in this case, although it does seem a plausible one for this type of problem in general. The reason it is plausible is that it makes the tacit assumption that the computational cost of expanding a node is roughly proportional to the number of its descendants.

In a tree with costs, a slightly more intelligent way to proceed is not expand nodes with lowest cost but to store the cumulative cost of the exploration so far and expand the node whose expansion keeps the costs at a minimum. This strategy restores to breadth-first search the optimality property. One can go one step further and make an estimate of the cost of completing the search from a particular node and then minimize the sum of the two functions. This is the basic idea behind the A^* algorithm. An algorithm designated B^* has been suggested by Berliner [22] which makes much more use of knowledge to terminate the search. These algorithms have been particularly important in game playing machines. Berliner's world champion backgammon machine used fuzzy logic in its evaluation of positions.

These are our first examples of intelligent search, although the only feature of intelligence being used for the most part is memory (of the costs). Knowledge about the particular problem at hand can often be used to guide a search in several ways. These include deciding which node to expand next in a search, and which sections of a tree to disregard or discard. The latter process is known as pruning. Best-first search seeks to construe an evaluation function for every node reached. This function is often a measure of how much the current state differs from a solution state.

Minimaxing and pruning are also the result of research into game playing. The minimax procedure applies to trees whose terminal states may be regarded as falling into three categories, usually labelled 'beat', 'lose' or 'tie' (B L T for convenience). The view is taken that the tree is balanced; i.e. that every node is a bifurcation unless terminal. Also the controller can only affect alternate moves. The controller must look ahead either to terminals or sufficiently to compute an evaluation function, and then make the move which maximizes the likelihood of a win or, if not, a draw. The alternate moves will be made to minimize this likelihood. Computing the successors of every node in a tree can be unnecessary in game-like situations. A procedure reminiscent of depth-first search involves cutting off these redundant branches of the search. This is the technique of $\alpha\beta$ pruning.

Table 7.1 summarizes some of the well known search strategies. For the gory details of how they work the reader is referred to Barr and Feigenbaum [16], Nilsson [163], and Berliner [22].

Table 7.1

Blind search	Intelligent search	Optimal search
Depth first	Best-first	Branch and bound
Breadth first	Means-ends analysis	Dynamic programming
Bidirectional	$\alpha\beta$ pruning	
Hill climbing	A^*	
	B^*	
	Minimaxing	
	Beam	

The hill climbing and branch-and-bound techniques of operational research have also found application in the area of tree search when optimality is a consideration.

Another useful technique in exploring large spaces of possibilities is constraint propagation. In any given problem, the physical characteristics of the problem often mean that certain assumptions are incompatible with one another. Winston [210] gives the example of the interpretation of line drawings where making the assumption that a particular junction is convex, say, will be incompatible with another one also being convex. The algorithm described exploits such facts as that there are only 18 ways to label a three line vertex. Similar methods can be applied to the removal of ambiguities in the interpretation of natural language sentences. The effect is to remove or prune certain branches from the search tree if they lead to contradictions. This class of techniques is often designated: 'exploiting constraints'.

We have made the implicit assumption in this section that knowledge representation is in the form of production rules, or some equally modular formalism. We will return to this question and other knowledge representation formalisms in Section 7.4. For now, we will pause to consider what is going on logically in all these search methods.

7.3 DEDUCTION, ABDUCTION AND INDUCTION

Using *modus ponens* and breadth-first search to arrive at conclusions is an example of deduction. So are all the other methods, providing that we are not reasoning in the presence of uncertainty, a point which we shall return to shortly. Forward

chaining lets us deduce the consequences of an assertion, and backward chaining
allows us to deduce a cause for some stated situation or to find a potential cause
for a goal. Mixtures of the two strategies also have this character. For example, in
the diagram shown in Fig. 7.3 of causal connections, we can infer D from G by
forward chaining and then backward chain to deduce that either G or the
combination of A and C could have caused F.

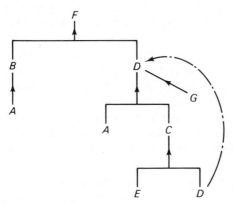

Fig. 7.3   Backward and forward chaining

On the other hand we can also see that, since D follows from G, if A and C are
true they support the truth of G even though they do not prove it in a strict
deductive manner. We are saying that if a consequence of a thing can be proven,
then at least there is nothing to contradict its truth, and that this provides
evidence of its plausibility. This kind of reasoning is called abduction. It becomes
especially important when multivalent logic is in use. Suppose that, in the above
tree we can only assign probabilities to propositions A, E and G. Then, it is
plausible that F is caused by them, but not certain. For example, if a friend says
she feels tired and hot and is sneezing we may abduce that she is suffering from the
common cold from the implication 'colds cause sneezing, high temperature and
lassitude'. The fact that she has pneumonia will be discovered by further
questioning, we hope. In other words, abduction is nonmonotonic. It is
nonetheless an invaluable method in expert systems as in human reasoning
about causes. As we have pointed out approximate reasoning with fuzzy
quantifiers can be used to give an alternative formulation: 'Most people who
sneeze etc. have colds.'

The inference method of the accumulation of evidence using Bayes's theorem
has been extensively covered in Chapter 4, so we need do no more than mention it
here.

The other principle mode of inference, in everyday thought as in logic, is
induction. The word 'induction' has two senses: the Aristotelian sense of a
syllogism in which the major premise in conjunction with instances entails the
generalization, or the sense of empirical generalization from observations. A third
sense, the principle of mathematical induction, need not concern us here. It is

with the second sense we shall be concerned. Most authorities (Braithwaite [225], Haack [86], Hempel [226]) talk about induction in terms of probabilities; if we observe that sheep on two hundred hillsides all have wool and four legs, then we may induce the generalization 'all sheep have wool and four legs'. Every observation we then make increases the probability of this statement being true, but never confirms it completely. Only one observation of a shorn three-legged merino is needed to refute the theory. From our point of view this cannot be correct. As we saw in Chapter 4 there are many kinds of uncertainty, and it can be said equally that our degree of knowledge, belief or the relevance of the rules is what is changed by experience rather than probability. The obsession with probability derives (probably) from the prevailing empiricist climate in the philosophy of science; experience as experiments performed by external observers trying to refute some hypothesis.

Another view is possible. The history of quantum physics shows that we can no longer regard observers as independent from what they observe. Marcuse [227] develops the alternative point of view especially clearly. Experience takes place in a world of which we humans are an internal part but from which we are able to differentiate ourselves. We do this by internalizing a representation of nature and checking the validity of the representation through continuous practice. But the very internalization process is a practice, and practice is guided by the representation so far achieved. This analysis leads to a ladder-like structure of concepts as shown in Fig. 7.4.

From this point of view induction is the process of practice which confirms our existing theories of all kinds. The other important general point to note is that the syllogism of induction moves from the particular to the general, whereas deductive and abductive syllogisms tend to work in the opposite direction: from the general to the particular.

The probabilistic definition of induction does have merit in many cases. Especially in the case of new knowledge, and it is this case that current computer learning systems always face. If we ever get as far as true artificial intelligence, then the situation may call for our broader definition. In nearly every case, computer programs which reason by induction are presented with a number of examples and expected to find a pattern, generalization or program which can reproduce and extend the training set. The complex question of the interaction between theory and practice has not arisen.

Suppose we are given the following training set of examples.

Eye colour	Hair colour	Sex	Job
blue	blonde	male	programmer
grey	brown	male	programmer
brown	black	female	analyst
brown	brown	male	operator
blue	black	female	analyst

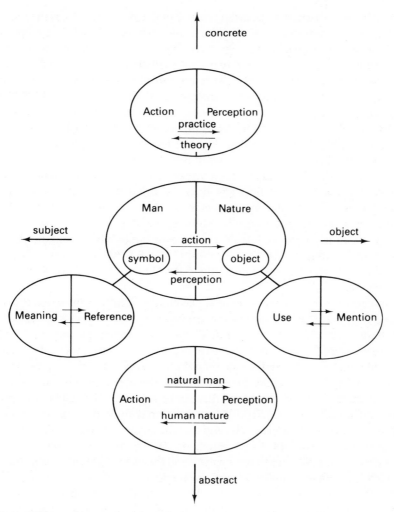

Fig. 7.4   Dialectical analysis of concepts

The simplest possible algorithm enables us to infer that:

IF female THEN analyst
IF male AND (blue eyes OR grey eyes) THEN programmer
IF brown hair AND brown eyes THEN operator

However, the addition of a new example (brown eyes, brown hair, female, programmer) makes the position less clear. The first and last rules must be withdrawn, but the second can remain although it no longer has quite the same force.

The first attempts at machine learning came out of the cybernetics movement of the 1950s. Cybernetics, according to its founder Wiener [229], is the science of control and communication in animal and machine. Several attempts were made, using primitive technology by today's standards, to build machinery simulating aspects of animal behaviour. In particular, analogue machines called homeostats simulated the ability to remain in unstable equilibrium; see Ross-Ashby [228]. Perceptrons [152] are hinted at in Wiener's work on neural networks, and, as the name suggests, were attempts to simulate the functionality of the visual cortex. Learning came in because of the need to classify and recognize physical objects. The technique employed was to weight the input in each of a number of dimensions and, if the resultant vector exceeded a certain threshold, to class the input as a positive example. Recently, neural network – or connection machine – technology has overcome the basic computational shortcoming of perceptrons discovered by Minsky and Papert [256], and impressive learning systems are beginning to be built.

Apart from perceptrons, one of the earliest examples of a computer learning algorithm is Langley's BACON program [147]. BACON was able to 'discover' Ohm's law of electrical resistance from a list of measurements of simple circuit parameters.

An algorithm with more general application is Quinlan's interactive dichoto-mizer, ID3 [142], which selects an arbitrary subset of the training set and partitions it according to the variable with the greatest discriminatory power using an information theoretic measure of the latter. This is repeated until a rule is found which is added to the rule set as in the above example on jobs. Next the entire training set is searched for exceptions to the new rule and if any are found they are inserted in the sample and the process repeated. The difficulties with this approach are that the end result is a sometimes huge decision tree which is difficult to understand and modify, and that the algorithm does not do very well in the presence of noisy data. A fuzzy analogue of ID3 might well overcome the latter objection, but it is difficult to see a way round the former one. ID3 forms the basis for Michie's widely available ExpertEase product.

Another algorithm which depends on searching a space of plausible descriptions is due to Dietterich and Michalski [257]. Their DEDUCE program uses a beam search technique to generate rules. This program was used to construct an expert system in the classification of soya bean diseases which achieved notoriety through outperforming an expert system built using conventional knowledge engineering methods. It uses a sophisticated method of generalization and a powerful predicate calculus representation language.

A completely different class of learning algorithm is based on the concept of adaptation or Darwinian selection. The general idea is to generate rules at random and compute some measure of performance for each rule relative to the training set. Inefficient rules are wasted and operations based on the ideas of mutation, crossover and inversion are applied to generate new rules. Various systems of this type are discussed in more detail in Forsyth [69], which also provides a general introduction to expert systems complementary to the treatment given in this book in the same series.

One of the problems with totally deterministic algorithms like ID3 is that, although they are guaranteed to find a rule to explain the data in the training set, if one exists, they cannot deal with situations where the rules can only be expressed subject to uncertainty. In complex situations such as weather forecasting or betting, where only some of the contributary variables can be measured and modelled, often no exact, dichotomizing rules exist. With the simple problem of forecasting whether it will rain tomorrow it is well known that a reasonably successful rule is 'if it is raining today then it will rain tomorrow'. This is not always true but it is a reasonable approximation for some purposes. ID3 would reject this as a rule if it found one single counter-example. Statistical tests, however useful, require complex independence assumptions and interpretive skills on the part of users. Statistical forecasting has not yet entered on the stage of artificial intelligence although many of its techniques are used internally by some systems. The Beagle system [70] is an attempt to fill the gap. Another approach is represented in RuleMaster which extends the basic approach of ID3 to include fuzzy attributes, although other aspects of fuzzy set theory are not included.

The most striking difference between ExpertEase and Beagle (which stands for Bionic [sic] Evolutionary Algorithm for Generating Logical Expressions) is that the former has a very nice user interface based on a spreadsheet approach and the latter has almost no user interface at all. This is represented in the difference in price, but does not reflect on the functionality of either system. Beagle is presented as a data analysis package designed to extract probabilistic rules from data which are principally numeric. The rules can then be used directly in, say, expert systems or Beagle will generate a subroutine in a conventional language such as C or FORTRAN. Both packages, in our opinion, have a role to play in knowledge acquisition, where a first stab at a rule set can be used to guide later knowledge elicitation as described in the previous chapter. With the current state of technology we thing it highly unlikely that pure rule induction systems will enjoy a wide success. ExpertEase has by now been applied to many problems including an advisory system on the postal services operated by Federal Express (a US courier service). Beagle has been applied to the analysis biochemical data in assessing the likelihood of survival of cardiac patients, predicting alcohol dependency from blood enzyme tests, analysing test bore-hole data in relation to oil exploration and to gambling on horse races [70]. Beagle is a package aimed at helping with forecasting or data analysis. It is not, however, intended for true time-series analysis and the author, Forsyth, recommends that trends and suchlike be computed in advance.

Since ID3 is well covered in the literature we will concentrate here on an explanation of the principles behind Beagle. Starting with a data file in comma delimited ASCII format and a target expression representing a hypothesis for testing, the data set is split into training data and a residue for later testing. The user creates, with the system editor, a file of rules representing *a priori* beliefs as to what good rules might explain the data. Beagle then generates more rules at random, if necessary, and proceeds to try out the rules and score their success at explanation of the data in the training set. The worst rules are replaced by an ingenious but simple procedure which 'mates' portions of the better rules at random to produce new ones. This generate and test procedure is then repeated many times while the rules get better and better at their job of explanation. The algorithm involves computing the correlation coefficient for the target (Chi-squared for a logical target) and applying a bonus for short (i.e. simple) rules, ranking them and excising the worse half. The survivors are mated to repopulate the rule-set and a small number are subjected to a random 'mutation'. The idea is that the process imitates Darwinian natural selection, and in doing so avoids the potentially huge search through the space of possible rules. Signature tables are constructed for the rule set and used to compensate for dependencies and interaction amongst the rules. Finally, a test report based on the earlier reserved data can be printed and the rules converted into a FORTRAN, PASCAL or C subroutine, if so desired. Beagle is not particularly adept at dealing with character data, and strings are converted to numbers prior to processing. This is done using an improved version of the SOUNDEX algorithm, which is based on the phonetic properties of words.

Another approach to machine learning is represented by the work of Lenat and his colleagues. As a graduate student Lenat produced a program called AM (which stood for Artificial Mathematician) whose remit was to discover number theory from a base of pre-numerical concepts from set theory [54]. AM succeeded, admittedly with a fair amount of guidance from its author, in pointing out the interestingness of prime numbers and conjecturing (it had no theorem proving capability) a number of results of number theory, including Goldbach's conjecture: every even number is the sum of two primes. No-one has proved or disproved this yet, incidentally, but we forbear setting it as an exercise to the reader. AM like most mathematicians thought it was fairly obvious. The next project was EURISKO which, like AM, was based on the idea of frames for which new slots can be created as part of the learning process and meta-rules or heuristics which affect the way rules are generated and generalized. An amusing example of this heuristic approach occurred early on in the development of EURISKO which noticed that rules inserted by humans were generally better than its own attempts at that stage. Thus it generated the meta-rule 'If a rule is machine-generated then delete it'. Fortunately, this was the first rule deleted under the new regime. EURISKO had a number of successes. It participated in the design of a new tesselated VLSI and embarrassed the Pentagon by winning the annual war game several times. On one occasion it did so by blasting its own crippled ships out of the water and steaming on to victory. The real success was that the rules were subsequently changed to disallow this rather bloodthirsty option. It should also serve to warn of the very real danger of entrusting dangerous activities like war or nuclear engineering to computer systems. But we digress. Lenat's latest project, CYC, is concerned more with knowledge representation than with learning, since it was the power of the representation language which made EURISKO so successful as well as the meta-rule approach to learning. CYC aims to encode and make available as an expert system all the knowledge contained in the Encyclopaedia Britannica.

Machine learning is at the forefront of research in artificial intelligence. Many of the difficulties faced by knowledge engineers, especially those of knowledge elicitation, may be overcome in the future as a result. For the present, though, we view the chief benefit of the commercially available induction systems as only an aid in the acquisition process. Just as human reasoning is a mixture of deductive, abductive and inductive reasoning, so will expert systems be for the foreseeable future. The subject of abduction will be dealt with again in the section on fuzzy reasoning strategies. We now turn to the meta-level of control strategies: if we are to use forward chaining, backward chaining, induction and what have you, how are we to choose among them dynamically? The related question of the formation of plans for problem solving also arises naturally at this point.

7.4 PLANNING AND HIGHER LEVEL CONTROL STRUCTURES

Saying that a knowledge-based system consists of a knowledge base together with a knowledge application system as we did in Chapter 2 is not quite enough. In the simplest cases we can conveniently confuse the knowledge application system, or inference engine, with the control mechanism. However, in systems where there is a need for more than one type of inference strategy or where that strategy cannot be asserted in advance of the setting of a particular task, then some distinct control mechanism must exist to supervise the process. There is no reason why the controller should not itself be a knowledge-based system, nor indeed why it might not consist in a simple inference mechanism based on logic. In general, however, the control of reasoning is a complex matter and to date mostly *ad hoc* methods have been used.

Clearly, a great deal of the subject of artificial intelligence is about problem solving in the most general sense. Thus, even if we have a number of inference mechanisms at our disposal, the need still arises to choose from them the most appropriate, to order our searches in the most promising way and to infer with the most pertinent knowledge. In other words there is a need for higher level strategies to control the interaction between models, data, knowledge and control methods. In this section we will look at some examples of meta-level control strategies, including a number of methods such as blackboard systems, actor systems and beginning with the field that has become known as planning.

Planning emerged as a core area of study quite early on with the work of Newell and Simon on GPS (the general problem solver) [162], and has suffered something of a revival following the development of knowledge-based methods and nonmonotonic logics. Also workers in the area of natural language have recently seen planning as important. In fact, people trying to establish theories of cognition have been able to utilize some of the insights that have derived from work on AI planning systems (Anderson [9, 10]). One particularly strong (and obvious) use of planning systems is in the factory scheduling and resources allocation problems. In this field fuzzy methods have been applied to scheduling repair work on aircraft (Grant [82]). Other domains where planning is important are responding to perceived threats in military contexts, and robotics in the context of multi-agent systems where the robots must avoid collisions and maintain performance in reaching defined goals.

The subject of planning has a distinctly dual nature. On the one hand, it can be viewed as a subset of the problem of search. On the other, it depends, as we will see, on the three key techniques of knowledge-based systems: knowledge representation, inference and the management of uncertainty.

All problem solving can be construed as a form of planned behaviour. A plan is often defined as an ordered sequence of potential actions to achieve a stated goal state. For humans planning is so much a part of our everyday life that it usually presents us with few problems. We have to form elementary plans even to carry out the most mundane of tasks such as typing a sentence or drinking a glass of beer. For computers this is not the case. They do better in the closed formal domains, such as game playing, which most humans find rather difficult. Also, highly parallel planning activities prove very difficult for computers but almost trivial for us. Here again the difficulty lies, at least partly, in the existence of linguistically expressed trade-offs.

There are several categories of problem solving. As with other AI problems the question arises as to how much its success relies on domain specific knowledge as opposed to general methods. As we have pointed out earlier this was the fundamental issue in the emergence of knowledge-based methods in AI.

The planning systems which we will consider are, roughly in order of appearance, GPS, STRIPS, ABSTRIPS, HACKER, INTERPLAN, NOAH, NONLIN and DEVISER [161, 194]. Several general lessons emerged from experience with these systems, among which we might mention the importance of propagating constraints and the notion of dependency directed backtracking and truth maintenance [210, 34].

The GPS approach [161] relies on a domain independent method which represents the world as objects and operators and uses means-ends analysis to reduce the difference between the initial and goal states. The usual example involves making a cake. We can represent the objects and operators in a logic based language as follows.

Initial state: *goals:*
have(eggs)   have(cake)
have(flour)   be_in(kitchen)
have(money)
have(car)
be_in(kitchen)
exists(kitchen)
exists(store)
exists(bank)
exists(delivery_service)

		Effects	
Operator	*Preconditions*	*Adds*	*Deletes*
buy_cake	in(store),have(money) exist(store)	have(cake)	have(money)
make_cake	have(eggs),have(flour)	have(cake)	have(eggs),have(flour)
order_cake			
etc.			

The operators can be applied to the states to bring about new states, as shown. The problem here is what fact to include as relevant in the representation: the classical frame problem.

Means-ends analysis determines the way various operators may be combined to achieve a goal using two fundamental techniques known as difference extraction and difference reduction. Computationally, a goal stack is constructed which starts containing the ultimate goals only. Difference extraction finds the differences between the goals in the stack and the world state. The result is placed on top of the stack. Then difference reduction is applied by looking for an operator which generates the top goal. If such an operator is found all its preconditions are added to the stack together with the operator. This cycle is repeated until the goal state is achieved.

This method often results in the generation of unwanted side effects which can produce unnecessary loops, and also we must be very careful in the order in which operators are selected. Domain specific knowledge can help with this. As with blind backtracking many dead ends might be fruitlessly explored. STRIPS extended GPS by introducing a method of hierarchical planning to reason about the more crucial operators first to produce outline plans. Levels of 'criticality' are assigned to the preconditions using domain knowledge to order the preconditions.

HACKER (Sussman [1941]) was originally intended to serve as a model of skill acquisition but introduced many new and useful planning techniques. It works by analogy with a programmer trying to write a new program. First existing procedures are tried to see if they work. If not 'patches' are developed to fix 'bugs' in the plan. This system marks a turning point in that it and subsequent systems tend to work in a space of plans rather than situations. It is important to note that HACKER does not obviously backtrack. It uses various libraries of standard methods, procedures, facts, bugs and patches. One important bug type occurs when the effects of one goal can seriously undermine another; so that the plan is not linear. HACKER does not necessarily construct optimal plans.

Suppose, in the blocks world for example, that we wish to transform the situation as shown in Fig. 7.5.

The goal might be expressed as make (on(B,C)). HACKER would look in its answer library for a procedure with the right effect and find that putting B on C requires that B is clear (has nothing on top) as a prerequisite. This kind of situation is known as a protection violation. A state is protected if it is required to

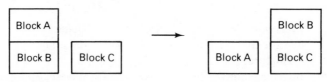

Fig. 7.5   Moving blocks

be true for a task in hand to succeed. It is *violated* if the state is false. In the above example we might generate a plan with steps, ordering and protections as shown below. The last line can be read as 'the top of block *C* must be clear at all times between the end of operation 2 and the start of operation 3'.

PLAN: put_on(B,A)
  Steps: 1. clear(B)
         2. clear[C)
         3. move[B,C)
  Order: precedes(1,3)
         precedes(2,3)
  Protect: clear_between(B,end(1),begin(3))
           clear_between(C,end(2),begin(3))

HACKER patches such bugs by inserting a procedure into the plan before the prerequisite is needed. Unfortunately, since HACKER builds stacks from the bottom up it sometimes undoes previously achieved goals in order to proceed with the solution. How can this be overcome? We need to be able to reorder goals at different levels in the plan. INTERPLAN (Tate [258]) achieves this with a mechanism that promotes subgoals which cause protection violations.

One of the most influential planners was the NOAH system (Sacerdoti [178]). This system uses hierarchical, or outline plans and a 'minimal commitment' strategy whereby ordering constraints are not established until absolutely necessary. The occurrence of protection violations is used to reorder the plan without having to backtrack. NONLIN (Tate [258, 41]) uses more complex methods to actually anticipate protection violations in advance. DEVISER [Vere [259, 41]) extends NOAH by introducing temporal reasoning. Goals such as 'make p true at time t_1 but no later than time t_2 and hold it true for duration d' can be expressed. As we have seen, temporal logic is an active and important area of research.

Doyle [57] has introduced the notion of 'truth maintenance' which depends on the ideas of default reasoning, or nonmonotonic logic (see Chapter 6), and on the realization that plans can be segmented into independent parts. For example, in planning meeting times for large numbers of people it might be discovered that only Tuesday and Thursday are convenient and that the only time that suits everyone is 10.30. Chronological backtracking would need to establish the Thursday answer twice should a room not be available on Tuesday because there is no realization that the day of the week and the time are independent. The implied strategy is known as *dependency directed backtracking.*

Other important issues in planning arise from its application to natural language understanding. Searle's speech acts, like plans, have prerequisites and effects. Understanding speech assumes that the actors involved are attempting to satisfy their own or other people's goals, and this involves reasoning about belief: epistemic logic. Hintikka has developed such a first-order logic of belief. For more details of this kind of extended logic see Chapter 6 and reference [103].

The list of important issues in planning is long and includes at least the following. How do you reason with time? How can problems such as protection violations be anticipated and allowed for? How best can you search the space of possible plans? How are plans to be translated into action? How can a plan's progress be monitored? How do you replan when things go wrong? When is one plan 'nearly' perfect? How can constraint propagation be best exploited? No one, to our knowledge, has investigated planning under fuzzy constraints yet, but this seems a promising line of research since planners so often have to reason in the present of incomplete and uncertain data (such as comes from visual sensors).

In the mainstream of research into and applications of planning, the only ways in which uncertainty is ever considered are via Bayesian probability theory, which arises in decision theory – *post hoc* planning, and via nonmonotonic and temporal logics. As we have pointed out the need for fuzzy methods arises whenever goals and constraints are uncertain due to non-stochastic effects (see Chapters 4 and 8).

The other chief meta-control technique is loosely referred to under the heading of *blackboard systems.* In complex, and especially in real-time, systems there may be many sources of knowledge and many plans and procedures. Typical application areas are fighter battle systems and financial trading rooms. If these components need to communicate there are essentially two methods of achieving this. Private-line or *actor* systems allow objects to send and receive messages which have definite destination objects when sent. In blackboard systems the messages are posted to a common data area which is accessible to other objects. Sometimes the blackboard is partitioned into *pigeonholes.* Usually, messages must be dealt with according to the order in which they arrive and the state of the receiving object at that time; thus all such systems tend to look like real-time systems and would benefit greatly from parallel hardware architectures. Having said this, the very earliest blackboard system was Hearsay-II [16] which was addressed to the problem of speech understanding which is only implicitly a real time problem. Most applications since then have been in military real-time communication, command and control systems, so that little has been published openly. Recently, however, work has begun on blackboard systems in plant process control and complex currency dealing decision support systems.

Blackboard systems run into problems in continuous reasoning because of the accumulation of information in the common data area and the global accessibility of that data. Actor systems, on the other hand, need to know in advance which objects will need to communicate. For these reasons there have been attempts to combine the formalisms in some systems. One programming environment, BLOBS, has been developed along these lines by Cambridge Consultants Ltd and applied to such problems as ship positioning control. It supports no obvious means of handling uncertainty however. BLOBS, like LOOPS and Flavours support an object-oriented programming style; so that instead of passing data to a program for manipulation messages representing methods are sent to objects. Objects are synchronized with a real-time clock and an 'agenda' object may be set up to schedule processing. An object (unsurprisingly in BLOBS) is called a 'blob'. Here is an example of a blob:

```
static blob Biggles

      private vars x,y,dx,dy

      on_message fly_north with s=speed do

          o --> dy; s --> dx;

          send 'biggles flies north to base';

      enddo

      ...

      on_message tick with t=time interval do

          x+t*dx --> x;

          y+t*dy --> y;

      enddo

      on_message where_are_you with s=sender do

          send 'biggles is at', x=x,y=y, to (s);

      enddo

   endblob
```

A typical way to implement a blackboard system is to set up a family of frames representing a community of co-operating experts. Each frame has a slot containing a 'trigger' and one indicating priority of execution of the procedures attached to the frame. Some frames will fire their procedures on the trigger value denoting the start of processing and these are *ceteris paribus* executed in order of priority. The priorities may be subject to dynamic alteration as earlier procedures write facts on the blackboard. Demons may be used to detect critical changes to the blackboard's data and amend the appropriate frames. Other frames are triggered directly by certain values in the database.

Strictly speaking object-oriented programming is a programming paradigm or methodology rather than a control or knowledge representation strategy. It is designed to promote modularity and reusability of code as well as facilitating better representation in the user interface as in systems such as Smalltalk, Objective-C and the Apple MacIntosh. However, in looking at systems like Xerox's LOOPS which combines object-oriented programming with INTERLISP, high quality graphics and a number of facilities for encoding knowledge-based systems it is difficult sometimes not to end up confusing the two. Objects are a little like the actors we have described above and at the same time a little like the frames described in Chapters 2 and 3. That is objects can send and receive messages, they are associated with *methods* which are procedures which can be performed on the objects, they support property inheritance, and they can have various attributes. If a generic object can inherit from multiple parents it is sometimes called a flavour. If all the attributes and methods associated with an object, flavour or blob can be filled in, then there is a case to be made for saying that we *understand* the object. The property attachment and procedural inheritance features lead us to a notion of *meaning* being inherent in an object-oriented description. Object-oriented control and meta-control strategies clearly have an interesting future. Much will depend on the theoreticians sorting out the terminological mess wherein there is no clear distinction between objects, frames, semantic nets and so on. Also, to date, no one has attempted to tackle the problem of fuzzy objects and, as with frames, uncertainty has either been handled by choosing high granularity representations or through techniques such as belief revision or defaults (see Chapter 4). It may well be that this will be seen as the true distinction between frames and objects in the future, for, after all, it appears too highly dangerous to introduce fuzzy concepts into programming itself. Knowledge may be vague but computers are going to require precise instructions in their programs for many years to come. We dealt with these points in Chapter 3.

As we suggested in Chapter 2 human reasoning uses a variety of logical processes and very often switches from one logical system to another during the course of the reasoning process. To simulate this on a computer requires a technological breakthrough that has not yet been made, although we seem to be approaching it. The fifth generation project is about parallel architectures: computers that can work on several problems simultaneously. This advance will undoubtedly allow the techniques described in this chapter to find their way into real applications. Several subgoals will be able to be explored simultaneously under backward chaining abductive strategies, simultaneously running expert systems will be able to communicate with each other via a blackboard. However, the fifth generation assumes that one logic will guide the process. We forecast that at some stage, the sixth, seventh or *n*th generation of computer systems will know which is the most appropriate formalism to use at any given stage of problem solving; be at first-order calculus, nonmonotonic logic, fuzzy logic, probability logic, epistemic logic or whatever. In bringing these together this work is, we hope, a modest contribution to this long-term goal. In the following section we turn to an extension of the backward chaining strategy where the usual logic has been replaced by one particular deviant: fuzzy logic.

7.5 FUZZY INFERENCE STRATEGIES

The theme of this book is uncertainty, so we now return to the question of how to propagate uncertainty through a search tree. This is problematical whether certainty factors, Bayesian probabilities or fuzzy sets are used due to the way that any measure of certainty is reduced under conjunction.

To illustrate the problem consider the situation in a courtroom where a jury is trying to reach a decision based on the evidence presented. It is known the witnesses have made the following two statements:

(1) There was mud outside the open window.
(2) The butler had mud on his boots.

However, statement (1) is corroborated by the independent evidence of several witnesses and statement (2) is based purely on the evidence of the housekeeper who, incidentally, stands to inherit a large fortune as a result of the untimely decease of the Major.

We might model this by assigning degrees of belief to each statement and, indeed, to our rules of inference. Suppose that we assign the values as follows.

Statement 1: 0.95
Statement 2: 0.30

Using the operations of standard fuzzy logic the possibility that 'the butler did it' cannot be greater than 0.30. Here we are invoking the judicial principle that one is innocent until proven guilty (which holds perfectly in whodunits if not in real life) and assuming that the jury will give the accused the benefit of any reasonable doubt. The outstanding difficulty is to set a 'cut off' point below which to acquit. Is 30% belief sufficient proof?

These difficulties apply in all backward or forward chaining inference schemes, and it is still a matter of experimentation to set cut-off levels in such a way as to reproduce expert decisions in knowledge engineering applications. The other problem is that one has to decide whether to backtrack if a truth value falls below a given level or only if it reaches zero. In practice there will be many more than two truth values and a whole stream of deductive inferences to process. How this problem is solved depends strictly on the particular application.

We propose here a method based on the theory of fuzzy sets.

7.5.1 Fuzzy backward chaining algorithms

The objective is to provide a convenient method of generating structure amongst a set of production rules which are fuzzy in nature, similar to the REVEAL syntax introduced in earlier chapters. Instead of being executed exactly once each in parallel, the rules are to be (effectively) compiled into a tree structure and evaluated using a generalized backward chaining algorithm. Adding some form of opportunistic forward chaining could easily be considered, but we do not do so here for reasons of clarity of exposition.

Consider a rule base containing several fuzzy productions. This system of productions is to be regarded as a complete description of our knowledge of how to compute the value of y, given the definition of the appropriate term sets. The rules are:

(1) if x is low then y is solution 1
(2) if a is medium then y is solution 2
(3) if b is medium then y is solution 3

Recall from Chapter 5 the method of approach, which can be summarized as follows:

(a) Obtain the (scalar) values of x, a and b.
(b) Compute the truth level of the antecedents of each production, based on these scalars and the definitions of the term sets. For example, if low = {1.0, 0.9, 0.7, 0.4, 0.2, 0.1, 0.0, 0.0, 0.0, 0.0, 0.0} over the interval [0, 100] and x is found to have the value 30, then the truth of the antecedent of production 1 is 0.4.
(c) Generate the consequent fuzzy sets for each production, according to the selected method of inference. Combine these sets using the selected disjunction operator, and thus generate the resultant fuzzy set representing the value of y.
(d) Using the selected method of defuzzification, reduce the resultant fuzzy set representing y to a scalar and an associated certainty factor for actual use.

If we now expand the system of productions by incorporating the three additional rules shown below, then we no longer expect to acquire the value of x as an immediate datum.

(4) if p is true then x is low
(5) if q is true then x is medium
(6) if v is true then x is high

Instead of this, we have to suspend the task of evaluating y, and compute x from its own set of productions. This is fine up to step (c) of the algorithm, but at stage (d) we must take note of a difficulty.

Suppose, at this stage, that

$$x = \{0.80, 0.90, 0.95, 1.00, 0.50, 0.20, 0.00, 0.00, 0.00, 0.00, 0.00\}.$$

Were we to use the 'maximum' method of defuzzifying x at this stage, x would be returned as 30 from this nested task. Then the computation of y would proceed as described above, and indeed yield an identical value. See Fig. 7.6.

However, a loss of information has occurred: representing the fuzzy set x as a

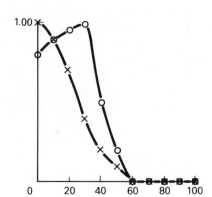

Fig. 7.6   Result of computation × low ○ x

scalar is an unwarranted approximation, and the earlier part of the task must return the full fuzzy set instead. Otherwise, later stages cannot begin with comparably rich data, since we have no really compelling evidence on the basis of which to assign a value in its domain to the variable in question. Evaluation of the antecedent clause 'x is low' is much better treated as a matter of comparing the output fuzzy set for x with 'low'.

There are obviously many ways in which this could be done. One way is to define the dissimilarity of two fuzzy sets, *A* and *B*, by the least-squares distance metric:

$$d(A, B) = \sum_{i=1}^{N} (\mu_A - \mu_B)^2 / N$$

where N is the number of sample points in the domain of *A* and *B*, and the μs denote their membership functions. This metric, although a somewhat arbitrary choice, has the virtues that, if $A = B$ then $d(A, B) = 0$ (in common with all metrics) and if *A* and *B* are such that $\mu(A) = 1$ and $\mu(B) = 0$ then $d(A, B) = 1$. In the current example $d(x, \text{low}) = 0.05$, and the similarity of the two fuzzy sets, defined as the complement of the dissimilarity, is thus 0.95. The impact on the computation of y is clear, since the truth of the antecedent in production 1 is now 0.95 rather than 0.4.

Thus, given an unstructured set of fuzzy productions, along with the nomination of a goal object, our fuzzy backward chaining algorithm differs from the classical formulation in the following significant ways.

(a) No goal object value (that is, no specific hypothesis) is fixed at the inception of the task. Rather, an evidence gathering mechanism is employed to seek the most plausible value of the goal object.
(b) Recursively, all productions contributing evidence as to the value of the current (sub-)goal object are processed together, in the manner of the forward chaining evaluation process discussed in Chapter 5.

(c) The full value (i.e. the generated consequent fuzzy set) of all objects is retained as the search unwinds, maximizing the value gained from the information obtained.

As with all backward chaining algorithms which permit multiple values in the antecedent, it becomes difficult to implement a 'what if' facility in a universally satisfactory way, but this is not a consequence of the use of fuzzy sets but applies equally to those algorithms based on probability or certainty factors. 'How' and 'Why' remain implementable.

EXERCISES

(1) Implement this algorithm in a suitable language; C, APL, PASCAL or LISP. If LISP is the target language, Schmucker [250] contains some useful hints on how to encode the fuzzy set representations. In the other languages an approach following the text here is suggested.
(2) Investigate the choice of different metrics from the one given above. Prove that it is indeed a metric.

We have now come very close to the nuts-and-bolts, software design and implementation concerns of computing. Let us now pause to consider some of the implementation issues surrounding inference methods in knowledge-based systems in a more human context.

7.6 KNOWLEDGE ENGINEERING ISSUES

In Chapter 9 we will discuss at length the question of how to elicit knowledge from human experts. A few words need to be said here about how to elicit from these people the kind of reasoning which they use in problem solving. This is especially true if the system builder envisages using some of the commercial products now available. If an expert system shell is chosen for the development, then it must be established that the logic and reasoning method incorporated in the shell correspond to those used by the human expert in problem solving, otherwise the project is almost certainly doomed to failure. If, on the other hand, a sophisticated knowledge engineering environment is considered necessary then not only must the extra cost be justified but the developers must have confidence that the tool is sufficiently flexible to model all the strategies which arise in the behaviour of the human subject. This can only be achieved if the knowledge engineers are really able to elicit the inference methods as well as the knowledge representations used.

Very little has been written, and we suspect little more than that is known, on how to elicit inference methods. Our own experience dictates that the two main prerequisites for knowledge engineers in this respect are a sound theoretical understanding of the various methods available and a good helping of common sense. The methods of interview, whether formal or informal, should be constructed to enable comparison of users' and experts' behaviour with a sort of library of standard methods. When no direct match between the standard methods and the real ones identified can be discerned, further investigation is indicated. Perhaps the computerization of the problem is beyond current technology or perhaps some novel combination of techniques can be derived. The watchword here is balance; don't give up too easily but don't be afraid to give up.

One of the most important considerations in this respect is that, as we have repeatedly emphasized, the choice of inference strategy and the choice of knowledge representation are inextricably bound together. This is why in blackboard systems we invariably find a frame or two lying around somewhere, and in production systems it is common to employ backward chaining and/or Bayesian inference. The selection of software tools should carefully balance the two. There is, as yet, no comprehensive theory of this interaction. When it emerges we are sure that it will include some logical features which are not standard and some advance in the theory of handling uncertainty, for the logic of opposites is the least well understood from a formal (and therefore computational) point of view.

We can distinguish at least three quite distinct types of human reasoning used for practical problem solving. These are reasoning based on highly specialized domain-specific knowledge, common sense reasoning based on rules of thumb and naive physics and the like and reasoning from the existence of prior examples or trends. Other types do exist but are beyond current computer technology; a good example is reasoning by geometrical analogy. Specialist knowledge is narrow but deep; the jocular definition of a specialist being someone who knows ultimately 'everything about nothing'. Common sense is the tool of the generalist, who knows 'nothing about everything'. This knowledge is broad but shallow. Most expert systems up to now have dealt with specialist inference techniques and not common sense reasoning. The role of uncertainty handling methods in computerizing common sense should be recognized. This is also the case with the third type of reasoning where the traditional techniques of statistical analysis, decision analysis and the less traditional methods of fuzzy forecasting, plausible reasoning and pattern recognition all involve the reduction of uncertainty in some way. Considerations of this type are necessary when assessing the suitability of a particular problem or expert for computerization, or the utility of a particular development environment.

The final question we intend to deal with on this score is the extent to which cognitive emulation can provide any benefits or compromise the efficiency of the resultant computer systems. Is it true that because humans reason in this or that way that an efficient computational solution should mimic their approach? Once again this is a largely unsolved problem and the remarks made already in Chapter 2 apply to it with some force. In some fields, such as computer chess, it is clear that cognitive emulation does have a role to play, as other methods tried so far have failed conspicuously. In others, most chiefly those where computers have been successful for decades, such as computation and data processing, this is clearly not the case. At the meta-level we have to extend the question of cognitive emulation to what might be loosely described as 'social emulation'. If a blackboard system is a community of co-operating experts, then are our systems to emulate the social interactions among experts in human societies? Clearly, lessons may be, and have been, learnt from such analogies but we have no clear answer to give at this stage.

Knowledge engineering is so called because it is an art rather than a science. When it becomes a science computers will have little more to learn from us, but that is a long way in the future.

7.7 SUMMARY

This chapter gave a very brief survey of AI chaining strategies and put them in the wider context of inference and logical systems. The basic notions of rules of inference, tree searching and forward, backward and other chaining strategies were introduced. The propagation of uncertainty in inference was discussed, concentrating on the notion of fuzziness – probability having been dealt with elsewhere in this book.

The differences between inductive, abductive and deductive logic were outlined, and there was a discussion of the application of induction in computer learning systems. We then considered AI planning and fuzzy inference strategies, concentrating on the applicability of these technologies. Blackboard systems were introduced, in preparation for the applications to be discussed in Chapter 10.

Finally, there was a short discussion of the interaction between the inference strategies to be used in an application and the activity of knowledge engineering; i.e. knowledge representation selection and knowledge acquisition.

7.8 FURTHER READING

As we said at the outset the subject of inference and chaining strategies is very thoroughly covered in the literature. Nilsson [163] gives several useful algorithms and details. Charniak and McDermott [41] have a good survey of this and of planning systems, but requires a knowledge of LISP to be comprehensible. Winston [210] is, of course, the classic text on artificial intelligence along with Barr and Feigenbaum [16], and both these cover the crisp inference strategies well. Addis [3] gives a refreshing perspective on the same subject from the viewpoint of database theory. On fuzzy inference we are afraid we can recommend nothing but the work before you now.

8

Simulation, decision support and knowledge engineering

'What will be the effect on human lifetime as the present level of global pollution increases? We cannot answer this question accurately, but we do know that there will be some effect. We would be more in error to ignore the influence of pollution on life expectancy in the world model, than to include it with our best guess of its magnitude.'

Limits to Growth, Fellows and Meadowes 1971

8.1 DECISION SUPPORT WITHIN THE ORGANIZATIONAL FRAMEWORK

Simon [230, 187] has suggested, and he is not alone, having a view similar to many economists, that we are undergoing an information revolution of significance equal to the development of language or that of writing. This revolution is characterized by the arrival of complex organizational structures, information processing technology and the merging of people and machines in the productive process. As with all such revolutions in technique there are good and bad human effects with profound social consequences; just as the industrial revolution increased the capacity of the human race to satisfy its material needs beyond all previous expectations, so the lag in the development of new social institutions caused the most dreadful human suffering. Similarly, the new possibilities of the information age for removing the most demeaning and dull aspects of productive labour are being accompanied by new structural unemployment, poverty and increased possibilities for repressive social control. Thus, for society, no really new issues are raised; merely new forms of old problems. For businesses this is not so. To compete in the new age is to absorb the new technology in a way which has and will continue to profoundly affect the very essence of the businesses.

Information processing can never be an end in itself. It is a tool in the process of decision making. In this sense a decision support system may be defined as an information processing system embedded within a decision making system. However this definition does not capture the essence of the term as it is currently

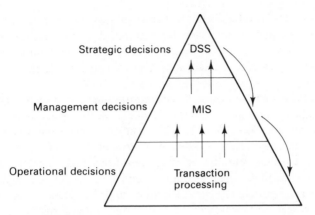

Fig. 8.1   Commercial activities

used. Commercial activities may be regarded as organized as a pyramid as shown in Fig. 8.1.

In this pyramid height is correlated with the reducing volume and increasing value of information. In general, information flows upwards through a process of aggregation and abstraction and control flows downward in the form of decisions. At the lowest level, the operational level, the activity is regarded as a complex of transactions, either abstract ones as in bookkeeping systems or physical as in, say, rivets penetrating steel plate in a factory. The transition to the line management level parallels the history of computing, wherein the earliest and most widespread uses of computers were the transaction processing systems, usually based on COBOL batch processing systems. The development of database and file management technology led to the concept of the management information system (MIS) currently still undergoing development. Even more recently the most senior decision makers have been provided with systems to support their strategic decision making, in the form of data enquiry languages, financial modelling systems and so on. Operational research and the now slightly unfashionable science of cybernetics have throughout this development contributed to the analysis of the information flow, control mechanisms and feedback within organizations. This has led to suggestions that fundamental organizational change could result in benefits for both the organizations and the social consequences of change mentioned above (see Beer [21]). Our definition of DSS encompasses only the top third of the pyramid.

A study of decision support, however, cannot exclude all management information system issues on which, after all, they are based. Management can be conceived as a mixture of planning and control. These categories require the resources of MIS, modelling, automatic information processing and decision making, and the latter require database management, learning and adaptation, logic, knowledge management, numerical methods, symbol manipulation and linguistics. Thus, it is striking how close the concerns of artificial intelligence come to those of DSS: What is the most appropriate way to represesnt knowledge? What human–machine interface is required? What applications are to be undertaken? How best can we manage uncertainty? Previous chapters have covered these topics. Now we will look at their application in the field of decision support.

It is patent that in any modern, large organization there is considerable division of labour; if there were not, smaller units could effectively compete against them to their detriment. Bonczek *et al.* [28] take the view that organizations are information and materials processors made up of abstract *roles* or jobs which may be filled by various humans or machines from time to time. These roles communicate through certain channels and may be related in a number of different ways; principally by definition and by association. Definitional relationships arise in hierarchical organizations and associative links arise in a context of co-operation. Most organizations have both aspects. Bonczek *et al.* point to an interesting analogy between these notions and AND/OR trees, links in semantic networks and database relationships. Roughly speaking, an OR node corresponds to a role filled by a replaceable decision maker, to an IS-A link in a semantic net or to a many–one database link. An AND node corresponds to a decision maker who has to consult other experts, to verbal links (such as 'wrote' in our earlier example based on Chaucer) in a net or to instances in a database. Terminal nodes are irreplaceable experts who need consult no other role. We should add that group decision making, which they do not consider, is a higher order, possibly recursive process.

All these roles require certain resources and abilities to participate in decision making. Bonczek *et al.* propose three basic aspects which give rise by combination to four further attributes; seven abilities in all. This is set out in Fig. 8.2.

An overlap indicates some sort of adaptive process between the abilities, so that

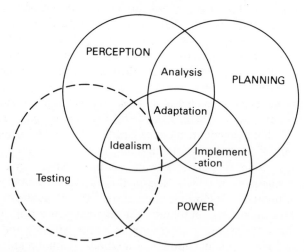

Fig. 8.2   Attributes of decision-support systems

implementation is 'a continuing adjustment between power and planning'. A moment's contemplation reveals that this classification may not be as comprehensive as is claimed. As with all analytical methods based on the number three, the ever present possibility of dividing categories into opposites leads to difficulties. In this case the important notion of testing (the opposite of designing) is omitted. A more satisfying analysis of decision making abilities is given in Fig. 8.3. It will be seen that infinite refinement is possible with this analysis and that it is symmetrical.

However we do agree with their more general point, that the number and degree of these abilities incorporated in the machine part of the system is a measure of its (artificial) intelligence. Of course, there are other aspects of intelligence which are not covered by this analysis, such as memory. Also, certain benefits arising from intelligent machinery are not strictly to do with its intelligence alone. Examples are filtered data, faster adaptation or response, consistency, and so on. But we are discussing decision support.

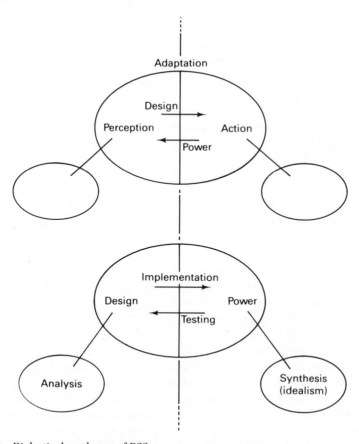

Fig. 8.3 Dialectical analysers of PSS

An important corollary of the high value of decision support data is that organizations cannot afford to ignore technical advances in its processing. For this reason the most advanced uses of computing tend to occur in this context rather than at the transaction processing level. Another characteristic feature of decision making at this level is the uncertainty which subsists in the goals and constraints under which the business operates. As Bellman and Zadeh [24] point out, statements such as 'Corporation X has a *bright future*' or 'the stock market has suffered a *sharp decline*' convey plenty of information despite the imprecision of the italicized words. Managers express themselves in this way and their computer systems must speak the same language to be ultimately useful in such contexts. The higher the level of the entity being organized the more this is true, and the more important an efficient solution becomes as more and more people's lives are affected. The quotation at the head of this chapter refers to the importance of handling uncertainty in ensuring the survival of the world.

The inability of classical decision support systems to handle uncertainty must therefore be of concern. In fact, at the very beginning of electronic computing, in the huts at Bletchley Park where the concern was code breaking, Bayesian probability was called into service. The current generation of expert system shells predominantly use this technique to handle uncertainty, as do such systems as PROSPECTOR which undoubtedly supports decisions. However, as we have shown, probability is only one of the kinds of uncertainty. The need for decision support to encompass other techniques such as fuzzy sets, nonmonotonic logic, frames and high levels of granularity is still a concern. We point up these issues in the remainder of this chapter, along with a general survey of decision-support systems.

8.2   CLASSIFICATION OF DECISION-SUPPORT SYSTEMS

One of the meanings given to the word 'decision' in *The Oxford English Dictionary* is that of a cut or separation. Taking a decision implies a definite break between the past and the future. Understanding how decisions are made is a fundamental human science, because it underpins all other human sciences: history, psychology, political economy, anthropology, and linguistics. The only possible exception is medicine, where only certain branches have the character of a human science. Decision support is about reducing the uncertainty of the transition. A classification of DSS should therefore centre on the handling, and resolution, of uncertainty.

There are three main sources of information to support decision making: these are accounting, which depends on the accurate, conservative storage of material information; modelling, which is accomplished through the computations of operational research and engineering; and intelligence, which applies reasoning to knowledge. These three sources correspond exactly to the main uses of computing machinery: storage, calculation and symbol manipulation. Despite its recent emergence into prominence, the field of artificial intelligence was tied up inextricably with the very earliest attempt to construct an electronic computer. Turing wrote [200] about the subject as early as 1948, when computers were being called, in the press at any rate, giant brains and when, in ordinary speech, a 'computer' was a human being who performed the dullest computational tasks such as the preparation of mathematical tables. It was not long, however, before the new machines were turned to computations for scientific and engineering applications; operational research and cybernetics emerged in this period also. A little later, the possibilities for commercial data processing were realized, principally in the USA but also in Britain slightly later on. The vision of replacing 'armies of clerks' by a single machine attracted huge funds into this area of computing, and the problem soon became how to increase the productivity of the new class of slaves to the valve-burning patricians: programmers. So it was that higher level languages than machine code (base 32 then) were developed. Assembly languages soon led to the third generation languages, starting with FORTRAN and closely followed first by LISP and then by COBOL. It is interesting that these three early languages parallel closely the classification given above, being primarily aimed at calculation, symbol manipulation and storage (data processing) respectively. From that time onward we have seen the emergence of ever higher stages of abstraction from the machine or physical level in computer systems.

According to Sprague [246] and Sprague and Watson [192] computer systems, and in particular decision-support systems, may be evaluated in three dimensions: in terms of logic management or modelling capabilities, data management ability and dialogue handling. Bonczek *et al.* [28] give a slightly different classification of the dimension of decision support and computer systems in terms of 'problem', 'knowledge' and 'language' processing systems. What we present here is a synthesis of these and our own views.

If we adopt the view that there are, indeed, three dimensions available for this classification, then each of these may be given a scale. In the case of problem processing or logic management the lowest point on the scale is where the model procedures are stated explicitly. This is the case with FORTRAN or COBOL routines where every step in the solution of a problem is specified algorithmically in terms of procedures; assignment, transfer of control, subroutine calls, loops and file access. The 1970s saw the introduction of packages in which it was possible to specify procedures by name without the need for a detailed knowledge of how to construct the requisite procedures. Thus in packages such as SPSS (Statistical Package for the Social Sciences) and finite-element analysis packages such as STRUDL, PAFEC and NASTRAN it was not necessary for the user to have any detailed knowledge of statistics or differential equations for useful results to be obtained, although this very lack of knowledge did sometimes lead to the results being misinterpreted. Despite this, in competent hands the increase in productivity over third-generation languages was considerable and worthwhile on the whole. Such developments introduced a less procedural style which culminates in the current trend towards non-procedural languages: database enquiry languages, PROLOG, functional languages, and so on. Thus we have identified a scale of languages for problem solving ranging from the totally procedural (assembler) to the totally non-procedural. Currently, non-procedural languages assume that there is only one underlying logic. The human ability to dynamically switch logical system according to the instantaneous needs of problem solving has not yet been computerized.

A similar scale can be uncovered in relation to data management. At the lowest level data is totally unstructured, consisting of numbers and strings fed into the machine in an order considered appropriate by its operators, or determined by the exigencies of the procedure to be run. This corresponds to early batch processing of sequential files. Next we have systems which permit richer data structures: vectors, arrays, lists, fuzzy sets, etc. It has been observed that a computer program is composed of (*inter alia*) algorithms and data structures, and it soon becomes apparent that the richer the data structures are, the less complexity need reside in the algorithmic part. For example, in spreadsheet systems such as Visicalc, Symphony and Framework the user is able to keep programming to a minimum due to the good match between the built-in data structures and the restricted range of problems which such systems are intended to address. A system which includes higher-order types such as fuzzy sets will again allow the system developer to avoid much of the chore of coding.

The highest point of this scale must be the system that recognizes the most appropriate data structures and generates them as required. To date only humans have this ability, but we may expect progress in the near future.

Thirdly, we have the dimension of language or dialogue management. At the bottom of the scale is the plug board or cathode ray tube display representing binary code. At the top is natural language. In the middle are such techniques as command or menu-driven systems, report writers and so on.

It is a useful exercise to plot a range of familiar systems in three dimensional space according to the criteria given above.

It is clear to us that these three dimensions fail to capture everything. There is a fourth dimension of knowledge which cannot just be lumped in with data, and a fifth concerning the degree to which the other dimensions involve uncertainty. In fact this aspect of knowledge is not a true dimension in the sense in which we have been using the word. Dimensions need to be mutually orthogonal, or independent of each other. Knowledge-based systems represent a move along the axis: data – information – knowledge – wisdom; a scale of increasingly complex structures and organization. If the scale on which data are evaluated is from no structure to the most appropriate structure then the knowledge-based content of a system can be regarded as ranging from explicitly stated rules up to systems of heuristics and strategies for learning and experimenting with rule systems. Uncertainty is a true fourth dimension, it affects all the other dimensions. Knowledge can be more or less certain. Data and data structures can be fuzzy. Procedures can be defined with a degree of imprecision and all speakers are aware of the imprecision of natural, and to a lesser extent, formal languages (because of the degree to which they are a restriction on the problem space).

Already, several expert decision support systems have incorporated methods of representing uncertainty. MYCIN has a means of propagating the degree of confidence with which its own rules can be taken to hold, and PROSPECTOR uses Bayesian probabilities to handle uncertain inferences. There are now a number of expert systems which use fuzzy logic in fields as diverse as internal medicine, rheumatology, earthquake engineering and hospital management (see Gupta and Sanchez [84] and Zimmermann [222]). Also, at least one of the British companies involved in the USA's 'Strategic Defence Initiative' research programme has been investigating the use of fuzzy logic in theatre battle management. It has been said by senior officials that a solution to this problem will determine the success or failure of the whole project.

System designers must, in the future, drive their systems upwards in all four dimensions wherever this is appropriate. Already we have seen systems such as MYCIN, PLANNER, and STRIPS pushing in this direction in the first three of our dimensions. The next generation of decision support systems must tackle the representation of uncertainty as well.

A different approach to the classification of decision support systems focuses on different approaches to problem solving itself. In a preliminary attempt to do this Bonczek *et al.* [28] identify three methods: state space, problem reduction, and production system approaches. Of course, other methods should be included and it is difficult to arrive at an exhaustive list, but the latter will certainly include inductive techniques and generate and test approaches. In the state space approach the user sets a goal in some non-procedural language and the system finds a solution using tree searching methods (see Chapter 6) based on a data management system which must be extended to include ways of representing the states of the system relevant to the application, the initial state and the rules for states to be altered.

Problem reduction involves the user in describing a problem in a descriptive language, whereupon the system must find ways of reducing the problem to soluble sub-problems or, in Sprague's terminology, to 'model building-blocks'. The usual method for doing this is a variant on the idea of AND/OR graphs and logic programming will clearly be useful. Production systems require facts from the user and rules which can be applied to these facts, either forwards to change the state of the global database or backwards to reduce the problem. This approach is just one way of unifying the former two. Inductive systems require the user to supply sets of examples, and the language interface must allow verification of conclusions reached.

It is interesting to note the parallels between the formal structures of these systems and the interactions between decision making modules in real organizations. Just as artificial intelligence sets out to model the human mind, so decision support sets out to model the 'mind' of complex human organizations. The two disciplines have much to learn from each other.

8.3   THE ROLE OF SIMULATION

Ackoff [2] defines a system as 'any entity, conceptual or physical, which consists of inter-dependent parts'. He then distinguishes behavioural systems which are subject to control by humans as the subject matter of systems theory, and goes on to define an organization as 'an at least partially self-controlled system' subject to four characteristics: humans are involved as components, there is division of labour in decision making, subsystems communicate and the system can choose means and ends. All these characteristics can be tuned to direct the efficiency of systems. The last one implicitly involves the notion of system purpose and this is directed by decision making. In other words systems are directed by *policy* and policies effected by a chain of individual decisions conforming to the policy rules. Given these notions of system and organization, we can see that both can be 'modelled' by systems which are isomorphic to the object of study in some respects only. Thus, we can build a scale model of a car which has the same number of wheels and the same superficial shape, but has no engine since the purpose of the model is to test the aerodynamic properties of the production model. Similarly, in modelling organizations models need only take account of factors relevant to the model builder's purpose. An organization chart of a company does not tell you what it makes, but is useful nevertheless. We will be interested in models of decision making in this section. Let us offer some definitions before proceeding with this.

The word 'model' has many shades of meaning in ordinary and in technical parlance. We can distinguish, following Petri [165], at least three:

- Simulation: A model car is a simplified system that simulates some pertinent characteristics of some other system in a real or possible world.
- Realization: A model for a set of axioms is a data structure for which those axioms are true. Consistent axioms may have many different models, but inconsistent axioms have no model. A proof in a complete model extends to all other models.
- Prototype: A model citizen is a standard for evaluating all other (less perfect) citizens or for improving them.

We have dealt with the last two types of model extensively already, realization in Chapter 6 and prototype under the heading of frames in the previous three chapters. Thus we will settle for the following definition of our own for the purposes of this book. A model is a description of some system or process which is isomorphic to a coherent subsystem and which simplifies and abstracts an important aspect of the total system's behaviour. A simulation model is one whose behaviour can be observed in less than (or more than in the case of ultra rapid phenomena) real time.

Models can be classified in three dimensions, by nature, structure and purpose and by mathematical basis. Following the presentation of Winch [209], the nature of models admits classification into the following types:

- Textual models, which can be verbal descriptions, diagrams or simple tabulations of aggregate data such as balance sheets.
- Iconic models, such as physical mock-ups or photographs.
- Analogue models.
- Symbolic or mathematical models.

Simulation models occur in two types; as accounting and representational models, the former being based on non-causal, definitional relationships and the latter on causal relationships which often cannot be determined with precision. Other models split into the optimization and answer-giving models. Both these kinds of systems often result in suggestions as to what decisions might be taken and expert systems often have precisely this property. What is not often realized is that this second group of models usually relies in some degree on the first group, the simulation models. The classification by mathematical basis boils down to determining whether the model is continuous or discrete, analytical or numerical, static or dynamic, deterministic or probabilistic and crisp or fuzzy. For example, financial planning models are deterministic, discrete, and numerical, while Black and Scholes's option pricing model is stochastic, continuous and analytical (see [51]).

An important part of the decision-making procedure involves the formulation and application of policy. In business environments this policy is often expressed as general rules or guidelines: 'We will conduct our business in a professional and honourable manner', 'Our main target is increased market share, subject to long-term profitability', and the like. The more exactly defined decision rules can often be expressed in models, but ultimately the output from models has to be compared with overall policy factors. The traditional approach of model builders to this need has been to incorporate techniques in the model control structure to permit scenario analysis, so that various options can be tried out and their consequences predicted or preconditions determined. The main techniques are conditional subjunctive (what-if) forecasts and targeting (backward iteration). These correspond to the state-space and problem reduction approaches mentioned above. Simulation models of this type give four principle benefits. They provide a safe, controllable, quick and understandable means of evaluating the concrete effects of policies. What they do not provide is any means to represent the interaction between policies and the detailed decision rules *within* the model. This is where knowledge-based systems come in.

The production systems approach to problem solving provides a starting point for the introduction of knowledge-based techniques into decision support and policy modelling. It also provides a platform on which can be built methods of incorporating uncertainty into simulation models.

Having looked at the theory of decision support we now turn, briefly, to the practical problems of implementing decision support systems, and to how a theory of uncertainty and knowledge-based techniques can help.

8.4   IMPLEMENTING DECISION-SUPPORT SYSTEMS

We have pointed out the correspondence between the abstract roles that are taken by decision makers and the models of expert and decision support systems. The assumption behind such an approach is that the individuals filling these roles are rational 'economic' beings, seeking to maximize some objective function compatible with the aims of the organization. In contrast to such normative theories it is possible to distinguish a descriptive, or behavioural, approach which is concerned with the actual reality of the manager in a social, economic, political and psychological context. Failure to explore this complementary viewpoint can be credited with many of the failures of decision-support systems during the 1970s. Various surveys have indicated that the failure rate has been as high as sixty per cent, and higher when the user was not the system builder. The chief reasons for failure are:

(1) The model is never completed, indicating bad performance at estimating and planning.
(2) The model is built but never used, indicating that top management are not convinced of the benefit or do not understand how to use the end-product.
(3) The model makes no contribution to strategic issues, indicating that mathematical modelling techniques are not suitable for dealing with policy modelling.

It has been observed by Mintzberg [231]), and others, that managers favour informal channels of information which are thought to be richer in data content. Interpersonal contact and direct observation are preferred to the use of reference books, computers, etc. This is precisely the area where knowledge-based systems are more at home: intuitive reasoning, naïve physics, qualitative models and so forth. Among the reasons for preferring informal sources of information are included the following:

• any formally encoded data must be a summary to some extent, so that data relevant to some unforeseen circumstance may not be accessible;
• emotional, political and other factors are not normally included in formal sources;
• visual and auditory cues are useful in face-to-face situations;
• most formal sources are not comprehensive enough; they do not have 'general knowledge';
• by the time information reaches a formal system it is often out of date, and forecasts rarely incorporate the sort of qualitative data obtainable in conversation.

All these concerns recall those of this book, and indeed of researchers in artificial intelligence.

The inherently fuzzy or qualitative nature of business goals is in contradiction with the crisp and quantitative ways in which they are stated in the context of organizational behaviour. For example, the stated goal of profit maximization in the short term may conflict with the need for long-term research and development or maintenance of capital equipment. This arises from the difficulty of combining manifold crisp goals simultaneously. As in process controllers, smooth adaptive behaviour may be more easily simulated using fuzzy or linguistic variables. Rigid and inflexible goals lead to a lack of congruence between the aims of individuals and the organization. Most traditional decision-support and management information systems are designed on the assumption that some crisp goal is to be maximized. In fact it is a complex of individual and business motivations which control the decision process. For example, analysis may be biased, or actually subverted, when a model does not support a particularly favoured capital project under the aegis of a powerful group within management.

In order to make decision-support systems acceptable to senior management the human–computer interface of these systems must improve and come to better reflect the actual behaviour of management. To do this there must be an attempt to understand the nature of managerial work itself.

Up to 75% of a senior manager's time may be spent in interaction with a complex network of personal contacts, mostly in short, often fragmentary, conversations. Furthermore, decision-making behaviour involves resolution into subdecisions, consciously sequenced over long intervals, and a good deal of parallel processing of tasks. This is one of the things that differentiates senior and junior managerial work and also one of the things that distances users from traditional modelling tools which, of course, do not behave in this way. Furthermore, formal planning is a 'bottom up' process; senior management does not generate or evaluate options, it merely approves or rejects them.

There are at least four distinct factors which contribute to the success or failure of DSS in organizations. These factors are the quality of the models themselves, the attitudes and styles of individuals, the decision-making environment and the support (or lack of it) offered by management. We have noticed in the course of many DSS projects that senior management support at the highest level is a key determinant of success. Not unrelated to this is the tendency towards inertia. Technicians in the data processing industry are often amazed by the slow rate of take up of patently sensible ideas. The fact that COBOL is still the most widespread means for system development at the time of writing demonstrates this phenomena. One of the reasons for this conservatism is the fact that managers do not generally have time to absorb all the details and implications of new technology themselves and are reluctant to delegate too much of the executive decision making. Thus a need is felt to base new departures on 'success stories'. Products which have achieved market leadership do well because of this and, sometimes, apart from any intrinsic merit. The introduction of systems based on AI technology is a case in point. Digital Equipment Corporation became a major advocate of the use of AI only after achieving real and substantial savings through the use of R1 (later EXCON) to configure VAX computers.

Implementation of decision-support and expert systems has to take account of resistance to change arising from misunderstandings of potential benefits, a desire to preserve some valuable aspect of the existing situation. These aspects must be understood and planned for in any real project. The most effective techniques for managing change may be summarized in the following guidelines.

(1) Identify all those individuals and groups likely to be affected.
(2) Obtain the clear commitment and support of senior management.
(3) Identify and educate potential users in the technology and the benefits. An individual should take clear responsibility for this.
(4) Select prototypes with high visibility and which can be built and delivered successfully in a relatively short time. Strict adherence to theoretical definitions should take second place to this in some cases. For example, if one has to build a small transaction processing system to get a DSS or KBS project off the ground (this often happens due to the inadequacy of existing systems) then worrying about whether it is 'really decision support' is usually unproductive and often disastrous.
(5) Avoid the 'complete solution' approach. An evolutionary and incremental one is nearly always better. However, this is not an excuse for not spending adequate time on preliminary analysis or ignoring all the usual accounting constraints with regard to cost. At each stage the results and benefits should be demonstrated – 'selling' must be done.
(6) Where possible get users to design and even write their own systems, but give them copious support and advice – 'hand holding' brings success.
(7) Do not make the users uncomfortable by ignoring the human factors in the situation, making them speak your technical argot, isolating them from the model building process, making them provide all the data and a precise definition of the problem or assuming that because their solution is facile it must be wrong.
(8) Do not force the problem to fit the tools available or the ones you feel comfortable with. Just because expert system shells are easy to use does not automatically mean that they can be used effectively for all purposes.
(9) Do not force new technology in for its own sake. If you have developed a system on the very latest LISP workstation and the organization has an entrenched policy of using IBM PCs, then port the system. The fact that it runs more slowly is probably not important in practice.
(10) Spend as much time as possible on the user interface. Bugs in functionality can be fixed more easily than overcoming the apathy of users towards a totally unfriendly system. Models should be simple, robust and adaptable. Having said this there is no case to be made for models which are not complete on the important issues; a system which consistently gives the wrong answers is *not* friendly.

Many of the remarks which we made in Chapter 2 about knowledge representation and, more especially, those which we make in the chapter immediately following this one on knowledge acquisition apply equally well to the data analysis and design stages of the implementation of decision-support systems. In the future systems builders will use many of the techniques of knowledge engineering as a matter of course.

8.5 DECISION MAKING IN A FUZZY ENVIRONMENT

The development of scientific techniques of business management has closely paralleled the development of computing and indeed of artificial intelligence. The ability of the computer to process large amounts of information rapidly has been the chief driving force in this development. However, the suspicion with which even the simpler techniques have been regarded by management is real. Partially, it is justified by the injudicious overselling that specialists have sometimes been prone to, but more importantly, it flows from the inability of techniques such as linear programming to handle judgement and intuition.

Behavioural science has evolved several theories as to how people reach decisions. Such descriptive theories usually conclude by stating that managers do not make decisions on a purely rational basis. To help managers improve their decision making however, a normative theory such as decision analysis is required. Decision analysis consists of three principal stages:

(1) determine problem structure;
(2) assess uncertainties and possible outcome states;
(3) determine a 'best' strategy for achieving a desirable outcome.

A decision problem is characterized as one of selecting one from several options so as to maximize some function of possibly many variables, attributes or criteria. The naïve formulation is to organize these into a matrix of options against attributes. We will see an example of this in the next chapter. Many methods are available to achieve the requisite selection: maximizing, minimaxing, regression and so on. The disadvantage of this method is that complex problems are sometimes over-simplified by it, a method of overcoming this will be considered in due course. The so-called modelling school of decision analysis would attempt to construct a more explicit model of the relationships, usually as a decision tree such as the one in Fig. 8.4.

In most professions and businesses, decision making takes place in an environment where the cost of obtaining precise information is unjustifiably high. In recognition of this fact the classical theories of decision analysis, operational research and decision theory make extensive use of normative, statistical techniques. The decision problem, as we have said above, is either a question of choosing an optimal course of action, such as the ideal mix of ingredients in animal foodstuffs, subject to constraints such as lowest cost and some requisite nutritional value; or it is concerned with generating a plausible set of alternatives. It is the first case which has received most attention. A decision problem, in this latter sense, is given by stating a set of *options*, a set of states, a transformation which to every pair consisting of a state and an option returns a

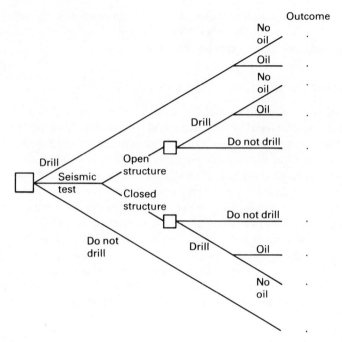

Fig. 8.4   The oilman's problem

new state representing the consequence of choosing that option *ceteris paribus*. Since the null option (do nothing) is always included this provides *inter alia* a model of the evolution of the system to which may be added feedback and/or feedforward control of options. Thus, we see that cybernetics becomes a special case of decision theory, and indeed many of the mathematical techniques are held in common. In addition decision models include a utility function which represents the ranking of outcomes with regard to their desirability in a given context. This function is analogous to the metrics required for homeostasis in cybernetic systems. In the few cases where decisions can be made in the presence of certain data the techniques of operational research, such as linear and dynamic programming and systems dynamics, are the most commonly used. We defer consideration of these until a later chapter. This leaves us with essentially only one tool: the decision tree. A decision tree is merely a hierarchy showing the dependencies between decisions. It is a shorthand description of some aspects of the general decision model whose chief value is to clarify our thinking about the consequences of certain decisions being made. However, with the introduction of probabilities the decision tree becomes a powerful tool.

To see this consider a very simple example. If one wishes to open a sweet shop, one must decide where it is to be located. There are, let us suppose, three options: near a school in an expensive suburb, in the busy high street or opposite a playground in a deprived inner city area. Let us call these options *A*, *B* and *C*. To each of these we can assign a probability of financial success, based on basic cost/revenue calculations and the history of similar ventures. In each case, however, there are other decisions to make, such as how much to invest in stock. Suppose the options and probabilities of success are as displayed in Fig. 8.5, where x, y and z represent these other decisions.

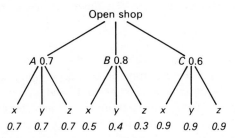

Fig. 8.5   Decision tree example

Combining the probabilities shows that option *C* is the most likely to succeed, despite the fact that on the basis of the first level of decision it was the worst option. Exploring the decision tree further might change the position again. Enhancement of this application of probability theory have proved most effective in attacking a wide range of decision problems.

Unfortunately life is not always that simple. Firstly, as we have pointed out so often in this book, the uncertainty which subsists in reality is not solely of a stochastic nature. Secondly, decisions are often multi-stage and options multi-attribute.

Bellman and Zadeh [24] put the first problem like this.

'Much of the decision-making in the real world takes place in an environment in which the goals, the constraints and the consequences of possible actions are not known precisely. To deal quantitatively with imprecision, we usually employ the concepts and techniques of probability theory and, more particularly, the tools provided by decision theory, control theory and information theory. In so doing, we are tacitly accepting the premise that imprecision – whatever its nature – can be equated with randomness. This, in our view, is a questionable assumption.

Specifically, our contention is that there is a need for differentiation between *randomness* and *fuzziness*, with the latter being a major source of imprecision in many decision processes. By fuzziness, we mean a type of imprecision which is associated with *fuzzy sets*, that is, classes in which there is no sharp transition from membership to nonmembership. For example, the class of *green objects* is a fuzzy set. So are the classes of objects characterized by such commonly used adjectives as large, small, substantial, significant, important, serious, simple, accurate, approximate, etc. Actually, in sharp contrast to the notion of a class or a set in mathematics [sic], most of the classes in the real world do not have crisp boundaries which separate those objects which belong to a class from those which do not. In this connection, it is important to note that, in [the] discourse between humans, fuzzy statements such as "John is *several* inches taller than Jim", "*x* is *much* larger than *y*", "Corporation *X* has a *bright future*", "the stock market has suffered a *sharp decline*", convey information despite the imprecision of the meaning of the italicized words. In fact, it may be argued that the main distinction between human intelligence and machine intelligence lies in the ability of humans – an ability which present-day computers do not possess – to manipulate fuzzy concepts and respond to fuzzy instructions.'

The theory they then introduce views goals and constraints as fuzzy sets, rather than the crisp sets found in conventional linear programming, say. Given a fuzzy goal, such as 'profits should be at least normal', and a fuzzy constraint, such as 'output will be about 1000', the resultant *decision* is the fuzzy set formed by conjunction. Recall that this is computed by taking minima. This set defines the fuzzy feasible region, and a maximizing decision can be generated by taking the supremum in the Cartesian product (see Fig. 8.6).

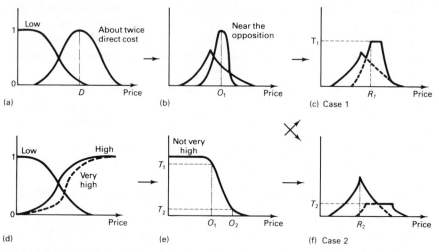

Fig. 8.6   Fuzzy inference

In general for several goals and constraints, taking the minimum of all of them together defines the decision. The method of defuzzification referred to above is, of course, not the only one available (see Chapter 5). The assumption here is that decision makers want to be presented with clear choices rather than a continuum of options. The method of 'moments' (see Chapter 5) is much more appropriate to situations of continuous control where sudden jumps in the output value are usually to be avoided for physical reasons. That engineering systems achieve goals under constraints is not in question.

Fuzzy sets have also been applied to multi-criteria analysis. We will get a glimpse of this at the end of Chapter 9, here we will look at the theory in a little more detail and mention some applications with a strong decision-support flavour.

A single-stage multi-criterion decision problem involves a set of attributes, a set of options and a weighting or priority value for each attribute. The degree to which each option possesses each attribute can be represented as a matrix, the decision matrix. Assuming that all the attributes are independent of each other, the valuation of an option can be achieved by multiplying the weights by the rating profile for the option and summing over all attributes. Following Mandic and Mamdani [221] this process can be represented in the schematic shown in Fig. 8.7.

If, on the other hand, the attributes do interact there is a need to represent some

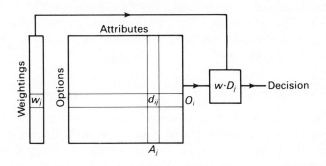

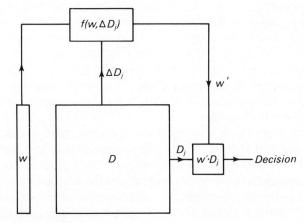

Fig. 8.7   (a) Constant weighting vector
                (b) Priority modification

notion of 'trade-offs'. The classical way of dealing with this is through Pareto optimality. A Pareto optimal solution is one where improvement of an objective function can only be achieved at the expense of another. There may be many such solutions, and the decision maker usually has to add some subjective judgement to select among them. The trade-offs involved express relative preferences for combinations of attributes. This means that the weighting vector depends on the relative levels of the attributes. Mandic and Mamdani [221] propose a method which uses a fuzzy rule-based inference mechanism to describe what they (misleadingly) call the 'topology of interaction' among the attributes. They propose a modification mechanism based on a graph describing the attributes which interact. The rules state degree of reinforcement of weightings; such as 'In a cheap car which is easy to break into a high quality stereo system is less important'. Such a rule can be thought of as a personal construct (see Chapter 9).

Bellman and Zadeh [24] develop a theory of multi-stage decision processes under both deterministic and stochastic control. Zimmermann [222] discusses a more general approach which allows different fuzzy set operations to be used when circumstances dictate that the minimum operation for intersection (and) is not the most appropriate one.

8.6 RECENT ADVANCES

Catastrophe theory [170] has been around for approximately the same length of time as fuzzy set theory. Possibly the same kind of dissatisfactions led to the need to develop such radically new mathematical paradigms. The basic idea behind catastrophe theory is that the commonly observed discontinuities in nature, such as the breaking of a wave can be described as the result of continuous phenomena in a higher dimensional state space. There are seven basic types of catastrophe of which the easiest to visualize is the cusp catastrophe. In a commercial context a very good example of a cusp catastrophe was the oil price hike of the 1970s. In Fig. 8.8 the supply curve for oil is represented as a slice through a surface plotting price against volume and a third dimension representing a surrogate political variable. At low (stable) values of this variable the supply curve is the conventional hyperbola of the micro-economics textbooks. At high values it has developed an S shape. It is conjectured that the oil curve was in that state and that as the volume declined beyond a certain point the price had to jump suddenly to remain on the supply surface.

The above explanation is all very well as a *post facto* description of what happened, but will it help us make decisions, does it have any normative potential? Up to now most applications have been purely descriptive. These simulation models do have predictive ability but the question as to how we are to construct the model *a priori* remains a difficult and mainly unsolved one.

Dimitrov [56] has proposed the use of a cusp catastrophe model for generating creative decisions. He also defines fuzzy catastrophes as the obvious generalization where the variables are linguistic.

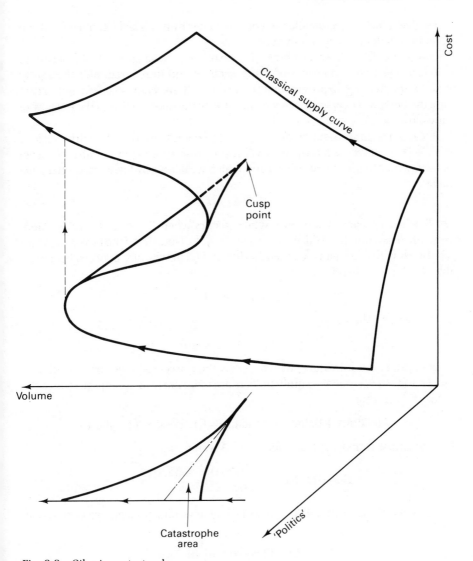

Fig. 8.8 Oil price catastrophe

Another interesting use of fuzzy set theory in this context is in corporate strategy. If we imagine representing a company's performance with a function similar to the one in Fig. 8.8 but where the variables are market share and profitability. Experience teaches us that we want to operate the business as close to the cusp as possible without entering the unstable region. In other words the decision rule amounts to stating that the business should operate 'close to', or within a fuzzy neighbourhood of, the cusp point. The surface itself may be regarded as a crisp constraint and the potential function as a rule of inference.

To give a little more detailed flavour, we present a worked example from the domain of balance sheet analysis.

Consider a firm whose earnings – i.e. cash flow – have an α risk classification. The firm has two main types of loans, secured and unsecured, and the equity holders are prepared to provide additional funds. Bank lending is used, but in that case the bank will oversee the business. Let Y be the net cash flow, D be the flow of funds from lenders and $Z = Y + D$.

If $Z < 0$ we may assume that equity intervenes, so that the firm fails iff $Z = Y + D \leqslant -K$ where K is the equity. Dividing this equation by the absolute level of borrowings to get the marginal rates which we denote by lower case letters, we have

$$z = d + y \leqslant k$$

Let F be the probability of failure which occurs when $F = \text{Prob}\{d + y \leqslant k\}$. More generally F is a function of d, y and k: $F = h(d, y, k)$. Note that if the firm moves into a business with a higher risk α then $F = h(d, \alpha, k)$. This will also concern lenders so that $d = d(\alpha, F)$. Therefore

$$F = h(f(\alpha, k) + d(\alpha, F), \alpha, k)$$

or, by Taylor's theorem,

$$F = h(f(\alpha, k) + d(\alpha, F))$$

Now consider bank lending, which makes the unsecured creditors sensitive to any change in α, while the equity holders are more likely to attempt to reduce the value of F, so that

$$F = h(\text{Equity} + \text{Debtors} - \text{Lending}) = f(\alpha, k) + d(\alpha, F) - g(\alpha, F))$$

Next we must transform F so that $F > 0$. Assume that

$$G(\alpha, 0) = d(\alpha, 0) = \frac{\delta G(\alpha, 0)}{\delta F} = \frac{\delta d(\alpha, 0)}{\delta F} = 0$$

that is when F is zero a small increase in F will have no significant effect on G or d. Now

$$G(\alpha, F) = g_2 \alpha F^2 + g_3 \alpha F^3$$

and

$$d(\alpha, F) = d_2 \alpha F^2 + d_3 \alpha F^3$$

where certain conditions on the d_i and g_i are necessary.

Finally,

$$f(\alpha, k) - \alpha(g_3 - d_3)F^3 + \alpha(g_2 - d_2)F^2 - F = 0$$

will be a cusp catastrophe surface iff

$$g_3 > d_3 \text{ and } d_2 > g_2.$$

That is to say: when the second-order removal of unsecured loans in reaction to an increase in F is greater than the firm's second-order borrowing ability from the bank, and when the third-order bank reaction is greater than the third-order depositor reaction to an increased F (see Fig. 8.9).

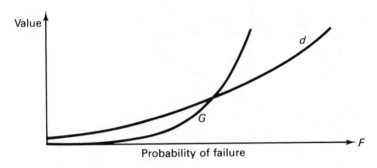

Fig. 8.9 Bank debt (d) and rate of change (e)

Suppose that for the firm, α increases. This will cause f to increase. Unsecured creditors will be reluctant to give further funds, and the bank will thus give loans up to a certain point. This causes the unsecured creditors to become even more cautious. The process then repeats iteratively.

In Fig. 8.10 the bank is initially at the point labelled 1. As α increases a steady increase in F takes place in equilibrium, and unsecured creditors reduce funds to be replaced by bank borrowing. However, beyond point 2 there is a sudden increase in the probability of failure if α increases further, the cause being the differentials in the slope (g_2, d_2) and in its rate of change (g_3, d_3).

This example shows, we hope, that catastrophe theory could have practical applications of enormous value. Its integration with fuzzy and knowledge-based methods has, as yet, hardly been explored.

We expect to see some exciting developments in the application of both fuzzy sets and catastrophe theory to decision making over the next few years. This development will be spurred on by developments in computer hardware and artificial intelligence software which will increase the potential of machines to compute more quickly and to permit more anodyne representations of complex problems. Perhaps, in this way, fuzzy catastrophe theory will be able to transform itself from a mainly descriptive to a prescriptive technique.

The last point we would like to make on future developments is a much more general one. Up to now, decision-support systems have shown a surprising reluctance to incorporate artificial intelligence techniques and expert systems products have usually exhibited a paucity of modelling and database manipulation abilities. We are confident that the distinction between the two will gradually

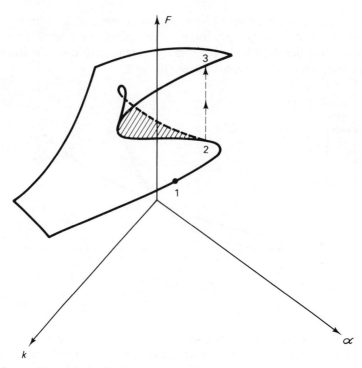

Fig. 8.10   Catastrophe surface

wither away, within ten years or so decision-support techniques and knowledge engineering methods will form merely a component in the general toolkit available to the data processing profession.

8.7   SUMMARY

This chapter has concerned itself with the subjects of decision-support systems, operations research and business modelling. All this under the assumption that all these are, in some sense, special cases of simulation. We have paid particular attention to the management of uncertainty and to the role that knowledge-based techniques have to play. We ended with a rather speculative look into the future for the decision sciences and their practical application.

8.8   FURTHER READING

On the question of the classification of decision-support systems the only worthwhile references seem to be the book by Bonczek *et al.* [28] and the papers of Sprague and his co-workers. The classic reference on systems and applications methodologies is Keen and Scott-Morton [110]. Another work it would be useful to consult on this topic is Alter [4]. The journal *Decision Support Systems* is also worth looking at.

On the related subjects of decision theory and fuzzy sets in this context we would recommend the original paper of Bellman and Zadeh [24] and the collection of papers in Zadeh, Fu, Tanaka and Shimura [219]. For a more recent collection see Zimmermann, Zadeh and Gaines [221].

For a first-class introduction to catastrophe theory the reader cannot do better than Poston and Stewart [170].

Part five

*Knowledge, uncertainty
and decision*

9

The practical implementation of knowledge-based systems

> 'Wisdom is the principal thing; therefore get wisdom:
> and with all thy getting get understanding.'
>
> *Proverbs i. 10*

9.1 KNOWLEDGE ACQUISITION

9.1.1 Elicitation methods

The subject of knowledge acquisition for knowledge-based systems falls conveniently into two parts depending on whether the knowledge is elicited from the experts by knowledge engineers or whether that knowledge is acquired automatically by the computer using some form of automatic learning strategy and algorithms. The latter subject was dealt with in Chapter 7 as part of our study of logical inference. Of course, knowledge engineers still have a role to play in automatic learning; they define the scope and set the parameters for the system, but the techniques used in that respect are either very simple or are covered by the techniques addressed in this section. There is one other method that has been used to acquire knowledge for expert systems and that is the centuries old one of going to school and reading books; in other words knowledge engineers can themselves become experts. Apart from the fact that we have nothing to add on how to go about learning things, this topic is not covered because we feel that while this method is perfectly acceptable in an academic environment it takes too long to be useful commercially. It has also been argued by some authorities that experts are often too close to the problem to be able to see it objectively and thus fail as system builders; they might be able to use their systems but no-one else can or wants to. The history of the MYCIN project provides an object lesson (see Chapter 1).

Thus, from now on in this section, we are talking about knowledge elicitation rather than acquisition in general.

Knowledge elicitation is a notoriously difficult activity and skilled knowledge engineers are hard to find and command good salaries. It is difficult for several reasons, among which are the facts that human knowledge is complex, unstructured and usually ill-formulated and that a lot of expertise operates at the level of the unconscious. Some experts have great difficulty in articulating their knowledge in words or diagrams and are often too busy to waste time talking to outsiders. Furthermore even the best knowledge engineers usually only have a partial understanding of the techniques of knowledge elicitation. One of the cases we will try to make here is that more of them should become familiar with the many methods developed by psychologists over the last hundred years. The objects of such techniques are to elicit knowledge in objective form, to uncover knowledge that is not stated explicitly and to impose some discipline on the interviewing process so that less is omitted and what emerges is understandable.

It is important to realise that knowledge engineers bring their own limitations and prejudices to the interview and that during the process of elicitation some interpretation necessarily takes place. Formal techniques help to minimize this although they cannot eliminate it entirely, no more than any scientific activity can be totally objective. The other thing to bear in mind is the importance of intermediate representations; that is the structures imposed on the knowledge by engineers and programmers because of their own mental processes and the exigencies of the software milieu in which they operate. Many expert systems make no *explicit* representation of some knowledge in them. For example the knowledge of the control structure is usually embedded deep in procedural code. In MYCIN the order in which questions are asked depends on the order of the conditions in the rules, and not on explicitly represented knowledge about what constitutes a sensible order to ask questions. Attempts to turn MYCIN into a tutoring system for medical students foundered on this particular reef. There is another sense in which the term 'intermediate representation' is sometimes used. In that sense the intermediate representation is the paper model of the expert's knowledge standing mid-way between the human expert and executable code. Some practitioners claim that the elicitation process is relatively easy compared to the problem of getting a good representation of it. There are some striking advantages to be obtained from using a representation which the expert can comprehend, whether it be a decision tree, production rules in some English-like syntax, predicate calculus or whatever. Thus an iterative cycle can be developed in which the expert can contribute to the paper model after the elicitation process to aid further refinement of the knowledge and further elicitation. However, with some applications this intermediate stage is difficult if not impossible because the task performance is itself unmediated; examples are language comprehension and image analysis.

The importance of thorough knowledge elicitation cannot be overestimated because most of the power of expert systems derives from the quality of the knowledge in them and, as with all computer systems, there is a grave danger that someone will accept their advice uncritically with potentially disastrous consequences. It is not, after all, worthwhile storing incorrect knowledge for subsequent use or even sale; no one will want it any more than they want the services of a charlatan once exposed as such. Well conducted knowledge elicitation often reveals facts that were not previously at the forefront of consciousness and can help sharpen the expert's own thought processes. On the other hand there is a tendency at present to see knowledge elicitation as a totally new skill. We feel strongly that people have been doing knowledge elicitation for years under the guise of systems analysis and that only the type of knowledge has changed as the software tools have changed to make this possible. Many of the skills of the analyst carry over unchanged into a knowledge engineering environment: rapport with the user, the ability to listen and suggest solutions, the conceptual mapping of informal understanding onto computer systems' structures, leading the user from simple to complex models, understanding the user's motivations and concerns and not talking down to people. From this perspective it is an important task of the knowledge engineer to insist on a clear definition of the objectives of the proposed system, and to establish a clear relationship with the expert and with potential users. It has been said that one of the problems with most knowledge engineers is that they know too much about AI and not enough about the common sense of experts. There is a grave temptation to try and force an expert to express knowledge in a form suitable for implementation in some well known knowledge representation formalism. This is usually a recipe for disaster.

The techniques available for knowledge elicitation break down into the following broad methods.

informal interviews,
interviews using scientific techniques (overtly or covertly),
presentations by the expert,
verbal protocols,
observational studies,
questionnaires,
introspection,
simulated consultations.

The advantages and disadvantages of each technique are seen to be as follows.

Informal interviews are the easiest kind to conceive and are conducive to a relaxed atmosphere. The difficulties arise because uncued recall is often incomplete and unstructured. Therefore it is difficult to get at details although this type of interview is good for getting a handle on the basic structure of the expert's knowledge. Due to the lack of structure they can be very time consuming and advance preparation can pay dividends. Our experience has shown that in these situations the meeting can seem to be going very badly for some time until a critical point is reached and then a lot of knowledge is acquired in the last 10% of the time available. This shows the importance of relaxing the interviewee.

If formal techniques are to be used they must be so well understood that they don't obtrude on the conduct of the interviewers; covert use is definitely to be preferred. The techniques available range from task analysis [35,224] to repertory grids [73, 183]. Usually experts will regard their knowledge as too subtle to be accessible to such crude methods, but used with discretion and in combination with other methods they can be highly successful, especially in uncovering latent knowledge. In this they have much in common with inductive techniques and we look forward to a growing together of the two.

As a first step in the elicitation process we have found that asking the experts to give a short presentation of their subject is invaluable. It provides a structure for subsequent meetings, an overview of the subject and enough insight to begin reading sensibly.

Verbal protocols are transcripts of sessions where the knowledge engineers ask an expert what she or he is doing and why she or he is doing it. The situation is a natural one for the expert and takes a minimum of time. This method is particularly useful when cases have been selected in advance and usually reveals a lot of detail. However, the questioning can interfere with the task if it is normally performed under pressure and often the expert will adopt an uncharacteristically systematic approach. If cognitive emulation is desirable this latter could be a problem.

Observational studies can only be done in certain circumstances but do help the engineer to break out of preconceived ideas and find out what the expert actually does. They provide information on the order in which tasks are carrried out, the expert's roles and the speed constraints. On the down side, they are time consuming and transcription of tapes or videotapes can be excessively time consuming. Some situations are ideal for this method. For example, one of us recently had experience of building an expert system for computer performance monitoring. In this situation we could not only ask the expert what he was doing and why, but had the computer record every action he took and keep an objective record of its consequences. The system was built very quickly and enjoyed some success.

Questionnaires are rarely used in this context but the (pseudo) science of psychometrics places heavy reliance on the way they objectify certain traits so their use should not be ruled out. Introspection is used as a last resort when the engineer asks 'how would *I* do that?'. That is always a useful question to ask, but we have already pointed out the danger inherent in the engineer trying to become an expert.

Another useful technique is to simulate a consultation between a user and an expert pretending to be the machine or, oppositely, asking the expert to set problems for the team members who then try to act the part of the expert under supervision. Also falling under the general heading of simulation is that technique where an artificial test case is fed gradually to the expert and his or her responses carefully monitored. This can help overcome the problem of post-rationalization; i.e. saying that you did something for reasons which were not in your mind at the time you did it, but emerged as rational with hindsight.

Over all, it is the case that no one technique will generally be adequate on its own. Furthermore we have found that machine induction, while limited in its usefulness, is very good at making a first stab at the rules (assuming rules are to be used) and combines well with other techniques. It is particularly useful for giving the knowledge engineer an early insight into the structure of the problem.

Further useful tips for knowledge engineers engaging in knowledge elicitation emerge from practical experience. It is helpful to approach interviews with a prepared strategy, it is this preparation and focus which often rescues a meeting which seems to be going badly at first. Make sure you tape or videotape or somehow record the interview. Transcription is tedious and exponentially time consuming and should be avoided if possible. The chief value of recordings is to clarify issues which are unclear after the interview, but they can also be used to brief colleagues on the domain. Case studies usually prove a useful way of focusing the discussion and aid understanding in the same way as protocols. Always be prepared to listen to the expert's cogitations, even if they seem to stray from the point. Sometimes a key piece of skill emerges in seemingly pointless ramblings and 'war stories' as they have been called. Make sure that the technical terms are clearly defined and that the domain's boundaries are understood. For example, in fault diagnosis the knowledge may be nothing to do with faults but only concern what tests are appropriate. Without attempting to become an expert, no knowledge engineer should attend a meeting with an expert without becoming familiar with the terminology of the subject; read some books. Structured walkthroughs and demonstrations can be useful if the expert has the time. Try to find out if you recognize the inference methods in use; backward chaining, induction, etc. Also try to find the most suitable form of knowledge representation to match the way the expert sees things; are they thinking in procedures, networks, causally or what? Lastly, ask yourself whether the expert's client is being considered? After all this will be the ultimate user – the expert system would be better for a model of the client as for example with tutoring systems we need to model the student's ignorance as well as the teacher's wisdom.

We have found that it is good practice to hold a knowledge engineers' meeting in advance of a knowledge elicitation session to focus the questioning sessions with a view to higher productivity. Also it is of value to hold another such meeting as soon as possible after the interview to discuss the results. This assumes that there is more than one engineer present and this we regard as *de rigueur* for such a meeting so that one can think up the next question while another continues to hold the expert's interest and continue the elicitation process. It is often considered that people are intimidated by being outnumbered in interview situations. Approaching experts in a manner sufficiently deferential to their status as experts seems to mean that even 'four to two' outnumbering will not be normally a problem.

9.1.2 Knowledge elicitation and the project management environment

Planning a knowledge elicitation session and the project environment is of crucial importance. At the first stages the following assessments have to be made:

- Are the experts suitable and readily available?
- Can they work together?
- Is the application a feasible one given current technology?
- Are the experts aware of the system builders' aims?
- Is it appropriate to produce a detailed project plan at the outset?
- Should knowledge elicitation be carried out at the outset or throughout the project?
- Is the information highly confidential?

Unless the system designers are confident that they have carried out many similar projects before, it is highly unlikely that a detailed plan can be prepared immediately. The project should be broken into stages with detailed plans being prepared only for the early ones. Naturally some knowledge elicitation must take place at the very outset, but since, following a philosophy akin to 'fast prototyping' or incremental development, the iterative nature of the development cycle overcomes many of the difficulties which arise from trying to elicit and formalize human knowledge all at once. This iterative procedure is best described by the flow chart in Fig. 9.1.

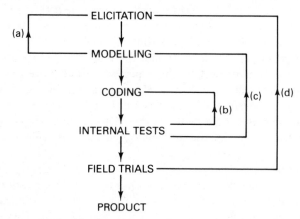

Fig. 9.1   (a) The model is inconsistent if misunderstood. (b) There is a fault in the code. (c) There is a logical failure in the organization of the model. (d) The advice given by the system is invalid.

As can be seen, there is a constant need to return to the experts during the project life-cycle. However, throughout such a project there will be times when the execution of plans is dependent on exogenous factors, among which one could be the availability of experts. Thus periods of expert involvement do have to be planned well in advance despite the remarks made above. In some ways this scheme dictates that the conventional system development methodologies must be partially abandoned. This does not mean, however, that a totally anarchic approach will suffice. Old methods must be adapted where possible and new ones developed where not. Of course the prototyping method is not entirely new. It has been extensively used in connection with the so-called 'fourth generation' languages which were one of the main results of database and modelling technology. Incremental development usually resulted in systems with a far higher degree of acceptance by users because they had been involved in every stage of the development, ensuring a system that met their requirements far more closely.

There are several questions to be answered when trying to decide whether the available experts are suitable.

- Are they genuinely experts?
- Are they available?
- Are they enthusiastic?
- Will there be a personality conflict amongst the experts or between experts and engineers?
- What is the nature of their expertise?
- How articulate or good at communicating their knowledge will they be?

For a knowledge engineer to decide whether someone is a true expert may be difficult in a field where he or she has only limited knowledge. It may be necessary to rely on reputation or the opinion of collegues in some cases. An unavailable, unco-operative or unenthusiastic expert will not be a great deal of use. The nature of the expertise should be evaluated in relation to available software tools; expertise involving geometric intuitions, for example, will be difficult to handle with existing technology. One useful test of this is to ask whether the expert could assist a client by telephone, so that image processing or the interpretation of subtle visual cues is not a part of the expertise. This is also important in estimating whether the knowledge is capable of being articulated.

One of the tasks which knowledge engineers have to perform early on in a project is domain analysis. This involves circumscribing the domain to be dealt with by the expert system to be built, establishing whether expert knowledge is deep and narrow or shallow and wide-ranging and evaluating the suitability of the application on technical and commercial grounds. In the early stages, this analysis is high level and breaks down into three main tasks:

analysis of the whole domain in terms of decision making activities;
selection of sub-domains for the early prototypes;
detailed analysis of the sub-domains.

In the first stage the objective is to analyse in terms of decisions made, rather than data flow, with the ulterior object of choosing the first prototype. It is necessary to ensure that the experts are aware of the aims of the knowledge engineers and what information they are trying to get hold of and what they will do with it. It can be useful to bring several experts together in the hope that discussions between them will reveal more facets of the domain and, as a secondary aim, reveal whether they could co-operate with each other. Some of the information typically required at this stage is:

information sources (such as conversations, documents, etc.);

decision factors, attributes and options;
time span of activities;
computer systems involved;
people and manual systems involved.

In the second phase the prototypes are chosen with a view to turning them ultimately into fully fledged expert systems. The sub-domain should be selected on the basis of the following criteria:

it must be an activity of importance to the aims of the client;
it should include most of the technical issues;
it should not be trivial;
it should not be unrealistically large or complex;
there must be some means of testing the results.

The third stage involves defining the domain boundaries and detailed technical assessments. The constraints of budget, time and personnel must all be taken into account. Other questions which will arise are the extent to which the knowledge is volatile or evolves, the projected size of the knowledge base and, most importantly the study of how uncertainty is coped with and how it may be classified. Attention to knowledge representation and inference is also required.

Recently Knight and Swaffield [116] have directed attention to the important principle of user independence in expert systems. That is to say systems ought to be independent of the data entered for processing by the knowledge base at run time. For example, in systems such as PROSPECTOR based on Bayesian inference the user is required to supply probabilities. As a result the sensitivity of the system to different probability estimates by users can be uneven and the system is not stable over time since humans are not usually very consistent about probability estimates. Use of a small term set as in the fuzzy sets approach will give some improvement in stability, but it is suggested that the knowledge elicitation technique of domain analysis promises even greater improvements in the same way that the introduction of data analysis techniques to complement functional analysis into conventional systems analysis resulted in more robust systems. The techniques of domain analysis may be summarized in Fig. 9.2.

Having dealt with the general activity of knowledge engineering, as thoroughly as is possible at this stage in the history of the subject, we now turn to some of the formal methods that can be used to assist knowledge engineers.

9.1.3   Interview techniques, task analysis and Kelly grids

> 'The splitting of a single whole and the cognition of
> its contradictory parts is the essence of dialectics.'
>
> Lenin, *Philosophical Notebooks*

There are, as we have mentioned, a number of formal techniques for structuring interviews which derive from psychology. The ones we consider here are protocol analysis, task analysis, multi-dimensional scaling and repertory grids.

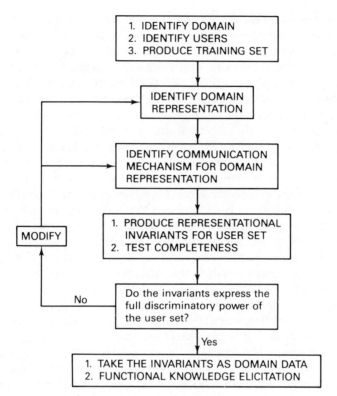

Fig. 9.2 Domain analysis (after Knight and Swaffield)

It is arguable whether protocol analysis is really a formal technique in the strictest sense. It was first described by Newell and Simon [162] as a method wherein problem solving behaviour is recorded 'on the job' and then analysed with the aim of identifying the solution states passed through during the analysis. The method of passing from one state to the next is then sought in the form of production rules. This formal structure imposes a certain discipline on the acquisition process so that if an expert has not mentioned explicitly some piece of knowledge or procedure its absence will show up more clearly in the formal paper model. However, it will be apparent from the remarks on production systems in Chapter 2 that not all knowledge can be represented readily in this way, and, as things stand at the present time, the knowledge engineer will need to devise a version of protocol analysis to suit the needs of the system under construction and the representations felt to be suitable. Much of what has been written in the preceding section concerns our own version of protocol analysis.

We distinguish between task and topic analysis. The former consists of breaking down tasks into steps to be performed in some sequence, and the latter is concerned with sets of inter-related elements not necessarily structured sequentially. Task analysis is usually applied to procedural knowledge while topic analysis is of more general application. By uncovering a network or hierarchy of objectives, the dependencies in the topic can be identified. There are several theories in this area. Bloom's taxonomy of educational objectives in training, in order of increasing complexity, into knowledge, comprehension, application, analysis, synthesis and evaluation. Gilbert's *Mathetics* classifies behaviour into three types: chains, discriminations and generalizations. Gagne expanded the classification of behaviours to eight elements: signal learning, response to stimulus, psychomotor chains, verbal chains, multiple discriminations, concept learning, rule learning and problem solving. These models were primarily aimed at applications in education, but it is clear that reversing the process in knowledge acquisition could be of value. Mathetics has been further developed for the analysis of tasks involving decision making related to physical operations such as operational control. There is an apparent similarity with Schank's conceptual dependencies which, as far as we know, has yet to be explored. Other methods worthy of mention are Seymour's skills analysis of industrial skills where repetitive operations are involved – this can be applied to robot programming applications – and Landa's analysis of mental operations, which extracts problem solving strategies by taking account of both rule following and heuristic behaviour. Lastly, Romiszowski has attempted a unified approach based on a classification model (Hopkins [102]). Knowledge is classified into facts, procedures, concepts and principles; skills into cognition, acting (psychomotor), reacting (attitudes) and interacting (communication). The movement between the categories of skills involves a cycle of perception (that a skill must be used), recalling which procedures or heuristics to use, planning and performance. These methods tend to be suited to eliciting knowledge in the form of production rules and a wider audience for them among knowledge engineers would almost certainly benefit the art.

In task analysis the objective constraints on problem solving are exploited, usually prior to a later protocol analysis stage. The method consists of arriving at classification of the factors involved in problem solving and the identification of the atomic 'tasks' involved. The categories which apply to an individual task might include: time taken, how often performed, procedures used, actions used, objects used, error rate, position in task hierarchy, etc. This implies that it is also necessary to identify the actions and objects in a taxonomic manner. For example, if we are studying poker playing we might start with the following crude structure:

Objects: Card, Deck, Hand, Suit, Player, Table, Coin
Actions: Deal, Turn, See, Collect, etc.

One form of task analysis has it that concepts are derivable from pairing actions with objects; e.g. 'See player', 'Deal card'. Once the concepts can be identified it is necessary to identify plans (win game, make money) and strategies (bluff at random) and use this analysis to identify the knowledge required and used by matching object–action pairs to task descriptions occurring in task sequences.

Multi-dimensional scaling is the general term which describes techniques which describe behaviour in terms of a possibly unknown number of variables or 'dimensions'. Attempts must be made to determine the minimal dimensionality of this set of variables and the rates of variation along each axis from the distribution of instances. The technique has been extensively used in marketing consumer goods where customer perception of products and markets is of key importance. In some ways this is knowledge elicitation 'in spades'; the people being asked for their knowledge are legion and inaccessible. Statistical techniques are required to collect and analyse data. The method has been more associated with eliciting opinions than knowledge, but could be of value in cases where there are multiple views held among experts who are required to reach a consensus before acting, or in cases where opinions and knowledge become indistinguishable (stock market speculation?).

Repertory grids, due to Kelly (see Shaw [183]) and thus also 'Kelly grids', are a special case of multi-dimensional scaling which have been applied to knowledge elicitation.

The technique generally proceeds as follows.

(a) *Step 1*

   Identification of a homogeneous, representative set of elements within each category involved in the knowledge. For example, if the knowledge concerns choosing suitable candidates for employment in some job the categories might be reduced to one; personality. Suitable elements might be the names of various careers. There are four general methods for specifiying elements:

   suggest a list of elements;
   provide a list of roles or situations;
   ask the expert to name specific instances;
   elicit through discussion.

(b) *Step 2: Identification of constructs*

   A construct is usually a quality that can be attributed to an object of thought or element. In the above example we might include: salary, difficulty, danger, job satisfaction, security, boredom. The constructs should be bipolar; e.g. extrovert/introvert, clever/dull, important/unimportant, etc. Once again there are four methods for generating elements:

   suggest a list;
   elicitation from triads;
   card sorts;
   laddering.

   In the example of career selection, a suggested list might well be as given above. In the triad method, the expert is invited to select groups of three elements from the list and say in what way two are alike and the third different. For example, if we consider the triad Engineering, Actuary and Accountant we might arrive at the construct 'mathematically complex – mathematically trivial', without committing ourselves to the extent to which each element satisfies this concept for the particular expert involved. Kelly maintained strongly that the bipolarity of constructs should be based on the idea of opposition rather than negation in the strict logical sense; not complex is not the same as trivial. It is for this reason that pairs of elements are rarely used in preference to triads, since this tends to encourage thinking in terms of simple logical negation. The Hegelian notion of negation is, of course, much closer to opposition and might be used with profit to formalize exactly what is meant by opposition. To illustrate the triad technique we include an extremely simple program (Fig. 9.3) which emphasizes the notion of personal constructs, and a sample run of this program applied to the problem of

```
 1: /* Personal construct elicitation by triads
 2: */
 3: £include stdio.h
 4:
 5: char esc='\33';                    /* declarations */
 6: char name[5][20],chr[5][2][20],order[5][7]={" First",
 7:         "Second",
 8:         " Third",
 9:         "Fourth",
10:         " Fifth");
11: int   value[5][5],nvalue[5][2],import[5][2];
12: int   cptr[5],nptr[5],i,j,v,ents,quals;
13: main ()                            /* control routine */
14: {
15:   puts("\nStarting execution ...\n");
16:         cls();
17:         instruct();
18:         getname();
19:         cls();
20:         getqual();
21:         cls();
22:         score();
23:         cls();
24:         result();
25:   printf("\nProcessing complete.");
26: }                                  /* end main routine  */
27: cls()                              /* VT52 screen clear */
28: {
29:   printf("%c%c%c%c",esc,'E',esc,'H');
30: }
31: instruct()                         /* print instuctions */
32:
33: {
34: printf("This program elicits personal constructs by the");
35: printf(" technique of Kelly grids.\n");
36: printf("\nYou will be asked to give the names of a number");
37: printf(" of entities and a number");
```

Fig. 9.3   Kelly grids in C

Fig. 9.3 *contd.*

```
38:  printf("\nof their qualities. Then you have to score each");
39:  printf(" entity against each quality.\n");
40:  printf("\n\n\n");
41:  }
42:  getname()                          /* prompt for names */
43:  {                                  /* of entities      */
44:    while(TRUE){
45:      printf("How many entities ?");
46:      scanf("%d",&ents);
47:      getchar();
48:      if(ents<6 && ents>0) break;
49:      puts("1 to 5 entities allowed");
50:    }
51:    printf("\nPlease type the names of the entities under");
52:  printf(" consideration\n");
53:    for(i=0;i<ents;i++){
54:      printf("%s entity: ",order[i]);
55:      gets(name[i]);
56:                      }
57:    printf("\nHit [RETURN]");
58:    getchar();
59:  }
60:  getqual()                          /* prompt for qualities */
61:  {                                  /* using triad method   */
62:    qual(0,1,2,0);
63:    if(ents==1) return;
64:    qual(0,2,3,1);
65:    if(ents==2) return;
66:    qual(1,4,3,2);
67:    if(ents==3) return;
68:    qual(0,4,1,3);
69:    if(ents==4) return;
70:    qual(4,2,3,4);
71:  }
72:  qual(a,b,c,r)
73:  {
74:    printf("%s %s %s",name[a],name[b],name[c]);
75:    printf("\nPlease type a quality that two of these entities");
76:    printf(" have but the third lacks\n");
77:    gets(chr[r][0]);
78:    printf("What is the opposite of %s ? ",chr[r][0]);
79:    gets(chr[r][1]);
80:  }
81:  score()                    /* prompt for subjective scores */
82:  {
83:    printf("Please score each entity's qualities\n");
84:    for(i=0;i<ents;i++)
85:    {
86:      printf("(1 is %s and 9 is %s)",chr[i][0],chr[i][1]);
87:      printf("%s %s\n",order[i],chr[i][0]);
88:      for(j=0;j<ents;j++)
89:      {while(TRUE){
90:        printf("%s ",name[j]);
91:        scanf("%d",&v);
92:        getchar(0);
93:        if(v<10 && v>0) break;
94:        puts("1 to 9");
95:        }
```

Fig. 9.3 *contd.*

```
 96:    value[j][i]=abs(5-v);
 97:    )
 98:  )
 99:  printf("\nHit [RETURN]");
100:  getchar();
101:  )
102:  result()                   /* calculate rankings, sort and */
103:  (                          /* print the results            */
104:   for(j=0;j<5;j++)
105:   (for(i=0;i<ents;i++)
106:    (
107:     nvalue[i][0]+=value[j][i];
108:     import[j][0]+=value[i][j];
109:    )
110:   )
111:  charsort();
112:  namesort();
113:
114:  printout();
115:  )
116:  charsort()
117:  (
118:   int score,temp;
119:   for(j=0;j<5;j++)
120:   (
121:    score=0;temp=0;
122:    for(i=0;i<ents;i++)
123:    (
124:     if(import[i][0]>score && import[i][1]!=1)
125:     (
126:      score=import[i][0];
127:      temp=i;
128:     )
129:    )
130:    cptr[j]=temp;
131:    import[temp][1]=1;
132:   )
133:  )
134:  namesort()
135:  (
136:   int score,temp;
137:   for(j=0;j<ents;j++)
138:   (
139:    score=0;temp=0;
140:    for(i=0;i<5;i++)
141:    (
142:     if(nvalue[i][0]>score && nvalue[i][1]!=1)
143:     (
144:      score=nvalue[i][0];
145:      temp=i;
146:     )
147:    )
148:    nptr[j]=temp;
149:    nvalue[temp][1]=1;
150:   )
151:  )
152:  printout()
153:  (
```

Fig. 9.3 *contd.*

```
154:    printf("\nThe quality at the top of the list, %s, is");
155:    printf("  most important to you.",chr[cptr[0]][1]);
156:    printf("\n%s is the entity you are clearest about.",
157: name[nptr[0]]);
158:    printf("\nIn the following list characteristics are");
159:    printf("  ranked in order of clarity");
160:    printf("\nfrom left to right and significance from");
161:    printf("  top to bottom.\n\n");
162:     printf("\n\n              ");
163:     for(i=0;i<ents;i++)
164:     {
165:      printf("%10s ",name[nptr[i]]);
166:     }
167:
168:    printf("\n\n");
169:    for(i=0;i<5;i++)
170:    {
171:     printf("%10s ",chr[cptr[i]][1]);
172:     for(j=0;j<ents;j++)
173:     {
174:      printf("%10d ",value[nptr[j]][cptr[i]]);
175:     }
176:     printf("%10s ",chr[cptr[i]][0]);
177:     printf("\n");
178:    }
179:    printf("\nHit [RETURN]");
180:    getchar();
181:   }
182:   £include ?stdio.lib?
```

----

assessing attitude to makes of automobile (Fig. 9.4). Most of the techniques of identifying constructs and elements and linking them in grids have proved susceptible to automation in this way. Interested readers are referred to Shaw [183] and Gaines and Shaw [73] for a fuller bibliography and information on these systems than it is possible to cover in a work of this nature.

The card sort technique involves writing the elements on cards and asking the expert to sort them into similar groups and to give, for each group, a verbal description where this is possible and natural. Lastly, the laddering method may be used once a first pass at elicitation of the constructs has been made. Here, the expert is asked which pole of the construct is preferable and why, so that the deeper constructs emerge. An exciting job may be preferred to a dull one because association with an exciting job (astronaut?) is a social asset while boring ones attach to a certain stigma (sewer records administrator?). All four techniques can, in principle, be used covertly during apparently unstructured interviews. The knowledge engineer might merely ask 'Do you think that people rate social kudos highly, or are they more concerned with the stigma attaching to this one?' during the course of conversation.

This program elicits personal constructs by the technique of Kelly grids.

You will be asked to give the names of a number of entities and a number of their qualities. Then you have to score each entity against each quality.

How many entities ?5

Please type the names of the entities under consideration
    First entity: Jaguar
Second entity: Rolls
  Third entity: Porsche
Fourth entity: Scimitar
   Fifth entity: Mini

Hit [RETURN]■

Please score each entity's qualities
(1 is Cheap and 9 is Dear) First Cheap
Jaguar 6
Rolls 9
Porsche 7
Scimitar 6
Mini 2
(1 is Sporty and 9 is Steady)Second Sporty
Jaguar 6
Rolls 7
Porsche 2
Scimitar 1
Mini 7
(1 is Cost and 9 is Economy) Third Cost
Jaguar 3
Rolls 1
Porsche 2
Scimitar 7
Mini 9
(1 is Comfort and 9 is Basic)Fourth Comfort
Jaguar 4
Rolls 1
Porsche 7
Scimitar 8
Mini 9

Fig. 9.4   The Kelly grid program in action

Fig. 9.4 *contd.*

(1 is Fast and 9 is Slow) Fifth Fast
Jaguar 4
Rolls 5
Porsche 1
Scimitar 3
Mini 6∎

The quality at the top of the list, Economy, is most important to you.
Porsche is the entity you are clearest about.
In the following list characteristics are ranked in order of clarity from left to
right and significance from top to bottom.

	Porsche	Scimitar	Rolls	Jaguar	Mini	
Economy	3	2	4	2	4	Cost
Basic	2	3	4	1	4	Comfort
Steady	3	4	2	1	2	Sporty
Dear	2	1	4	1	3	Cheap
Slow	4	2	0	1	1	Fast

Hit [RETURN]∎

(c) *Step 3: Linking the constructs to elements*

The grid is the method of linking. First it is necessary to decide which method
of rating where the elements fall along the dimensional axis of each
construct. There are three methods:

• dichotomizing: a binary assignment to each element;
• ranking: putting the elements in order for each concept;
• rating: assigning truth values or fuzzy intervals to each element.

(d) *Step 4: Analysing the grids*

There are essentially two methods available for grid analysis: manual or
computer assisted. Within this distinction many analytical techniques are
available, and it is generally held that interpretation is more of an art than a
science. This means that the engineer conducting the interview will normally
be the only person in a position to analyse and interpret the results. Consider
the following grid elicited from our careers adviser using the dichotomizing
method.

	Accountant	Actuary	Engineer	Sales Rep.	Lawyer	
Boring	1	1	0	0	1	Exciting
Well paid	1	1	0	1	1	Badly paid
Secure	1	0	0	0	1	Insecure
Satisfying	0	0	1	1	0	Frustrating
Difficult	1	1	1	0	1	Easy

First, rearrange the grid so that similar constructs appear side by side, according to some measure of pattern similarity.

	Accountant	Actuary	Engineer	Sales Rep.	Lawyer	
Boring	1	1	0	0	1	Exciting
Frustrating	1	1	0	0	1	Satisfying
Well paid	1	1	0	1	1	Badly paid
Difficult	1	1	1	0	1	Easy
Secure	1	0	0	0	1	Insecure

Note the way in which the satisfying/frustrating concept has been reversed. Now count the number of matches for each pair of elements to get the similarity matrix:

	Accountant	Actuary	Engineer	Sales Rep.	Lawyer
Accountant		4	1	1	5
Actuary			2	2	4
Engineer				3	1
Salesperson					1
Lawyer					

where high numbers denote greatest similarity. A similar matrix can be deduced for constructs.

The analysis of the grid depends on the purpose for which it was elicited. In the above example, we have seen that the expert regards Lawyer and Accountant as similar professions. This could guide his or her decision-making when giving career guidance. For example, he or she might ask fewer questions as a result of this insight, needing only one last question to discriminate. What that question should be may require further elicitation.

We have based our example on the dichotomizing method so far. Much more interesting are the various versions of the rating technique. One method of analysis due to Boxer [33] and known as reflective analysis is illustrated in Fig. 9.5 as coded in REVEAL.

As an example of the use of linguistic variables in REVEAL, we have illustrated a session with a system called 'option analysis' wherein the user is trying to choose a new car. The interesting point to note is that after the user is interrogated for his preferences in vague terms, like high and low, the system generates new rules dynamically. Bear in mind when looking at the sample session that the rankings given to each type of car represent the subjective ideas of the user, and are in no way a comment on the qualities of the particular vehicles.

Another, related, development is the application of repertory grids to multi-attribute decision making under uncertainty (see Eshragh [62] and Zimmermann *et al.* [221]). Typical problems to which this technology has been applied are selection of micro-computer software and fertilizers. This can be useful for a knowledge engineer trying to understand the decision making involved in an expert's problem-solving behaviour or during top-level domain analysis. This method basically involves assigning linguistic truth values which describe the degree to which certain options satisfy or possess certain attributes. As an example, if the problem is the selection of software, we might construct Table 9.1.

Table 9.1

		Attributes					
		Report Generator	*Enquiry Language*	*User Friendly*	*Modelling Abilities*	*Speed*	*Price*
O	Dbase III	Good	Average	Average	Average	Good	Good
P	Framework	Average	Poor	Good	Poor	Good	Good
T	Micromodeller	Good	Poor	Poor	Excellent	Average	Average
I	Micro-FCS	Good	Poor	Poor	Excellent	Average	Poor
O	Rapport	Good	Excellent	Average	Average	Good	Poor
N	Reveal	Average	Poor	Poor	Excellent	Average	Poor
S	Symphony	Average	Poor	Average	Poor	Average	Good

(The values shown in this table are not intended to reflect on the products mentioned.)

Fuzzy set theory then enables the transformation of the linguistic values into numerical form. The next question is how important each attribute is for the application envisaged. Suppose that the weightings are expressed as shown in Table 9.2.

```
MODE  > option.analysis

...WORKSPACE CLEARED
...CONTEXT LOADED
...VOCABULARY INSTALLED

...Do you wish to load an existing dataset? > no

...Option/concept analysis system

...Enter the options you wish to evaluate, ending with a c/r
a   > Fiat
b   > Golf
c   > Fiesta
    > Metro
e   >
...Enter the concepts over which you wish to evaluate, ending with a c/r
1   > Comfort
2   > Economy
3   > Finish
4   > Cost
5   > Reliability
6   >
```

...For each concept, give an approximate ranking of the way you perceive the various options
Do it by entering the option codes (a,b,c etc) along a line; for example, your entry for the first concept ' Comfort' might look like:

```
Comfort                                   > ------b------e--------c-d -------- a------
```

...If you have numeric values for a concept, just hit c/t and you will be prompted later for the values

```
                                          LOW                              HIGH
Comfort                                   > ------a--b--c--d
Economy                                   > -------a-c----b--------d
Finish                                    > ------------a----b---c----d----
Cost                                      > --------------b---a---------d-----c
Reliability                               > ----a---c---d---b
```

...A cluster analysis of the options is as follows:

```
Fiat                                      > a-------b------c------d------------------
Golf                                      > b------ca------d-------------------------
Fiesta                                    > c------d-------a -------------------------
Metro                                     > d------c-------b------a------------------
```

...The similarity of concepts is:

		(1)	(2)	(3)	(4)	(5)
Comfort	(1)		68	34	68	14
Economy	(2)			48	6	64
Finish	(3)				51	32
Cost	(4)					67
Reliability	(5)					

...Based on the similarity matrix, we can build up a structured set of more general concepts. Try to enter the name of some new concept which embraces each pair of concepts which are presented:

...Economy and Cost	> Expense
...Comfort and Reliability	> Engineering
...Finish and Engineering	> Good Manufacture
...Expense and Good Manufacture	> Value for money

...This structured set of concepts can now be displayed as a tree diagram:

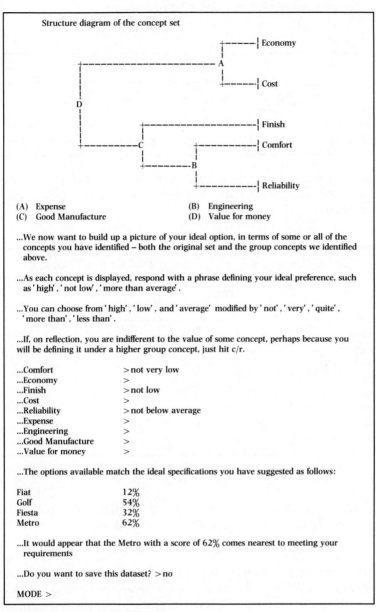

Structure diagram of the concept set

```
                                              +------| Economy
                                              |
     +------------------------A               |
     |                        |               +------| Cost
     |                        |
  D  |                +-----------------------| Finish
     |                |
     |                |       +----------| Comfort
     +----------C     |
                |     +-------B
                +-------|     |
                              +----------| Reliability
```

(A) Expense   (B) Engineering
(C) Good Manufacture   (D) Value for money

...We now want to build up a picture of your ideal option, in terms of some or all of the concepts you have identified – both the original set and the group concepts we identified above.

...As each concept is displayed, respond with a phrase defining your ideal preference, such as ' high' , ' not low' , ' more than average' .

...You can choose from ' high' , ' low' , and ' average' modified by ' not' , ' very' , ' quite' , ' more than' , ' less than' .

...If, on reflection, you are indifferent to the value of some concept, perhaps because you will be defining it under a higher group concept, just hit c/r.

...Comfort	> not very low
...Economy	>
...Finish	> not low
...Cost	>
...Reliability	> not below average
...Expense	>
...Engineering	>
...Good Manufacture	>
...Value for money	>

...The options available match the ideal specifications you have suggested as follows:

Fiat	12%
Golf	54%
Fiesta	32%
Metro	62%

...It would appear that the Metro with a score of 62% comes nearest to meeting your requirements

...Do you want to save this dataset? > no

MODE >

Fig. 9.5   Reflective analysis in REVEAL

Table 9.2

	Attributes					
	Report Generator	Enquiry Language	User Friendly	Modelling Abilities	Speed	Price
Importance	Very high	High	Average	High	Low	Fairly low

Suppose further that from the definitions of the fuzzy sets High, low, average, excellent, good and poor we are able to arrive at the following numerical representations:

Table 9.3

	Attributes					
	Report Generator	Enquiry Language	User Friendly	Modelling Abilities	Speed	Price
O Dbase III	7	5	5	5	7	7
P Framework	5	3	7	3	7	7
T Micromodeller	7	3	3	9	5	5
I Micro-FCS	7	3	3	9	5	3
O Rapport	7	9	5	5	7	3
N Reveal	5	3	3	9	5	3
S Symphony	5	3	5	3	5	7
Importance	9	8	5	8	2	3

The valuation of each option is computed as the weighted sum of the attribute values. So, in the cae of Reveal the normalized valuation is:

$$(5*9+3*8+3*5+9*8+5*2+3*3)/60 = 175/60 = 2.91$$

EXERCISES: Compute the valuation of the other options and select the best one under the assumptions given. Write a computer program to generalize this to any multi-criteria selection problem of the same form. What is wrong with the method of normalization used above; i.e. dividing by a constant?

The valuation arrived at by this process can readily be converted back to a linguistic expression. The advantages of using the fuzzy set approach should be fairly obvious in terms of the facility of problem description, but one weakness of this particular application is the need to convert to numerical form prior to valuation. In this case they are not being used to deal with any intrinsic vagueness in the knowledge only in the way it is expressed.

Gaines and Shaw [73] report a method of using repertoire grids to elicit entailments or production rules automatically. We have already seen that the process of grid elicitation can be automated to a considerable extent. This method goes further and automates part of the process of analysing the grid, which results in the automatic induction of a ranked set of rules with a single antecedent and a single consequent. Since Gaines and Shaw emphasize the role of fuzzy sets in their analysis it is, perhaps, surprising to find that they have not attempted to induce rules with compound antecedents. The poles of a grid are regarded as representing predicates defining fuzzy sets. A measure of the distance between two fuzzy sets based on the Lukasiewicz fuzzy logical operators. A generalization of the notion of Shannon entropy is given the name *surprise*, and entailments are ranked in such a way as to minimize surprise or reduce uncertainty. This method, which allows a neat combination of fuzzy and probabilistic hypotheses, holds out the promise of reducing the labour involved in knowledge acquisition without dehumanizing the result, as could happen with pure rule induction. This is a necessary consequence of the very personal nature of the repertoire grid.

Recently, Boose [30] has applied the techniques described above to automate knowledge acquisition in a system called ETS (Expertise Transfer System). ETS uses laddering and triads, induces rules and generates code for a number of expert system shells and languages, such as EMYCIN and OPS5. Boose points out that the technique, as it presently stands, is only good for a small class of knowledge engineering applications which come under the general heading of 'classification' systems; fault diagnosis is an example. Planning problems would not be amenable to this approach, but the development is exciting nevertheless. ETS was implemented in InterLisp.

We have given a very brief overview of the use of formal methods and hinted at some of the ways in which they can be employed in knowledge engineering applications. In addition to the above techniques the following practical guidelines follow from the technique of domain analysis and good project management practice.

Before an interview, set and clarify the objectives to be achieved and the techniques to be employed. Make sure the experts are aware of your aims and provide an agenda. Ask permission before any recording (tapes, videos, shorthand, etc.) is started and be ready to discuss how you will ensure the security of the recordings in the case of sensitive information. Start with a summary of progress to date and the conclusions drawn from earlier sessions. In most cases, meetings of over two hours should be avoided, on the other hand they should not be too brief to create a relaxed and friendly atmosphere and leave time for an adaptable strategy to be implemented if necessary. Do not build up unreasonable expectations in the experts (i.e. don't tell them they can have a system which will play golf, mix Martinis and forecast the weather before doing the washing up). Above all be a nice person; i.e. read up the subject, show genuine interest and listen carefully and with respect for their greater knowledge (just because you know what a multi-bus is doesn't put you above walking occasionally). After a session meet with your team as soon as possible to plan the next stage and discuss the results while still fresh in your memories.

9.1.4   Knowledge tuning

Having built a successful expert system the question then arises of maintaining it, as with all computer systems. In particular there is the problem of maintaining the knowledge contained in it. In this section we take a very brief look at this problem about which, in practice, little is yet known.

In most fields of human endeavour, knowledge is subject to more or less rapid evolution which can take three forms: additions to existing knowledge, amendments to fragments of the knowledge or deletion of redundant knowledge. Also possible is a revolutionary restructuring of knowledge following on some fundamental new discovery or paradigm shift in theory. In the latter case it is almost certain that an expert system would have to be rebuilt from scratch and so this case is not considered here.

In the case of additions to knowledge, the primary concern is that the new chunks added will not contend with the existing ones or with the basic structure of the knowledge base. In rule-based systems some means of consistency checking or contention breaking is often provided. In the case of fuzzy production or frame systems there is some extent to which the assimilation of new rules is catered for automatically. Even so, care must be taken that the consolidation of truth values through fuzzy operators does not submerge a rule whose content requires that it is handled as an exception. We dealt with this point in Chapter 7.

An analogous problem arises with deletions where a rule may be of structural significance in some inferences the system might perform, and if removed would emasculate the remaining knowledge. Since amendments may be regarded as a superposition of delete and add operations, any special problems relating to amendment can easily be overcome.

The other problems and anomalies that arise can be regarded as identical to those which arise in ordinary database management which were dealt with in Chapter 3.

9.2   SUMMARY

In this chapter we surveyed some of the existing types of knowledge-based software tools available and commented on their strengths and weaknesses. The bulk of the material was taken up with various techniques for knowledge acquisition, with the exception of the inductive methods which were covered in Chapter 7.

The emphasis has been on the interplay between formal and informal methods and the manner in which they can be utilized. We also stressed the importance of appropriate methods of project management for knowledge engineering applications.

9.3 FURTHER READING

Wellbank [208] provides a survey of several practical methods for knowledge elicitation. Shaw [183] is interesting to read on the application of personal construct theory in this area. Boose [30] is a fascinating and controversial attempt to almost totally automate knowledge elicitation using these techniques. He also gives a useful general introduction to expert systems. Unfortunately there is a poverty of literature on the subject at the time of writing. Useful background material on Kelly grids is to be found in Kelly's own work [112]. Our treatment follows that of Easterby-Smith [60].

In fact, at the time of writing, the only book available solely on the subject of knowledge acquisition is the one by Hart [235]. This contains little that cannot be found in the above mentioned works and is an elementary introduction suitable for undergraduate students studying knowledge engineering for the first time. It is, however, extremely readable and concise.

10

Selected applications of fuzzy sets and knowledge engineering

> 'You must bring out of each word its practical cash value, set it at work within your stream of experience.'
>
> William James

10.1 FINANCIAL APPLICATIONS

This section surveys as nearly as is possible every important application of artificial intelligence techniques to the practical solution of problems in the financial sector. This sector includes banks of all types, insurance companies, traders and intermediaries in intangible instruments such as securities and service companies peripheral to the above industries. Related roles in other industries such as those of corporate treasurers or accountants are considered to fall within the scope of our coverage. It would be impossible to give a complete coverage of a wider field and this specialization merely reflects the authors' recent experience and interests. It is also the case that we believe that this is one of the sectors where there is the greatest scope for the application of this technology.

One major difficulty in surveying financial applications is the secrecy and even paranoia which surrounds successful ones. Because one of their chief benefits is the competitive edge they provide this is hardly surprising, but as with the defence sector a certain amount of knowledge is in the public domain. Although this is manifest it is also possible that some of the secrecy could have arisen from the vested interests of the developers, who are concerned not to expose their infant and struggling applications to the glare of publicity until they are proved to be robust.

The information contained in the remainder of the chapter will be useful to those discussing the potential applications of knowledge-based computer systems in the financial sector. It combats the view that the technology is impractical and will give a feel for the scale of applications and likely development costs.

In the next section we turn to a range of applications where fuzzy methods have been employed. Some of these could be regarded as financial applications as well.

They again are selective in that they reflect the authors' earlier connection with the REVEAL product mentioned hitherto.

The following survey includes applications and products with particular pertinence to financial applications. We begin by naming the products, services, users and suppliers covered in Tables 10.1 and 10.2. In subsequent sections we deal with some of these applications in sufficient detail to support discussion with the informed layman.

Table 10.1 Suppliers of knowledge-based systems for financial applications

Product	Supplier	Domain
Le Courtier	DEC/Generale de Banque	Stock and investment distribution advice
ATRANS	DEC/Cognitive Systems	Telex interpretation
PlanPower	APEX	Personal financial planning
—	Arthur D. Little	Various
—	Logica	Various
—	DataLogic	Nostro reconciliation
K:Base	Gold hill/Symbolics/ DRI/Lehman Bros	Interest rate swaps
—	Syntelligence	Underwriting
—	Index Systems	Financial products
Promoter	Management Decision Systems	Sales promotions
—	Inference Corp.	Asset and liability management
REVEAL	ICL	Policy modelling

Table 10.2 Live users

User	Problem addressed
Lehman Bros/Shearson/AmEx	Interest rate swaps
	Mergers and acquisitions
American Int. Groups Inc.	Underwriting risk assessment
Arthur Anderson	Audit (pilot in 1985)
Travellers Insurance	Product advice
CitiCorp	Credit checking/training
AmEx	Credit filtering
ARIES	Fire Risk Assessment
	Security Selection
ALFEX	Company health assessment
Leonardo Creative Logic	Financial planning and evaluation
The Stock Exchange	TOPIC\SEAQ fault diagnosis
Salomon Bros.	Program trading on stock indices

10.1.1 Interest rate swaps

Lehman Brothers is a huge American investment bank which transacts about $15 million worth of fees for interest rate swaps on behalf of its clients. They estimate that use of K:Base contributes about $1 million to this figure. K:Base is a system which was developed jointly by Lehman, Gold Hill Computers, Symbolics and Data Resources to run on IBM PCs backended by Symbolics machines.

Two organizations will find an interest rate swap attractive when each of them is able to borrow funds at interest on different bases, due perhaps to structural or geographical differences between them, and each finds that the basis on which the other can borrow would suit its need better than what it has in fact been able to negotiate. A typical example is that of a bank which can borrow at fixed interest but would prefer to pay interest in line with current LIBOR. If a company with a floating rate loan of the same magnitude can be found then the basis for a swap exists. Specialist brokers exist to find such matches and receive a fee for so doing. The companies involved in the swap then contract to pay each other's interest repayments. Repayments of principal are not affected and usually a bank will underwrite the arrangement to guarantee the security of the lenders. While the basic idea is very simple, there are many different kinds of swap possible and in practice matching partners can be a complex task.

The Lehman Brothers system uses a general purpose system called K:Base. K:Base is capable of inducing rules from examples. The system runs on IBM PCs which can be, optionally, connected to a central Symbolics. The underlying technology is LISP. K:Base has also been applied to portfolio management.

Typical data required for the analysis of a swap matching decision on behalf of a client, apart from the client's name and bankers, include the following.

> principal;
> years to maturity;
> type of loan (fixed or floating);
> maximum interest rate;
> maximum spread over treasury;
> repayment frequency, repricing cycle and basis;
> arrangement fees;
> credit rating;
> whether collateral is required;
> company size.

Data on actual swaps are entered and the system induces decision rules which are used to query the brokers about new applications for swaps in order of the importance of the attributes. The system returns advice in the form of a description of the attributes a company must have to provide a suitable match. Suitable companies are then retrieved from the database and presented to the broker for consideration. For further details of this application see Rauch-Hinden [175].

This application is a good example of a decision-support system. Similar methods could be applied to dealer decision support where the induction base is taken from the stock wire services and 'interesting' companies sifted out.

10.1.2 Personal financial planning

In the United States and, to a lesser extent, in Europe there has been a burgeoning of companies which make their living by offering advice to wealthy individuals on how to manage their investments. This area has become known as personal financial planning (PFP). The expertise required cuts across the fields in which accountants, tax planners, investment analysts, pensions advisers and solicitors are able to offer professional services. Much of the success of a PFP project depends on the ability of the planner to gain a full picture of both the financial situation and the personal goals of the client. Also required is a detailed knowledge of the products, services and techniques available on the market. The end product of PFP is a personalized report giving recommendations, to be reviewed annually as circumstances change.

Skilled planners take a long time to train both in terms of inter-personal skills and knowledge of the task. Thus, two principal benefits are to be obtained from the use of knowledge-based systems. First, a computer system can alleviate some of the chore of the analysis and comparison of options. Secondly, the training of junior consultants can be accelerated by giving them access to an automated version of the logical processes used by their more experienced colleagues.

A computerized PFP support system should map the analytical portion of a planner's expertise and, at some level of generality, select the most appropriate mix of strategic and product-based solutions to help a client reach his or her goals. It should allow for subjunctive conditional analysis and be able to gather data from various sources such as public wire services and internal records concerning clients and products. It will need to incorporate data on taxation regimes and economic indicators across various countries. At a minimum it will take account of a client's overall goals for retirement, wealth maximization, tax shielding, estate planning, risk protection, school fees, liquidity and consumption. The results, because of the psychological profiles of typical clients' have to be presented in a high quality format tailored to the client and showing both the recommendations, the reasoning behind them and how they meet the client's objectives.

The system should simulate the feedback and interaction which takes place during a real planning session by asking confirmational questions based on its reasoning so far. An important requirement is that the planner is able to inspect and alter the reasoning strategy used. This will at least involve changing the knowledge contained in the system and possibly the routes taken through the knowledge. It is also desirable that the system is sensitive to the subjective factors involved in setting the client's goals and constraints. These factors should be incorporated in any goal seeking strategies.

A typical data flow structure for a personal financial planning system is shown in Fig. 10.1.

Applied Expert Systems (APEX) was founded jointly by expert financial planners and Randal Davies, an authority on knowledge-based systems responsible for Teiresias. APEX have released a product, PlanPower, which is claimed to broadly match the above requirements. Its more obvious weaknesses are in the international dimension and in the way it handles vague goals and constraints. While suitable for a US client, a UK client would need to modify the package considerably. It is an open question as to whether a new UK product could be written more quickly than it would take to do the modification. A considerable number of man-years went into the development in LISP on a Xerox 1108 workstation. The delivery vehicle is a Xerox 1186 with HP laser printer packaged at around $50,000.

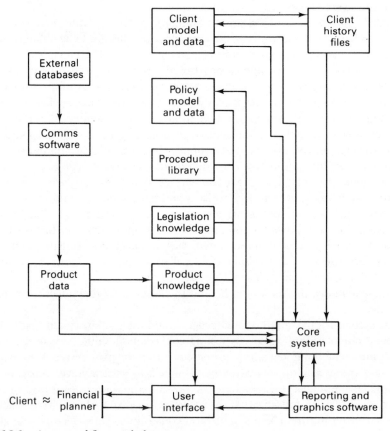

Fig. 10.1   A personal financial planning system

Arthur D. Little and Vanilla Flavour Ltd have both also been engaged in the production of a PFP package.

10.1.3   Portfolio management and asset and liability management

The services offered by stockbrokers to their clients, personal or otherwise, include giving recommendations on portfolio distribution. An inductive approach can be useful here also. If the input data are taken to be age, income and tax bracket and the output is a recommendation, then data from real decisions can be converted by a package like K:Base into production rules or a decision tree. The difficulty here is that K:Base uses an induction algorithm based on Bayes's theorem and the usual problems about data independence arise. Beagle would almost certainly be a more appropriate technology. Conventional knowledge acquisition based on preference ratings could also be advantageous here. It is an 'automated questionnaire' application similar to the ARIES system described below.

DEC are well known by now as proponents of AI technology, following their internal success with XCON. Recently they have joined up with Générale de Banque (GB) in Belgium to promote a system called Le Courtier (The Broker) which offers advice on stock purchases and investment distribution based on data about the Belgian stock market.

This prototype system is aimed at gaining a competitive edge for GB in the lucrative retail banking sector by enabling clients to receive specialist advice without attending at a central branch. The user is asked to supply information on his other current portfolio and the amount to be invested. Based on rules entered by the bank and some subjective rules supplied by the user a recommendation as to the best current purchases is given. The system can also answer factual questions asked in a subset of natural language, although the control program is menu driven. The alternative mode offers advice about the percentage of the available cash which should be invested in different instruments, such as stocks, bonds and precious metals. This is based on forward chaining on built-in rules. The stock advice rules can be modified by the bank. Delivery is likely to be accomplished via viewdata terminals. The system runs on a VAX which accounts for the interest shown by DEC.

One of the collaborators with GB on Le Courtier was Schank's company, Cognitive Systems. Another of their products is ATRANS, a system which automatically extracts information from unstructured natural language telexes, about interbank and customer funds transfers. The data extracted are converted to SWIFT or other formats for automated processing. This can be accomplished at present in any one of six European languages. The object of this system is to reduce the amount of human labour required to check incoming messages and reduce re-keying errors. Since the volumes for some banks can be as high as 4000 messages per day and ATRANS success rate is reported as over 82%, it is easy to see that the saving might be substantial. Having said this, we should point out many organizations already receive nearly all input in SWIFT or similar format nowadays so that the benefits may not apply uniformly to all organizations. One of the founders of cognitive systems was Roger Schank and his well known work on natural language understanding using scripts is evident in this work.

10.1.4   Alvey projects

Two Alvey projects partially funded by the UK government under its information technology programme are directly pertinent to the financial sector and both of them were community clubs; ARIES and ALFEX. ARIES was the club of companies in the insurance sector. The main contractor was Logica. ALFEX was a more broadly based financial club comprising mostly banks. It aimed to construct a system to advise on the financial health and stability of small companies. The main contractors were Helix Expert Systems and Expert Systems International, suppliers of Expert Edge and PROLOG II respectively.

ARIES set out to look at two applications, one in general insurance and the other in life assurance. Two working prototypes exist now, the first of which advises risk assessors on the rating decision for fire risks of buildings. Basically the system is an automated intelligent questionnaire. It was originally written in KEE on a Unisys (badge engineered Texas Instruments) Explorer workstation in about six months including planning and knowledge acquisition. Subsequently it was transported to run in Crystal on an IBM PC/AT. The prototype restricts its expertise to fire risks in the garment trade. A number of questions are asked about various attributes of premises; what kind of heating is in use, whether waste is tidily stacked for disposal, whether smoking is permitted and if so whether it is adequately controlled, and so forth. The output is either acceptance of the risk with an appropriate loading or rejection. In the case of a rejection the underwriter can perform conditional tests with the system to see if there are means of improving the risk so that an acceptance becomes possible. For example, in a warehouse where it has been observed that ashtrays lie around unemptied, banning smoking may make the risk acceptable. Thus relatively inexperienced underwriting staff can use the system to help obtain the kind of medium risk business that can be very profitable if difficult to assess correctly. Undoubtedly, the ARIES member companies will now extend the prototype to meet their own objectives, first into industries other than the 'rag' trade and perhaps later for risks other than fire. There are many domains where automated questionnaires are appropriate; such as audit risk (see below).

The second application to be tackled was a system to assist portfolio managers select new securities on which to spend a funds income. The deliverables from ARIES were not programs but methods to assist insurance companies in the club with building their own systems. However a prototype system was successfully completed. This system, again in KEE, takes data from public information services such as EXTEL on companies deemed to be of interest and enters into a dialogue with the fund manager on issues such as the nature of the company's management as well as its financial condition. The result is a buy signal and the reason why the purchase is appropriate (e.g. for growth). The 'port' in this case used the LEONARDO II expert system shell [263], because of the greater complexity of the KEE system compared with the fire risk advisor. This type of system could also be of use to researchers in stockbroking firms, at least to the extent that the stock market is not just an insider market.

In neither of the two ARIES systems discussed above is there any significant management of uncertainty, except by using high granularity linguistic labels. This was due to the nature of the experts' knowledge and the way it was expressed in the fire risk system. However, it is the view of the present authors that, in the fund management system, the manipulation of probabilities and possibilities would have been advantageous, and it was chiefly the limitations of KEE and the lack of LISP tools that prevented the team at Logica from proceeding in this way. When the systems are ported onto their ultimate development environments on conventional mainframes or micros this question will almost certainly be readdressed. Curiously many second-generation micro shell products are actually better in this one respect than the large-scale knowledge engineering packages like ART and KEE. Another surprise is that they often run faster. This is not to deny the utility of the large-scale tools in the development cycle, only to question their appropriateness in the end product.

The large-scale demonstrator project concerned with DHSS regulations may turn out to have some financial implications, but this is not its prime aim so it is not considered further here.

10.1.5 Knowledge-based systems in the dealing room

We now turn to look, in some detail, at the application of knowledge-based decision support in financial dealing rooms. We start by addressing the nature of the problems faced by dealers and their management, and attempting a classification of their functions in terms of decision making and of information processing. Particular attention will be paid to the question of risk and the types of risk involved. Next we explore ways in which decision support systems can be utilized in the trading environment. In particular we address a few specific applications where knowledge-based techniques have a role to play. For simplicity we concentrate mainly on foreign exchange dealing, but the principles will be seen to be more widely applicable. Lastly we speculate about systems which combine many separate decision support and expert system modules into a comprehensive dealer support system, using the notion of a blackboard system.

The primary objective of any trading activity is, of course, to produce profits. Having said this, we observe that this objective is influenced, *inter alia*, by the following factors:

(1) turnover maximization;
(2) control and minimization of costs;

(3) elimination of errors;
(4) minimization of risk; both credit and market risk;
(5) minimization of working capital and debt;
(6) sustenance of 'reputation'; this being achieved by offering competitive rates and avoiding scandal and/or fraud.

The roles within a trading organization which address these issues may be summarized as follows:

(a) back office accounting;
(b) treasury management;
(c) marketing;
(d) trading room management;
(e) dealing.

We shall see in what follows that each role can be evaluated, or described, in two dimensions; decision making and information processing, of which the latter is the more fundamental since it provides the background against which all decisions are made.

The back office accounting role is concerned with the administration of debt and the elimination of errors. It will in addition report on risks such as late settlement. The treasury has the responsibility of ensuring that surplus funds are well invested and that shortfalls are met at the lowest cost. Both these activities have an impact on trading activity through global positions. The marketing function requires information from the other areas in order to arrive at commission and fee rates applicable to customers in such a way as to ensure future business. This function will not be discussed further here. Instead we will concentrate on the dealing room activities. The relationships between roles and functions is summarized in Fig. 10.2.

The dealing room manager, or head dealer, has to absorb the constraints set by the treasury, customer's requirements, corporate policy and strategy and a large quantity of information concerning the market. The latter includes:

		Roles				
		a	b	c	d	e
Functions	1			●		●
	2	●				
	3	●			●	●
	4				●	●
	5		●		●	
	6				●	●

Fig. 10.2 Incidence of trading functions within roles

- current positions;
- customer orders;
- market rates (prices and quotes);
- world news;
- competitors' activities;
- trends and market sentiment;
- trading history;
- individual securities (research);
- risk.

As a decision maker the head dealer has the task of selecting which instruments to hold and to what extent to be exposed; subject to the organisation's policy. She or he may also be responsible for issuing buy/sell to the traders themselves. Another important task is the reconciliation of all the traders' positions.

The trader's main tasks are as follows:

- offering quotes, on request;
- maintaining predefined positions;
- ensuring that profits exceed losses.

To do this successfully, the trader needs the following resources:

- the ability to perform fast arithmetic;
- information on competing quotes;
- information on trends, volatility, etc.;
- forecasts of price movements;
- knowledge of factors influencing the market;
- knowledge of risk avoidance strategies;
- knowledge of which information sources to observe and interpret;
- client and counterparty knowledge;
- information on limits;
- *and* some means of combining all these factors to reach trading and pricing decisions.

Thus, the trader's decision process may be described as follows. There are three stimuli to trading (focusing here on FX trading): (a) a requirement to cover a position, (b) a price request from another dealer or broker, and (c) a customer order. For cases (a) or (c) we can observe the following decision process:

(1a) Select a counterparty who deals in the market concerned, usually offers a good service, seems to be offering a good rate on the wire and – perhaps more importantly than should be the case – is a 'good fellow'.
OR
(1b) Select a counterparty who seems to be offering an extreme rate and is a 'first class name'; e.g. a major bank.
  (2) Confirm rate by telephoning several names.
  (3) Check counterparty limits against proposed positions.

(4) Decide if price is right.
(5) Deal.
(6) Record deal details.
(7) Compute Profit and Loss (P&L).

For case (b) the process is as follows:

(1) Broker requests bid/offer prices.
(2) Decide if position is long or short of desired levels.
(3) Compare with perceived market prices and estimated trend.
(4) Guess if counterparty is likely to be a seller or a buyer.
(5) Arrive at a price at a level and spread likely to result in a bargain only if it moves the position in the desired way and will make a profit.
(6a) If the quote is accepted deal, record it and compute new positions and P&L
OTHERWISE
(6b) Modify view of market in accordance with the new information obtained.

Viewing the dealer as an information processor, we can construct the model shown in Fig. 10.3.

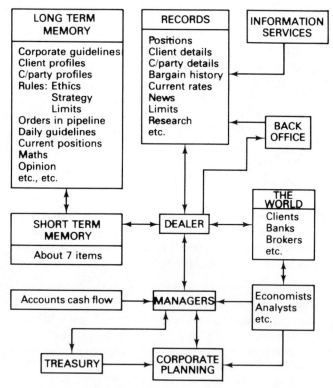

Fig. 10.3 The dealer as an information processor

We will attempt to relate these models of the trader as decision taker and information processor to the questions of how trading room skills can – or cannot – be subjected to a degree of automation, and what decision-support facilities may be provided. But first we must digress to give the promised analysis of risk exposure in this context.

Trading organizations are subject to a diverse and interacting range of risks, especially in the new deregulated and increasingly international markets. For our purposes risk may be classified according to the following schema:

- positional (systematic and unsystematic market) risk;
- counterparty risk;
- fraud.

Conventional systems exist which handle positional risk [51], but have shortcomings due to the difficulty of evaluating forecasts. Positions can be easily summed across the organization and reported by counterparty, etc., using database and modelling software. However, most companies do not yet have the sort of real-time, worldwide systems which can detect, for example a counterparty approaching limits in three time zones; New York, London and Tokyo, say. In practical terms, what is needed is a method of warning local offices of the possibility of this arising, but intelligently enough to only report *abnormal* trading patterns. This type of exception reporting, which can also be applied to local exposure, is characterized by the volatility of the rules; those rules which determine what constitutes an abnormal pattern or those which the house may wish to specify from time to time. Systems with changing rules are notoriously problematical for conventional programming languages, because of the huge maintenance costs implied. Thus it becomes attractive to utilize the modular rule bases of expert systems products to implement such systems. Shells of course will not always provide the necessary power for the pattern matching algorithms, so that recourse to full programming languages is also a requirement in some cases.

The preceding analysis of trading activities and risk has prepared us to address the question of the technologies appropriate for the dealing room of the (immediate) future. We will not cover conventional technologies such as video switching or information systems since these are already well covered in the specialist literature. Instead we concentrate on a few areas where expert systems can be applied to solve the key problems we have uncovered; namely risk management, forecasting, decision making and strategy.

In principle, there is little difference between the problem of assessing the risk of a counterparty going bankrupt or defaulting and that of rating the fire risk for a clothing factory. If the right questions are asked in the right order it is possible to compute whether the risk will be an acceptable one. The ARIES prototype mentioned above could form the basis of a counterparty risk evaluation system. Other unsystematic risk could be dealt with similarly.

Forecasting is a notoriously difficult art. Because of the vast amounts of data and the independence assumptions required statistical forecasting has failed significantly to provide accurate price forecasts for securities; so much so that some investment firms have been known to resort to astrology. Aside from this there are two principal methods for arriving at a decision on whether a given instrument should be bought or sold. These are known as *fundamental analysis* and *technical analysis.*

Fundamental analysis betokens the collection and assimilation of data on the firm or firms under consideration, including their management, product range, financial condition, sales prospects, position in the economy, and so on. A pension or investment trust fund manager and an investment analyst both use such data to arrive at buy/sell decision criteria. From the point of view of knowledge-based systems the problem is an interesting one in that it contains a mixture of numerical and fuzzy parameters. The ARIES prototype fund manager's assistant addresses precisely this problem area, taking data from EXTEL and from the fund manager and turning it into a buy/no-buy decision signal. One can easily envisage the time when the fund manager will arrive at the office, having read the financial press on the journey to work, and turn to the dedicated AI workstation to enter the list of companies to analyse. When the initial screening is complete he or she will turn to it again for an interactive session to complete the analysis.

Technical analysis is quite a different way of arriving at the same end; a buy/sell signal. Whichever particular theory is used, Dow theory or the Elliott wave principle [261], the assumption is roughly that the underlying determinants of prices are so complicated that a reductionist approach cannot predict market behaviour. Instead the macro behaviour of the price curve, or price action as it is often called, and other indicators are used empirically to determine a qualitative forecast. There are four ways in which artificial intelligence techniques can be brought to bear on technical analysis:

- To permit the effects of a combination of different, recognizable buy/sell indicators to be analysed. For example, to generate a sell signal when the crossing over of the price action and a moving average is confirmed by movement out of a head and shoulders pattern or when the penetration exceeds some percentage threshold, whichever occurs the sooner. More complex combinations involving trading volumes or other momentum indicators can easily be envisaged.
- To allow the incorporation of non-numerical, subjective or fuzzy factors, such as the trader's view on market sentiment, into the decision hierarchy. Input expressed via linguistic variables is used to modify the sensitivity of the technical indicators, according to the trader's policy and current view of the market.
- To carry out pattern matching on price action or point and figure charts, compare segments of the charts with prestored templates for the recognized patterns such as head-and-shoulders, double bottom, flag, pennant, etc. Fuzzy pattern matching algorithms are obviously essential here, and each pattern will have associated with it a rule base for the determination of subsequent processing when a successful match occurs. The information derived can be

utilized to draw in trend, support and resistance lines, which in turn contribute to the generation of signals as described above. Also the user's attention can be drawn to a breakout from a pattern as it occurs.

- To use data on prices and actual deals done over a period of time to generate optimal trading rules, using some rules induction techniques.

The benefits of the system implicitly described above are few in number but huge in value. Apart from enabling performance to be analysed and improved upon, there is really only one. That is that traders can reach their buy/sell decisions a few minutes, or seconds, earlier than their competitors. This is particularly important in foreign exchange and commodity markets where chartist activity can itself move the market; the profits accrue to the dealer who trades earliest.

Having dealt with the fundamental questions of risk and forecasting, we now step to a slightly higher, or more abstract, level to consider the question of strategy. There are many ways in which expert systems could be deployed to assist in the generation and maintenance of trading strategies. Rather than attempt to list and classify all these we will restrict ourselves to just one example in an area where technical expertise is currently in very short supply: traded options.

Options are traded for many reasons but the chief ones are speculation and hedging. For example, if you have every confidence that the price of DEC shares or pork bellies is going to rise and you can buy a call option at the money, then you have an unlimited profit potential with a maximum risk equal to the relatively small premium paid for the option. That is the speculative use. Hedging occurs when trading or production activity forces the holding of futures of uncertain value. Options can then be used to eliminate any market risk. However, exactly what combination of options and futures to hold is a difficult question, even if we leave aside the complex mathematics needed to value an option – see Copeland and Weston [51] or Smith [262] for details of how to solve the stochastic differential equation involved. The option strategy chosen will also depend on the trader's view of the market, trends, volatility, transaction costs, taxation, etc. It is possible to express option strategy selection criteria in the form of a mixture of crisp and fuzzy production rules.

The option strategy selection system for options on currency futures takes as input user opinions on trends in the dollar and the cross rates, volatility and costs. It picks a suitable strategy and optimizes its profile in terms of strike prices, deltas, etc. Warnings are given when a strategy needs maintenance; e.g. due to unexpected changes in volatility or price. It can offer explanation as to why a particular strategy was selected and display the strategy graphically and numerically to show P&L forecasts and risk exposure. Most importantly, perhaps, it is designed to bring mathematical trading within the grasp of the non-mathematically inclined trader. It can be used to bring trainee traders up to speed more quickly; at present this often takes over a year of practice.

It should be becoming clear by now that all the systems mentioned will need to interact to some degree. Technical and fundamental analysis can both contribute to profitable trading decisions; option strategy involves elements of risk analysis and could use technical analysis to trigger maintenance routines following trend reversals. What is required to achieve this integration conforms very closely to the blackboard model discussed earlier. Blackboard systems have been applied in a military context where, for example, a fighter pilot has to process a vast amount of incoming data in order to select from a limited range of actions. The model is of several independent knowledge-based systems monitoring the input and advising the pilot when something interesting occurs; e.g. when a real target or threat is identified among many dummy targets or threats. The dealer is in a similar position, being the recipient of a vast amount of data from several information feeds all of them in need of analysis to determine (a) if anything interesting has occurred requiring further analysis and (b) what the appropriate action should be.

A blackboard system imitates a group of highly specialized experts sitting around a blackboard in order to solve a problem. As new information arrives it is written up in the blackboard where all the experts can look. When an expert sees that she or he can contribute a new fact based on specialist knowledge she or he raises a hand. This might be to confirm or refute an hypothesis already on the board or to add a new one. The new evidence will now be available to the other experts who may in turn be prompted to contribute to the discussion. The leader of the group monitors the experts and selects their contributions in order, according to an agenda visible on the board. In this context our experts are represented by a technical analysis expert system, a fundamental analysis system, an option strategy adviser, and so on. Common storage is the blackboard and the agenda is under the control of a specialized inference program. If, for example, new price information arrives from the wire, the chartist might detect a possible reversal but need to await confirmation before a sell signal is issued. However, the fundamental analyst only needed this small piece of confirmatory evidence to suggest a flagging in the security's fortunes. The combined evidence may be enough to generate a valid signal and thus, incidentally, beat all the pure chartists to the winning post. Perhaps also this action of selling the security will attract the attention of the option strategist who now sees a need to modify positions in order to maintain a risk-free hedge or to avoid an otherwise unexpected exercise in now unfavourable market conditions.

This brings us to our last application in the dealing room: demon driven presentation of data. The most noticeable thing about a modern trading room is the large number of screens on the dealing desks. These screens provide access, typically, to half a dozen data services each containing tens of thousands of pages. Some traders watch only one page all day long, but others, notably options traders, need to constantly flick from one page to another. Even in the currency markets where this is less the case it is difficult to spot arbitrage opportunities involving several currencies before they are traded away. Knowledge-based systems with 'demons' have a ready application in the background analysis of price movements so that significant changes result in the trader's attention being directed to a particular page of information, or perhaps the attention of a specialist expert system in the case of the blackboard system discussed above. The purely algorithmic development of such a demon driven system would not be difficult but would be of limited value. This is principally because of the need to combine forecast evidence with the actual data, which are often slightly out of date by the time they reach the screens. Also, as we have said, forecasting prices is an art dependent on much subjective judgement where conventional systems are singularly inappropriate.

Thus we have arrived at a picture of the dealing room of the 1990s. Dealer workstations networked to information feeds and demon driven information filters. Also on the network are computers containing specialist expert systems in the areas we have described. These are controlled by a blackboard system which throws up their advice on the dealer screens alongside the price services and price change warnings. Special routines or computers are available to assist with strategy selection or risk analysis for the senior traders, and researchers have their own powerful analysis machines. In the background, attracting little attention, is a small rule induction system which watches every change and every trade. Every now and then this system suggests an improved trading strategy. Possibly the same data are analysed by another expert system which is looking for fraud, insider trading and other rule breaches. It is to be hoped that this system never produces any output.

10.1.6   Other applications

Several management consultancies are currently experimenting with systems to help them with audit risk management. We expect to see some announcements on this by the end of 1987.

NMB in Holland has developed prototype systems which advise on mortgage applications and medium size commercial loans. These applications have received consideration from several other banks but no information has been

```
• Dealer decision support

• Personal financial planning

• Insurance

• Currency swaps

• Database enquiry

• Financial modelling
```

Fig. 10.4   Typical applications (financial sector)

made public, which probably means either outstanding success soon to emerge as a commercial product or stupefying failure.

Another area of application which has attracted attention in the management services departments of some banks is job evaluation. Here the rules and regulations can be excessively complicated and hard to remember. A text-based expert system could be of great value. Also fuzzy matching techniques could be of use in aggregating scores in different attributes of job performance.

Arthur D. Little are building a decision-support system for dealers using an AI workstation which will capture on one screen the data feeds normally spread across several with clear ergonomic advantages. There are obviously opportunities here to incorporate intelligence into such systems so that data may be automatically screened for opportunities and positions and rate misalignments spotted at high speed. In FX markets the rate of transactions is so high that some sort of blackboard architecture may be required to keep up. Dealer decision support is certainly an area where we expect growth. It is particularly interesting because it involves potentially high gains and several technologies: modelling, KBS, graphics, communications, real time computing, etc.

Information providers who supply financial information often provide hardware support for the delivery vehicle for their services; typically a videotext terminal. When the client's livelihood is dependent on the equipment, as will be the case in the new deregulated, highly electronic capital markets, fast response to reported faults becomes of great importance. Thus, that favourite expert systems' application, fault diagnosis, could be of great interest to parts of the financial community. Often the manual systems are sufficiently refined to eliminate most of the need for knowledge acquisition. In fact the Stock Exchange in London has implemented a small expert system as part of its SEAQ equipment fault reporting system. A small network of micros captures incoming fault reports and compares with a customer and equipment database. Job sheets are then issued to engineers. In the case of common simple faults the operator can eliminate the need to send an engineer to the site by utilizing a simple decision tree to suggest an immediate remedy. This part of the system was quite rapidly implemented using an expert system shell.

More complex network management systems for large users and specialist installations, such as dealing rooms, are currently under development.

10.2   FUZZY SET BASED APPLICATIONS

In this section we shall present a number of illustrative practical applications of fuzzy modelling. At least one of them deserves the appellation 'expert system' in that it was able to tell its authors [43] things about the machine they were using that were not previously realized by even very experienced programmers at the site. This is the VAX performance monitor described in Section 10.2.2. It has also enabled a company to make modest savings on the cost of additional memory boards. All the applications presented here were written using REVEAL. Of course there have been other, more ambitious, applications of fuzzy sets to real-world problems but these are well covered by the literature and we unceremoniously consign them to the section on further reading. The material we cover in this section first appeared as papers [80, 81].

10.2.1   Knowledge-based corporate modelling

Most modern companies today use some sort of computerized corporate models which represent in quantitative terms the state of the business at any particular time or the changes occurring between times. The models are, in general, descriptive rather than normative and as such are based on the manipulation of forecast or historical time series which represent corporate or exogenous variables. Sophisticated languages now exist for the manipulation and representation of these vectors and the relationships between them. Commonly used financial functions are supplied as part of the languages and usually refined reporting and data manipulation tools are provided. However there is a significant defect in these models which arises from the fact that corporate goals are often stated in very vague terms.

The planning process itself can be divided into the formulation of strategic plans, the formulation of tactical plans and a feedback from operational data allowing these plans to be revised at these two levels.

At a more practical level, the process consists of the statement of relationships to give a 'model' which can be applied to data present at any given time period, actual or hypothetical. The computed figures are then offered up in the form of reports or graphs which may, in turn, be the subject of statistical or sensitivity analyses leading to modification of the data (Fig. 10.5).

The difficulties begin when the analysis of output indicates not a change to the data but a change in the model logic itself. Theoretically, a well constructed model should not require this kind of alteration, but the 'theory' referred to here is a highly abstract one that does not allow for such catastrophes as changes in the regime of tax allowances and what have you.

Furthermore, the decision makers often do not express themselves in crisp quantitative terms and even less understand the modelling languages used by their aides. This is not necessarily a weakness on the part of the decision makers either. As Bellman and Zadeh [24] point out, most business activity takes place in an environment in which the goals, the constraints and the consequences of possible action are not known with precision. Statements such as 'Corporation X has a *bright* future' or 'the stock market has suffered a *sharp* decline' convey plenty of information despite the imprecision of the italicized words. Any attempt to turn these vague statements of policy into precise quantitative terms will indubitably lead to the need to rewrite the models as time goes by. In other words there is a need to review results at each stage in terms of informally stated company policy as well as against the quantified plan. A number of systems have been written using the REVEAL system which exemplify this approach. The details of such

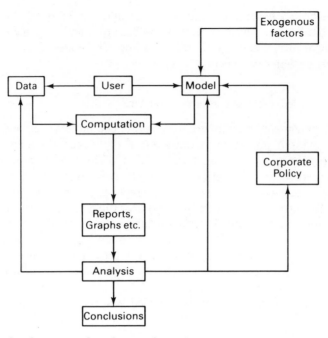

Fig. 10.5   The planning and analysis cycle

commercial systems are often highly confidential, involving as they do the business plans of corporations, but we are able to give within these pages an overview of the essentials, the techniques used and the areas of application.

Consider a company which is viewed as the agglomeration of several large capital projects which may or may not be companies in their own right. Mining, oil and construction companies are often of precisely this nature. Every project in this case may have a significant effect on the overall balance sheet and careful planning is vital. The problems facing the planner include both engineering and financial aspects; resources are consumed, loans have to be drawn down and, in both cases, risks taken account of. The classical methods of financial project evaluation (cf. Merrett and Sykes [149] or Copland and Weston [51]) involve the computation of the net present value (NPV) of the project's net and equity cash flows and usually the calculation of the discounted cash flow yield (DCF) or internal rate of return. The latter is a relative measure of the opportunity cost of a project expressed in terms of interest on capital. Theoretically projects with the highest NPV should be selected but where funds may only flow into projects with similar capital structures the DCF is often a good if not better measure. Unfortunately, this method does not take into account the many uncertainties facing the planner. Where the uncertainty is of a statistical nature a favourite method has been that of Monte Carlo simulation or risk analysis, a technique originally developed by physicists to study the movement of particles in cloud chambers. As an aside, it is interesting to note that predating the development of quantum theory by Einstein, studies of random movements of securities on the Bourse had resulted in equations very similar to those of the Brownian motion; this illustrates the profound links between financial theory and particle physics in a striking way. With Monte Carlo methods deterministic input is replaced by a sequence of input sampled from some probability distribution of known shape. For example one might take the view that the forecast value of the dollar exchange rate is normally distributed about the trend. In practice this means that the model is run several (often hundreds of) times leading to painfully slow execution on most machines in current use. Also the output is given as a distribution which is not always meaningful to management without the appropriate statistical background even assuming that the selected input distributions are based on reliable data. Worst of all, there is the consideration of non-probabilistic uncertainties and the planner's views on factors such as the political financial stability of both markets and the countries in which the investment is to be made. A project which is based on the assumption that El Supremo of this or that banana republic will be able to continue to reign unchallenged must be open to question even if he keeps labour costs lower than elsewhere in the world where a stable democratic government gives greater confidence at the cost of lower rates of exploitation of labour power. Hitherto, models have not allowed for such variables and skilled business analysts have been required to incorporate such vague and elusive influence with the output from financial models and engineering analyses.

One mining company has developed a model using REVEAL which on the one hand is a conventional program handling the financial and engineering aspect of mining projects but also incorporates policies covering the effects of political and socio-economic factors. We cannot print the actual policies here for reasons of commercial secrecy but an early prototype contained such statements as:

```
IF POLITICS IS GOOD THEN FINANCIAL.RETURN IS REDUCED

IF FINANCIAL.RETURN IS VERY GOOD THEN POLITICS IS SHAKY

IF LEAD.TIME IS SHORT THEN PROJECT.DESIRABILITY IS HIGH
```

and so on.

If you have read the chapters dealing with fuzzy sets and REVEAL it will not be difficult to infer the general structure of this system. The system runs on an IBM PC/XT.

Another REVEAL application in area of corporate modelling is the CONCEPT system written by MacNamara [138]. This package, which runs on IBM mainframes, helps marketing managers in the consumer goods industry build models of their perceptions of the effects on their market of advertising and promotions.

In his seminal paper on decision calculus, J. D. C. Little [131] suggested that the big problem with models was that managers 'practically never used them' and went on to say that a good model should 'represent an extension of his ability to think about and analyse his operation'. MacNamara points out that discussions with marketing executives showed that however much they appreciated the benefits of modelling they disliked using statistical techniques. Most managers had a good idea of the general effects of marketing variables, such as price or advertising, on sales. The problem with statistics was that often adequate data were not available, or absolute effects could not be isolated owing to interaction between variables and competitive activity.

As Little pointed out [131, 132], ignorance of advertising response phenomena, inability to make good measurements and the lack of a theory to organize existing knowledge contribute to great waste in advertising and in marketing in general. We often come across statements such as 'That market should receive more attention because industry sales are strong and our sales are low'. Recognizing the fuzzy production rule format of this common locution led to REVEAL as the natural choice for the development vehicle. CONCEPT allows each user to generate his own market model, incorporating expert judgement where appropriate, and to calibrate this model against historical performance. Once the basic dynamics of the market are satisfactorily accounted for, the effects of alternative advertising, pricing and promotional schemata may be evaluated until planned performance is optimized. A session proceeds in question and answer format allowing the user to modify assumptions as the dialogue proceeds. Mechanisms are incorporated to allow for such effects as trialist attraction/conversion, forward buying and so on. Consumer Panel or Retail Audit data are used to compare forecast with actual performance and if required to equate these with ex-factory shipments via the profit and loss statement. Although the user never need know it, fuzzy sets are used intrinsically throughout much of the perceptual model building stage. This occurs both in the development of suitable advertising response curves and in interrrogating the user for levels of such variables as advertising 'share of voice'. Here is a fragment of the policy dealing with share of voice.

```
IF ADV.SOV IS LOW THEN ADV.MULTIPLIER IS LOW.MUL

IF ADV.SOV IS MED.LOW THEN ADV.MULTIPLIER IS MED.LOW.MUL
```

etc.

See Fig. 10.6.

The last application we deal with under this heading is an expert system due to Wong [212] which analyses the income statement and balance sheet of a company to provide diagnosis and recommendations for corrective management action in the areas of management, operations, profitability, sales, liquidity, gearing, coverage and specific expense.

Wong states that this system was conceptualized, designed, and built in

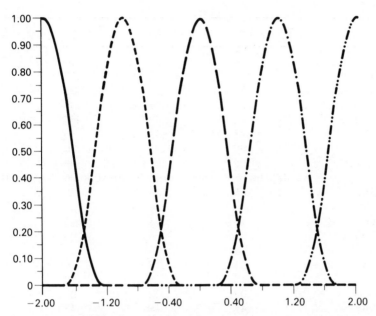

Fig. 10.6 Graph of advertising multiplier fuzzy sets: * low mul, = mid high mul,
+ med. low mul., @ High mul., − med. mul.

approximately five weeks and contains about 100 rules. Although essentially
only a prototype it is claimed to be a genuinely useful system in its own right. The
original idea was to use it as a building block to more complex expert systems in
such areas as commercial loan decisions, acquisitions and so on. Wong contrasts
his short development cycle with 'the litany sounded by the academically
oriented AI products which require that expert systems be built by highly
specialized knowledge engineers with the equivalent of a Ph.D. in computer
science, requiring months and even years to develop a prototype, and requiring
expensive and exotic LISP machines'. Wong's system ran on DEC, IBM and Prime
minicomputers before REVEAL was withdrawn for machines other than those in
the ICL range.

The upper part of Table 10.3 shows data from an income statement and
balance sheet for a firm over a period of four quarters in a common size format, i.e.
assets are expressed as a fraction of total assets, liabilities are expressed as a
fraction of total liabilities, and income data are expressed as a fraction of net sales.
This income statement and balance sheet data are followed by various standard
financial ratios beginning with the current ratio. These financial ratios are not
input to the program but are calculated using the DSS language in REVEAL.
Other ratios shown in Table 10.3 include: quick, sales/receivables, cost of
sales/inventory, sales/working capital, earnings before interest and taxes/annual

Table 10.3

	4Q.83	1Q.84	2Q.84	3Q.84
CASH	.10	.10	.10	.10
ACT.REC	.22	.22	.19	.22
IVENT	.21	.21	.23	.22
OCUR.ASET	.04	.04	.05	.03
TCUR.ASET	.58	.58	.57	.57
FIX.ASET	.33	.33	.35	.35
INTANG	.00	.00	.00	.00
ONCUR,ASET	.08	.08	.08	.08
T.ASET	62,500.000.00	62,500,000.00	62,500,000.00	62,500,000.00
STNOT.PAY	.08	.08	.09	.08
CUR.MAT	.04	.04	.05	.04
ACT.PAY	.13	.13	.10	.13
ACRU.EXPEN	.06	.06	.06	.06
OCUR.LIA	.04	.04	.05	.04
TCUR.LIA	.35	.35	.35	.35
LT.DEBT	.15	.15	.18	.13
ONCUR.LIA	.02	.02	.02	.02
NET.WOR	.48	.48	.45	.50
TLIA.NWOR	62,500.000.00	62,500,000.00	62,500,000.00	62,500,000.00
NET.SALE	100,000,000.00	100,000,000.00	100,000,000.00	100,000,000.00
COST.SALE	.80	.80	.85	.80
GR.PROF	.19	.19	.15	.20
OP.EXPEN	.16	.16	.11	.17
OP,PROF	.03	.03	.04	.03
O.EXPEN	.02	.02	.02	.01
PBTAX	.01	.01	.02	.01
CUR	1.80	1.80	1.80	1.80
QUICK	1.00	1.00	1.00	1.00
SALE\REC	7.27	7.27	7.27	7.27
CSALE\INV	5.99	5.99	5.99	5.99
SALE\WCAP	6.20	6.20	6.20	6.20
EBIT\INT	2.29	2.29	2.29	2.29
CFLO\CMAT	16.11	16.11	16.11	16.11
FIX\WOR	.75	.75	.75	.75
DEBT\WOR	2.09	2.09	2.09	2.09
PBT\NWOR	5.06	5.06	5.06	5.06
PGT\TASET	2.24	2.24	2.24	2.24
SALE\NFAS	4.82	4.82	4.82	4.82
SALE\TAS	1.60	1.60	1.60	1.60
DDA\SALE	3.20	3.20	3.20	3.20
LRE\SALE	.60	.60	.60	.60
OC\SALE	3.50	3.50	3.50	3.50

interest expense, cash flow/current maturities long-term debt, fixed/worth, debt/worth, percentage profit before taxes/tangible net worth, percentage profit before taxes/total assets, sales/net fixed assets, sales/total assets, depreciation depletion amortization/sales, lease rental expenses/sales, and officers' compensation/sales.

The knowledge base portion of REVEAL utilizes 'if-then' production rules in an English-like format. The rules have the format: If condition/situation is true, then conclusion/response is true.

In order to write these rules in an English-like format, we need a vocabulary of words which we define using the theory of fuzzy sets. For each of the numeric variables in Table 10.3 we define three fuzzy variables: high, average and low. For example, the first numeric variable in Table 10.3 is cash for which we define the three fuzzy variables: high.cash, average.cash, and low.cash. Wong used data from Robert Morris Associates (RMA) segmented by industry type (SIC Code) and sales volume to establish the possibility curve (see Fig. 10.10)) which relates the truth value (vertical axis) of high.cash for various cash amounts as a percentage of total assets (horizontal axis). In particular, RMA provides industry statistics on upper, mid, and lower quartile ranges for the various financial ratios. In Fig. 10.7 the possibility curve for the fuzzy variable high.cash is denoted by the symbol *. We see that this possibility curve indicates that if cash on hand as a percentage of

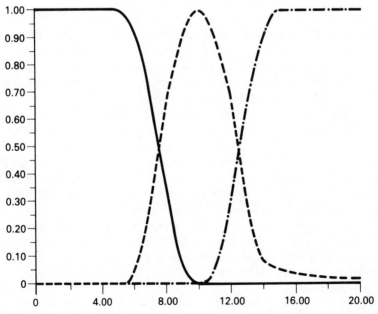

Fig. 10.7   Example fuzzy variables: * HIGH. CASH, + AVE. CASH, − LOW CASH

total assets is 15% or greater then high.cash has a truth value of 1.0, if the percentage if 10% or less then high.cash has a truth value of 0.0, and there is a smooth transition of truth from 0.0 to 1.0 for percentage values between 10% and 15%. Using this example, fuzzy logic is to be contrasted with traditional crisp logic in which high.cash is defined based on an arbitrary cut-off (say 15%), and one has high cash on hand only if the percentage is greater than 15%. In this situation, 14.99% misses the cut-off and is not considered as having high cash on hand even though it misses the cut-off by only 0.01%! The possibility curve for this crisp logic is a step function with a truth value of 0.0 up to the cut-off of 15%, jumping to 1.0 at 15% and remaining at that value. The fuzziness in the way variables are defined is considered to be more natural than the arbitrary cut-offs forced upon us by traditional crisp logic.

Using a similar process, the fuzzy variables average.cash and low.cash can be defined using RMA data. The associated possibility curves are also shown in Fig. 10.7. These three fuzzy variables provide a vocabulary which can now be used to write rules dealing with cash on hand as a percentage of total assets.

This same paradigm (based on RMA statistics) is used to establish the three fuzzy variables (high, average, and low) for all the numeric variables in Fig. 10.7. In addition, the fuzzy variables increasing and decreasing are defined to capture the rate of change of a numeric variable over two successive time periods. Thus, in using these fuzzy variables one can write rules which take into account the relative value of a numeric variable (high, average, and low) and the rate of change (increasing, decreasing) of a numeric variable over successive time periods. The list of fuzzy variables is displayed in Table 10.4.

REVEAL uses if-then production rules to encode expertise into its knowledge base. There are other methods to encode knowledge (e.g., frames, semantic nets); however, production rules appear to be the form which is the most easily understood by the business/financial end user. Second-generation products are beginning to show the realization that frames and (in the case of LEONARDO) procedures are also useful and aid user understanding.

Because REVEAL uses fuzzy variables, the if-then rules can be written entirely with words; these words have meaning as defined by the possibility curves of fuzzy set theory. Thus, the efficacy of fuzzy sets is to allow the user to model the vagueness and ambiguity of business/financial relationships using words. In fuzzy set terminology, this is often referred to as semantic of linguistic modelling. That is, we model the business/financial concepts with words which the computer can understand. Scientists do not understand completely the human reasoning process; however, we do know that the most convenient form to convey this knowledge is through words. Thus, fuzzy sets and the linguistic modelling they afford through rules written in English-like form give a natural basis on which to encode the heuristics and rules-of-thumb of the business/financial reasoning process.

The rules in this application are grouped into the following policies; a policy is a REVEAL term for a group of rules:

Table 10.4   List of fuzzy variables

TRUE	AVE.TCUR.LIA	HIGH.CSALE\INV
HIGH.CASH	HIGH.TCUR.LIA	LOW.SALE\WCAP
AVE.CASH	LOW.LT.DEBT	AVE.SALE\WCAP
LOW.CASH	AVE.LT.DEBT	HIGH.SALE\WCAP
LOW.ACT.REC	HIGH.LT.DEBT	LOW.EBIT\INT
AVE.ACT.REC	LOW.ONCUR.LIA	AVE.EBIT\INT
HIGH.ACT.REC	AVE.ONCUR.LIA	HIGH.EBIT\INT
LOW.IVENT	HIGH.ONCUR.LIA	LOW.CFLO\CMAT
AVE.IVENT	LOW.NET.WOR	AVE.CFLO\CMAT
HIGH.IVENT	AVE.NET.WOR	HIGH.CFLO\CMAT
LOW.OCUR.ASET	HIGH.NET.WOR	LOW.FIX\WOR
AVE.OCUR.ASET	LOW.COST.SALE	AVE.FIX\WOR
HIGH.OCUR.ASET	AVE.COST.SALE	HIGH.FIX\WOR
LOW.TCUR.ASET	HIGH.COST.SALE	LOW.DEBT\WOR
AVE.TCUR.ASET	LOW.GR.PROF	AVE.DEBT\WOR
HIGH.TCUR.ASET	AVE.GR.PROF	HIGH.DEBT\WOR
LOW.FIX.ASET	HIGH.GR.PROF	LOW.PBT\NWOR
AVE.FIX.ASET	LOW.OP.EXPEN	AVE.PBT\NWOR
HIGH.FIX.ASET	AVE.OP.EXPEN	HIGH.PBT\NWOR
LOW.INTANG	HIGH.OP.EXPEN	LOW.PBT\TASET
AVE.INTANG	LOW.OP.PROF	AVE.PBT\TASET
HIGH.INTANG	AVE.OP.PROF	HIGH.PBT\TASET
LOW.ONCUR.ASET	HIGH.OP.PROF	LOW.SALE\NFAS
AVE.ONCUR.ASET	LOW.O.EXPEN	AVE.SALE\NFAS
HIGH.ONCUR.ASET	AVE.O.EXPEN	HIGH.SALE\NFAS
LOW.STNOT.PAY	HIGH.O.EXPEN	LOW.SALE\TAS
AVE.STNOT.PAY	LOW.PBTAX	AVE.SALE\TAS
HIGH.STNOT.PAY	AVE.PBTAX	HIGH.SALE\TAS
LOW.CUR.MAT	HIGH.PBTAX	LOW.DDA\SALE
AVE.CUR.MAT	LOW.CUR	AVE.DDA\SALE
HIGH.CUR.MAT	AVE.CUR	HIGH.DDA\SALE
LOW.ACT.PAY	HIGH.CUR	LOW.LRE\SALE
AVE.ACT.PAY	LOW.QUICK	AVE.LRE\SALE
HIGH.ACT.PAY	AVE.QUICK	HIGH.LRE\SALE
LOW.ACRU.EXPEN	HIGH.QUICK	LOW.OC\SALE
AVE.ACRU.EXPEN	LOW.SALE\REC	AVE.OC\SALE
HIGH.ACRU.EXPEN	AVE.SALE\REC	HIGH.OC\SALE
LOW.OCUR.LIA	HIGH.SALE\REC	INDICATED
AVE.OCUR.LIA	LOW.CSALE\INV	DECREASING
HIGH.OCUR.LIA	AVE.CSALE\INV	INCREASING
LOW.TCUR.LIA		

- sales,
- management,
- coverage,
- leverage,
- operations,
- profit,
- liquidity,
- specific expense.

Figure 10.8 shows some examples of these policies and rules written to evaluate liquidity and operations. To be noted is the English-like form of the rules.

```
MODE  >policy liquidity
*>t *
   1 : !Policy to determine liquidity -- ability to meet obligations on tim
   2 : !
   3 : if cur is low.cur then liquid.p1 is indicated
   4 : if cur is ave.cur and f.cur is decreasing then liquid.p2 is indicated
   5 : if cur is high.cur then liquid.p3 is indicated
   6 : if cur is ave.cur and f.cur is increasing then liquid.p4 is indicated
   7 : if quick is high.quick then liquid.p5 is indicated
   8 : if quick is ave.quick and f.quick is increasing then liquid.p6 is
       indicated
   9 : if quick is low.quick then liquid.p7 is indicated
  10 : if quick is ave.quick and f.quick is decreasing then
       liquid.p8 is indicated
  11 : if cur is high.cur and quick is ave.quick then liquid.p9
       is indicated
*>end

MODE >policy operations
*>t *
   1 : ! Policy to determine operational problems--ability to
   2 : ! control inventory, accounts receivable, cost of goods sold
   3 : ! operating expenses
   4 : !
   5 : if csale\inv is high.csale\inv then operate.p1 is indicated
   6 : if csale\inv is ave.csale\inv and f.cost.sale is increasing
       then operate.p2 is indicated
   7 : if cscale\inv is low.csale\inv then operate.p3 is indicated
   8 : if csale\inv is ave.csale\inv and f.csale\inv is decreasing
       then operate.p4 is indicated
   9 : if sale\rec is low.sale\rec then operate.p5 is indicated
  10 : if sale\rec is ave.sale\rec and f.sale\rec is decreasing
       then operate.p6 is indicated
  11 : if cost.sale is high.cost.sale then operate.p6 is indicated
  12 : if cost.sale is ave.cost.sale and f.cost.sale is increasing
       then operate.p7 is indicated
  13 : if op.expen is high.op.expen then operate.p8 is indicated
  14 : if op.expen is ave.op.expen and f.op.expen is increasing
       then operate.p9 is indicated
```

Fig. 10.8   Example rules

This facilitates the ability of the non-computer oriented end user to write rules for REVEAL and to examine and modify rules without the need for a computer professional to act as intermediary. The rules written in an English-like form are compilable code in the REVEAL rule-based language. Thus, the end user can have confidence that if she or he can write down the reasoning process in words, then the computer will execute the reasoning process as the end user conceives it.

A typical advice-giving session of Corporate Analyser is shown in Fig. 10.9. Here, the confidence levels are, of course, fuzzy possibility values.

The rules developed by the user to evaluate and analyse the income statement and balance sheet are evaluated using the methods explained in Chapter 5. Any problem situations as identified by the rules which have a confidence level (truth value) of greater than 50 (on a scale of 0 to 100) are printed out for the attention of the decision maker.

The mathematical theory of fuzzy sets allows one to combine the ambiguity and uncertainty in the facts and evidence with the appropriateness of a rule to a given situation to determine the overall confidence level of a piece of advice or recommendation.

Corporate Analyser is a prototype for an expert system which helps a manager to cope with the information explosion. In particular, data processing departments can produce volumes of data and reports which can inundate the corporate manager. The approach taken in Wong's system is intended to make this unnecessary.

10.2.2   Continuous diagnosis and tuning

In some sense Wong's corporate analyser is an example of a whole class of problems which we designate as those of continuous diagnosis and tuning. Another example is provided by Chestnut's PEX system which diagnoses and tunes the performance of a VAX supermini [43]. This system is currently in daily use at a number of sites and has resulted in significant if relatively modest cash savings in hardware purchases.

It is based, in terms of methodology, on documentation provided by Digital Equipment Corporation with the VMS operating system (VAX performance monitoring manual) but also utilizes REVEAL's ability to program with fuzzy variables to handle such concepts as 'poor response time'' and so forth. The system consists of four modules. The first, the configuration module, tailors the second, the continuous diagnosis module, to the particular installation having regard to the amount of memory, number of disk drives attached, etc. This latter module runs as a background job and constantly (every few seconds) samples the copious monitoring data made available by VMS. This is of course exactly analogous to the corporate analyser except that there the sample rate is annual. Fuzzy policies are applied and if degradations are detected it can either report to the operator at a user-selected level of detail or automatically start up the third module. This, the tuning module, is able to make use of the remarkable features of

* LIQUIDITY *

Liquidity problems may exist --ability to meet short term financial
commitments. If so, diagnosis follows

Quick is decreasing, probably not enough cash or accounts
receivable   Confidence factor is   100.00

* PROFITABILITY *
Profitability prolems may exist. Prices too low or cost
goods sold, operating expense, interest charges too high.
If so, diagnosis follows

Gross profit too low.
Price too low or cost of good sold-material, labour,
overhead-probably too high.   Confidence factor is: 100.00

Operating profits too low.
Price too low or cost goods sold or operating expenses
probably too high.   Confidence factor is   100.00

Profit before taxes low.
Price too low or cost goods sold or operating expenses
or interest charges too high.   Confidence factor is: 100.00

* LEVERAGE *

Leverage problems may exist--vulnerable to business
downturns. If so, diagnosis follows.

Debt\worth is high. Possibly too high proportion of debt.
                                       Confidence factor is: 100.00

* OPERATIONS *

Operational problems may exist--inventory, accounts receivable,
cost of sales, and operating expenses. If so, diagnosis follows.

Cost sales\inventory low. Possibly problems in over stocking,
obsolescence, and selling.   Confidence factor is: 60.40

Cost sales\accounts receivables low. Possibly deliquencies
in credit collection.   Confidence factor is: 99.01

* COVERAGE *

Coverage problems may exist--ability to service debt
If so, diagnosis follows.
----

* MANAGEMENT *

Management problems may exist. Inefficient use of resources:
assets, equity, debt, working capital. If so, diagnosis follows.

Profit before taxes\total assets is low. Inefffficient use
of assets.   Confidence factor is: 100.00

Profit before taxes\net worth is low. Inefficient use of
net worth.   Confidence factor is: 100.00

Net sales\working capital is low. Inefficient use of
working capital.   Confidence factor is: 58.42

* SALES *

Sales problems may exist. Low sales volume generated from assets.
If so, diagnosis follows.

Sales\fix assets low. Ineffective use of fixed assets
                                      Confidence factor is: 100.00

Sales\total assets low. Ineffective use of total assets
                                      Confidence factor is: 100.00

* SPECIFIC EXPENSE *

Specific expense problems may exist--Depreciation, depletion,
amortization, lease/rental, officer compensation. If so,
diagnosis follows.

DDA\sales too high. Depreciation, depletion, or amortization
expenses too high.   Confidence factor is: 100.00

OC\sales too high. Officer compensation probably too high.
                                      Confidence factor is: 100.00

Fig. 10.9   Example advice

VMS in that, unlike many operating systems, many of the VMS system parameters can be altered without regenerating the operating system. It is thereby that PEX can either try to find the cause of the problem and suggest remedial action or actually go in and make beneficial changes to the system parameters. Of course, checks are performed to make sure that this automatic process does not result in hunting or oscillation back and forth between two equally unsatisfactory states. At the time of writing the fourth module was only at the specification stage. This module deals with the crucial problem of capacity planning, taking information from the other three modules to project medium to long term hardware needs and incorporating the views of system staff and management on future requirements.

A fundamentally similar system has been written to deal with the IBM/MVS operating system, although the automatic tuning capabilities could not be implemented in this package due to the exigencies of MVS. It was for this reason as well as for economy that it was considered wise to build the system to run on a remote micro-computer. The RMF logs are passed from the MVS system to REVEAL running on an IBM PC which then diagnoses and reports faults and problems at the required level of detail (see Fig. 10.10).

10.2.3   Scheduling and network maintenance

In the example which we considered in Section 10.2.1 we spoke of the consideration of political and socio-economic factors in the context of capital project assessment. Another important aspect of that application is the allocation of resources between and the time of different projects. Most large corporations have many more opportunities than they can possibly fund and subjective factors play a decisive role in deciding not only on the best project but on the relative proportions of capital to assign to different concurrent projects. Purely quantitative methods seem to fail significantly in this area of endeavour and the results obtained so far with fuzzy models promise much for the future.

Parallel to this is the problem of managing large and complex projects. The traditional methods of critical path or PERT techniques assume that sufficient resources exist but very often this is not the case and yet humans still manage to complete the projects on time and within budget (well, sometimes!). A good example of such a project is the US space shuttle whose project deadlines are sometimes set not by the fickle whim of government but by the very movement of the celestial orbs in their spheres. The whole area of project management is over-ripe for a revolution in technique based on fuzzy modelling techniques. The question of what constitutes a 'late' project is among one of the fuzziest notions we have ever encountered; it depends on context and on the predelictions of the manager concerned. Many of the skills used by experienced project managers can be captured in a readily understandable way in fuzzy policies.

Apart from the project evaluation example the nearest these ideas have come to practical realization is a prototype system written by Sean Stanley as part of a

Program Reveal VAX/VMS performance limitations

Memory Limitation Policy
  1: ! Initial policy to determine if a performance problem
  2: ! is a memory limitation problem
  3:
  4:     If   Free.memory is substantial
           and   page.fault.rate is low.page.fault.rate
           and   inswap.rate is low.swapping
           then   a memory.limitation is not indicated
  5:
  6:     If free.memory is not substantial
                              then a memory.limitation is
                              indicated
  7:     If inswap.rate is not low.swapping
                              then a memory.limitation is
                              indicated
  8:     If page.fault.rate is not low.page.fault.rate
                              then a memory.limitation is
                              indicated
  9:     If num.como is many.como
                              then a memory.limitation is
                              indicated

I/O Limitation Policy
  1: ! Initial policy to determine if a performance problem
  2: ! is an i/o limitation problem
  3:
  4:     If direct.io is high.direct.io
                              then an io.limitation is indicated
  5:     If buffered.io is high.buffered.io
                              then an io.limitation is indicated
  6: ˙
  7:     If direct.io is zero
                              then an io.limitation is not
                              indicated
  8:     If buffered.io is zero
                              then an io.limitation is not
                              indicated

CPU Limitation Policy
  1: ! Initial policy to determine if a performance problem
  2: ! is a cpu limitation problem
  3:
  4:     If number.computable is many
                              then a cpu.limitation is strongly
                              indicated
  5:     If user.mode% is high.user
                              then a cpu.limitation is indicated
  6:     If idle.time is near zero
                              then a cpu.limitation is indicated

Fig. 10.10   Rules for VAX tuner

student project at the University of Surrey which attempts to schedule work on the repair and maintenance of sewers. In the UK this is a critical problem. Most of the sewer network was laid down in the reign of Queen Victoria or earlier and the costs of removing waste water are second only to the costs of pumping it in. In a situation where resources are scarce and skilled civil/water engineers even scarcer the problem of deciding whether to and when to repair or even inspect old sewers is difficult at the best of times. Exact mathematical methods have proved to be as good as useless, one of the problems being the messy nature of the data (sorry about that one, folks!). The engineers work by assessing each site according to its known condition, geographical location, proximity to locations where flood is abnormally costly (e.g. under motorways) and date of construction among other factors. This system uses fuzzy rules to weigh the various factors and recommends the order of inspection.

Once again the scheduling and maintenance class of problems seems to be a generic one so far as fuzzy modelling is concerned. See for example Grant [264] and Elleby and Grant [61].

10.2.4   Multi-attribute and multi-stage decision making

There is by now a huge literature on the application of fuzzy mathematics to this general class of problems. We present here just five practical applications which have been implemented using REVEAL.

The first is based on the work of Briggs and Hale (unpublished) at Coopers and Lybrand Associates. It is a decision-support system for the management of a restaurant which assists with the planning of menus and ordering the required quantities of food. The authors point out that in this case if the wrong decisions are made the results can be spectacular; if there is a shortage then angry customers may be the problem and any surplus must be destroyed with a significant effect on the budget. The task of the manager consists of deciding on the menu, the likely demand and the order quantities. He or she must take into account the weather, the day of the week, the general preference of customers, calorific and nutritional values, cost, colour and texture, existing stocks, preparation time and labour supply. Some parameters are fixed; seating and customer capacity and the number of menus for example. Various rules of thumb are also embedded in the system; the same meal should not be offered twice in the same week, a proportion of customers do not take the full meal, there is a correlation between customer preferences and the weather, trade is seasonal. The problem thus is not as trivial as it may appear at first sight. The parameters are ill defined and the solution is never perfect. It is also a problem typical of a large class of concerns in services and distribution. In Fig. 10.11 we show a sample session with the prototype.

Systems based on the more classical matrix approach to decision making, whereby there is a matrix of rows representing options and columns representing attributes which each option must possess, and where each cell of the matrix

---

Day of the week is Thursday

Season is Autumn

Temperature is 17 degrees Celsius

Weather is damp

Menu
selected: main course   chilli
                   starter   avocado
                   sweet   apple pie

Number of customers expected today are 121

(Establishment caters for a minimum of 50, a maximum of 180, and an average of 120 customers per day)

Number of main meals taken today will be 96

Quantity of chilli required is 4 tubs
  Waste is 24 portions (80% of tub)

Quantity of avocado required is 48 single units
  No waste

Quantity of apple pie required is 16 single units
  No waste

Meal preparation for Thursday is complete

Fig. 10.11   Sample menu planner output

contains a number representing the degree to which the options possess the attributes, have been written. The fuzziness almost goes without saying. We mention three examples.

The first lies in the area of personal portfolio management. Every investor has certain personal preferences such as high capital gain, low risk, or minimal short term volatility. Assuming that the problem is to add a security to an existing portfolio this system enquires for these preferences and then interrrogates a database of stocks to find a best match between product and customer.

Similarly given a particular business problem such as cash flow planning or cost allocation the problem is to find the best software package and the best hardware to run it on.

Some decision criteria are easy to deal with, like price, but when it comes to deciding where a particular package has a 'sufficiently good' report generator or other functionality or is 'easy' to learn, then Approximate Reasoning becomes a useful technique. Of course further fuzziness enters when the user is asked to say how he or she weights the importance of the various attributes. This system was written by a software consultancy on an IBM PC for internal use.

The last system only reached the demonstration stage but uses exactly the same techniques to advise on the selection of suitable fertilizer based on considerations such as weather conditions, soil type and humidity and exposure to pests.

10.3 SUMMARY

In this chapter we have seen how the techniques of knowledge engineering, fuzzy sets and decision support can be applied to a limited range of problems. We selected finance for most of our examples and then gave a number of examples using a fuzzy sets approach.

Among the most important applications where we expect considerable developments to take place are those in financial dealing rooms, where we gave an analysis of the conceptual problems and an outline design for a comprehensive dealer decision support system, drawing on the material of earlier chapters for inspiration.

The applications covered show the importance of the decision support viewpoint, rather than that of artificial intelligence, and underline the importance of a calculus of imprecision in genuinely practical applications that are not amenable to conventional decision-support system treatment.

10.4 FURTHER READING

There are a vast number of books which purport to deal with applications of knowledge engineering to practical problems. The most comprehensive we have found is Rauch-Hinden [175]. Johnson [104] is a costly but thorough review of the state of the art. Reference then reduces to more scattered material on specific applications, such as Bintley [23] and Burns and Williams [39].

The major fuzzy sets based expert systems now in successful operation, such as CARDIAC-2 are described in Zimmermann [222].

Because of the evanescence of the state of the art, when it comes to applications, there is little doubt that a good source of further reading is the trade press. The reader must beware however of exaggerated claims. Even the artificial intelligence literature is on occasion guilty of this misdemeanour, so how can we expect journalists to be any better. *The Economist, Expert Systems User, International Business Week, Banking Technology* and *Computing* are publications forming part of a very long list indeed that are worth scanning from time to time. Several academic journals also now carry reports on applications as a matter of editorial priority. Among these we might mention *Expert Systems, Fuzzy Sets and Systems* and many, many more.

References and bibliography

1 Abrial, J.R. (1974) Data Semantics, in *Data Base Management* (eds Klimbie and Koffeman), North-Holland.
2 Ackoff, R.L. (1969) Systems, organisations and interdisciplinary research, in *Systems Thinking* (ed. F.E. Emery), Penguin Books.
3 Addis, T.R. (1985) *Designing Knowledge Based Systems*, Kogan Page.
4 Alter, S.L. (1980) *Decision Support Systems: Current Practice and Continuing Challenges*, Addison-Wesley.
5 Alexander, I. (1986) *Designing Intelligent Systems*, Kogan Page.
6 Allen, J.F. Maintaining knowledge about temporal intervals, in Brachman and Levesque [34].
7 Alwood, J., Andersson, L-G. and Dahl, O. (1977) *Logic in Linguistics*, Cambridge University Press.
8 Anderson, A.R. (ed.) (1964) *Minds and Machines*, Prentice-Hall.
9 Anderson, J.R. (1976) *Language, Memory and Thought*, Erlbaum.
10 Anderson, J.R. (1983) *The Architecture of Cognition*, Harvard.
11 Arbib, M.A. and Manes, E.G. (1975) Fuzzy Machines in a Category, *J. Aust. Math. Soc.,* **13**, 169–210.
12 Atkin, R. (1981) *Multidimensional Man*, Penguin Books.
13 Ayer, A. J. (1952) *Language, Truth and Logic*, Dover.
14 Bachman, C.W. (1969) Data structure diagrams, *Data Base*, **1**(2).
15 Baldwin, J.F. (1985) *Support Logic Programming*, ITRC Report 65, University of Bristol.
16 Barr, A. and Feigenbaum, E. (1981) *The Handbook of Artificial Intelligence* (3 vols), Pitman.
17 Bartlett, C.W. (1985) Artificial intelligence and knowledge engineering, in *Knowledge Engineering and Decision Support* (ed. M. Small), Tymshare UK and ICL Ltd.
18 Barwise, J. (ed.), (1977) *Handbook of Mathematical Logic*, North Holland.
19 Barwise, J. (1977) First Order Logic, in *Handbook of Mathematical Logic* (ed. J. Barwise), North Holland.
20 Beckman, F.S. (1981) *Mathematical Foundations of Programming*, Addison-Wesley.
21 Beer, S. (1975) *Platform for Change*, Wiley.
22 Berliner, H. The B* tree search algorithm: a best-first proof procedure, in Webber and Nilsson [206].
23 Bintley, H. (1985) Fuzzy Modelling Applied to Time Series, in *Knowledge Engineering and Decision Support* (ed. M. Small), Tymshare UK and ICL Ltd.
24 Bellman, R. and Zadeh, L.A. (1970) Decision making in a fuzzy environment, *Management Science*, **17**(4).
25 Bobrow, D. and Winograd, T. (1977) An overview of KRL, a knowledge representation language, *Cognitive Science*, **1**(1), 3–46.

26 Bochvar (1939) On three valued logical calculus and its application to the analysis of contradictions, *Matematiceskij Sbornik*, **4**, 353–69.
27 Boden, M.A. (1977) *Artificial Intelligence and Natural Man*, Harvester Press.
28 Bonczek, H., Holsapple, C.W. and Whinston, A.B. (1981) *Foundations of Decision Support Systems*, Academic Press.
29 Boole, G. (1854) *An Investigation of the Laws of Thought*, Dover, New York.
30 Boose, J.H. (1986) *Expertise Transfer for Expert System Design*, Elsevier Science Publishers.
31 Bossu, G. and Siegel, P. (1984) Saturation, nonmonotonic reasoning and the closed world assumption, *Artificial Intelligence*, **25**, 13–64.
32 Boulden, J.B. (1975) *Computer Assisted Planning Systems*, McGraw Hill.
33 Boxer, P.J., *Reflective Analysis*, in Shaw [183].
34 Brachman, R.J. and Levesque, H.J. (1985) *Readings in Knowledge Representation*, Morgan Kaufmann.
35 Bramer, M.A. (ed.) (1984) *Research and Development in Expert Systems*, Cambridge University Press.
36 Buchanan, B.G., Sutherland, G.L. and Feigenbaum, E.A. (1969) Heuristic DENDRAL: a program for generating explanatory hypotheses in organic chemistry, in *Machine Intelligence*, Vol. 4 (eds B. Meltzer and D. Michie), Edinburgh University Press.
37 Bundy, A. (1983) *The Computer Modelling of Mathematical Reasoning*, Academic Press.
38 Burge, W.H. (1975) *Recursive Programming Techniques*, Addison-Wesley.
39 Burns, N.A. and Williams, C.E. (1986) Use of Artificial Intelligence to diagnose, hardware, in *IBM RT Personal Computer Technology*, IBM Austin.
40 Carrega, J.C. (1983) The categories Set-H and Fuz-H, *Fuzzy Sets and Systems*, **9**, 327–32.
41 Charniak, E. and McDermott, D. (1985) *Introduction to Artificial Intelligence*, Addison-Wesley.
42 Chen, P.S. (1976) The entity-relationship model – towards a unified view of data, *ACM TODS* **1**, 9–36.
43 Chestnut, R. and Okuma, A.T. (1984) *VAX/VMS Performance Analyser*, MacDonnell Douglas Knowledge Engineering Division.
44 Chomsky, N. (1980) *Rules and Representations*, Basil Blackwell.
45 Clarke, K.L. and McCabe, F.G. (1984) *Micro-PROLOG: Programming in Logic*, Prentice-Hall.
46 Clark, K.L. and Tarnlund, S-A (eds) (1982) *Logic Programming*, Academic Press.
47 Clocksin, W.F. and Mellish, C.S. (1981) *Programming in PROLOG*, Springer.
48 Codd, E.F. (1970) A relational model of data for large shared data banks, *Communications of the ACM*, **13**(6).
49 Codd, E.F. (1979) Extending the database relational model to capture more meaning, *ACM TODS*, **4**, 397–434.
50 Cole, J.C. (1971) *Categories of Sets and Models of Set Theory*, Doctoral Dissertation, Sussex.
51 Copeland, T.E. and Weston, J.F. (1980) *Financial Theory and Corporate Policy*, Addison-Wesley.
52 Coste, M.-F., Coste, M. and Parent, J. (1974) *Algebres de Heyting dans les Topos*, Seminaire Jean Benabou.
53 Date, C.J. (1981) *An Introduction to Database Systems*, Addison-Wesley.
54 Davis, R. and Lenat, D.B. (1982) *Knowledge Based Systems in Artificial Intelligence*, McGraw Hill.

55 Davies, N.G., Dickens, S.L. and Ford, L. TUTOR – A prototype ICIA system, in Bramer [35].

56 Dimitrov, V. Creative decision making through fuzzy catastrophes, in Gupta and Sanchez [85].

57 Doyle, J. *A Truth Maintenance System*, in B.L. Webber and N.J. Nilsson [206].

58 Dreyfus, H.L. (1979) *What Computers Can't Do: the Limits of Artificial Intelligence*, Harper Colophon.

59 Dubois, D. and Prade, H. (1980) *Fuzzy Sets and Systems: Theory and Applications*, Academic Press.

60 Easterby-Smith, M. The design analysis and interpretation of repertory grids, in Shaw [183].

61 Elleby, P. and Grant, T.J. (1985) *A Knowledge Based Scheduling System for Aircraft Repair Jobs*, Brunel University.

62 Eshragh, F. Subjective multi-criteria decision making, in Shaw [183].

63 Eytan, M. (1981) Fuzzy sets: a topos-logical point of view, *Fuzzy Sets and Systems*, **5**, 47–67.

64 Eytan, M. (*c* 1983) *Fuzzy sets: a topos-logical point of view II*, Unpublished manuscript.

65 Expertech Limited (1985) *Xi User Manual*, Expertech.

66 Fain, J., Gorlin, D., Hayes-Roth, F. and Waterman, D. (1981) *The ROSIE Language Reference Manual*, Tech Rep N-1647-ARPA, Rand Corporation.

67 Flannagan, T. (1985) *The Consistency of Negation as Failure*, Manuscript.

68 Forgy, C.L. (1981) *The OPS5 User's Manual*, Tech Rep CMU-CS-81-135 Computer Science Dept, Carnegie-Mellon University.

69 Forsyth, R. (ed.) (1984) *Expert Systems: Principles and Case Studies*, Chapman and Hall.

70 Forsyth, R. and Rada, R. (1986) *Machine Learning*, Ellis Horwood.

71 Fourman, M. (1973) *Logical Aspects of Topoi*, mimeographed notes, Oxford.

72 Freyd, P. (1972) Aspects of topoi, *Bull. Austral. Math. Soc.*, **7**, 1–76.

73 Gaines, B. R. and Shaw, M.L.G. (1986) Induction of inference rules for expert systems, *Fuzzy Sets and Systems*, **18**.

74 Gabbay, D.M. and Reyle, U. (1984) N-Prolog: An extension of prolog with hypothetical implications I, *J. Logic Programming*, 319–55.

75 Goguen, J.A. (1981) Concept representation in natural and artificial languages: axioms, extensions and applications for fuzzy sets, in *Fuzzy Reasoning and its Applications* (eds E.H. Mamdani and B.R. Gaines), Academic Press.

76 Goguen, J.A. and Meseguer, J. (1986) EQLOG: equality, types and generic modules for logic programming, in *Functional and Logic Programming* (eds DeGroot and Lindstrom), Prentice-Hall.

77 Goodman, I.R. and Nguyen, H.T. (1985) *Uncertainty Models for Knowledge Based Systems*, North Holland (1985).

78 Graham, I.M. (1985) *Reveal Introductory Guide*, McDonnell Douglas, London.

79 Graham, I.M. (1987) Fuzzy sets and topoi, towards higher order logic programming, *Fuzzy Sets and Systems*, **23**(1).

80 Graham, I.M. and Jones, P.L.K. (1985) Commercial applications of knowledge engineering, *Proceedings of AI Europa*, Wiesbaden.

81 Graham, I.M. and Jones, P.L.K., Reveal and its applications, in [172].

82 Gray, P.M.D. (1984) *Logic, Algebra and Databases*, Ellis Horwood.

83 Grothendieck, A. (1972) *Theorie des Topos et Cohomologie Etale des Schemas* (SGA4), Lecture Notes in Mathematics 269, Springer.

84 Gupta, R. and Sanchez, E. (eds), (1982) *Approximate Reasoning in Decision Analysis*, North Holland.

85 Gupta, M. and Sanchez, E. (eds), (1982) *Fuzzy Information and Decision Processes*, North Holland.

86 Haack, S. (1978) *Philosophy of Logics*, Cambridge.

87 Harmon, P. and King, D. (1985) *Expert Systems: Artificial Intelligence in Business*, Wiley.

88 Hatcher, W.S. (1982) *The Logical Foundations of Mathematics*, Pergamon.

89 Haugeland, J. (ed.), (1981) *Mind Design*, MIT Press.

90 Hayes, P.J., The logic of frames, in Brachman and Levesque [34].

91 Hayes-Roth, F., Waterman, D.A. and Lenat, D.B. (1983) *Building Expert Systems*, Addison-Wesley.

92 Hegel, G.F. (1973) *The Logic*, translated from the Encyclopaedia of the Philosophical Sciences by W. Wallace, Oxford University Press.

93 Heijenoort, J. van (1967) *From Frege to Gödel – A Source Book in Mathematical Logic* 1879–1931, Harvard.

94 Henry, D.P. (1972) *Mediaeval Logic and Metaphysics*, Hutchinson.

95 Hersh, H.M. and Caramazza, A. (1976) A fuzzy set approach to modifiers and vagueness in natural language, *J. Experimental Psychology, General*, **105**(3).

96 Heyting, A. (1956) *Intuitionism, An Introduction*, North Holland.

97 Hintikka, J. (1973) *Time and Necessity*, Oxford.

98 Hodges, A. (1983) *Alan Turing: the Enigma of Intelligence*, Burnett Books.

99 Hofstadter, D.R. (1979) *Gödel, Escher, Bach: An Eternal Golden Braid*, Harvester.

100 Hofstadter, D.R. (1985) *Metamagical Themas*, Basic Books.

101 Hohle, U. (1985) Fuzzy topologies and topological space objects in a topos, *BUSEFAL*, **21**.

102 Hopkins, I. *Expert systems and instructional technology*, Manuscript.

103 Jackson, P. Reasoning about belief in the context of advice-giving, in Bramer [35].

104 Johnson, T. (1984) *The Commercial Application of Expert Systems*, Ovum Press.

105 Johnson-Laird, P.N. and Wason, P.C. (eds), (1977) *Thinking: Readings in Cognitive, Science*, Cambridge.

106 Johnstone, P.T. (1977) *Topos Theory*, Academic Press.

107 Johnstone, P.T. (1982) *Stone Spaces*, Cambridge University Press.

108 Jones, P.L.K. (1985) *Reveal Users Manual*, Tymshare Inc.

109 Jones, P.L.K. (1984) REVEAL: An expert systems support environment, in *Expert Systems: Principles and Case Studies* (ed. R. Forsyth), Chapman and Hall.

110 Keen, P.G.W. and Scott-Morton, M.S. (1978) *Decision Support Systems*, Addison-Wesley.

111 Keisler, H.J. Fundamentals of model theory, in Barwise [18].

112 Kelly, G. A. (1955) *The Psychology of Personal Constructs*, W.W. Norton, New York.

113 Kickert, W.J.M. (1978) *Fuzzy Theories on Decision Making*, Martinus Nijhoff, Leiden.

114 Kleene (1952) *Introduction to Metamathematics*, Van Nostrand.

115 Klimbe, J.W. and Koffeman, K.L. (eds), (1974) *Data Base management*, North Holland.

116 Knight, B. and Swaffield, G. *Knowledge Elicitation Based on the Principle of User Independence*, to be published.

117 Kock, A. and Wraith, G.C. (1971) *Elementary Toposes*, Aarhus Universitet Lecture Notes 3.

118 Koestler, A. (1970) *The Ghost in the Machine*, Pan Books.

119 Kohout, L.J., Keravnou, E. and Bandler, W. (1982) Information retrieval system using fuzzy relational products for thesaurus construction, *Proceedings of NATO Advanced Study Institute.*

120 Kohout, L.J., Keravnou, E. and Bandler, W. Information retrieval system using fuzzy relational products for thesaurus construction, in Zimmermann, Gaines and Zadeh [221].

121 Kolmogorov, A.N. (1967) On the principle of the excluded middle, in J. van Heijenoort, *From Frege to Gödel – A Source Book in Mathematical Logic 1879–1931,* Harvard.

122 Kowalski, R. (1979) *Logic for Problem Solving,* North Holland.

123 Kowalski, R. (1980) *SIGART Newsletter,* **70.**

124 Kroenke, D. (1977) *Database Processing,* Science Research Associates.

125 Lakoff, G. (1973) Hedges: A study in meaning criteria and the logic of fuzzy concepts, *J. Philos. Logic,* **2,** 458–508.

126 Lang, S. (1967) *Algebraic Structures,* Addison-Wesley.

127 Lawvere, F.W. (1970) Quantifiers and sheaves, *Actes du Congress Int. des Math. tome,* **1,** p. 329.

128 Lawvere, F.W. (1964) An elementary theory of the category of sets, *Proc. Nat. Acad. Sci. U.S.A.,* **52,** 1506–11.

129 Levi-Strauss, C. (1963) *Structural Anthropology,* Basic Books.

130 Lindberg, D.C. (1978) *Science in the Middle Ages,* University of Chicago Press.

131 Little, J.D.C. (1974) Models and managers: a decision calculus, *Management Science,* **16,** 466–85.

132 Little, J.D.C. (1979) Aggregate advertising models: the state of the art, *Operations Research,* **27**(4).

133 Lady Ada Lovelace (1842) *Notes upon the memoir 'Sketch of the Analytical Engine Invented by Charles Babbage',* Geneva.

134 Lowen, R. (1976) Fuzzy topological spaces and fuzzy compactness, *J. Math. Anal. Appl.,* **56.**

135 Lukasiewitz (1920) On 3-valued logic, in *Polish Logic* (ed. S. McCall) (1967), Oxford.

136 MacLane, S. (1971) *Categories for the Working Mathematician,* Springer.

137 MacLane, S. and Birkhoff, G. (1967) *Algebra,* Macmillan, New York.

138 MacNamara, J.M. (1984) *CONCEPT User Guide,* Vol. 1, Tymshare UK.

139 Mamdani, E.H. and Gaines, B.R. (eds) (1981) *Fuzzy Reasoning and its Applications,* Academic Press.

140 Martin, J. (1977) *Computer Data-base Organisation,* Prentice-Hall.

141 Martin, T.P., Baldwin, J.F. and Pilsworth, B.W. (1985) *FPROLOG – A Fuzzy Prolog Interpreter,* ITRC Report 50, University of Bristol.

142 Michalski, R.S., Carbonell, J.G. and Mitchell, T.M. (1983) *Machine Learning – an Artificial Intelligence Approach,* Tioga Publishing Company.

143 McCarthy, Circumscription – a form of non-monotonic reasoning, in Webber and Nilsson [206].

144 McCarthy, J. (1960) Recursive functions of symbolic expressions and their computation by machine, *Communications of the ACM* (April).

145 McDermott, D. and Doyle, J. (1980) Non-monotonic logic I, *Artificial Intelligence* **13,** 41–72.

146 Zadeh, L.A. (1987) *Fuzzy Sets and Applications: Selected Papers,* Wiley.

147 McCorduck, P. (1979) *Machines Who Think,* W. H. Freeman & Co.

148 Mendelson, E. (1964) *Introduction to Mathematical Logic*, Van Nostrand, New York.
149 Merrett, A.J. and Sykes, A. (1963) *The Finance and Analysis of Capital Projects*, Longman.
150 Minsky, M.L. (1968) *Semantic Information Processing*, MIT Press.
151 Minsky, M.L. (1969) A framework for representing knowledge, in Haugeland [89].
152 Minsky, M.L. and Papert, S. (1969) *Perceptrons*, MIT Press.
153 Moore, R.C. (1985) Semantical considerations on nonmonotonic logic, *Artificial Intelligence*, **25**(1).
154 Morton, J., Hammersley, R.H. and Bekerian, D.A. (1985) Headed records: a model for memory and its failures, *Cognition*, **20**, 1–23.
155 Negoita, C.V. (1982) Fuzzy sets in topoi, *Fuzzy Sets and Systems*, **8**, 93–9.
156 Negoita, C.V. (1983) Fuzzy sets in decision support systems, *Human Systems Management*, **4**.
157 Negoita, C.V. (1985) *Expert Systems and Fuzzy Systems*, Benjamin Cummings.
158 Negoita, C.V. and Ralescu, D.A. (1975) *Applications of Fuzzy Sets to Systems Analysis*, Birkhauser Verlag.
159 Negoita, C.V. and Stephanescu, A. (1982). On fuzzy optimisation, in *Fuzzy Information and Decision Processes* (eds M. Gupta and E. Sanchez), North Holland.
160 Newell, A. and Simon, H.A. (1956) The logic theory machine, *IRE Trans. on Information Theory*.
161 Newell, A. and Simon, H.A. (1963) GPS: A program that simulates human thought, in *Computers and Thought* (eds E.A. Feigenbaum and J.A. Feldman), McGraw Hill.
162 Newell, A. and Simon, H.A. (1972) *Human Problem Solving*, Prentice-Hall.
163 Nilsson, N.J. (1980) *Principles of Artificial Intelligence*, Springer.
164 Norwich, A.M. and Turksen, I.B. (1982) Stochastic fuzziness, in *Approximate Reasoning in Decision Analysis* (eds Gupta and Sanchez).
165 Petri, C.A. (1977) Modelling as a communication discipline, in *Measuring, Modelling and Evaluating Computer Systems* (eds Berliner and Gelenbe), North Holland.
166 Piaget, J. (1971) *Structuralism*, Routledge and Kegan Paul.
167 Pitts, A. (1982) Fuzzy sets do not form a topos, *Fuzzy Sets and Systems*, **8**, 101–4.
168 Ponasse, D. (1983) Some remarks on the category Fuz-H of M. Eytan, *Fuzzy Sets and Systems*, **9**, 199–204.
169 Poston, T. (1971) *Fuzzy Geometry*, Doctoral Dissertation, Warwick.
170 Poston, T. and Stewart, I. (1978) *Catastrophe Theory and its Applications*, Pitman.
171 Prade, H. (1983) *Approximate and Plausible Reasoning: The State of the Art*, Unpublished manuscript.
172 Prade, H. and Negoita, C.V. (1986) *Fuzzy Logic in Knowledge Engineering*, Verlag TUV Rheinland.
173 Price, R. *Observations on Reversionary Payments*, British Museum BM-8229.bbb.36.
174 Rasiowa, H. and Sikorski, R. (1963) *The Mathematics of Metamathematics*, Warsaw.
175 Rauch-Hinden, W.B. (1985) *Artificial Intelligence in Business, Science and Industry*, Prentice-Hall.
176 Reiter, R. On reasoning by default, in Brachman and Levesque [34].
177 Robinson, J.A. (1965) A machine-oriented logic based on the resolution principle, *J. of the ACM*, **12**.
178 Sacerdoti, E. (1975) The nonlinear nature of plans, *Proceedings of IJCAI*, **4**.
179 Searle, J. (1969), *Speech Acts*, Cambridge University Press.

180 Schank, R.C. and Abelson, R.P. (1977) *Scripts, Plans, Goals and Understanding*, Lawrence Erlbaum Associates.
181 Schotch, P.K. (1975) Fuzzy modal logic, IEEE Int. Symposium on Multiple-Valued Logic.
182 Schwartz, D.G. (1985) The case for an interval-based representation of linguistic truth, *Fuzzy Sets and Systems*, **17**.
183 Shaw, M.L.G. (ed.) (1981) *Recent Advances in Personal Construct Technology*, Academic Press.
184 Shipman, D. (1979) The functional data model and the data language DAPLEX, *ACM TODS*, **6**, 140–73.
185 Shoenfield, J.R. Axioms of set theory, in Barwise [18].
186 Shortliffe, E.H. (1976) *Computer Based Medical Consultations: MYCIN*, American Elsevier.
187 Simon, H.A. (1977) What computers mean to man and society, *Science*, **195**.
188 Slatter, P.E. (1985) Cognitive emulation in expert system design, *The Knowledge Engineering Review*, **1**(2).
189 Sloman, A. Why we need many knowledge representations, in Bramer [35].
190 Small, M. (ed.) (1985) *Knowledge Engineering and Decision Support*, Tymshare UK and ICL Ltd.
191 Smorynski, C., The incompleteness theorems, in Barwise [18].
192 Sprague, R.H., Jr. and Watson, H.J. (1975) MIS concepts, *J. of Systems Management*, **26**.
193 Sowa, J.F. (1984) *Conceptual Structures*, Addison-Wesley.
194 Sussman, G.J. (1975) *A Computer Model of Skill Acquisition*, American Elsevier.
195 Taylor, A.E. (1927) *Plato, The Man and his Work* (2nd edn), London.
196 Thompson, G. (1955) *The First Philosophers*, Lawrence and Wishart.
197 Tierney, M. (1972) Sheaf theory and the continuum hypothesis, in *Toposes Algebraic Geometry and Logic*, Lecture Notes in Mathematics 274, Springer.
198 Tong, R.M. and Efstathiou, H.J. (1982) A critical assessment of truth functional modification and its use in approximate reasoning, *Fuzzy Sets and Systems*, **7**, 103–8.
199 Troelstra, A.S., Aspects of constructive mathematics, in Barwise [18].
200 Turing, A.M. (1950) Computing machinery and intelligence, *Mind*, **LIX**(236) and in A.R. Anderson [8].
201 Turner, R. (1984) *Logics for Artificial Intelligence*, Ellis Horwood, Chichester.
202 Ullman, J.D. (1982) *Principles of Database Systems*, 2nd edn, Computer Science Press.
203 Wagner, H.A. (1972) *Principles of Operations Research*, Prentice-Hall.
204 Wallace, M. (1984) *Communicating with Database in Natural Language*, Ellis Horwood.
205 Warren, D.H.D. (1984) Higher order extentions to PROLOG: are they needed? in *Machine Intelligence 10* (eds Hayes and Michie), Ellis Horwood.
206 Webber, B.L. and Nilsson, N.J. (eds) (1981) *Readings in Artificial Intelligence*, Tioga Publishing Company.
207 Weissman, C. (1967) *LISP 1.5 Primer*, Dickenson Publishing Company.
208 Wellbank, M. (1983) *A Review of Knowledge Acquisition Techniques for Expert Systems*, Martlesham Consultancy Services, Ipswich.
209 Winch, G. Modelling for Policy Evaluation, in Small [190].
210 Winston, P.H. (1984) *Artificial Intelligence*, 2nd edn, Addison-Wesley.
211 Winston, P.H. and Horn, B.K.P. (1985) *Lisp* (2nd edn), Addison-Wesley.

212 Wong, P. (1984) *Corporate Analyser*, MacDonnell Douglas Knowledge Engineering Division.

213 Woods, W.A., What's in a link: foundations for semantic networks, in *Representation and Understanding* (eds D.G. Bobrow and A. Collins).

214 Zadeh, L.A. (1978) PRUF – a meaning representation language for natural languages, *Int. J. Man–Machine Studies*, **10**.

215 Zadeh, L.A. Calculus of fuzzy restrictions, in L.A. Zadeh, K-S.Fu, K.Tanaka, and M. Shimura [219].

216 Zadeh, L.A. (1983) Commonsense knowledge representation based on fuzzy logic, *IEEE Computer*.

217 Zadeh, L.A. (1983) A computational approach to fuzzy quantifiers in natural languages, *Comp. & Math. with Appls.*, **9**(1).

218 Zadeh, L.A. (1984) *A Computational Theory of Dispositions*, Proceedings of the conference of the Association for Computational Linguistics.

219 Zadeh, L.A., Fu, K-S., Tanaka, K. and Shimura, M. (eds) (1975) *Fuzzy Sets and their Applications to Cognitive and Decision Processes*, Academic Press.

220 Zeman, J.J. (1973) *Modal Logic*, Oxford.

221 Zimmermann, H.-J., Zadeh, L.A. and Gaines, B.R. (eds) (1984) *Fuzzy sets and decision analysis*, North Holland.

222 Zimmermann, H.-J. (1986) *Fuzzy Set Theory and Its Applications*, Kluwer-Nijhoff.

223 Duda, R., Hart, P. *et al.* (1976) *Development of the PROSPECTOR system for mineral exploration*, SRI report projects 5822 and 6415, SRI, Palo Alto, Ca.

224 Johnson, P. *et al.* (1984) *Tasks, skills and knowledge: Task analysis for knowledge based descriptions*, Manuscript.

225 Braithwaite, R.B. (1953) *Scientific Explanation*, Cambridge.

226 Hempel, C.G. (1966) *Philosophy of Natural Science*, Prentice-Hall.

227 Marcuse, H. (1985) *Reason and Revolution*, Oxford.

228 Ross-Ashby, W. (1956) *An Introduction to Cybernetics*, Chapman & Hall, London.

229 Weiner, N. (1948) *Cybernetics*, MIT Press.

230 Simon, H. (1981) *The Sciences of the Artificial*, 2nd edn, MIT Press.

231 Mintzberg, H. (1965) *The Nature of Managerial Work*, Prentice-Hall.

232 Lenin, V.I. (1961) *Philosophical Notebooks, Collected Works*, Vol. 38, Lawrence and Wishart, London.

233 Lenin, V.I. (1967) *Materialism and Empirio-Criticism*, Progress Publishers, Moscow.

234 Brodie, M.L. and Mylopoulos, J. (eds) (1986) *On Knowledge Based Management Systems*, Springer.

235 Hart, A. (1986) *Knowledge Acquisition for Expert Systems*, Kogan Page.

236 Weizenbaum, S. (1984) *Computer Power and Human Reason*, 2nd edn, Penguin Books.

237 Leith, P. (1986) Fundamental errors in legal logic programming, *The Computer Journal*, **29**(6).

238 Zadeh, L.A. (1965) Fuzzy sets, *Information and Control*, **8**.

239 Kelly, J. (1955) *General Topology*, Van Nostrand.

240 Bonissone, P.P. and Brown, A.L. (1986) *Expanding the Horizons of Expert Systems*, General Electric Corporation.

241 Shackle, G.L.S. (1961) *Decision Order and Time in Human Affairs*, Cambridge.

242 Keynes, J.M. (1921) *A Treatise on Probability*, Macmillan.

243 Cohen, P.R. (1985) *Heuristic Reasoning about Uncertainty: an artificial intelligence approach*, Pitman.

244 Shafer, G. (1976) *A Mathematical Theory of Evidence*, Princeton.
245 Buchanan and Shortliffe (eds) (1985), *The MYCIN Experiments at Stanford*, Addison-Wesley.
246 Sprague, R.H. (1980) Framework for the development of decision support systems, *MIS Quarterly*, **4.4.**
247 Nowakowska, M. (1986) *Cognitive Sciences*, Academic Press.
248 Buckley, J.J., Siler, W. and Tucker, D. (1986) A fuzzy expert system, *Fuzzy Sets and Systems* **20**(1).
249 Yager, R.R. (1986) Paths of least resistance in possibilistic production systems, *Fuzzy Sets and Systems*, **19**(2).
250 Schmucker, K.J. (1984) *Fuzzy Sets, Natural Language Computations, and Risk Analysis*, Computer Science Press.
251 Marx, K. (1983) *The Mathematical Manuscripts*, New Park (London).
252 Winograd, T. (1983) *Language as a Cognitive Process*, Addison–Wesley.
253 McCawley, J.D. (1981) *Everything Linguists have Always Wanted to Know about Logic*, Basil Blackwell.
254 Eshragh, F. and Mamdani, E.H. (1979) A general approach to linguistic approximation, *Int. J. Man–Machine Studies*, **11.**
255 Zadeh, L.A. (1971) Quantitative fuzzy semantics, *Information Science*, **3.**
256 Minsky, M. and Papert, S. (1972) *Perceptrons*, MIT Press.
257 Michalski, R. *et al.* (1983) (eds), *Machine Learning*, Tioga Publishing (Palo Alto).
258 Tate, A. (1977) Generating project networks, *Proc. IJCAI*, **5.**
259 Vere, S.A. (1983) Planning in time: windows and durations for activities and goals, *IEEE Trans. on Pattern Analysis and Machine Intelligence*, **PAMI-5**(3).
260 Graham, I.M. and Jones, P.L.K. (1987) Fuzzy frames, *BUSEFAL*, **31**, 32.
261 Pring, M.J. (1985) *Technical Analysis Explained* (2nd edn), McGraw Hill.
262 Smith, A. (1986) *Trading Financial Options*, Butterworths.
263 Creative Logic Ltd. (1987) *Leonardo Reference Manuals*, Creative Logic, Brunel Science Park, Uxbridge, Middx.
264 Grant, T. J. (1986) An Expert Fuzzy Planner for Scheduling Aircraft Repair Work, *Proceedings of the First International Expert Systems Conference.*
265 Romiszowski, A.J. (1981) *Designing Instructional Systems (Decision Making in Course Planning and Curriculum Design)*, Kogan Page, London.
266 Gilbert, T.F. (1961) *Mathetics: The technology of education*, Journal of Mathetics Vols 1 & 2.
267 Gagne, R.M. (1965) *Conditions for Learning*, Holt Rinehart Winston.
268 Gagne, R.M. (1975) *Essentials of Learning for Instruction*, Dryden Press.
269 Gagne, R.M. and Briggs, R. (1974) *Principles of Instructional Design*, Holt Rinehart Winston.
270 Bloom, B.S. (1956) *Taxonomy of Educational Objectives, Handbook 1: Cognitive Domain*, David McKay Inc, New York.
271 Landa, L.N. (1974) *Algorithmization in Learning and Instruction*, Education Technology Publications.
272 Landa, L.N. (1976) *Instructional Regulation and Control: Cybernetics, Algorithmisation and Heuristics in Education*, Education Technology Publications.
273 Seymour, W.D. (1966) *Industrial Skills*, Pitman.
274 Seymour, W.D. (1968) *Skills Analysis Training*, Pitman.

275 Kernighan, B.W. and Ritchie, D.M. (1978) *The C Programming Language*, Prentice-Hall, Englewood Cliffs.
276 Kandel, A. and Lee, S.C. (1979) *Fuzzy Switching and Automata*, Edward Arnold, London.

Note:
The Bibliography is *not* in alphabetical (or any other) order. However, in order to provide easy access, it is cross-referenced in the Name Index which is in alphabetical order. For instruction on how to use the cross-referencing system see the remarks at the head of the indexes.

Computer systems index

Reference numbers are given in square brackets.

Name index

Reference numbers of which the person is an author or in which the person's work is included are given in square brackets.

Abelard 162
Abelson, R. P. 32, 33, 34, 42, [180]
Abrial, J. R. [1]
Ackoff, R. L. 260, [2)
Addis, T. R. 51, 73, 80, 221, 251, [3]
Alexander, I. 16, [5]
Allen, J. F. 196, [6]
Alter, S. L. 275, [4]
Alwood, J. 219, [7]
Anderson, A. R. [8], [200]
Anderson, J. R. 23, 239, [9], [10]
Andersson, L-G. 219, [7]
Anthony 11
Aquinas, St. T. 162
Arbib, M. A. 211, [11]
Aristotle 73, 162, 163, 168, 174, 175
Atkin, R. 42, [12]
Ayer, A. J. 219, [13]

Babbage, C. 3, [133]
Bachman, C. W. 47, [14]
Bacon, R. 162
Baldwin, J. F. 29, 60, 218, [15], [141], [172]
Bandler, W. 61, [119], [120]
Barendregt 200, [18]
Barr, A. 42, 228, 232, 251, [16]
Bartlett, C. W. 42, [17]
Barwise, J. 166, 219, [18], [19]
Bayes 94
Beckman, F. S. 220, [20]
Beer, S. 253, [21]
Bekerian, D. A. 34, [154]
Bellman, R. 150, 218, 256, 267, 270, 275, 321, [24]
Berliner, H. 231, 232, [22]
Bintley, H. 338, [23]
Birkhoff, G. [137]

Bloom, B. S. 288, [270]
Bobrow, D. G. 80, [25]
Bochvar, 175, [26]
Boden, M. A. 16, [27]
Boethius 162
Bonczek, H. 254, 257, 259, 275, [28]
Bonissone, P. P. 86, 108, [240]
Boole, G. 162, 219, [29]
Boose, J. 301, 303, [30]
Bossu, G. 190, [31]
Boulden, J. B. 9, [32]
Boxer, P. J. 297, [33]
Boyce 56
Brachman, R. J. 42, 80, [34]
Braithwaite, R. B. 234, [225]
Bramer, M. A. [35]
Bran 67
Brodie, M. L. 75, 80, [234]
Brouwer 163, 164, 194
Brown, A. L. 86, 108, [240]
Buchanan, B. G. 116, [36], [245]
Buckley, J. 158, [248]
Bundy, A. 204, 219 [37]
Burge, W. H. 220, [38]
Burns, N. A. 338, [39]

Cantor 163, 164
Caramazza, A. [95]
Carbonell, J. G. [142]
Carrega, J. C. 208, 214, [40]
Charniak, E. 24, 251, [41]
Chaucer, G. 29
Chauntecleer 30
Chen, P. S. 50, 51, [42]
Chestnut, R. [43]
Chevalier de Mere 90
Chomsky, N. 44, [44]
Church 37, 45, 194, 198, 199

Subject index